PRAISE FOR *THE ANATOMY OF EVIL*

"The fluid, articulate style of this studious yet accessible volume attests to the impressive breadth and depth of Dr. Stone's knowledge about the people who've committed the world's most evil acts. Using psychology, religion, philosophy, and neuroscience, he dissects this complex concept in the form of case study and presents a concise and profound analysis. A great read for scholars and laypeople alike. You won't forget these stories! It's everything you ever wanted to know about evil but were too afraid to ask."

—Dr. Katherine Ramsland,
professor of forensic psychology and chair of social sciences,
DeSales University; author of *Confession of a Serial Killer*

"Only a person of Dr. Stone's stature could address so complex an issue. For years he has led the effort to better understand the perverse depth of the most heinous of criminal minds. This book sheds a bright light on the darkness of those same minds."

—Roy Hazelwood, FBI (ret.)

"In this fascinating and compelling work, Dr. Michael Stone leads the way on a dark and irresistible journey. Down each path and around every corner the Face of Evil is ever changing—everything from the fresh 'innocent' faces of the seemingly benign Karla Homolka and Paul Bernardo . . . to the malicious and haunting faces of Charles Manson and Richard 'Night Stalker' Ramirez. . . . Powerful and riveting!"

—Carol Rothgeb-Stokes, author of *Hometown Killer*

"Dr. Stone's groundbreaking work is a must read for everyone involved in the criminal justice system, and for everyone else who wants to better understand the concept of evil and those to whom it applies."

—Peter Davidson, journalist and true crime author

The ANATOMY *of* EVIL

22
21
20
19
18
17
16
15
14
13
12
11
10
9
8
7
6
5
4
3
2
1

The ANATOMY *of* EVIL

MICHAEL H. STONE, MD

Published 2017 by Prometheus Books

Cover image © PhotoDisc, Inc.
Cover design by Jacqueline Nasso Cooke
Cover design © Prometheus Books

Inquiries should be addressed to
Prometheus Books
4501 Forbes Boulevard, Suite 200
Lanham, Maryland 20706
www.rowman.com

Distributed by NATIONAL BOOK NETWORK

Library of Congress Cataloging-in-Publication Data

Names: Stone, Michael H., 1933- author.
Title: The anatomy of evil / by Michael H. Stone, MD.
Description: Amherst, New York : Prometheus Books, [2017] |
Includes bibliographical references and index.
Identifiers: LCCN 2017023636 (print) | LCCN 2017036525 (ebook) |
ISBN 9781633883369 (ebook) | ISBN 9781633883352 (pbk.)
Subjects: LCSH: Criminal psychology. | Good and evil.
Classification: LCC HV6080 (ebook) | LCC HV6080 .S85 2017 (print) |
DDC 364.3—dc23
LC record available at https://lccn.loc.gov/2017023636

for Ben Carey
and for Meg

CONTENTS

INTRODUCTION

Canto III, ll. 3–9

Per me si va nella citta dolente
Per me si va nell' eterno dolore
Per me si va tra la perduta gente
Giustizia mosse il mio alto Fattore;
Fecemi la divina potestate,
La somma sapienza e 'l primo amore.
Dinanzi a me non fuor cose create
Se non etterne, ed io etterno duro.
Lasciate ogne speranza, voi ch'intrate.

Through me the way to the grieving city,
through me the way into eternal sorrow,
through me the way among the lost people.
Justice moved my high Maker;
divine power made me,
highest wisdom and primal love.
Before me were no things created
except eternal ones, and I endure eternal.
Give up all hope, ye who enter.

Tr.: Robert M. Durling
The Divine Comedy of Dante, vol. 1: *Inferno*
New York: Oxford University Press, 1996

The aim of this book is to understand evil. To demystify evil altogether would be much too ambitious a task. I am committed, however, to the belief that we can make sense of a good portion of what goes by the name of evil, though there will remain areas that will continue to baffle us. We can assume that those territories on the grand map of evil will, through scientific inquiry, be rendered smaller with each succeeding generation.

Along the path of our investigation, there will be several high hurdles to clear. We need, for example, to reach an acceptable definition of evil. The question must be addressed: who, if anyone, is qualified to make judgments about evil? There is also the problem of how to agree upon the legitimate domain within which evil can meaningfully be said to exist. If evil emerges as a legitimate topic for discussion, as I believe it is, are there important differences between what is considered evil in times of war or group conflict and what we may regard as evil committed by individuals in peacetime?

DEFINING EVIL

There is a close connection between our ideas about evil as an abstract concept and the religious sources in which these ideas are rooted. The very term itself occurs some 604 times in the Bible (Old and New Testaments together) but covers a wide array of human failings and crimes—from seemingly minor acts, like touching creatures that crawl, to abominations like incest and murder. There are lengthy lists of evils to be found in Leviticus and Deuteronomy, including those embodied in the Ten Commandments. In the New Testament we find another such list in Paul's Epistle to the Galatians.[1] There, Paul inveighs against fifteen wrongful attitudes and behaviors: among them jealousy, debauchery, selfishness; religious acts such as idolatry and heresy; and also acts associated with violence: hatred and murder. In the Bible "evil" is equated with "wrong" or "bad" and is not limited as a label to be reserved for the *worst* of the bad or wrong actions to which we are prone. This same global use of evil is found in the Koran as well.[2] The third-century Persian prophet Mani[3] (from whom *Manichaeism* is derived), divided human experience, as had Zoroaster[4] before him, into Good and Bad. Zoroaster ascribed Good and Bad to two twin gods representing these influences: a god of light and the good (Ahura Mazda), and a god of darkness and the bad or evil (Ahriman). Buddhism emphasizes, besides lust as a primary sin, a tripartite concept that gives special weight to anger, greed, and foolishness.[5]

Religion has played a powerful role in shaping our ideas about evil. Many insist that discussion of the subject is legitimate only when put forward either by religious leaders—whether the clergy or professors of theology—or else by philosophers. Philosophers are the other group to whom we have ceded over the centuries the privilege of instructing us on matters of good and evil. Meanwhile, one will search in vain for a useful working definition from the earlier of these sources. There are, however, a few contemporary philosophers, most notably Susan Neiman, who have contributed importantly to the problems inherent in creating a useful definition.[6] Neiman states, in fact, that her book will not offer a definition, nor does she think an intrinsic property of evil can be defined, though she adds that to call something evil is a way of marking the fact that "it shatters our trust in the world."[7] Similarly controversial: how to draw the line where the "very bad" ends and the "truly evil" begins.

There might be near-universal agreement about the *opposite* ends—the somewhat bad (slapping one's child) and the extremity of evil (Auschwitz in wartime; raping a child, in peacetime), as Delbanco mentions[8]—but there will always be a gray zone in the middle, where opinion is far from unanimous. Further on, Neiman helps us distinguish between *natural* versus *moral* evil, reminding us that earthquakes and floods had been seen in the past as natural evils, often inflicted upon us by a deity as a punishment for our sins. Moral evils are those that we ourselves initiate. Since most of us no longer consider natural disasters as stemming from divine retribution, if we speak of them as "evil," we are doing so metaphorically. This book concerns only the evil acts for which we are alone responsible—the moral evils. Religious doctrines converge in holding us responsible in this sphere, as conveyed in the Koran, where it is written: "Whatever benefit comes to you, o Man, it is from Allah, and whatever misfortune befalls you, it is from yourself."[9] Passages like that, also found in the Old and New Testaments, situate evil in us, where it admittedly belongs, but do not further define its nature or boundaries.

Brian Masters, who wrote an excellent biography of the serial killer Dennis Nilsen, is no stranger to the concept—and the enigma—of evil.[10] Evil, for him, is "an occult word meaning little more in reality than conduct which is so bad that it is better left unexamined."[11]

It would be convenient if we could at least define "absolute evil" and if we could answer the equally elusive question: can one be born "evil"? Answers to such questions would be comforting to philosophers and to the legal community. But the answer to the first question is not to be found, and the second answer is simply "no."[12] To define and describe absolute evil would require, it seems to me, a universal agreement among people of good will—philosophers, theologians, medicolegal experts, and people in ordinary life—as to what the characteristics of this extreme phenomenon might actually be. One would like to think that the death camps of Auschwitz or one of the other twentieth-century genocides would earn this kind of unanimity, but we know that there remain groups here and there who think differently. Perhaps the rape and murder of a child would serve as our high-water mark for an absolute evil. And for 99 percent of us that probably would fit, but there is still that 1 percent who would differ. To be "born evil" could only mean that some infant, crippled by a perverse twist of the genetic code, would grow up, in no matter how loving, harmonious, and even prosperous a family, to commit acts, repetitively and undeterrably, that the community regarded as evil. This would be the "vicious mole of nature" that Hamlet spoke of to Horatio, cited by Masters in his persuasive argument that "good and bad are co-existent and part of one another, and harmony emerges from the correct and decent balance between the two."[13] Born evil? I know of no such person, even in the annals of crime or in the biographies of despots. The answer here is no.

So far, this may seem like an exercise in futility—we cannot define evil in a useful way or even establish a meaningful hierarchy or scale of evil acts. But before I share with you my working definition of evil and my approach to measuring evil, I need to say something about what it means to make judgments of this sort in the first place.

MAKING JUDGMENTS ABOUT EVIL

Some people feel strongly that no one has the right to make judgments about evil. Religious people in particular hold to the view that God is the final, perhaps the only rightful, arbiter of such decisions. Since He does not speak to us directly, many religious people are willing to make the compromise, allowing for clergymen, God's earthly representatives, to make such judgments. Philosophers, because of their wisdom, and especially those far in the past, have also been privileged in this regard. Within Christianity, Saint Augustine and Saint Thomas Aquinas were doubly privileged, since they were men of holy orders in addition to being philosophers. In Judaism, certain revered rabbis like Maimonides occupy almost as hallowed a place in making such decisions. In Islam, the word of Mohammed, as Allah's prophet, enjoys more than respect: it has the force of law.

People raised in a humanistic but not-so-religious a tradition may give more weight to the opinions of philosophers than of clergymen. It is rare, however, for either leaders of the various faiths or secular philosophers to get down to actual cases. What we are left with are guidelines and prescriptive comments, such as the generalities of St. Paul's Epistle to the Galatians or the outlines for good and bad behaviors in Leviticus and Deuteronomy. Detailed clinical descriptions of individuals—what we would consider case histories—are seldom found before the late eighteenth century, except in the biographies of kings and aristocrats.[14]

Another complicating factor lies in the different tone of the Old and New Testaments. Although God is still the Final Judge in both, in the Old Testament, men of blameless lives are accorded the privilege of making judgments. "In righteousness shalt thou judge thy neighbors"—as we are told in Leviticus.[15] The prophet Ezekiel strikes a more ominous note in his diatribe against what he saw as the sinfulness of Israel in his day: "Now is the end come upon thee [land of Israel] and I will send mine anger upon thee, and will judge thee according to thy ways, and will recompense upon thee all thy abominations."[16] ("Recompense" here means to pronounce sentence or to penalize, not to repay someone a debt.) The tone is not as harsh in the New Testament. In fact, we find Jesus saying: "Judge not that ye be not judged,"[17] adding a little further on: "And why beholdest the mote in thy brother's eye, but considerest not the beam that is in thine own eye?"[18]

Writing as a psychiatrist and a psychoanalyst, I face another high hurdle. Psychiatrists are taught not to make moral judgments about their patients. This cautionary note is sounded even more emphatically in psychoanalysis. The early generation of psychoanalysts recognized, however, that people who habitually violated societal norms were not good candidates for their method of treatment. Freud had said a hundred years ago, for example, that if one were to benefit from psychoanalysis, it was essential to have a good character. As a method of understanding the inner workings of people, irrespective of their moral standing, psychoanalysis retains its usefulness. In subsequent generations, a few psychoanalysts did begin to work with delinquent adolescents, modifying their treatment methods so as to encourage the development of "prosocial" habits that would replace the earlier antisocial habits. Other forms of therapy might still prove effective for patients of a more questionable character. The physician's model of offering treatment to all, while withholding judgment, is no less honored in psychiatry than in medicine in general. But psychiatrists, in their other role as ordinary citizens, make moral judgments all the time, the same as everyone else. Men committing rape or serial sexual homicide seldom make it to the analyst's couch. Such men avoid self-revelation and generally commit their acts unburdened by the shame or guilt that would propel someone else to seek psychiatric help. Psychiatrists and psychoanalysts, reading about such individuals in the newspapers or hearing about them on the television, certainly make moral judgments: "Those were atrocious things to do," or perhaps even, "That was an evil act."

As for this kind of shift between a doctor's professional versus public self, I am reminded of some incidents in New York's Bellevue Hospital half a century ago. One incident concerns a police van that had brought a prisoner to the parking lot within view of the unit where I was working as an intern. When let out of the van, the prisoner, his arms and legs bound in chains, tried to escape, hopping as best he could away from the van. The police shot the man in the back. That was their job: to prevent escape. Thus immobilized, he was carried straightway to the emergency ward just on the other side of the parking lot. There, the surgeons immediately began stanching the bleeding and extracting the bullets. That was their job: to save the man's life, never mind that he was a prisoner. Some time later, I was working in that emergency ward, where an alcoholic man, drifting in and out of consciousness, was getting care for a nasty cut on the palm of his hand. Whenever the man was unconscious, the surgeon was busy stitching up the large wound. Whenever the man awoke for a bit, he would hurl vehement curses and racial epithets at the surgeon—who paused momentarily in his efforts until the man became stuporous again. This back-and-forth routine continued a few times until the stitching was completed. It would have been unethical for the physician to have refused to treat the man because of his insulting behavior.

In the face of all the religious injunctions and moral constraints against making judgments about evil, what is a psychiatrist writing on this subject to do? How might I extricate myself from the ethical quicksand that grips whoever enters this territory? The way out, I believe, is to be found by turning to the public. People in everyday life, as it turns out—including authors of books on crime, journalists, commentators in the media—all use the word *evil* quite frequently and freely, in describing certain varieties of violent crime and certain perpetrators of these crimes. And they—or, rather, we—do so without much attention to the supernatural, metaphysical, ineffable, "occult" overtones with which the term is otherwise so loaded. And in their reactions to violent crimes of a particularly depraved nature, clergymen, philosophers, judges, attorneys, psychiatrists, and other physicians, reacting as private citizens to the events of the day, also speak of evil, and do so with great regularity.

It is on this general usage that I base my own impressions about evil. The philosopher Ludwig Wittgenstein once said: "The meaning of a word is its usage."[19] Well and good. So besides the (maddeningly vague) use of evil in religion and philosophy, there is also the often quite specific use of the term, authorized, as it were, by the public in everyday speech. Reminiscent of the Hungarian saying, "If three people call you a horse, buy a saddle!" if a judge, journalist, and the public concur that a particular crime was evil—well, then, it was evil. For that establishes the meaning of evil—down here on earth. If we can accept this as a working definition of the concept, we need not feel so self-conscious in calling certain acts "evil," as though we had intruded upon a space reserved for the clergy.

As I will show in more detail in the first chapter, this is the approach I will rely on in my discussion of evil. Further, I hope to show that certain acts of violence or otherwise hurtful actions are seen as underlying this notion of evil—to a greater extent than other not-quite-so-dreadful actions. This makes the fashioning of a scale for capturing these community-based distinctions at least a *thinkable* enterprise—one that is worthy of scientific inquiry. And these community-based distinctions, legitimate as they appear in the here and now, are not necessarily permanent or eternal.

CULTURE AND ERA

Because a community is an organic entity that grows, changes, and evolves over time, prevailing opinions about what is or is not evil are subject to modifications from one geographic setting and from one historical period to another. Perhaps the closest we come to a universal is murder—regarded as wrongful (by definition) and often enough as evil across all cultures and in all eras. With rape, in contrast, the story is different. The position of women was hardly the same in the times of the Old Testament as it is now in the "developed" countries. Wherever women cease to be men's property or chattel, attitudes toward rape undergo corresponding changes. There wasn't a separate word for rape in the Old Testament, but there are references to forced sex. Fine distinctions were drawn. If a man forced sex on a betrothed virgin in the field, she was considered blameless. If she cried and there was none to save her, the man was put to death. But if a man forced sex on a virgin that was *not* betrothed, then the man must pay fifty shekels (about a third of a year's wages) to her father and must marry her—without the possibility of divorce.[20] Presumably the sex was not consensual (this was three thousand years before the Pill and Women's Liberation, after all), so the girl was in effect compelled to marry her rapist, without much thought being given to her feelings in the matter. What we now view as a big evil was in that era and culture a relatively small evil.

In the biblical period (of both Testaments), people tended to live in small tribes, usually of around 150 people. A tribe, if it were not to be conquered by a larger tribe nearby, truly needed to be fruitful and multiply (so its sons outnumbered the sons of the would-be aggressor tribe). This meant that the laws and warnings against masturbation, prostitution, abortion, homosexuality, and adultery—all of which interfered with fertility or optimal child rearing—had a compelling rationale in those days.[21] These activities endangered group survival, even individual survival (a conquered tribe might be slaughtered or enslaved). Practices that threatened reproductive success constitute violations of an evolutionary principle. For similar reasons infanticide and child sacrifice, as were practiced by the heathens, were abominations to the Israelites.[22] Infanticide is still practiced or sanctioned in many parts of the world; it is not yet regarded as a crime *universally*. Incest is close to being universally regarded as wrong—stronger language is used in holy books ("an abomination," "evil")—but the punishment was much more severe in biblical times (death by burning or stoning) than now.

The need for group survival underlies the importance of group cohesion. One way to ensure group cohesion is for the leaders of a community to insist on unity of values and beliefs. Ideally, each member of the group should be willing to do anything necessary to strengthen that unity—including to die defending the group's values or to destroy those who threaten the solidarity of the group's customs and beliefs. This accounts for the persecution of heresy in the situation where a new religion is taking shape while its membership is still small and vulnerable. In much of the developed world, heresy belongs to the moldy books of bygone times, when it was punished by expulsion (following excommunication) if you were lucky; by death, if you were not. And that death might include being burned at the stake.[23] Heresy was a very big evil, as it still is in certain parts of the world today. If the group was a national rather than a religious one, the comparable crime was dissidence, or simply being different from those accepted by the leader. Not to be an Aryan in Nazi Germany, not to be a Communist in totalitarian Russia led to the same kinds of persecution, death penalty included, that once awaited heretics.

The threat to the group from supposed witches led to their persecution and execution (often by the most cruel means) in times past. Here the threat lay in the supernatural powers people attributed to them. This meant that witches, even though few in number, could—according to people who believed in witchcraft—create havoc in the community.[24] Now and then even in contemporary America there are a few people (mostly women) who profess to be witches, and others, not in great number, who fear their powers and regard them as evil handmaidens of the devil (in whom they also believe).

We would like to think that as citizens of the twenty-first century we have outgrown the superstitions that led people to stigmatize, persecute, and all too often kill "outsiders" whom their communities saw as "evil." And we would like to think that whenever we use the word in our culture and in our day, it applies to those who are "really" evil and who would be properly labeled so for the rest of eternity. There should never be a time, for example, when child rape, serial killing, torture, wife bashing, and the like become acceptable. This is an understandable hope. Given the history of the world, however, I do not think it is a reasonable hope. Still less reasonable is the hope that the large-scale evils that unfold in times of war and conflict—where torture, mutilation, and enslavement suddenly seem "justifiable"—disappear from the earth. The Four Horsemen of the Apocalypse have yet to be unseated.

GRADATIONS

Susan Neiman's hesitation in drawing a line between the *very bad* and the *evil* stems in part, I suspect, from the inherent vagueness in how such phrases have been used in religious and philosophical texts. Codes of law, both in ancient times and modern, make many fine distinctions—gradations, if you will—between the bad, the very bad, and the extremely bad. But the law avoids the word *evil*, preferring a vocabulary that corresponds pretty closely to what the community might call evil: words like *heinous* and *depraved*. Side by side with "evil" in books and journals there is a similar set of strong words, such as *fiendish*, *diabolical*, *monstrous*, *abominable*, which also overlap quite closely with the public's use of "evil." At the very least, there have always been simple systems for placing unacceptable or "wrong" behaviors into categories such as *misdemeanors* and *felonies*. And then there are those felonies that are so serious as to amount to *capital cases*—or in places where the death penalty has been abolished, what *used* to be capital cases—for instance, treason and certain forms of murder. What the law identifies as an extreme felony the public often identifies as evil—but the connection isn't that close. An unintended murder during the course of an armed robbery might be spoken of as "terrible," whereas "evil" might be reserved for the rape and murder of a child or the murder of a kidnap victim. Two thousand years ago, the Talmudic triad of incest, murder, and taking the Lord's name in vain—all punishable by death—was set off against a host of lesser crimes, but all were called *ra*: a word that meant "bad" but could also mean "evil," for which there was no special word that set it apart from *ra*. There is a graded system in the Catholic Church in which sins are divided into "venial" (forgivable, minor ones) and "mortal." But the "mortal" list contains more than thirty examples. Some of these are, to modern attitudes, much less serious than others. Envy, drunkenness, and cowardice are not at the same level as defrauding, robbery, and murder. For whatever reason, rape, arson, and assault are not mentioned specifically. There is no easy way to draw a connection between our current notion of evil and the various mortal sins.

Our word *evil* today does set apart the bad from the beyond-the-merely-bad. The next chapter will also reflect my efforts to hold a magnifying glass, so to say, over the realm of the beyond-the-merely-bad, in hopes of finding meaningful differences within this otherwise blurry region of smudged-together "evils."

TO DO EVIL IS HUMAN

Before I offer you my working definition of evil, there are two ideas about evil that need to be put forward first, as a kind of prelude to this definition. First, I believe we can make a solid claim that evil applies only to human beings.[25] We reserve the word *evil* now for describing certain acts done by people who clearly intended to hurt or to kill others in an excruciatingly painful way. That pain might be physical or it might be emotional or mental, involving extreme humiliation as well. Either way, the perpetrator must have a knowledge of death and an awareness that his or her action might bring about the death of the victim. Another requirement for using the term *evil* is that the perpetrator be aware that the victim would suffer intensely, experience agony—the same as the perpetrator knows he would feel if the tables were turned and he were the victim of those same actions. But ours is the only species that has this kind of conscious awareness and imagination about death and suffering. Ordinarily, humans also have a sense of shame, which acts as a braking mechanism to prevent us from carrying our violent or vengeful fantasies into action.[26] Some people who commit evil acts have a sense of shame, but in dire circumstances this sense of shame seems to go temporarily "off-line." In others who commit such acts, this sense of shame was never properly developed to begin with.[27] As humans, we can also hate, which means we can think how much better life would be if the object of our hatred were put out of the way. Animals lack these qualities, so they are not capable of evil. The lion chasing after a gazelle, the cat pouncing on a mouse—they are prompted to do so for their supper. They do not hate the gazelle or the mouse, nor are they vividly aware that what they are about to do will bring about suffering and death to their victims. Actually, predatory animals like the cat family try for a coup de grâce: one quick scrunching of the neck so that death comes instantly. Perhaps chimpanzees have the capacity to plot, singly or in groups, to kill other chimpanzees or even to bash them in ways that must hurt a great deal. I'm not so sure they experience shame or have the ability to mull over such actions way ahead of time and then to act "with malice aforethought," using our kind of elaborate language—to rape another chimp's mate and then bludgeon the rival with a tree branch. Even so, I am not ready to call this evil. In the same say, I know that a cat will sometimes seemingly tease a mouse it has captured, pouncing on it, letting it go for a second, pouncing on it again, until it finally does what it set out to do, which is to eat the mouse. This may look "sadistic" to us, as we imagine what people would call us if we behaved that way to someone else. But the cat is probably just engaging in a kind of practice-play, honing its skills the better to catch another mouse on another day. Without malice, without awareness of suffering and the finality of life, without shame or guilt: that is, without our uniquely human qualities.

The second point I have already hinted at: people tend to agree closely about which acts are evil when committed by individuals in ordinary civilian life—that is, in *peacetime*. In times of group conflict, including war, there will be two sides—each thinking the other is "evil." It is sometimes very difficult to get around this subjectivity. We would like to think that some neutral observer could size up a situation, say, where Country A invaded Country B and committed atrocities against the citizens of B and declare that, viewed from the mountaintop, clearly the A-people involved in these acts were the evil aggressors. History often agrees with such a choice. There are no longer many people who endorse the goals of the Spanish Inquisition, claiming that its victims were the evil ones who got what they deserved. But wars, including the "asymmetric" wars of a terrorist group versus a strong country, that are going on in our own time may have as many supporters as detractors. Islamic extremists are as ready to praise 9/11 as we are to condemn it: our "hijackers" are their "*shaheedis*" (holy martyrs). The net effect of this subjectivity is that it will be easier and more convincing to create a scale for the gradations of evil in peacetime than for evil in times of war. Do I believe that the Nazi genocide was evil, the earlier Turkish genocide of the Armenians was evil, that Stalin's starvation of the Ukrainians and the millions he sent to the gulag were evils, that the Japanese Rape of Nanking and Mao's destruction of tens of millions of his own people in the *Lao-Gai* (Labor-Reform) camps were evils? Of course I do (and this is just the short list). But here is where it would be helpful to have a God that *everyone* looked up to and who periodically sent us memos to the effect of: "I have looked over the situation between the A-people and the B-people, and I am letting you all know that I consider the A-people to be the evil aggressors here and the B-people to be their victims. Signed, God." Alas, even the most devout members of any and all religions must ruefully acknowledge that we do not receive such final judgments.

Instead we must often make do with the consolation that comes (within our lifetime, if we're lucky) from the consensus of respected historians. To do justice to this complicated topic—to analyze the kinds of evils perpetrated in wartime—would be beyond the scope of this book and would, in fact, warrant a book of its own.

Returning to the situation in peacetime, I will submit here a definition of evil that I think captures the essence of what people in everyday life—the final arbiters of what is meant by "evil"—see and experience before they spontaneously intone this dreaded word. Owing nothing to religious or philosophical teachings, the definition is purely pragmatic.

A WORKING DEFINITION OF EVIL

"Evil" is a word we apply to *situations* or *specific acts* that have the quality of horrifying or shocking whoever witnesses or hears about these acts. In today's parlance, the term is less commonly applied to the *persons* who are guilty of these acts. "Evil," in other words, is reserved for acts that are breathtakingly awful: breathtaking, because the degree of violence, suffering, or humiliation imposed so greatly exceeds what would be needed to express one's irritation or animosity or to subdue the victim.

This element of excess is crucial to the customary use of the word *evil*. The root meaning of *evil* from its Anglo-Saxon origins (the word was then spelled *yfel* but pronounced the same way we do) was "over" or "beyond."[28] To be categorized as evil, there must be a flagrant deviation from the standards of acceptable behavior within the community of the particular culture and time period. The deviation, that is, must be over and beyond what the ordinary people in the community could even envision as something another human being could ever do.

Usually, though not always, evil acts are those preceded by intention or premeditation. This means there was usually malice aforethought: the contemplation of injuring—physically or psychologically—another person in a malign, "over-the-top" way. People will generally know more about the details of the evil act before they get to know something about the person responsible. And as far as the perpetrators go, the more clearly sane (in the legal sense of knowing right from wrong as opposed to being "crazy") they are, the more readily we will conclude that they or their acts were indeed evil. If we find out later on that the persons in question were insane[29] or seriously mentally ill,[30] we end up thinking their *acts* were evil but they themselves were not.

We feel on surer ground in calling an act evil when it results in intense physical suffering, mutilation, or death. But certain nonviolent acts may also reach the level of excess and outrageousness that will call forth the response from people that those acts were evil.

For a more concise definition we can try to get down to the very *essence* of evil. For an act to be evil

1. it must be breathtakingly horrible;
2. malice aforethought (evil intention) will usually precede the act;
3. the degree of suffering inflicted will be wildly excessive;
4. the nature of the act will appear incomprehensible, bewildering, beyond the imagination of ordinary people in the community.

With regard to the first item, there will rarely be universal agreement within any given community or large group of people as to what is "breathtakingly horrible," but there will often be near-universal agreement if the act involves the kidnapping and torture of a child. Ironically, certain crimes amounting to less than murder will be experienced as more clearly evil than murder itself, because of the suffering involved—coupled with our very human tendency to identify with the victim and to imagine how the crime would have affected us, had we been the victim. Here is an example to illustrate the point.

Some years ago I interviewed a man who went to prison for having gone on a crime spree. Under the influence of methamphetamine and cocaine, he had become suspicious and hostile, thinking everyone was out to get him. In that frame of mind, he shot three men who had been working on the street. They had been repairing some electrical cables, while standing with their backs to him. One died, but of the two that lived, one was blinded in both eyes. He had just gotten married the week before. The sympathies with the jury during the ensuing trial—as with most people who became aware of the case—were particularly strong for the blinded man. The family of the dead man would mourn for him, of course, but in the fullness of time, they would make their peace with their loss and get on with their lives. But those who knew about the blinded man (with whom I spoke and sympathized) found themselves imagining what it would be like to live the next fifty years as that blinded man, less able than before to earn a good living and to take care of his wife—whom he would never again be able to see. He would be forced to live with the memory of how his life was turned upside down in an instant—thanks to the senseless violence of some "maniac." The journalists who wrote about the case—for the three days it still was "news" on the inner pages—also spoke of the evil in having blinded the bridegroom. Little was said about the murder victim.

As a footnote to the definition I mentioned above, we can add that when people call a certain *person* "evil" (in contrast to calling certain *acts* evil), we imply that the person can be counted on to commit such acts habitually and often. Even so, it will only rarely be true that every moment of that person's waking day is spent doing evil acts. Some persons of this sort may turn out to have been unassuming and helpful neighbors or pleasant and innocuous-seeming coworkers who have led (as we eventually learn)—unsuspected and undetected for many years—a "secret life" devoted to the commission of evil acts.

EVIL AS A TERM OF EMOTION

When hearing the story of a particularly gruesome act (or having witnessed it), we will often respond by saying (often enough by gasping) *That was evil!* We are not putting forth some philosophical comment here. We are not reciting a chapter from the Good Book. *We are expressing an emotion.* Evil, in everyday speech, means something to the effect: "I feel a horror beyond my ability to understand, beyond my ability to put what I feel into words."

The meaning of the word *evil* in everyday speech can be grasped most readily from the accounts in newspapers and in the biographies of those who have committed murder or other violent crimes. From these sources, we can look for common features in the crimes themselves and even in the people responsible for them. Here is a small sampling, culled from hundreds of examples in books and papers:

Derrick Todd Lee, a serial killer from Louisiana, when finally arrested and convicted, was called "evil incarnate."[31]

Ronald Kennedy and Jerry Jenkins in Casper, Wyoming, lured Becky Thompson and her half-sister, Amy Burridge, to a remote spot near the Freemont Canyon Bridge, raped Becky, and then threw both girls over the bridge. The author who wrote of the incident spoke of his having been a child, living in Wyoming, when the crime occurred, and mentioned that he was "splashed by the unexpected evil of it all."[32]

Phillip Skipper, with his wife, brother, and stepson, in northeast Louisiana, bludgeoned a black neighbor—a woman who had actually helped them financially and had included them in her will. Phil then paid a black man to masturbate into a cup, the contents of which Phil then tossed over her, to mislead the police into thinking her assailant was a black man rather than her white neighbors. People, including Sheriff Bunch, who knew the family, spoke of the wife, Lisa, as "an evil woman from an evil family."[33]

Nancy Kissel, living with her wealthy husband, Robert, in an upscale "ex-pat" community in Hong Kong, had been cheating on her husband. He learned of this through the help of a private investigator. When confronted, she then bludgeoned Robert to death with a lead statuette and then tried to make it appear as though the murder were "self-defense" from his "abusiveness." When her lies were exposed and she was convicted, the Hong Kong newspapers wrote of Nancy: "Evil foreign woman murders husband."[34]

Skylar Deleon conned a retired couple into selling him their yacht and then into meeting them on the yacht to "close the deal." He then subdued them and tossed them into the ocean. Skylar had conned a notary into backdating documents that would appear as if the couple had granted Skylar power of attorney over their assets. Described as "pure evil" by his own cousin, Skylar was also depicted by a detective on the case as "a complete sociopath guilty of a kind of pure evil that is rare."[35]

Gary Ridgway, the serial killer from Washington State, escaped justice for many years. During that eighteen-year stretch, he killed (by his own estimate) some seventy women. When Sheriff David Reichert—the man who helped capture Ridgway—confronted him, he called him "an evil monstrous murdering coward," to which Gary replied, "Yeah, I am."[36]

Dennis Rader, who gave himself the moniker "BTK" (for bind-torture-kill), when finally captured, spoke openly to FBI expert Roy Hazelwood about his bondage fantasies. At his trial, attorney general

Phil Kline told the audience: "In a few minutes, you will look face to face with pure evil; victims whose voices were brutally silenced by the evil of one man will now have their voices heard again."[37]

Ray and Don Duvall, two brothers from Michigan, savagely beat up two hunters in a bar in the northern part of the state and boasted of having then "fed them to the pigs." Whether they did or not is unclear, but the Duvalls were so intimidating that no witnesses came forward for seventeen years. When the brothers were finally arrested, the prosecuting attorney, Donna Prendergast, told the jury: "There is no understanding of evil, there is only the recognition of what evil is."[38]

In the chapter that follows, we will see numerous examples of evil acts, many that end in murder, though not all of them. And we will examine many additional examples of people whom—because of the numerous and grotesque acts they had committed—the public, including journalists, authors, and the victims themselves or their relatives, unhesitatingly called "evil."

Chapter One

EVIL IN PEACETIME

Canto II, ll. 7–12

O muse, o alto ingegno, or m'aiutate;
O mente che scrivesti ciò ch'io vidi,
Qui si parrà la tua nobilitate.
Io cominciai: Poeta che mi guidi
guarda la mia virtù s'ell' è possente
prima ch'a l'alto passo tu mi fidi.

O muse, o lofty mind, now help me;
O memory that wrote down what I saw,
here will your nobility appear.
I began: "Poet who are my guide,
consider my strength, if it is powerful enough
before you entrust me to the deep pass."

I will be concentrating throughout these pages on evil in peacetime in its various forms and degrees. I am using "peacetime" here as a shorthand term for acts committed either by individuals or by several perpetrators working together. There are plenty of evil acts carried out by rioters, members of opposing street gangs, political protesters and the police who try to subdue them, and the like. All of these situations can be considered something just short of a declared war, but the individuals involved in the clash are nameless and are usually acting more as people swept up in the heat of the moment. In a riot, for example, the sense of personal responsibility for whatever one side does to the other—and that may include brutality of the most gruesome and shocking sort—is pretty much lost. Questioned later, one at a time, the participants may say, "*We* did it," rather than "*I* did it." Or they might say, "Well, *they* started it!" The point here is that in a riot, people from ordinary life—with no criminal record, who had no forethought as to what they were going to do and no idea they were even going to get involved—are seldom disturbed or vicious. A terrible situation arose, forces got unleashed in otherwise ordinary law-abiding folk who never dreamed themselves capable of pummeling or maiming others, and lo and behold, they ended up doing things that the bystanders and commentators later on called "evil." I don't feel there is much we can learn about the evil that may emerge in the crowd, the mob, the gang—except to say that in extreme circumstances almost all of us can take part in regrettable actions that would (or should) later move us to shame and remorse.

Cultural and historical factors count in the equation of what we regard as evil in times of peace. Some actions in the past by those in positions of great power were seen—by them—as necessary, even though many at the time felt those actions were evil. Reading about these events centuries later, we also regard them as evil. History is filled with examples of what we now, looking back, regard as evil—as when general or kings order bloody punishments, including torture, to "wrongdoers" as a warning to the populace. England's King Henry the Eighth provides one such example. Desperate for a son and heir, he had his first marriage annulled (never mind that Catherine of Aragon had given him a daughter, later to be known, ironically, as Bloody Mary). After his second wife, his then beloved Anne Boleyn, miscarried what would have been his son and heir, he had her beheaded though she gave him a healthy daughter (the future Elizabeth I).[1] He had his fifth wife, the teenaged Catherine Howard, beheaded when she was caught cheating on him.[2] Was there evil here? Certainly not in the executioner: he was just doing his job, one that he did as efficiently and painlessly as that job allows. As for the beheading of Catherine Howard, some kings look the other way at an adulterous mate. Henry was not of that mold. His fury was at least understandable to us, though we may feel he went a bit too far. Perhaps there was evil in beheading Anne (and her equally innocent brother, George), since he did this for selfish motives. To weasel out of a marriage that seemed unlikely to bear (male) fruit, Henry, exercising his powers, compelled his inner circle to conjure up tales of adultery and treason about his guiltless wife, Anne, and her brother. There were no poll takers in sixteenth-century England, so we don't know how many would have voted (anonymously!) that Henry's action here had been "evil." As for Catherine Howard, very few in those days would have objected to her beheading. Her public execution was anyway meant as an act of terror, warning anyone with eyes to see that they had best not take liberties with their king. And Henry was not a mad monarch in any case. What he did was in keeping with his personality: he could be loving to those he cherished and who respected him, yet, insistent upon having his way, brutal to those who crossed him. Perhaps to justify his ways, he took a page from Machiavelli's *The Prince*, written when Henry was twenty-two and filled with advice for how a ruler should rule and when the ruler, to restore order, must be harsh or even cruel.[3]

Notwithstanding the above examples, the people I want to draw attention to throughout these pages are people the great majority of whom have acted as individuals and who have done the kinds of things to others that most people would call evil. What drew my own attention to this particular subject was a murder case some twenty years ago, in which I was called to serve as an expert witness in a court of law. The defendant had stabbed to death his pregnant wife and children, so there was little hesitation in the press or in the minds of most people who knew of the case in referring to the crime as "evil." As for motive, this man had felt threatened with exposure: he had cheated on his wife and had done some other disreputable acts—but the murder of his family had an unplanned, "spur-of-the-moment" quality.

The case stimulated my interest in murder. I thought it might be useful if I could get the members of the jury to think of an imaginary line along which different kinds of murder (and different murderers) could be categorized, starting with the most understandable and least horrific murders and stretching all the way to those that were the most mind-boggling and horrific. This was the beginning of the scale that I was to call the "Gradations of Evil." I began to read full-length biographies about famous murderers—the ones found in the true-crime section of a bookstore—because these books generally give a great deal of personal detail about each murderer. There would be material about the childhood background of the man or woman in question, about what the family had been like, about what crimes may have preceded the murder. And I would learn whether the murderer abused drugs or alcohol, was mentally ill, had suffered a head injury when young, or had tortured animals or set fires. As a psychiatrist with a specialty in disorders of personality, I combed through each biography for impressions and reminiscences of the people who knew the murderer—friends, relatives, and also lawyers, doctors, and (if the person had been in prison) jailers and other inmates—who could give a picture of what the murderer had been like. Was the person shy or outgoing, able to care about others, or totally self-centered, open or secretive, candid or habitually lying, calm or hot-tempered, forgiving or vengeful, submissive or domineering? Was the person jealous, greedy, violent . . . ? Were there other malignant personality traits? I paid close attention to whether the author of the true-crime book used the word *evil* in describing either the crime or the murderer. Was the word used in other accounts about the same killer in newspapers and magazines? And if so, was that the impression of the writer, or of the police, the judge, and the prosecutors, or of the relatives of the victims? Above all, what was the special quality that had prompted anyone to say the word *evil*: Was it the cunning way used to lure the victim? The callousness of the killer? The extreme suffering endured by the victim?

My idea was to give the jury a better grasp of who the murderer really was in everyday life and of where the murder fit along this imaginary line from least to most horrifying and inhumane. Could I identify, in other words, divisions, or "gradations" that made one type of murder more evil-seeming than others, in the opinion of the authorities and the public? When I gave my impressions to the jury, I had not as yet read more than a few dozen biographies of murderers. There were not so many different natural divisions I could make along that line, but I felt they could be put into perhaps half a dozen such categories, or "compartments." As dreadful as it was to murder one's pregnant wife and two small children, the husband had acted impulsively and had not subjected his family to torture. So this crime, though it was called evil, struck me as less deplorable than, say, the serial murders of children that had been committed in the mid-1960s by Ian Brady and his girlfriend-accomplice, Myra Hindley, in the English moors.[4] Brady had first strangled his victims and had then recorded their screams on a tape recorder, for use later as a kind of aphrodisiac for him and Myra.[5] That was torture and callousness of a sort that went beyond anything I had heard of in the crime literature up until that time. That was twenty years ago. Worse was to come. But at the time, I placed that example at the far end of my evolving scale: evil at the extreme.

At the other end, I made a category for people who had killed someone but whose action could be viewed as a justified homicide and therefore not technically murder (which refers only to unlawful killing), let alone "evil." This category would "anchor" my scale at the absolute lowest point, where the notion of evil disappeared. The case that attracted my attention as I was creating the scale had occurred in Wyoming: a teenage boy, Richard Jahnke Jr., had killed his abusive father.[6] Richard Sr., besides constantly beating his son and daughter, whipping his wife, and going around the house with a pistol pointed at them, also sexually molested his daughter. Sixteen-year-old Richard Jr. saw no way of escaping the abuse: his father, after all, was an agent for the IRS. The mother lacked the courage to admit her husband was abusing the entire family. Richard had gone to the authorities, but they turned a deaf ear (as is quite common in such cases). So in November of 1982, Richard Jr. shot his father to death with a rifle. The case shows how our ideas about right and wrong, and about evil, can undergo change over the generations. Richard's act clearly violated the Bible's fifth commandment: *Honor thy father and thy mother*, as well as the seventh: *Thou shalt not kill*. The punishment in biblical times for killing one's father or mother was not light: such a child "shall surely be put to death."[7] Even cursing one's parents or stubbornly disobeying them could get a child stoned to death "by the men of his city"[8]—as a stern warning to any like-minded youngster.

I am unwilling to believe that there were no abusive parents in Moses' time; however, no allowance was made then or for the next three thousand years for that contingency. Even in 1982 Richard was convicted of voluntary manslaughter and was sentenced to five to fifteen years in prison. The governor of Wyoming, a man ahead of his time, quickly commuted the sentence to time served at a state-run boy's school "till he was twenty-one" and where Richard would win a conditional release in less than a year. So what fifty years ago would have been a clear-cut murder case was, in 1982, still not considered close to an instance of "justified homicide." The law has begun to recognize that severely abused children and wives sometimes have little recourse except to kill their more physically powerful adversary—the husband or father—using surprise or deception. But any kind of planning or premeditated element has always earned, until very recently, a first-degree murder conviction. This, despite the law having a vague grasp of the fact that a hundred-pound woman, when under murderous attack by her two-hundred-pound husband, has no real chance of winning or even surviving. If escape is impossible, she (or a child under similar attack) must take the aggressor by surprise. The Jahnke case and those similar to it became my "zero-point" for what was to become my Gradations of Evil Scale.

So far my scale had three points: the two extremes and a case in the middle, where there was evil but no torture and little if any planning. Before showing my rudimentary scale to the jury, I added a few more points: one for jealousy murders, another for men and women who clearly had schemed—with "malice aforethought," that is, with "guilty mind" and prior intention[9]—to kill someone they regarded as an obstacle to some important goal. And then, an additional point for serial killers who, unlike Ian Brady, did not engage in torture.

Jealousy murders, the sort where someone surprises a spouse in bed with a lover and then kills the spouse or the lover (or both), are the most understandable to the public and the most likely to earn a measure of sympathy—even though the public recognizes that the murder was morally indefensible and wrong. People reacting to such a story are likely to think: *If I were in your place, I'd do the same, or I'd at least feel like doing the same*. Murders of this sort are considered the least "evil" or perhaps not evil at all. People committing a murder prompted by jealousy feel they are engaged in a kind of "righteous slaughter," where the killing becomes an antidote to the unbearable humiliation and emotional pain of the betrayal.[10] We might be moved to say that the *act* was evil, but the *person* was not. The example I had used at the time was Jean Harris's murder of her lover, the "Scarsdale Diet" doctor, Herman Tarnower, when she discovered he had been cheating on her with another woman.[11]

For a schemer driven by malice aforethought, I used the case of Steven Benson. The son of sixty-three-year-old tobacco heiress Margaret Benson, Steven had racked up big losses in a number of failed business ventures. He had embezzled several millions from his mother already, and she was about to have her books examined to see where the shortages were coming from. For Steven, that lent some urgency to the problem. The way he figured he could even the financial balance sheet was to accelerate his inheritance, so to speak, by advancing the date of his mother's death ahead of God's schedule. To that end he planted two pipe bombs in the car she was about to take a ride in. His mother died in the explosion, as did a nephew; his sister survived, badly burned.[12] Benson, convicted two years later, collected two life sentences rather than the ten million dollars he was counting on. Because of the diabolical planning that went into Benson's scheme (if his sister had died too, then *all* the heirs except himself would have been put "out of the way"), he belongs to a higher (i.e., worse) spot on the evil scale—higher even than the man who killed his family.

I saw the need for another category, one that covered crimes people found more disturbing than the murder of one's mother for monetary gain but less disturbing than a serial killer who tortured his victims. I chose Ted Bundy, since he was a serial killer with many victims, but he did not subject them to torture.[13]

At this stage of its development, the scale had some six points, or compartments. If we put them next to each other, with the most horrific cases at the far right—the ones people would just about unanimously find "evil" and somehow worse than those in the compartment just to the left—we would end up with a simple scale that would look something like this:

A	B	C	D	E	F
Justified homicide, not evil at all	Jealousy-driven and other impulsive murders	Murder to get someone out of the way, without planning.	Murder to get someone out of the way; malice aforethought	Serial murder, repetitive vicious acts, but without torture	Serial murder, with torture the main goal

I chose to focus on murder initially, not just because the case I was asked to comment on for the jury happened to involve murder, but because people are quicker to use the word *evil* when they hear about a murder than if they hear about a civil crime such as fraud. And the more diabolical the murderer (meaning the more scheming and malice involved) or the more intense the suffering of the victim, the more readily we tend to add the word *evil* to our description of the event.

There is plenty of evil "out there" that has nothing to do with murder. We already saw that in the Jahnke case. If there had been a passerby who witnessed the Jahnke boy raise his shotgun and kill his father, that person might conclude there was "evil" present, as personified by the son. But if the passerby's curiosity were piqued and he looked into the matter further, he would learn that the father had beaten every member of his family repeatedly, had intimidated them all with the pistol that he toted around the house, on top of which he also committed incest with his own daughter. *Now* where was the evil?! It would strain most people's sense of justice to "honor thy father" in the Jahnke case, and indeed, the term *evil* is often applied to cruel parents, vicious bullies, and bosses who humiliate their employees to the point of mental breakdown and even suicide. This is not the complete list, but I will devote a later chapter to uncommonly cruel parents (whose actions sometimes fell short of murder).

By the time I had read a few hundred true-crime biographies, it became clear that more points on the gradation scale were needed to do justice to the variety of murders that have occurred. The number of categories began to expand, eventually reaching twenty-two. This does not mean that there exists in nature altogether twenty-two distinct types of evil involving murder—or actually twenty-one, since Category 1 is set aside for cases that appear at first to be murder but are better understood as justifiable homicide. The number is really arbitrary: someone else reading the same literature might decide there were fewer or even more varieties. And now that I have read over six hundred such books and have interviewed many violent criminals in hospitals and prisons, I now and then encounter persons who don't fit neatly into the original categories. Some have committed shocking acts of violence but were obviously mentally ill—so much so that they were scarcely aware of, and not legally responsible for, what they had done.

By "mentally ill" I refer to people who suffer from a psychiatric condition (often called a "psychosis") that grossly impairs their sense of reality. This impairment might come in the form of delusions: rigidly held beliefs that are contrary to all reality and impervious to reason. For instance, thinking that airplanes flying overhead are capturing your thoughts by special sensors and then broadcasting them to the world would be such a delusion. Hearing imaginary voices (hallucinations) would be another symptom of a psychosis. Some people who have committed violent crimes have done so under the false belief that God's voice or the devil or the voice of some powerful "leader" was commanding them to kill a certain person, and that it was right and necessary to obey this voice.

A brief example: a young man from a home where the father had been cruel toward both him and his brother became acutely delusional. In this state he grabbed a large knife and severed the head of his father, throwing it out the window. His fear was that if he did not do so, the head might somehow become reattached to his father's body, and the trouble would start all over again. This was a dramatic crime, and it was called "evil" in the newspapers. But the young man, before his mental breakdown, had been a good student, caring and supportive toward his younger brother, and had never been in trouble with the law. There was no matchup, in other words, between the act and the person. His was an impulsive murder occurring in a psychotic state: a kind of "one-off" totally at odds with the man's character before he became mentally ill.

Other exceptional cases that didn't fit neatly into the scale I had developed involved men, in no way mentally ill, who had made lifelong careers of subjecting others to excruciating tortures, using complicated machinery of their own devising, and whose acts begged for a category that went beyond even my "extreme" number of 22. For reasons of simplicity I have left these cases at number 22, acknowledging that even among torture-murders, some are seen by the community as considerably more evil than others. In other words, these cases are similar in *type*, but different in *intensity*. Torture-murderers—basically serial killers who are sexually stirred up by inflicting torture—are almost never mentally ill, meaning they are not delusional, do not hear voices, nor do they show any other signs of a radical departure from reality. In large part, the public does not readily grasp this distinction, assuming instead that anyone acting in such a way must be "crazy." Put another way: the public is just about unanimous in defining certain *acts* as evil. But it requires a measure of familiarity and sophistication about mental illness to distinguish between those evil acts (the vast majority) that are committed by people whose mental faculties are intact and other evil acts (much less numerous, but often quite spectacular) that are committed by the mentally ill. The opinion of the public is quite trustworthy as to what acts can be considered evil. But the act is more directly visible than is the nature of the person committing the act. One of my goals in fashioning the scale was to fine-tune the estimation of evil, taking into consideration not only the quality of the act and the degree of suffering it imposed on the victim, but also the nature of the offender. Was the offender mentally ill? If not, was the person impetuous, or instead calculating and cold-blooded? I regard these nuances as important in creating such a scale, which means accumulating information that is not always immediately apparent to the public when the news of a murder or other extremely violent act is first made known through the media.

Here is an example that illustrates this point:

> Many years ago a man was arrested for having assaulted and castrated another man. When the case came before the court, the judge assumed the man must have been mentally ill (specifically, schizophrenic) to have committed such an act. This was years before there was a better understanding by either psychiatrists or legal experts about sexual sadism, and about how the men carrying out acts of sexual sadism are rarely mentally ill. All involved—the public, the media, the professionals concerned with the case, including the judge—had the reaction: this was evil. But the judge understandably (in that era), yet incorrectly, concluded the assailant was mentally ill and recommended psychiatric treatment in a special hospital, rather than placement in a correctional facility.

We would like to think that people who learned of prolonged torture, whether or not it ended in murder, would all react the same way—that this was an evil act. The closer the public's reaction approaches the unanimous, the less "subjectivity" there is. There are nevertheless certain situations where the public reaction to a murder, and its assessment of how "evil" the crime was—depends more than we might care to admit on the characteristics and on the social status of the victim. Our Constitution laudably says that all men are created equal; our religions tell us that all are equal in the eye of God. But we do not always react as we assume God and our noble Constitution would have it. This leads to a measure of confusion as to where certain acts belong in any scale of evil.[14] Here are two examples that highlight the problem. The first concerns a veteran who, on his return to the United States, stabbed to death a homeless black man who had been sleeping in the street. The veteran, relating this incident to me while in his prison cell, said, "I was mad because the blacks are taking over the country" (he expressed himself in much coarser language than I have indicated here). His deplorable act—a racial hate crime—earned the label "evil" in a brief note on one of the inner pages of the local paper. And that was all. Contrast this with another murder, this time the murder of Sharon Tate and her friends at her Los Angeles home in the summer of 1969 by the followers of Charles Manson. This was no inner-page murder. The Tate murder was not only headline material for an extended period, but it electrified the whole nation and spawned books and articles for years afterward.[15] Sharon Tate was white; blonde; eight months pregnant by her husband, the famous movie director Roman Polanski; and was in addition an extraordinarily beautiful woman and by all accounts extraordinarily sweet. No one hesitated to call her murder evil, and, judging from the public reaction, an evil of greater magnitude than the unheralded murder of the anonymous black man. Both murders were, viewed from one perspective, equally senseless and despicable. This would be the supremely fair perspective of God and the Constitution. But from the more subjective reaction of the public, the murder of a beautiful, pregnant celebrity weighed heavier in the balance of evil. There was of course the element of terror in the Tate case, and indeed Manson had meant to strike terror in the public. That was the meaning underlying his "Helter Skelter." Manson, no more a friend of the blacks than was my veteran, had imagined in his crazy vision that the blacks were going to rise up and kill all the whites (except Manson and his followers, that is). And then—because the blacks were, in Manson's jaundiced view, incapable of governing, he—Manson—would assume leadership of the remaining population. So in a way, one can understand how the Tate murder seemed to belong to a higher notch in the scale of evil than the murder of the homeless man. Yet—when you take full stock of the veteran's bigotry and cowardice in killing a sleeping black man, just as innocent and defenseless in his way as Sharon Tate was in hers, the scales of evil are not so far apart.

WHY "CATEGORIES" OF EVIL?

One may well ask, what is the point of breaking up the concept of evil into all these categories in the first place? Once we accept the new way of defining evil—taking it outside the realm of religion and philosophy, that is, and reexamining it in the light of everyday speech—then we all see that some violent crimes, some forms of cruelty to women and children in particular, are worse than others. The measure of these differences might be a stronger gasp when we hear certain stories, our jaw dropping lower, our eyebrows raised higher—the changes in facial expression that accompany our hearing an "evil" story. Those changes in expression correspond quite closely with the degree of shock, the reaction of horror that we register when we first hear such a story. But this alone would not justify making twenty-two categories of evil acts.

My argument for making distinct categories rests on the fact that in other areas of human behavior, something useful often emerges from making these distinctions. There are several important questions that might be more easily answered if we take this approach to evil as well. If all the individual cases that get labeled "evil" are simply lumped together, it becomes harder to discover the origins of the different varieties of evil behaviors. If we are dealing with prisoners who have committed horrific crimes, how can we best decide which ones are salvageable—and which ones can most safely be restored to the outside world as functioning members of the community? Which of these criminals are best kept under lock and key for extended periods, or even for the rest of their lives? Can one inherit certain tendencies or be marred by certain experiences early in life that heighten the risk for cruelty? The first step toward answering such questions is to find common features—of background, of behavior, of personality—shared by one group of individuals who have committed evil acts but not often found in some other group. Those fitting into the half-dozen categories already mentioned ought to differ from one another in ways that go beyond the mere differences in the types of murder. My guess at the outset is that serial killers are not the same as the kind of men who lie awake thinking up schemes to kill their wives, and that the latter are probably quite different from those who kill on impulse in some dramatic but once-in-a-lifetime way. It is only when we separate the groups that show these *outer* differences that we can then take the magnifying glass and look for subtle differences and, ultimately, *inner* differences. By "inner differences" I mean the various hereditary, early-background, and even brain-structure differences that would not be at all apparent when the people behind the evil actions were first identified.

This is the same process that has already begun to pay big dividends in psychiatry. The system of classification in psychiatry was still so broad in America even fifty years ago that most patients who showed a break with reality were lumped together as "schizophrenic."[16] Worse yet, the supposed "causes" of this loosely defined condition were narrowed down (mostly) to one: destructive mothering. There were a few patients in that era whose breakdown took the form of grandiose delusions so flamboyant ("I am Napoleon," "I am the Virgin Mary") as to be labeled "manic." There wasn't much one could do for either type of patient, so an accurate diagnosis wasn't a high priority. Once medications like chlorpromazine[17] were developed in the 1950s, that was what the patients were prescribed. Not many types of psychotherapy were available either, so most patients who were called schizophrenic were given a form of therapy based on psychoanalysis. This one-size-fits-all treatment didn't change much until lithium was found to be useful in the treatment of mania. In mania one sees such symptoms as an abnormally elevated mood, often with grandiosity or irritability (or both), along with excessive rapidity of thought and speech. The delusions of manic persons may take the form of believing they are some exalted figure, like the Messiah, the Queen of England, Napoleon, or the Virgin Mary. At this point it became important to make careful distinctions in diagnosis: many patients who had been labeled schizophrenic were finally recognized (in the 1950s in Europe but not until the late 1960s in the United States) as manic and given an effective medication.[18] Alongside this improvement, better forms of psychotherapy for both schizophrenic and manic patients were also developed. As more was understood about causative factors for these conditions, the role of inheritance came to overshadow improper parenting. Mothers were no longer blamed for making their children schizophrenic. In recent years magnetic resonance imaging (MRI) techniques have made it possible to show in an even more dramatic way the differences in how the brain works in these two separate conditions, not so long ago thought of as just one condition.[19]

It is by applying a variety of methods to the area of severe mental illness that we have developed a better understanding of its dynamics. By applying similar methods to the shadowy realm of evil, I hope to develop a better way of understanding the complex forces that lead to it: What are the varieties of evil? What are the underlying factors peculiar to each of these varieties?

In the search for a violent criminal who has so shocked the public as to call his act evil, the police are mainly concerned with the questions: who, when, where, and how. As a psychiatrist, entering the picture well after there has been a capture, and well after those four questions have been answered, my interest is: why? In the case of murder, to the police, to the prosecutor, and even to the judge, the *why* question is usually of less interest. To the defense attorney, the *why* question is of interest, since the defense will try to show "mitigating circumstances," based on such things as having suffered a grievous loss, or being the object of bigotry, or having had a history of terrible abuse or neglect in childhood. Where psychiatry and the law come together—in "forensic psychiatry"—there is the all-important question of dangerousness. This outweighs even the issue of treatability, as significant as that is. With the focus here on murder, we want to know whether the persons in a particular category of the scale are likely to harm others again if they were released. That is, after all, one of the major reasons why the categories were created: in *which* persons, having committed an evil act, does dangerousness remain a compelling issue? In which persons, who have committed a violent act, can we expect eventual rehabilitation and the reduction of dangerousness to a minimum?

By looking at the histories, and the subsequent fate (in the case of released prisoners) of persons in different categories, we can begin to answer such questions as this: is a person who has committed so gruesome a murder as to place him in one of the more extreme categories of the scale—but who has done so only once—more dangerous than someone who has performed less shocking crimes of violence but has done them more often? Another relevant issue concerns the legal tradition. There is a centuries-old custom of shaping the length of sentencing purely on the nature of the crime and whether it is a first-time offense. Of course many judges are more sensible and more strict. But there are plenty of examples in the crime literature where someone committing a seriously violent act, such as rape of a stranger with mutilation, is given something like "ten years with three years off for good behavior." What if a young man of nineteen commits rape, and he is freed at age twenty-six? Still in the prime of life, that is, with all of his masculine juices flowing as ardently as before? We know from studies what happens with rapists in the years after release from prison: they have high rates of re-offending ("recidivism"). Depending on the report, a third, perhaps a half, will commit another rape or another violent crime within two or three years.[20] Viewed in this light, "ten years with three off for good behavior" looks pretty generous. Too generous. Especially, when in the all-male environment of the men's prison, there are no women with whom the rapist's "improvement" can be put to the test. Prisons nowadays, incidentally, are often called *correctional facilities*, a phrase built on the hope that during their incarceration prisoners will emerge "corrected" of their tendency to behave in antisocial, let alone violent, ways. And this does sometimes happen. The older term for prisons was *penitentiary*—implying that prison was a place where you were to feel sorry (from the Latin *paenitet*, "to make sorry") for what you did.

And that sometimes happens, also. But there are many exceptions to these hopeful beliefs. One of the aims of making more accurate categories of serious crimes, including the ones people call "evil," is to improve the guidelines about whom to keep in prison, and for how long, versus whom to release back into the community. In all fairness, I would have to say that there are incarcerated men and women who, despite having committed acts widely felt to be "evil," have become truly both penitent and "corrected." They are no longer dangerous, yet they are ironically serving immensely long sentences because of the same kinds of technicalities that released some dangerous persons prematurely. Before presenting the Gradations of Evil Scale in its currently more expanded state, I would like to share with you two examples: one of a man who should never have been released, but was, and another of a man who will never be released (as far as I can tell), but who I believe now deserves return to society.

The first example concerns a Massachusetts man, David Paul Brown, who began showing violent behavior when he was six: he choked a six-year-old female pupil. He grew massively obese and was a social misfit, mocked in school for his awkwardness and obesity. At fifteen he tried to lure two boys to a cemetery for lewd purposes. He was not able to carry through his intentions, and the boys' mother did not press charges.[21]

Later he took to impersonating policemen in order to lure young boys, and at eighteen almost choked one to death. For that offense he was given merely a year's probation. At twenty he lured two adolescent boys, with the same ruse of being a "cop," and, using a knife and handcuffs, attempted to kidnap and sodomize them. One was able to play dead, and later ran off and summoned the authorities. Both survived. Brown was arrested and sent to a prison for sex offenders with the recommendation from a psychiatrist that he be retained indefinitely. While at that facility, he changed his name to "Nathaniel Benjamin Levi Bar-Jonah."[22] After fourteen years, during which time he showed himself to be treatment-resistant, refusing to participate in the various therapeutic programs, he was nevertheless released. This was in part thanks to efforts of his mother. By that time he weighed 375 lbs (170 kg). His mother managed to find two independent psychiatrists from outside the prison who testified that he was no longer a risk to the community. Based on their testimony (made without delving into Brown's criminal record), the judge was persuaded—bamboozled would be a better word—into granting Brown's release. Scarcely a month and a half later, he was rearrested, this time for entering a parked car and sitting atop a seven-year-old boy who was awaiting his mother to return from shopping. Brown's mother pleaded with the boy's mother not to pursue the charges, on the promise that her son, now thirty-four, would relocate to Montana. Not long after he moved to Montana, Brown was arrested for pedophilia involving an eight-year-old boy; for this he spent only five months in jail. A year later, again impersonating a policeman and standing outside a school, Brown lured a ten-year-old boy, immobilizing him with a stun gun. Accused of molesting the boy sexually, killing, and cannibalizing him, Brown could not be convicted of murder, since no body was ever found, and the boy's grief-stricken mother, still unable to accept that her son was dead, would not cooperate with the prosecution. Convicted instead of child molestation among other offenses, Brown began serving a life sentence.[23] He remained to the end in denial of the crimes he committed and incapable of telling the truth about the least controversial things. When I interviewed Brown a few years before his 2008 death in prison, I asked him why he had moved to Montana. He said, "Oh, I was getting sick of Massachusetts." To my reply, "And I guess Massachusetts was getting sick of you," he had no answer.

As I will show in a later chapter, this picture of incarceration for a violent crime, followed by imprudent release and then the commission of still more—and more shocking—crimes is actually common in the literature on men ultimately convicted of serial sexual homicide.

The second example centers on a man, Ronald Luff, who got swept up in a small Ohio cult whose leader was a con man-turned-preacher. The leader, Jeff Lundgren, was a self-styled prophet of a Mormon offshoot called the Reorganized Church of Jesus Christ of the Latter Day Saints. A stranger to modesty, Lundgren claimed that he was a prophet of God, heard God's voice, and—toward the end—that he *was* God.[24] Lundgren set up his base of operation near one of the holy places in Mormonism: Kirtland, Ohio (some forty miles east of Cleveland). There, a church had been erected by the early Mormons during their westward trek in the nineteenth century. Among the two dozen people he mesmerized into joining his cult was a devout man from a more traditional Mormon background, Ronald Luff. Married with children, Luff had been a deeply religious, hardworking, industrious man with a sterling record in his Missouri hometown. He fell under the spell of Lundgren, taking him for the prophet he claimed to be. In time he became the second-in-command member of the cult. Another Missouri family that felt the same enchantment with Lundgren's grandiose and controlling qualities was Dennis and Cheryl Avery and their three children. The Averys fell afoul of Lundgren, who was trying to con them out of their savings. Lundgren would not tolerate such "disobedience" and ordered the whole family to be executed. Luff, whose moral values had been swamped and overridden by Lundgren, participated, with an obedience worthy of Hitler's henchmen, in this murderous plan. One evening, in April of 1989, Lundgren commanded Luff to lead the members of the Avery family, one at a time, from the main house to a farmhouse farther off on the grounds. Once the entire family was in the farmhouse, Lundgren shot each one so that the bodies fell into a pre-dug pit that was then sealed over.[25] Lundgren and his flock then fled. Arrogating to himself the privilege of marriage and sex with whoever struck his fancy, Lundgren tried to make one of his married flock's members into his "second wife." As a result, this woman's husband broke down and revealed the murders to the authorities. Lundgren was executed for the massacre in 2006. Ron Luff was given a life sentence—actually a "170-year" sentence, which is very much the same. An intellectual, thoughtful, and remorseful man who had never been remotely in trouble with the law before, Luff has already served over twenty years. He shows every sign of being able to resume his place in society as a worthy and law-abiding citizen—someone who could be of special use, given his experience, in warning other susceptible people against submitting to power-hungry cult leaders. But it is not likely he will ever be released.

The difference between these two men is that the dangerousness of the one was ignored until it was too late, and the non-dangerousness of the other was not taken fully into consideration. The great judge Oliver Wendell Holmes once said, "May Justice triumph over Law." Ron Luff has felt the full weight of the law but was not served the full cup of justice. At least that is my opinion. There was, of course, no miscarriage of justice here: he was unquestionably guilty as an accomplice to a massacre. It is appropriate that he serve a long sentence for that crime: perhaps the twenty years he has thus far been in prison. But from the standpoint of our main topic—evil—it is clear that evil was quite evident in the pedophile and equally so in the cult leader. Lundgren, in fact, was one of those rare individuals who behaved atrociously on a day-in day-out basis throughout most of his adult life. (We will have more to say about him later.) Clearly, Ron Luff also participated in an evil act. But since we are interested in *gradations* in the domain of evil, Luff belongs at a lower level than the utterly callous leader, Lundgren, who dominated him.[26] Luff did know ahead of time what Lundgren was planning. This means that Luff might have somehow found the courage to escape and tell the authorities about Lundgren, perhaps even saving the Avery family. So our sense of the level of evil here, in Luff, is still quite high. A more dramatic example of a "lesser" evil is a man who has had the opportunity to demonstrate his rehabilitation: Billy Wayne Sinclair.[27]

Briefly put, when he was twenty, Billy Sinclair killed a store owner in a bungled holdup in Louisiana. It was an impulsive and unintentional murder. He had fired his pistol over his shoulder without looking where it was pointed as he tried to escape the owner. Through terrible luck, the bullet struck and killed the man. Billy was arrested, spent seven years on death row and twenty-eight more years there when the death penalty was temporarily abolished. He eventually became the editor of the prison newspaper, exposed the pardons-for-sale scandal at the infamous "Angola" (Louisiana State) prison, and was befriended by a journalist whom he later married. A man of unusual integrity, he refused the offer of early release if he paid the pardon price and so spent more years in prison, until he was released on merit when he was approaching sixty. He and his wife now live in Houston, where I interviewed him and got a chance to learn how he has been working at a law firm, helping other inmates who have had to struggle with the kinds of unfairness that for so long had characterized the criminal justice system in his area. The book he and his wife have written is a testimony to the possibility of self-transcendence and redemption in some men and women who have committed an evil act—a stark contrast to the life of Jeff Lundgren and others like him, for whom redemption is unthinkable, whom age does not mellow, and whose propensity to evil actions remains at full tilt throughout their life span.

—∞—

THE GRADATIONS OF EVIL SCALE

This would be a good point to show the Gradations of Evil Scale in its expanded form with twenty-two compartments. Since murder cases formed the inspiration behind the creation of the scale, its focus remains on murder. There are a few exceptions for cases involving multiple rapes and a strong *suspicion* of murder, the latter never proven in court. Some of the cases concern people regarded as evil by the community—people who were exceptionally cruel to a spouse, to children, or to other family members. Their actions fell short of murder, though they sometimes precipitated a suicide. Some cases involved spouses (usually husbands) whose evil consisted of "gaslighting" their wives. The term *gaslight* comes from the famous play *Angel Street*, by Patrick Hamilton, later made into the novel *Gaslight*, by William Drummond.[28] The word has now become a verb, meaning to drive someone mad (usually one's wife) through malicious acts designed to make that person doubt her own perceptions. As it says on the back cover of Drummond's book: "Trapped in the evil mansion on Angel Street, Bella suspects that her own husband, sinister Mr. Manningham, is driving her mad." If the victims of gaslighting survive, as they usually do, no murder has been committed. Hence the evil in these cases does not fall within the scale. But these and other examples of prolonged cruelty, deserving perhaps a separate scale, fall readily under the larger umbrella of Evil—with a capital "E"—covering every known variety.

The terms *psychopathic traits* or *psychopath* occur in most of the descriptions of the categories from number 9 on. A century ago the word *psychopath* meant little more than its root meaning of "mental illness."[29] But about the time of World War II the meaning changed: it was now reserved for people who used deception to "con" others (like the *con*fidence men who sell fake Rolex watches on the street), people who are socially irresponsible and who show no remorse for the offensive or, often enough, violent, things they habitually do.[30] The definition got much more specific after 1980 when the renowned Canadian psychologist Robert Hare and his colleagues refined the original description, creating a scale called the Psychopathy Checklist. This checklist consists of twenty items, some dealing primarily with personality; others more with behaviors. Since each item can get a score (depending whether it applies considerably, only a little, or

TABLE 1.1. Gradations of Evil Scale	
Killing in Self-Defense or Justified Homicide	
Category 1.	Justifiable homicide
Impulsive Murders in Persons without Psychopathic Features	
Category 2.	Jealous lovers, egocentric, immature people, committing crimes of passion
Category 3.	Willing companions of killers, impulse-ridden; some antisocial trait
Category 4.	Killing in self-defense, but extremely provocative toward the victim
Category 5.	Traumatized, desperate persons who kill relatives or others, yet have remorse
Category 6.	Impetuous, hotheaded murderers, yet without marked psychopathic traits
Persons with a Few or No Psychopathic Traits; Murders of a More Severe Type	
Category 7.	Highly narcissistic persons, some with a psychotic core, who murder loved ones
Category 8.	Murders sparked by smoldering rage—resulting sometimes in mass murder
Psychopathic Features Marked; Murders Show Malice Aforethought	
Category 9.	Jealous lovers with strong psychopathic traits or full-blown psychopathy
Category 10.	Killers of people "in the way" (including witnesses); extreme egocentricity
Category 11.	Fully psychopathic killers of people "in the way"
Category 12.	Power-hungry psychopaths who murder when "cornered"
Category 13.	Inadequate, rageful psychopaths; some committing multiple murders
Category 14.	Ruthlessly self-centered psychopathic schemers
Spree or Multiple Murders; Psychopathy Is Apparent	
Category 15.	Psychopathic, cold-blooded, spree or multiple murderers
Category 16.	Psychopathic persons committing multiple vicious acts (including murder)
Serial Killers, Torturers, Sadists	
Category 17.	Sexually perverse serial killers; killing is to hide evidence; no torture
Category 18.	Torture-murderers, though the torture element is not prolonged
Category 19.	Psychopaths driven to terrorism, subjugation, rape, etc. short of murder
Category 20.	Torture-murderers but in persons with distinct psychosis (such as schizophrenia)
Category 21.	Psychopaths committing extreme torture but not known to have killed
Category 22.	Psychopathic torture-murderers with torture as their primary motive. The motive need not always be sexual.

not at all) of 2, 1, or zero, the maximum score would be 40. Anyone scoring 30 or more is considered a *psychopath* proper. Others with lower scores—in the teens or twenties—are said to show *psychopathic traits* (but not the full-blown condition). For our purposes, the most important items are those having to do with personality. Taken together, they paint a picture of extreme egocentricity, or "narcissism," with ruthless disregard for the rights and feelings of others. These personality items are: glib speech or superficial charm, grandiosity, conning or manipulativeness, pathological lying, lack of remorse or guilt, callousness or lack of empathy, and a failure to accept responsibility for one's actions. Some of the behavioral items include impulsivity, sexual promiscuity, poor behavioral controls, and a parasitic lifestyle.[31] The characteristics seen again and again in people whose actions rise to the level of evil are those extreme narcissistic traits, especially conning, callousness, and lack of remorse. Armed with those dreadful qualities, a person is capable of just about anything.[32]

A brief example that brings this point home is that of the serial killer Ted Bundy.[33] When Bundy would troll for likely victims, one of his tricks was to put his arm in a sling, pretending it was broken. Standing outside a shopping mall with a bag of groceries, he would then ask a young woman if she could help him get the bundle in his car. Once she got into the car to place the grocery bag on the seat, Bundy would then snap the lock on her side and drive off to some remote place, where he would proceed to rape and kill the woman, with no more regret than if you were to step on a roach in your kitchen.

As we go through the descriptions of the various men and women who occupy the higher-number categories in the evil scale, we will see psychopathy, or at least some of its key traits, over and over again. Some of the worst offenders—those whose actions prompt the word *evil* most quickly and uniformly—also show "sadistic" traits. The terms *sadism* and *sadistic* come from the life and writings of the infamous eighteenth-century Marquis de Sade, whose novels contained much more cruelty than did his actual deeds.[34] Having been caned and whipped a good deal in the private schools he was sent to as a child, he took to whipping many of the "loose" women he later associated with. But he murdered no one and would have found our serial killers of today revolting. The essence of sadism, as we now use the term, is the taking of *enjoyment in hurting others*. Two other main qualities of sadism are *humiliation* and *control*—each carried to an extreme. As it happens, a person can be psychopathic without being sadistic (as in the fake-Rolex salesman who is nice to his wife and children), or one can be sadistic without being psychopathic. We see the second type in families where a parent may be verbally or even physically cruel to others in the family, yet behave decently at work and in most other social situations. Robert Jahnke Sr., from the example given earlier, was such a person: abusive toward his whole family but honest and reputable in his work with the IRS. At the most he may have had a few psychopathic traits, but he did not come up to the level of the full-blown psychopath.

The common thread that runs through almost all of the categories from number 9 to number 22 is the element of malice, or "intentionality." Even some of the rageful and impulsive murderers of Category 13 had the intention of maiming or killing others, although they had no idea in advance who the victims might be—or they were ready to kill anyone who tried to resist them as they committed a robbery. Richard Speck, the alcoholic drifter who killed eight nurses in a Chicago hospital dormitory, had broken into the dorm intending to cadge money from the nurses.[35] He then bound them and held them at gunpoint. When some of them resisted, he killed all eight that he could find, though there was another nurse who had hidden under a bed and who survived.

Since the Gradations scale was built only from published biographies, it represents just a fraction of all the people who have committed a murder. Americans make up 89 percent of the men and women in the biographies I've studied, but compared with the different murderers in the United States each year, not even one in a thousand achieves the notoriety that leads to having a biography written about them. This means that the members of the "biography group" are quite special: their murders were spectacular in some way, either because of the cunning they used to conceal the crime, or the horrific nature of the crime, or the large number of victims (as in the case of a massacre). The great majority of murders would register much lower on any scale of evil and are usually impulsive acts, like barroom brawls that went too far or spousal murders that resulted from a passionate argument. The latter often occur at the very moment when the wife with packed bags is about to leave the house and divorce her husband. The tearful husband then calls the police and tells them he'd done a terrible thing. Thus the element of malice aforethought is not nearly as often present in murders of the more "everyday" type.

AN EARLIER ATTEMPT TO CREATE A SCALE OF EVIL

I first published the Gradations of Evil Scale in 1993, essentially in its present form.[36] Occasionally I come upon a case that does not fit neatly into one of the original categories, especially when there was severe mental illness in the picture. In those cases I have given a lower number to the case, acknowledging that the act was widely considered evil but that the offender could not really be held fully responsible for what he had done. Murderous cult leaders are also difficult to place on the scale because they have often persuaded their followers to do the killing—without the leader firing a shot. Charles Manson, for example, did not participate physically in the murders he authorized. Jeff Lundgren was the exception, since, although he used an accomplice, he personally murdered the Avery family.

My efforts in creating such a scale were not, however, the first. Though there have been very few such attempts, there was an earlier one that earned considerable—and lasting—fame. Without having meant to, this earlier scale shows us quite vividly how society's values as to what is absolutely evil, fairly evil, or not so evil are subject to change over time. I refer to the *Divine Comedy* of Dante Alighieri, the first book of which—the *Inferno*—was composed seven hundred years ago (in 1310).[37]

Dante's vision of hell (his Inferno) was inspired in good part by the biblical references to the Seven Deadly Sins, outlined some two thousand years before Dante's time in the Book of Proverbs. There we read: "These six things doth the Lord hate; yea, seven are an abomination unto him: A proud look, a lying tongue, and hands that shed innocent blood, / a heart that deviseth wicked imaginations, feet that be swift in running unto mischief, / a false witness that speaketh lies; and he that soweth discord among brethren."[38] The Seven Deadly Sins, as they were spoken about in early Christian times were, and remain, Pride, Envy, Greed, Sloth, Lust, Anger, and Gluttony. As with the longer list in the Epistle to the Galatians of the New Testament, the Seven are also merely a list, with no ranking as to which might generally be worse, more partaking in evil, than some of the others.[39] Anger, for example, spawns hatred, vengeance, the wish to do evil or harm to others, sometimes in the forms of assault or murder. Whereas Proverbs mentions murder per se, the

Seven Deadly Sins are not actions, let alone evil actions in our modern sense. They are only attitudes or emotions that happen to nudge those who harbor them in the direction of committing certain actions. The Seven do not lend themselves to any scale, though one would like to think that Anger, to the extent that it is associated with murder, would merit far more social disapproval than would Sloth or Gluttony. But obviously the overlap between Anger and Evil is only partial. Anger, in less vehement forms, also motivates us to protest against social injustice. That said, Dante, as he journeys down through his Nine Circles of Hell in the company of the great Roman poet Virgil, does offer us a ranking, or a scale, of bad attitudes and actions, going from the mildest (and to our way of thinking, the least akin to "evil") to the most abominable or repugnant (and thus closer to what we now mean by "evil").

Dante divided the sins and vices of which people could be guilty into three broad sections, also anchoring his system to a "zero point"—of essentially guiltless persons whose only fault, or rather, misfortune, was to have been born before Christ.[40] Virgil was in fact the standard bearer of these too-soon-born virtuous pagans: with Virgil as his guide, Dante

Table 1.2. Types of Persons in Dante's Inferno	
Guiltless Persons from the Pre-Christian Era	
Circle 1.	Virtuous Pagans
Incontinence: Wrong Action Due to Inadequate Control of Desires	
Circle 2.	The Lustful
Circle 3.	The Gluttons
Circle 4.	The Avaricious and the Prodigal
Circle 5.	The Angry and the Sullen
Circle 6.	The Heretics
Brutishness: Morbid States in Which What Is Naturally Repulsive Becomes Attractive	
Circle 7.	The Violent against Neighbor, Murderers, War-Makers, Usurers
Malice or Vice: Evil Actions Which Involve the Abuse of the Specifically Human Attribute of Reason	
Circle 8.	Seducers, Flatterers, Simonists,[41] Grafters, Hypocrites, Thieves, Sowers of Discord, Impersonators, Counterfeiters, False Witnesses
Circle 9.	Traitors to Family or to Country, Murderers of Guests, Traitors to Lords and Benefactors

could look at all humankind of the pre-Christian period as well as all humankind born later—up through the time of Dante's own life. Table 1.2 shows Dante's "Gradations" in schematic form.

There are a number of crucial differences between the graded divisions of Dante's *Inferno* and the Gradations of Evil I have sketched above. My schema concentrates on evil actions committed in peacetime and throws the spotlight on murder or acts of violence that are a little short of murder. I equate evil with *that-which-horrifies*. Dante includes wrong actions done either in peacetime or in times of group conflict and war. "Evils" for him also include all the mortal sins emphasized by the church, both the noninjurious and the sanguinary. He does not insist on an act being shocking or horrifying before he will include it among his list of wrong behaviors, though if he were to do so, he would apparently find heresy (in Circle Six) more repugnant, perhaps more horrifying, than anger (Circle Five) or avarice (Circle Four). The values of thirteenth-century Florence when Dante grew up are not all the same as ours. Also, we know there were rare cases of serial sexual homicide at the time of Joan of Arc in the fifteenth century: her chief lieutenant, Gilles de Rais, the richest nobleman in France, was a pedophile who seduced and killed several hundred boys before he was finally executed.[42] And Countess Erzsébet Báthory in sixteenth-century Hungary sexually violated and killed some four hundred virgins in her castle.[43] Whether there were such people active in Dante's time, we do not know. It is hard to imagine he would have overlooked them, if they existed. The influence of religion was so strong in Dante's time, that for him the worst person imaginable was Judas Iscariot, who betrayed Jesus. Dante put evils caused by perversions of Reason in a lower circle than the Brutish. Hence he saw the simonists[44] as somehow worse than murderers. Compared with our worst murderers, who torture their victims, Dante's worst were those who killed a relative in order to hasten an inheritance. A modern example would be Steven Benson (his case is mentioned earlier in this chapter), whom I placed in Category 14 for "ruthlessly self-centered psychopathic schemers." The impatient legatee that Dante mentions was a Florentine man, Sassol Mascheroni. As so often happened in those days, the punishment was more gruesome than the crime. Sassol had murdered a cousin hoping to inherit from his uncle (Canto XXXII, 65).[45] Once caught, he was rolled through the city in a barrel full of nails and then beheaded[46]—which gives some idea of how seriously such a crime was taken in Dante's era.

We are now ready to take a closer look at the Gradations of Evil as I have outlined them, approximately in the order in which they appear in the scale. I am not so fortunate as to have Virgil as my guide, but I do have Dante as my inspiration.

Chapter Two

CRIMES OF IMPULSE

Murders of Jealousy and Rage

Canto XII, ll. 46–51

Ma ficca li occhi a valle, ché s'approccia la riviera del sangue in la qual bolle	But probe the valley with your sight, for we are approaching the river of blood, in which are boiling
qual che per vïolenza in altrui noccia Oh cieca cupidigia e ira folle, Che sì ci sproni ne la vita corte E ne l'etterna poi sì mal c'immole!	those who harm others with violence. Oh blind cupidity and mad rage, that so spur us in this short life, and then in the eternal one, cook us so evilly!

As we have just seen, the Gradations of Evil scale includes a category where evil is not present at all, plus twenty-one others. The higher the number, the more likely people will use the word *evil* in describing the murders and other acts belonging to that category. We then reduced those twenty-one categories to five groups: the impulsive without psychopathic traits, the impulsive with a few psychopathic traits, those showing malice aforethought and many psychopathic traits, psychopaths committing multiple violent crimes, and finally, psychopaths committing either torture alone or else serial sexual murders that also include torture.

To simplify matters even further, we could speak of just *two* very broad groups: those with few or no psychopathic traits versus those with many or full-blown psychopathic traits. Another broad division concerns those who acted on *impulse* and those who *planned* the hurt or the violence they then committed. Here we will turn our attention to impulsive persons whose evil acts were not accompanied by psychopathic traits, or, if they were, the traits are minor. As always, I am using the word *evil* here in response to the reactions of the public in general and to the reactions of the people who came to be involved with the various cases, including journalists, members of the court, and relatives of the victims.

In the courts and in books about crime, certain phrases are used over and over that have almost identical meaning. An *impulse* crime may also be spoken of as a crime of *passion* or a crime done in the *heat of passion*. The "passion" may concern a love relationship and sexual passion or may mean no more than a strong emotion of any kind, such as anger or rage. A less commonly used word is *expressive*—which merely indicates that the act was done by way of expressing some intense feeling. Crimes preceded by planning, and done with malice aforethought—that is, with the conscious intention of hurting another person—are often called *instrumental* crimes. This does not mean the crime was carried out using an instrument; rather, the crime itself was the "instrument" for achieving some goal. Hiring a hit man to kill a spouse so as to free oneself to be with a lover is, for example, the "instrument" the killer uses to carry out his or her plan of a new life with the other partner. This is quite different from the situation, mentioned in the last chapter, where a woman tells her husband "out of the blue" she is leaving him, and, as she tries to leave the house, he kills her with a blunt object. In that example, the crime is said to be impulsive/expressive/done in the heat of passion.

JEALOUSY AND OTHER CRIMES OF PASSION

People are more tempted to use the word *evil* when speaking of a crime that not only involves great cruelty but is also preceded by conscious intention. The same is true for acts of cruelty, often carried out within a family, that go unnoticed because the authorities are not summoned. Crimes of intention are placed under the heading of *instrumental*. The term *premeditated* is regularly used in the same connection.[1] Rape, kidnap, and robbery would come under the heading of instrumental crimes. Acts of this sort are most often premeditated, in contrast to crimes or other damaging actions that are called *expressive*, where the common characteristics are lack of forethought and spontaneity. These acts are said to have been done in the heat of passion.[2]

Before people regard an event as evil, they are apt to take into consideration the *motive* that seemed to have set the harmful act in motion. Certain motives are regarded as more understandable and more forgivable; others are regarded as more vile and inhuman.

To get a better grasp on why we tend in our minds to create a hierarchy of more or less forgivable acts—in effect, lesser or greater evils—we can take a brief page from psychiatry; specifically, from the comments of Sigmund Freud.

Toward the end of his long life, Freud was approached by a journalist who inquired of the great man what life was all about. I suspect the man expected a rather lengthy disquisition—distilled presumably from Freud's half century of exploration into the human mind. What the journalist got was two words. Well, three, if you count the "and." Freud said: "*Liebe und Arbeit*"—Love and Work. When matters go very wrong in the sphere of love, we may find jealousy. And where jealousy is extreme, serious crimes including murder can be the outcome and may occur quite suddenly—literally in the heat of passion. Stalking an intimate partner following a rejection is another act of love-gone-wrong—one that may also escalate to a serious crime or murder, though here there is more conscious planning—making the stalker's actions "instrumental."

In everyday speech people do not always make fine distinctions between jealousy and envy. This was apparently so in Old Testament times, when the term *qin'ah* was used for both words and also meant "ardor" or "heat," in the emotional sense. The equation between passion and heat goes back to our earliest days. The equation worked (as it still does) in both directions: we burn with passionate love; if the love turns sour, we burn with anger (and the switch can happen in the fraction of a second). The Romans also made little distinction between jealousy and envy, using the word *invidia* for both. For them, the root meaning was to see (*vidēre*) in a *negative* way; figuratively, to look upon someone with the evil eye. But currently envy is usually reserved for two-person situations—where you have something (your Ferrari) that I wish I had (instead of my Chevy)—in this case, coveting your neighbor's car. Jealousy refers more to a three-person situation: I resent you because I thought you loved me, but now I see you have turned away from me and love another. I have lost you and I hate the other for having taken you from me—or I hate you for having deserted me for that other person. Because each of us can identify with how devastating it is to lose the object of one's love, especially in the context of a long partnership or marriage, we tend to be less shocked when we hear that jealousy was the motive for a murder. We also realize that a loss in a love relationship is harder to replace than loss of a job. This makes us more sympathetic in the case of a jealousy murder (especially if the killer found a spouse in bed with a lover) than with a workplace murder where the killer shot the boss after being fired. The word *evil* is not so often used when commenting about a jealousy murder, unless the circumstances are extraordinary. Two examples might be: the victim had in reality done nothing to evoke jealousy,[3] or the victim had indeed cheated on the killer—who nevertheless resorted to extremes of mutilation or torture in exacting "revenge." Absent this kind of excess, jealousy murders seem the least evil and fit into the lowest categories of the Gradations of Evil scale: Category 2, or perhaps a little higher.

There are other types of spontaneous, or "expressive" violence and murder unrelated to jealousy: violence during a brawl or in the course of an argument. Family fights that end in murder belong in this category; we shall see a few such examples in chapter 8. Murders of this type seem more avoidable and often enough closer to what we mean by evil. Many of the spur-of-the-moment murders and other acts of violence committed by people with severe mental illness fall under this *expressive* heading and are sometimes so spectacular as to smack of evil—until we learn that the person in question was acting under the command of imaginary voices or something similar. This was the case with the young man who threw his father's head out the window—or with another mentally ill person who slit open her mother's abdomen in the belief that the mother's exterior was the devil and that the "good" mother was inside, waiting to be released.

When things go very wrong in the sphere of *work*, we may find a different set of responses, and different motives for criminal acts. Greed is a common motive, as in arson carried out in the expectation of getting the insurance money, as well as in the more mundane crimes of theft, burglary, and robbery. The motives behind certain work-related murders are to get rid of a business rival or to avenge a real or fancied wrong—of which retaliation for being fired is a common example. Schoolwork is work, too, in the broader sense of the word; many of the mass murders committed on campus are in retaliation for being dismissed from high school or college for failed grades. Mass murders are almost universally regarded as evil no matter the motive (which is almost always revenge), and no matter if mental illness is a factor—given the enormous amount of destruction and loss of innocent life occurring in the wake of such crimes.[4] In all but the rarest of cases, these murders are instrumental.

Before we flesh out the theme of jealousy with actual examples, it should be recognized that both an expressive and an instrumental motive may get compressed together in one violent episode. This may happen when someone else's action ignites an overwhelming rage, sparked usually by an intolerable feeling of humiliation and a consuming hunger for revenge (the "expressive," heat-of-passion component). This is quickly followed by a methodical plan to undo the humiliation by a violent act (short of or including murder) that will then "even the score" and restore the person's sense of self-worth. The accomplished forensic psychologist Reid Meloy has written about this reaction, and the crimes that occur in the aftermath, under the heading of *catathymic crisis*.[5] There is a close connection between this violence-inducing crisis and what Jack Katz had spoken about under the heading of "righteous slaughter."[6]

JEALOUSY—WHERE ITS POWER COMES FROM

An Evolutionary Look

Jealousy is best understood as the extreme of an emotional state for which our brains are wired to safeguard what is most precious to us: a sexual mate by whom we hope to have children who will carry our genes (half of them, anyway) into the next generation. For most of us, this is our best hope of immortality. A few geniuses can manage immortality of a different kind without children—like Michelangelo or Beethoven or Schubert. Most of us, however, rely on our children. Our brain has not changed appreciably from the days long back in the African savannah from which we began to spread out some fifty thousand years ago. In that setting, survival of the group and of the individuals within the group was dependent upon division of labor between the sexes. Women bore children and nurtured them. Men safeguarded the perimeter and hunted and gathered for food supplies to guarantee the group's survival.[7] It has been important for men to have assurances that the children they are working to support are truly their own. For women it has been important to have assurances that their mates will be loyal and devoted to them during the vulnerable period when their children are small and need maximal care and protection. Jealousy relates to the resentment stirred up if a man loses his sexual partner and if he is forced to worry that the children he has been working to support really belonged to some other man. For the woman, she, too, will feel threatened if she loses her sexual partner, but she will feel especially threatened if she is abandoned and left without the vital support she needs when her children are young and helpless. It is an elementary fact that women at least know that the children they bear are indeed their own. Fatherhood is a dicey business—for which reason men go to great lengths to ensure that they are truly the fathers of the children born to their mates. Until DNA testing became available the mid-1980s to resolve paternity disputes, just about the only men who could be completely certain of their paternity were the Ottoman sultans.[8] Each sultan had a harem (the word means "forbidden") safeguarded by eunuchs (of a different race than that of the sultan, to further guard against cheating). Girls were brought into the gilded prison of the harem before puberty, to be "harvested" when they reached childbearing age by the sultan and only the sultan. Other men have had to make do with long engagements, preceded by the careful guarding of a girl's chastity via the vigilance of her father and brothers. Marriages in many cultures were arranged. Prior "dating" was unheard of; virginity of the bride was demanded. Sexual cheating by a spouse, that is, adultery, was punished with great severity or even by death. Socially we've come a long ways. But our brains, having evolved to ensure the continuity of our treasured genes, are still prone to react with violence when faced with the fact—or even the hint—of sexual betrayal. There are still many parts of the world where killing a mate caught in bed with another sexual partner is not even considered a crime. Sometimes, even killing when there is no more than a suspicion of infidelity may be tolerated as a "justified homicide." When I was in Bogotá, Colombia, many years ago, I read on page 7 of the local paper a two-inch column describing how a judge shot his wife to death at a cocktail party when he saw her "looking at another man" (hard for a wife to avoid when she is hostess at a large party). In that locale the incident was not a crime, nor was the judge reprimanded.

There are still other reasons why either the fact or the worry about sexual betrayal may make jealousy rise to such a fever pitch. One's chances of finding a replacement for an abandoning mate may be drastically lowered because of one's (advanced) age, disadvantaged social position, or unattractiveness of physique, personality, and behavior. To be young, high in social rank, well to do, good looking, and pleasing in personality is to be less vulnerable (usually) to feeling murderous jealousy. There are exceptions, however. If a person occupies high public office or a prominent social position, betrayal may cause such loss of face, such public humiliation that drastic action (including the murder of the deserting mate) may seem, to the victim at least, the only acceptable solution. This was the situation with Shakespeare's Othello. As a Venetian general and governor of Cyprus, he could easily have found another woman to marry, once he thought Desdemona had cheated on him with Cassio. Of course the audience knows that Desdemona has done no such thing, and that it was the evil, scheming Iago who planted the seed of jealousy in his hated superior. But in the culture of that place and time, and because of his public visibility, Othello could not shrug off being cuckolded with calm and grace. To save face, Othello kills his wife. We see this as murder. Othello would see his act as the simple administration of summary justice—until, that is, Desdemona's handmaiden makes Othello aware of Iago's treachery. Now faced with having murdered, rather than "rightfully killed," his wife because of his baseless suspicions, Othello commits suicide.

The power of Shakespeare's play stems in no small part from the plot's similarity to what happens all too often in real life and is based on feelings with which almost all of us have one time or another struggled. In Verdi's opera *Othello* we see the instantaneous switch from burning love to burning anger. We sense the fatal consequences that jealousy will swiftly bring in its train. The very adjective we use—"burning"—describes perfectly the powerful impulses here: the consuming urge to make love and the explosive urge to kill, separated only by a razor-thin partition in the jealous soul.

We should not overlook yet another factor that can raise jealousy to the point of murder. This is the phenomenon sometimes spoken of as a grand passion, sometimes as an obsessive love. It is more a characteristic of the young—who may fall in love with such intensity (as in *Romeo and Juliet*) that *no other person on earth could ever satisfy as a replacement* for the beloved.[9] This kind of love harkens back to the uniqueness of the bond between mother and infant in its earliest days—for whom, after all, mother *is* the only irreplaceable figure. But whatever its psychological underpinnings, this kind of all-consuming (and to that extent, morbid) love can readily inspire the urge toward murder and suicide, should the beloved suddenly desert one for another. One is reminded of the Spanish saying: *el raton que no sabe mas de un agujero, el gato lo coge presto*—the mouse that only knows one hole, the cat catches quickly. This is the situation with the person who knows one and only one option, one solution, to the quest for a mate. When one loses their beloved—especially if the beloved has rejected one for another—life loses all meaning. Reduced to one option, there is only death, and whether that occurs by suicide, murder, or murder-suicide is a mere detail. The technicality of interest here is that because two of the choices involve murder, the issue of evil is evoked.

There are many examples of jealousy murder to be found in the crime literature, to say nothing of the less-prominent cases in magazines and daily newspapers. These cases have a way of touching us, because

Table 2.1. Jealousy Murders and Suicides in Opera

OPERA	COMPOSER	LOVE TRIANGLE	OUTCOME
Othello	Verdi	Othello; his wife, Desdemona; Cassio* *(in the mind of Othello)	Othello strangles Desdemona, then commits suicide
Carmen	Bizet	Carmen; Don José; the matador Escamillo	Don José stabs Carmen to death
Il Tabarro	Puccini	Michele; his wife, Giorgetta; her lover, Luigi	Michele kills Luigi
Katya Kabanova	Janáček	Katya Kabanova; her husband, Tikhon; her lover, Boris Grigoryevitch	Katya drowns herself after confessing her adultery
Medea	Cherutini	Medea; Jason; his new wife, Glauce	Medea kills Glauce and then her two children by Jason
Cavalleria Rusticana	Mascagni	Lola; her husband, Alfio; her lover, Turiddu	Alfio kills Turiddu
I Pagliacci	Leoncavallo	Canio; his wife, Nedda; her lover, Tonio	Canio kills Nedda

they can so easily stimulate the thought that *there but for the grace of God go I*. Our susceptibility to jealousy is a quality shared by all peoples from all cultures—and this is why we find it so often the major theme of operas, plays, and novels. The table below shows the details from just seven among the hundreds of operas built around jealousy.

We can speak of a *biological* push in the direction of jealousy, when we view this emotion as an early-warning device that evolution steered us to by way of minimizing the tendency to cheat. As a species, we are inclined—men probably more so than women—to a certain measure of sexual promiscuity. The poet Dorothy Parker[10] understood this as well as any evolutionary psychologist, when she penned her famous quatrain:

Higgimus hoggamus
Women—monogamous;
Hoggamus higgamus
Men are polygamous.

Chimpanzees—our closest primate cousins—are notably more promiscuous than humans;[11] geese and prairie voles (small mouselike creatures), in contrast, mate for life. We occupy a position in between, perhaps nearer to the geese and voles. Chimpanzees would think operas about jealousy were crazy; prairie voles wouldn't understand what they were all about. Most human cultures encourage us strongly to mate for life, which for many will create a conflict between what we ought to do and what we might like to do. The rules we are supposed to live by were given to us long ago: the Old Testament tells us "Thou shalt not covet thy neighbor's wife nor his maidservant."[12] Those who recite the Lord's Prayer ask of him: "Lead us not into temptation."[13]

JEALOUSY MURDERS

The jealousy murders described in this section are of the expressive, or *heat-of-passion* type, driven by sudden impulse and showing little or no planning. What planning was involved, if any, had mostly to do with hiding evidence so as to escape being brought to justice.

George Skiadopoulos

The story concerns a wild and beautiful "pin-up" girl, Julie Scully, who had modeled for magazines and then married a wealthy businessman, Tim Nist. Men found Julie "foxy," but she was also very bright and had a fabulous memory. Still, she abused drugs, had a theatrical temperament, and was one of those people whose engine required novelty and thrills to keep it running. She became bored with her husband after a few years, and while on a cruise in the Caribbean, she met a younger Greek sailor, George Skiadopoulos, with whom she quickly fell in love. Soon after, Julie and Tim divorced. Julie began to live with George. An intensely jealous man, George would listen in on her phone calls and became argumentative—even with Julie's mother, whom he once tried to choke. Tim, who was still in Julie's life because of their daughter, advised Julie's mother to press charges. As a result George was made to return to Greece, where he implored Julie to join him. This she did, but she found the little town where George lived wearying and dull. She insisted on returning to the United States to see her daughter, realizing that she no longer loved George anyway. At this point George lured her to a remote spot, strangled her to death, and dismembered her, throwing her body parts into the Aegean Sea. Police saw through his claim that she just "went missing," and he was sentenced to life in prison without parole. The dramatic nature of the murder gives it the ring of evil, though Skiadopoulos's flaws were those of jealousy, anger, and impulsiveness—plus, in linking his fate to Julie, he had tackled more than he could handle. I placed him in Category 2 on my scale. His story resonates remarkably with that of Carmen, the seductive gypsy so similar to his Julie, whom George, as the counterpart of Don José, killed the moment she flung him aside.[14]

Clara Harris

The only child of an affluent Colombian family, Clara Suarez Harris became a dentist and married another dentist, David Harris. They lived and flourished in an upscale enclave in Houston, Texas. Childless for several years, Clara eventually had twins. A tall, attractive woman, she got busier than ever with motherhood and her practice. David felt sidelined and entered into an affair with his receptionist, Gail Bridges. They were not very discreet, and word got out to Clara. Thanks to a private investigator, Clara discovered that David and Gail had checked into a hotel. She drove there, and when she saw the two emerge from the hotel, she revved up her car and drove into her husband, running over him three times, killing him. Like other jealousy murders where someone suddenly "snaps," Clara Harris is not so different from Jean Harris (no relation to Clara) who murdered Dr. Tarnower, or George Skiadopoulos. But there was a modest degree of intentionality in her act (driving to where she assumed he and the other woman would be and thus putting herself into a state of higher emotion and risk for violence). Also, there was a measure of "overkill": backing up her car in order to run him over two more times as he lay on the road.[15] Taking these aspects into consideration, I placed her in Category 6.

Jeremy Akers

Born in Mississippi to a working-class family, Jeremy Akers was a straight-A student, a bodybuilder, and a highly competitive man. Self-conscious about his height, he became an "overachiever"—working twice as hard as necessary to achieve his potential. He graduated law school and served in Vietnam, winning several medals. Upon his return he married Nancy Richards, who came from a wealthy family in the northeast. Her parents were against the marriage because of his abrasive, hot-tempered behavior. Macho to the point almost of caricature, Akers was brash, domineering, and opinionated, but also jealous and possessive. The marriage began to deteriorate. Nancy was depressed after the birth of her third child and she gained a great deal of weight. Her husband grew critical and disparaging, even though she managed to get back down to her original weight and underwent some cosmetic surgery. Ever more dissatisfied in her marriage, she struck up an acquaintance with a truck driver, Jim Lemke, twenty years her junior. Love of writing formed part of their bond: he wrote poetry, Nancy wrote novels. They became lovers, and for a time Jim even lived in the Akers's own home, as though he were just a "friend." Jeremy suspected Nancy's infidelity despite Jim's denial of it, and his already jealous feelings escalated when Nancy sued for divorce. Jeremy begged her to reconcile, but she refused and went to live elsewhere with Jim—despite Jeremy's warning that he would kill her rather than submit to divorce. Finally, after luring Nancy back to their house under the pretext of discussing divorce details, Jeremy shot her to death with a .38, which he then turned on himself, committing suicide a few hours later.[16] Here is another example of an "evil" act by someone no one considered evil (nasty, maybe, but not evil). Pride and jealousy contributed to his conviction that there was "no other option" but murder—the "righteous slaughter" of which Professor Katz wrote. Besides Jeremy's intense egotism, there was careful planning here, as well as deceit (tricking Nancy to return to their house), making this case appropriate for Category 7 of the scale.

Jonathan Nyce

The eldest of four boys from a working-class family in Pennsylvania, Jonathan Nyce was studious, quiet, awkward, and lacked confidence around girls. He suffered no abuse or losses during his formative years. An excellent student, he eventually earned a doctorate in molecular biology. As an asthmatic himself, he turned his efforts to asthma research. His first marriage failed after seven years. He then began corresponding with a Filipino girl, Mechily Riviera, and eventually flew to Manila to meet her and propose marriage—which she accepted. At forty, he was twice her age, but he pretended to be thirty-two. In the early 1990s they had two children, and Jeremy founded a company for producing what he hoped would be an asthma cure. He obtained considerable venture capital, and they moved to a huge house, living in luxurious circumstances. The business began to fail, however, especially when venture capital dried up after 9/11. Even so, Jonathan installed a gym inside their house because he worried that Mechily would attract other men if she went to the local gym. She was, after all, very attractive. But the real problem resided in his behavior toward her. He limited her freedom as though she were a harem concubine; to make matters worse, she found out he had lied about his age. And money problems aggravated the situation.

In these unsettled circumstances, Mechily developed an attraction for the landscape gardener she had hired. Again she ended up with a man who lied to her, only this time, the lie concerned his name. She knew him only by one of his aliases, "Enyo," though his real name was Miguel DeJesus. Jonathan—already depressed because he was voted out of the directorship of his company—suspected Mechily was cheating on him. This was confirmed by a private investigator. One night, when Mechily came home late after having been with Miguel, Jonathan smashed her skull with a baseball bat. Placing her body into the driver's seat of his car, he then pushed the car down an embankment, and told the police that her death resulted from an accident. When the real cause was discovered, he was arrested and then convicted—though the judge was unusually lenient, sentencing him to only five years for "passion/manslaughter." He continues to deny having killed his wife. The murder was impulsive but was followed by "staging" of the crime scene—to fool the police and to escape arrest: an "expressive" act followed by an "instrumental" act. Still, Dr. Nyce, though jealous and narcissistic, was not psychopathic.[17] The case fits in Category 8 of the scale.

IMPULSE MURDERS OF OTHER TYPES: EMPHASIS ON RAGE

Murders done on the spur of the moment do not all derive from jealousy. The driving force can be rage that is ignited in a few seconds, or it can be a smoldering anger that gradually builds up and crosses the threshold into murderous rage. The following murder was done in a state of what is called "blind rage"—a state in which all semblance of rationality and self-control is momentarily lost. It is as if someone were driving a car without brakes, the accelerator pedal to the floorboard, and with a blindfold firmly in place. The trigger can be an overpowering humiliation or else a feeling of entrapment in an intolerable life situation. Most of the people in these situations have no psychopathic traits. But as we ascend to the higher categories on the scale, we see some extreme egocentricity along with a few psychopathic traits (such as callousness or a lack of remorse). We are dealing with evil *acts*—committed by people whom others would rarely call "evil" in any general, day-in day-out way. As we shall see, in some of the cases, rage led to repeated stabbing with mutilation of the body or to destruction of the body through burning. As we try to imagine what the victims must have felt in such circumstances, the notion of "evil" comes more quickly to mind than if the murders were (relatively) painless, say, from a stab to the heart or a shot to the temple.

Susan Cummings

One of fraternal twin daughters born to a billionaire arms dealer and his Swiss wife, Susan Cummings lived on a huge rural estate in Virginia where she owned and managed a horse farm. Whereas her sister was pretty and popular, Susan seldom dated and was shy, tomboyish, and not as attractive. She fell in love with an Argentine polo expert, Roberto Villegas, hired originally to teach her how to play. He had come from a poor background but now moved among the people in Virginia's well-to-do "horsey set." In 1995 they moved in together, but the "honeymoon period" was short-lived. Each became increasingly irritated with the other. Roberto was ill-tempered and verbally abusive. Rumor had it that he was also cheating on Susan. She became sexually indifferent and tended to alienate him as well as others by her tightness with money. Local farmers would complain, for example, that she haggled over a $5,000 horse, offering only $500, despite being immensely rich. By 1997, the situation between the two became explosive, culminating in Susan shooting Roberto to death (with four bullets) in her kitchen. Her upbringing with her arms-dealer father had made her quite handy with her 9mm Walther semiautomatic. Claiming she had acted in self-defense, she showed some cuts on her body and produced a knife when apprehended. Some thought she had done the cutting herself to make her reaction seem more justified. Though declared guilty of manslaughter at the trial, she was sentenced to a mere sixty days in jail.[18] Hers is not the story of an inoffensive woman maltreated by a bitter and vindictive brute, the way Heathcliff treated Cathy's daughter in Emily Brontë's *Wuthering Heights*.[19] Roberto was no ideal mate, but Susan contributed in good measure to the tension that finally precipitated the murder. For this reason I felt her story conformed to that of Category 4 of the scale: *killing in self-defense, but extremely provocative toward the victim.*

Robert Rowe

Robert Rowe was an attorney, one of two brothers raised in a Protestant family. He married a Catholic woman, Mary, over the stringent objections of his bigoted mother. They had two sons: Bobby, the normal one, and Chris, who was born blind and deaf, owing to Mary's having contracted rubella early in that pregnancy. Robert proved unusually stoical in the face of so handicapped a child. He formed a support group for other similarly affected couples, who took inspiration from his cheerfulness and self-transcendence. When he was forty, he and Mary adopted a girl, Jenny. Rowe's mother died three years later, but not before humiliating him with her "confession" that she wished she could have aborted him as she had done with her first two pregnancies. Added to that, she told him she saw him as just a lowly bureaucrat, a fake, and the head of a damaged household. As her final coup, she disinherited him, leaving what little she had to his brother, Kenny. Robert had several disturbing dreams in which his mother urged him to kill his whole family. He became seriously depressed, began to hear voices, and once fled the house after he had started to pick up a kitchen knife.

Under the care of a psychiatrist, he was given medications for depression and anxiety. No longer able to work as an attorney, he took a job as a cab driver in New York. Through his carelessness, his cab was stolen, so the $25,000 he spent for the taxi medallion was lost. Reduced to being a house husband while Mary worked, he sunk deeper into depression, and deeper still when he learned that Bobby, his "normal" son, had a congenital hip disease that might consign him to a wheelchair. Robert stopped taking his medication, causing him to plunge to the very bottom of depression and despair. He thought of placing Chris in an institution, but Mary wouldn't hear of it. It was this endlessly deteriorating situation that culminated in February of 1978 with his taking a baseball bat and crushing to death his three children. When Mary came home, he put a blindfold on her, telling her he had a "big surprise" for her—the surprise was killing her with the bat as well. Rowe then made a suicide attempt with gas from the oven but was rescued by a neighbor who summoned help. He confessed to the murder of his family and was sent to a forensic hospital.

Released three years later, he was able to gradually rebuild his life. He remarried and had a son. Rowe died five years later at age sixty-eight. His is the story of murder under tragic circumstances, remorse, and redemption. Though he had been temporarily in the grips of a psychotic depression[20] (one in which he heard voices), Rowe had no psychopathic characteristics. His case corresponds to Category 5 on the scale: *desperate persons who have killed (usually relatives) but who are without psychopathic traits*. What made the murder appear more "evil" was the public's reaction to the bludgeoning of one's whole family with a blunt instrument. There was also some premeditation—in the blindfolding of his wife so that she would have no idea what he had in store for her.[21]

Susan Wright

As a young and pretty woman of eighteen, Susan Wyche had worked for a time as a go-go dancer. Jeff Wright, who had met her at the discotheque where she worked, became enamored of her. In the stormy affair that ensued, she became pregnant, but to her irritation Jeff put off marrying her till she was eight months along. Jeff was a fairly successful salesman, so they were able to live in a pleasant area of Houston, Texas. But Jeff was addicted to cocaine and to other women. These avocations were ruinous to their finances. Susan caught a sexually transmitted disease as a result of one of his escapades. She also complained that he was physically abusive, partly because, infidelity aside, he was very jealous of her. The abuse history was corroborated by her mother and denied by his mother.

In January of 2003 Susan's anger reached the boiling point. One evening she enticed Jeff with the promise of sex into a bondage game in which he let himself be tied to the four corners of the bed. In a paroxysm of rage, Susan then sliced at his penis and stabbed him almost two hundred times all over his body. Becoming panicky, she then dragged his body to their backyard where Jeff had for some reason dug a pit. She placed his body there, thinking to tell people he had "disappeared." Their dog dug up the body a few days later. At the trial that took place after her arrest, the prosecution argued that she killed him for insurance money, but this was far-fetched. If the burial had been successful, Jeff would not have been declared officially dead for seven years. The defense argued that she was a battered woman who had "lost it" in a fit of rage but had to resort to trickery because he was twice her size and much stronger. Some courts, recognizing the "unfair fight" element when a large man is abusive to a small woman, show leniency; others do not. Susan was given a twenty-five-year sentence with the possibility of release in half that time. She was not psychopathic. The case has the features of an impulse murder, but some planning was evident just before and just after the attack as a result of her physical weakness compared to her husband's size and strength.[22] Category 5 seems the appropriate level for Susan Wright.

Ed Gingerich

Married to an Old Order Amish wife from the Pennsylvania Amish community, Ed Gingerich was befriended by an evangelical Christian man, David Lindsey, from the surrounding non-Amish population. David hoped to proselytize Ed, who in the process began to feel torn between the two ways of life. Ed had ambitions to be more "free," like the "English"—as he called the non-Amish people, yet he felt strong ties to the Amish ways, which included avoidance of cars, telephones, electricity, and doctors from the outside. In this context Ed suffered a nervous breakdown and began to have visions and dreams about leaving the old religion. He was sometimes abusive to his wife, Katie. Though the breakdown led at first to Ed's going to a conventional hospital, his wife and brother persuaded him to stop taking the medications the doctors there had given him. Instead they insisted he see an Amish chiropractor and healer who prescribed molasses for his condition (as the healer did for all other conditions as well). Ed's paranoid preoccupations with visions and the devil quickly resumed. He became combative at times or would crawl on the floor sobbing. In 1993 Ed had wanted to attend a wedding, but Katie insisted he go instead to an herbalist far away.

That man was honest enough to say he could offer nothing of help, urging that Ed be hospitalized instead. The family refused, forcing him to see the molasses doctor instead. The actual day of the wedding, Ed became enraged and beat Katie to death with his fists, tore her abdominal organs out in front of his children, and smashed her skull. At trial he was called "guilty of involuntary manslaughter, but mentally ill," and was sent to a forensic hospital unit in a Pennsylvania prison, where he spent about two years. It was discovered that when Ed was about ten, he had fallen off a horse and was unconscious for a time; this may have played some role in his eventual breakdown. Some people in his community still consider him an unstable and potentially violent man.[23] The Gingerich case conforms to Category 6*: *impetuous, hotheaded murderers, yet without psychopathic features*. I add an asterisk here to draw attention to the presence of mental illness. In the last section of this chapter, I will have more to say about the way certain crimes committed by the mentally ill elicit from us the reaction: *evil!* more predictably than do the crimes of others.

Dr. Bruce Rowan

The youngest in a large Idaho family, Bruce Rowan had been depressed most of his life, grappling with suicidal feelings and convictions of being "unworthy." His depression continued through his medical school days, in the middle of which he was hospitalized briefly because of suicidal thoughts. At one point he made a suicide attempt with pills. He had a girlfriend, Debbie, who stood by him, partly out of love, partly out of fear that if she were to leave him he would kill himself. They married, and for a while they went around the world doing charitable work among the poor in various countries. Once back in the United States they adopted a baby girl. His wife wanted to get a house and settle down. Bruce was still eager to roam the world, his lofty ambition—to help the poor—being driven in part by the hope this would alleviate his chronic feelings of unworthiness. Debbie of course spent considerable time with the baby. Bruce grew increasingly resentful at having to do chores around the house and at having less "quality time" with his wife.

In March of 1998 his resentment crossed a threshold into rage, and he killed Debbie with an axe. He then put her body into their car, pushing it down a hill to make it appear as an accident. Afterward he stabbed himself in the abdomen, using his medical knowledge to avoid spots that might prove fatal. All this happened the day a half-million-dollar insurance policy he had taken out for Debbie (for which he was beneficiary) had come due. At trial Dr. Rowan was declared not guilty by reason of mental illness and was sent to a forensic hospital. His long-standing depression outweighed, in effect, the planning that accompanied what was otherwise primarily an impulse murder born of rage. The lenient decision was in all likelihood a reflection of his being, in general, neither psychopathic nor sadistic, despite his extreme egocentricity.[24] The Rowan case fits into Category 7 on the scale: *highly narcissistic but not distinctly psychopathic persons, often with a psychotic core, who kill loved ones or family members.* Killing his wife with an axe, even factoring out the "staging" of the murder to resemble an accident and the insurance windfall, was enough to earn the label of "evil" from the public, even more so because the killer was a physician who once had taken the Hippocratic Oath: *Do No Harm.*

Gang Lu

One of four children from a middle-class family in mainland China, Gang was an outstanding student. This enabled him to attend an American university for graduate studies in physics. Enrolled at the University of Iowa, he earned his doctorate, but he had hoped to get a certain physics prize as well. He was barely beaten out for the prize by another Chinese student, Lin-hua Shan. Gang became progressively embittered and paranoid, insisting that the heads of the physics department had been conspiring against him to deny him the prize. In the fall of 1991, twenty-eight-year-old Gang obtained a pistol permit, not a difficult accomplishment in this country for someone with a "clean record." Then in November, Gang calmly shot to death the chairman of the physics department, a professor who had sat in when Gang defended his PhD thesis, yet another professor who was his mentor, a female dean who Gang regarded as "dismissive" of his (frankly paranoid) letters of appeal, and last but not least, his archrival, Lin-Hua Shan. He then committed suicide.

People who knew him on campus described his personality as a collection of the following traits: combative, argumentative, envious, bitter, difficult to live with, shy, a "loner," quiet, brooding, resentful, slovenly, "know-it-all," self-centered, nit-picking, abrasive, rigid, aloof, critical, hotheaded, a "spoil-sport," overly proud, and paranoid. A devotee of pornographic and violent films, Gang was narcissistic and possibly personally repellent, but he was not psychopathic. This configuration is very common in persons committing mass murder—a topic I will expand upon later. We know less about the personal lives of mass murderers than we do about most other types of murderers, because they usually die at the time of the murders, either by their own hand or by the police. The appropriate category for Gang Lu would be 8: *non-psychopathic murderers with smoldering rage, who kill when the rage is ignited.* The general sentiment surrounding this case; namely, that an evil had been committed, reflected both the enormity of the crime—five lives lost—and the fact that the victims were all highly placed and highly valued members of the academic community.[25]

IMPULSE MURDERS AMONG THE MENTALLY ILL

In commenting on murderous or other violent acts by mentally ill persons—acts that reach the level of "evil" in the public's opinion—our first task is to try to take the vagueness out of the inherently vague phrase "mentally ill." People in ordinary life are inclined to call anyone "crazy" or "mentally ill" who commits a violent act of particular gruesomeness, especially if it is unprovoked. Someone who castrates a man and then eats the genitals or other body parts will unfailingly be called "crazy" not only by the public and by journalists covering the story, but also by most judges who might preside at the subsequent trial. But this is because the act was so repugnant and primitive, nauseating, even, and so rare, that it goes beyond the imagination of most people to think such a person could be "sane." *Sane*, however, is no longer a psychiatric term so much as a legal term, indicating that the person in question knew right from wrong and understood the nature of his act.[26] Most mentally ill people are not so far out of touch with reality as to lose those distinctions, so legal insanity is rare indeed. For our purposes, we will restrict the phrase *mentally ill* just to those persons who suffer from a condition that, for some extended period, causes them to be in poor contact with reality and to suffer certain symptoms such as delusions, hallucinations, and peculiarities of speech—as seen commonly in schizophrenics or people with a mood disorder so profound as to cause the rapid-fire speech and grandiose ideas typical of the manic person. The extreme self-disparaging thoughts of the seriously depressed or melancholic person would be another type of mental illness, as we saw with Robert Rowe and Dr. Rowan in the examples above. In some mentally ill people, both thought and mood are morbidly affected.

I recall a particular case as an example. A woman had been in a psychiatric hospital shortly after her husband divorced her. Now at home, she fell into a deep depression, but she also came to believe that her ex-husband, who lived miles away, was sending poisonous rays from his eyes that went through her windows and made her ill. Another example: a man took his rifle and shot his neighbor, convinced that God had commanded him to kill "Satan" (the neighbor having, in his mind, somehow morphed into the devil) so that the world could be "saved." Every so often one will hear of a mentally ill man who stabs his pregnant fiancée or wife to death, believing that God, or perhaps some secret terrorist organization, has ordered that the woman die because she is "really" the whore of Babylon or else the enemy of the state, who must be killed so as not to bring destruction upon the world. These are all examples of mental illness. Although the bulk of mentally ill people, defined in this way, suffer from schizophrenia (which primarily affects thought processes) or manic-depression (which primarily affects mood), some will develop conditions with similar symptoms that result from serious head injury or from abusing drugs such as methamphetamine, cocaine, LSD, or alcohol. Extremely heavy, repeated use of marijuana can induce mental illness of this sort as well. All these conditions come under the heading of "psychosis," which is simply a technical term indicating a condition that seriously disturbs one's grip on reality. When a psychosis is connected with a chronic condition such as schizophrenia, the more serious forms of mood disorder, or head injury, we are on more certain ground in speaking of mental illness. The situation becomes more murky and controversial in many cases of drug abuse, because of the seemingly voluntary nature of the abuse. One could presumably have chosen not to get drunk and therefore chosen not to have committed whatever act of violence the alcohol "made" him do (as the offender might try to argue in court). Public opinion is divided on this point. There was a young man from North Carolina, some years ago, for example, who got drunk, and while inebriated shot his rifle through his car window as he was driving, killing a passenger in a car that had been driving alongside his. In court, the shooter was called by his attorney "temporarily mentally ill because of the alcohol" and thus not capable of exercising judgment as to right or wrong—hence not responsible. Surprisingly (surprising to me, anyway) the judge accepted this interpretation and sent the man to some treatment program rather than to prison. In my view, the man had effectively willed himself into a state of lowered self-control, where he was more at risk to do something foolish and dangerous—and was therefore doubly guilty and doubly dangerous.

But if we now turn our attention to the unequivocally and chronically mentally ill, controversy and disagreement will evaporate. It turns out that some of the most horrifying and repellent acts of violence, where the word *evil* comes immediately to almost everyone's mind, are committed by mentally ill—especially schizophrenic—people. Those laboring under bizarre delusions or who have succumbed to psychotic rage may act as though freed from all inhibition, or as though the victims they are attacking or mutilating are not really "people" at all. All restraints are off; no "punishment" is too great. And when a psychotic person commits mayhem in this way, through dismemberment, cannibalism, mutilating disfigurement, and the like—the scene will be splashed on the front page of the tabloids as a combined titillation and warning about what shocking things crazy people are capable of. And herein lies a problem of immense consequence to the general public. In the minds of many people, events that make headlines appear to be precisely the kinds of events that "happen all the time" against which we must be perennially on guard. Yet the hard facts and the statistics tell a different story—one that has great meaning for our discussion of mental illness, evil, and the supposed overlap between the two. Apart from the crimes of serial killers and mass murderers (most of whom are disgruntled loners but not necessarily psychotic), it so happens that the term *evil* is applied with particular frequency to certain acts of violence by the mentally ill. We saw this in two of the examples above: the schizophrenic man, Ed Gingerich, and the psychotically depressed man, Dr. Rowe. But if we looked at our entire population, what would we see?

In the whole population of America, there were about 20,000 murders in a year during the 1992–1998 period. This decreased to approximately 17,000 in 2003.[27] If one looks at the larger number of victims of violent crime in that year (since most victims survived), 480,000—one in five—needed care in an emergency room or in a hospital. The offenders were usually an intimate partner (48 percent) or family member (32 percent), and less often a stranger (20 percent). Firearms were the instruments behind most of the murders (72 percent) in the United States. Most of the killers were male (90 percent) as were the victims (77 percent). The murder rate per 100,000 persons dropped from about ten (1972–1994) to five and a half or six in recent years. Whereas most murderers in Sweden had a record of mental illness (90 percent), the figure is very low in the United States owing largely to the much easier access to guns in this country such that many mentally fit people can easily obtain pistols or rifles. The best recent estimates for the number of homicides committed by those with "severe persistent mental illness" in the United States suggest a figure of about 1,000 per year. Compared with the figure of 17,000 in the year 1998, this would mean approximately 6 percent of the murders were committed by the severely mentally ill. This number is misleading, however, because the mentally ill without substance abuse account for barely 3 percent of the murders; those who abuse alcohol or other drugs may account for 9 percent to even 15 percent.[28] In Britain as well, one is much more likely to be killed by an alcoholic than by a "crazy person."[29]

Another important figure to keep in mind is that the rate of violence (including the much larger number of minor to moderate injuries, not just the rare murders) among the mentally ill (among schizophrenic and manic-depressive persons, for example) is about 3 to 5 percent.[30] Of one hundred mentally ill people, if followed for several years after release from a hospitalization in the United States, three to five will have engaged in a violent act—meaning that ninety-five to ninety-seven will not have done so. This should be reassuring to the public, who may fear the risk posed by the mentally ill.[31] But it is not. Why? To begin with, most acts of violence by the mentally ill are done on impulse, lending them a disturbingly unpredictable, and thus more frightening, quality. Secondly, their violent acts, rare though they be, all too often are not only unpredictable but unnerving and spectacular. And the headlines will often contain the word *evil*. It is not easy to avoid sensationalism in describing these headline-grabbing cases. The examples I am about to relate I have accordingly toned down as much as I can without obscuring the nature of the violent acts altogether.

In a case that earned national attention, a schizophrenic man, Andrew Goldstein, pushed a woman, Kendra Webdale, off a New York City subway platform into the path of an oncoming train, killing her. He had lived for a time in a supervised residential setting where he took his prescribed antipsychotic medications, but after a time he chose to live on his own. From that point on he stopped taking his medications and relapsed, experiencing delusions and hallucinations, and engaging in unprovoked aggressive behaviors. There were many emergency-room visits and a "revolving-door" situation where he would spend a little time in the supervised residence and then leave of his own accord, always neglecting to take his medications when on his own, and always spiraling down into active psychosis as a result. The death of the woman he pushed later spurred legislators to enact "Kendra's Law," authorizing long-term assisted outpatient treatment for patients with severe mental illness.[32] The program, where implemented, has had good success in reducing (though by no means eliminating) the frequency of harmful behaviors.[33]

In a news item from Seattle in March of 2007: "a mentally troubled woman accused of drowning her six-year-old daughter, cutting off her head and throwing the remains off a bridge, has pleaded guilty to first-degree murder."[34]

A schizophrenic man in his forties, with a long record of being abusive toward his mother—physically attacking her on a number of occasions—had been in and out of mental institutions many times. In a similar pattern to Andrew Goldstein's case, above, he would be released, would stop taking his medications, and would then experience a relapse. In his psychotic state, he imagined the FBI was following him and that he could save the world by getting people to give up their money and credit cards, since without them, "there would be no war or crime." He would walk around the city looking for the rainbow or else feeling he had turned into a bear. Finally, he began to believe his mother was "Satan," and in that state of mind, he attacked her with a knife, stabbing her many times and cutting out both her eyes—with the rationale that "now the World could see again." He felt compelled to attack his mother in this way so as to satisfy terrifying hallucinatory voices, as if from God, commanding that he "kill Satan." Shortly before the fatal attack he had complained in a hospital emergency room that radioactive emissions from a satellite were entering his brain and bothering him, making him feel that his own life was in danger. The murder was characterized as an evil act by the media immediately thereafter, but public reaction softened when it became apparent that the man was severely psychotic. Neighbors testified that when he was taking his medication, he was polite and friendly and helpful toward his mother, with whom he lived during his adult years when not in hospital.

A man in his late twenties had recently become a father. The burdens of the new responsibilities and demands that accompany fatherhood—being able to relate lovingly to the infant, working consistently so as to support the growing family, accepting the necessary shift of attention on the part of his wife toward the new baby—pushed this fragile man beyond his coping capacity. Already struggling with depression before he married, he now fell into a psychotic depression. Hearing God's voice urging him to destroy both himself and the infant so as to save the world from even bigger destruction, he jumped out the window, clutching his six-month-old son. He survived; the infant did not. The man was then sent by the courts to a forensic hospital.

Though marijuana is not often implicated in crimes of the "heinous" or "depraved" sort that would place them in the realm of "evil," heavy use in vulnerable persons may result in violent acts. A gifted young artist, for example, began to abuse marijuana several times a day every day in a deteriorating family context, one aspect of which was his mother having become extremely seductive toward him after the death of his father. As his tension mounted and his self-control weakened under the influence of the cannabis, he one day "lost it," and on impulse bludgeoned his mother to death. While smoking the marijuana so heavily, he began to show psychotic symptoms: delusions that his mother was the devil and that it was his mission to kill her. He has now spent many years off marijuana and on appropriate medication in a forensic hospital, where he has made an excellent adjustment. He has had one-man shows of his paintings in various galleries. In this case, what made for such a favorable recovery was the *absence* of psychopathic traits, along with the freedom from psychotic thinking, once he stopped the marijuana.

Heavy marijuana abuse in a psychopathic person can lead to a quite different result, and to the kinds of violent crimes that in the public eye smack of evil. This was the case with what the papers described as the "grisly slaying of dancer, Monica Berle" in 1989.[35] Her killer, who had met the dancer through a friend and who had begun to live with her, both used and dealt marijuana heavily. He had developed grandiose delusions, imagining he was "the Lord," whose mission he felt was to "take leadership of the satanic cultists to make sure they do everything that has to be done to destroy all those people who disagree with my church . . . those who call me evil, who say I am not the New Lord." He called himself "966" because he said that three lords came floating out of a wall to appear to him in 1966. After killing the dancer, he dismembered her body, boiled her head in a kitchen pot, and placed bits of her flesh in buckets he then kept in storage facilities. Having cooked her flesh, he then, in an act of grotesque generosity, dispensed some to the homeless in his neighborhood as "meat." As an earlier indication of his contempt for the suffering of living creatures, throughout his adolescent and adult years he had tortured cats and dogs. This may have served as a prelude to the manner in which he murdered and desecrated his victim. Because this man was psychopathic, but had been psychotic only temporarily owing to the effects of drug abuse, he should be placed in Category 16: *multiple vicious acts that may include murder*. Curiously, he did not, to the best of our knowledge, indulge in cannibalism himself. Instead, he dismembered his victim's body to destroy evidence. That he gave some of her flesh to strangers as though it were properly edible meat created a kind of cannibalism-by-proxy. This, of course, also contributed to the disappearance of her body, so as to thwart the authorities in their prosecution of the case.

Sometimes chronic abuse of powerful illicit drugs such as "crack" cocaine can lead to a psychotic state resembling paranoid schizophrenia: delusions of persecution are prominent, as are hallucinations commanding one to commit violent acts. Whether Lom Luong was hearing such voices is not known, but he was a heavy crack user. He had gotten into an argument with his wife (both were immigrants from Vietnam) and one day threw all four children off a bridge in Mobile, Alabama. Their ages ranged from three to just four months. He initially confessed, then retracted, claiming a certain woman had taken the children to feed and clothe them. But then over a period of several days, the bodies of the four children were found. Luong was called a "monster" in the press, and people who were against the death penalty wrote letters stating that they were still basically against it but wanted to make an exception in Luong's case.[36] Luong's murder of his children, shocking because he killed all four at once, made headlines—but only briefly, because of his humble socioeconomic position. The situation was quite different when Andrea Yates drowned all five of her children in Texas in June of 2001. She had been valedictorian of her high school class and had worked as a nurse until she married Russell Yates in 1993. Her husband persuaded her to remain at home caring for the children, even home-schooling and home-churching them. Russell was a computer specialist at NASA earning what was then an upper-middle-class income. For a time, however, he insisted they all live in a Greyhound bus that he had converted into a mobile home. There was a family history of depression on Andrea's side; she'd had postpartum depression (leading to a suicide attempt) after the birth of her fourth child, and a more severe depression after the last child, who was only six months old. It couldn't have been easy to live—almost imprisoned—in such cramped quarters.

This may have contributed to her final depression, which reached psychotic proportions. She heard voices and had felt for some time like killing her children, which was most inconsistent with her otherwise unusually caring nature. The psychiatric care she received toward the end was not of the best quality: she was given two different antidepressants and an antipsychotic drug, but the latter was dropped, unwisely as it turned out, shortly before the murders. By that time, the family had moved to a house—where she drowned her children one by one in the bathtub.[37] Granted that killing four or five of one's children makes a bigger impact on the public than killing only one, the publicity in the Yates case, in contrast to the Luong case, was a function of the higher social position of Andrea and her family. Described as a "shy woman, bereft of self-esteem, overwhelmed by raising her five children with little help, yet unable to admit her frustration,"[38] she, as a person, hardly met any of our criteria for "evil." Once the matter came to trial, the shocking nature of the act, however, coupled with the publicity, led to an initial rejection of the insanity defense and to a sentence of life imprisonment. This was eventually overturned, and Andrea was sent to a forensic hospital, where she should have been sent in the first place.

There is something about cannibalism in the course of a crime that many of us react to with a revulsion more intense even than our reaction to incest, and not matched by any other act of violence, with the exception possibly of castration or other types of mutilation. Perhaps this has to do with the primitive nature of cannibalism, as though it represents our earliest, yet socially taboo, longing. In my psychoanalytic training, I was taught the developmental stages through which, in Freud's understanding, the infant passed on the way to psychological maturity. The first stage was called oral cannibalism, based on the assumption that the newborn wanted not merely to suckle at its mother's breast but to devour all of her. But newborns can't talk; they can only give us hints about what they're longing for. I think the jury is still out on this one. But I understand how predictable it is that we shudder when we hear about cannibalism: the crime involves, after all, the total annihilation of a human being—someone just like ourselves—not by an alligator or a tiger (which we don't hold to the same standard) but by *another* human being who was willing to trample on this most sacred prohibition in the social code. This is what underlies, I believe, the universal reaction of horror, and of evil, when we hear of a cannibal murder—especially when committed by a "crazy" person acting on impulse. He could, to our way of thinking, attack anyone at any time in a totally unpredictable fashion. When twenty-one-year-old Mark Sappington began killing on impulse and then cannibalizing four people in Kansas City, Kansas, and drinking their blood as well, he quickly earned the soubriquet "the Kansas City Vampire."[39] Sappington was schizophrenic: someone whom most people knew as a charming young man with a ready wit. But under the influence of his psychosis, he heard voices commanding him to drink the blood and devour the flesh of whichever stranger he might meet next on the street. Some of the victims, however, were people he knew. As with many high-profile and particularly horrific crimes by mentally ill persons, the disposition in court is a mixed one: he will be held in a forensic hospital—but for the rest of his life.

Despite improvements in the care of the severely mentally ill over the past twenty years, imperfections in psychiatry and the law still allow some dangerous persons to slip through the cracks. We are, however, much more aware of risk factors in mentally ill people that either lower or heighten the likelihood of a violent outbreak. Many of these factors have been worked out by law enforcement personnel[40] and by mental health professionals.[41] Some of the risk factors one watches for in trying to predict violence in the mentally ill include command hallucinations (in which a person hears a "voice" urging him to do a certain act, often enough a violent act); delusions of persecution (the belief that people are out to do you harm, for example); recent purchase of a weapon or camouflage gear; fantasies of revenge; abuse of alcohol or drugs; a criminal history—especially if marked by previous episodes of violence; head trauma; being male; and conditions such as schizophrenia or manic-depression. Other risk factors include personality abnormalities where certain traits are in abundance, such as paranoia, antisocial behavior, or psychopathic behavior. Mentally ill people showing only a few of these factors may be no more at risk for violence—much less for murder—than any average person. Others, showing many such factors, especially if previous violence and recent drug abuse are in the picture, are at far higher risk. In some tragic cases, however, our awareness of just how many of these red flags were present is raised only after a violent or lethal act has occurred. The next example shows how a tragedy could have been averted, had we known beforehand what we knew only in retrospect.

A thirty-nine-year-old man had first been diagnosed as schizophrenic when he was twenty-two. He had been in and out of hospitals numerous times in the interval, sometimes because of outbursts of anger and violence toward his parents. He had never worked and lived at home all during this period. It was his refusal to keep taking the medications he had been given that led to his becoming actively psychotic again and again, ending up for brief stays in the hospital on each such occasion. He would often hear accusatory voices and felt people were "after him." He had peculiar habits, such as wandering the streets at all hours, picking up cigarette butts, or taking twenty showers a day. His parents divorced during his adolescence, after which he lived alone with his mother. It was when she had to be placed in a nursing home that his life unraveled once again. By this stage, his mother had grown afraid of him and insisted he not visit her. When he attempted to do so, he was restrained by the staff, toward whom he then lashed out, necessitating police intervention. This happened twice, and both times he was taken to an emergency room to have his mental state evaluated. He was then admitted for observation and given appropriate medications, but was released after two days. Little inquiry was made into his lengthy psychiatric history. Nursing a grudge against the first psychiatrist who had examined him years before—and who had recommended he be hospitalized involuntarily—he now decided to rob that doctor and use the money to spirit his mother and himself far away where they could continue to live together. To that end, just two weeks after the episodes of violence at the nursing home, he gained entrance to the doctor's office, carrying a suitcase filled with knives, duct tape, and other paraphernalia related to a crime and to escape. Whether his initial intention was to harm or kill the doctor was unclear, but he did begin to attack the doctor with knives. Hearing the commotion, a doctor who shared the office suite ran to the rescue of her partner—only to be attacked by the man with a meat cleaver and knives, and with greater force than had been used against the first doctor. The first doctor survived. The second died. Whereas a good deal of planning went into the attempted robbery of the first doctor, the murder of the woman was done on impulse. The attacker escaped from the building and was at large for several days before he was captured. Given that the victim was a well-known and highly respected psychologist, her murder instantly became headline news.[42] The first headlines were all the more glaring because the "madman was still on the loose," a phrase that maximized the element of fear in the public.

As for the killer, the thorough examination he underwent *after* the murder showed that he had—with the exception of drug abuse—almost every known risk factor for predicting violence (including those specific for the mentally ill). There was a fantasized rehearsal of the crime, acquisition of weapons, lowered inhibition (thanks to his having stopped taking his medication), obsessional preoccupation with the doctor from the past, recent and past violence, involuntary hospitalizations on many occasions, a perception of injustice, active delusions, and command-type hallucinations. These were all within the context of chronic paranoid schizophrenia, in a male, where the risk is greater than it would be for a female. Unfortunately, the emergency room doctors who saw this man in the days before the murder had neither the time nor perhaps the intuitive sense to know that this man was at high risk for imminent violence. He belonged to a small group of mentally ill persons whose risk for violence in the near future was perhaps 90 percent, though their risk for actual murder would be much lower. He did not belong to the vastly larger group of mentally ill people for whom the violence risk was 1 or 2 percent, and for murder risk—negligible. Doctors in private practice don't have metal detectors as you enter their offices, nor would they always be of help. Dr. Wayne Fenton, associate director of the National Institute of Mental Health in Maryland, was killed by a schizophrenic patient he saw in his private office in 2006; the patient had used only his fists.[43]

What is hard for the public to understand is that for any given individual, going about the business of ordinary life, the risk of being harmed seriously, let alone killed, by a mentally ill person who has gone berserk is of about the same order as being killed by lightning. Yet the first seems evil and disproportionately high; the lightning strike we regard (more accurately) as bad luck and exceedingly rare. This has much to do, I believe, with the fact that within the animal kingdom, the animal of greatest danger to a human being is of course another human being. And since we are the only animal capable of evil, death—especially a brutal one born of impulsive rage at the hands of our fellow man—is often interpreted as . . . evil.

To put this point in clearer perspective, the public's emotional reaction to a shocking murder, especially to one that involves mutilation, extreme suffering, and degradation of the victim(s), torture, and the like, is altogether understandable. Accompanying this emotional reaction is, often enough, the word *evil.* Evil, when we say the word, is the verbal counterpart of the horror certain acts elicit. The public needs no education about this: the reaction is part of our culture, part of our nature. I say "our" here, referring to the fact that the vast majority of people, whatever murderous thoughts they may have from time to time when angered or grievously disappointed, do not lose control and *do* something evil. People have less reason to be afraid of the mentally ill person who kills a family member, however gruesomely, than of a psychopathic serial killer or a recidivist rapist—whose danger to the public is far greater. In between the once-in-a-lifetime act of the psychotic person who kills a parent and the psychopathic killer is the mentally ill person who is violence-prone and resistant to treatment. He, like the schizophrenic man who bludgeoned the psychologist, lives in a chaotic manner, does not comply with his treatment regimen, and is at great risk of harming others in the future. The mentally ill person committing an act of the sort we call evil is responsible for that act—but is considered to show "diminished responsibility" because of the illness. A good deal of the responsibility in a case such as that of the man who killed the psychologist rests on the shoulders of the "system" that was imprudent in releasing him from residential care in the first place. He had a long track record of defying medical advice and of menacing others. The medical system had a long track record of failing to ensure that he was kept within the four walls of a hospital setting—that protected him from his tendency to become ill and violent again, and that protected the public from what he was likely to do if prematurely released into the community.

Chapter Three

OTHER CRIMES OF IMPULSE

Emphasis on Antisocial Persons

Canto XI, ll. 79–84

Non ti rimembra di quelle parole	Do you not remember the words
con le quai la tua Etica pertratta	with which your Ethics treats so fully:
le tre disposizion che 'l ciel non vole	the three dispositions that Heaven refuses
incontinenza, malizia e la matta	—incontinence, malice and mad bestiality?
bestialidade? E come incontinenza	and how incontinence offends God
men Dio offende e man biasimo accatta?	less, and acquires less blame?

We just examined cases of impulsive violence prompted primarily by motives such as jealousy, fury arising between sexual partners, or rage at specific individuals. Jealousy does not always involve a sexual triangle: men can sometimes be so jealous, within a family triangle, of the attention a new mother devotes to her child, as to kill either child or wife or both. In some of the examples, it was mental illness that had helped release the brakes on self-restraint.

Here we will turn our attention to crimes of impulse, particularly violent crimes carried out by people with a more distinct antisocial twist to their personalities. The persons we will confront here will be more likely than those we met earlier to stretch out their actions to include some planning *after* the fact, often to hide the evidence of what they have done. Hence their violence was born of an ungovernable impulse but was followed by what we might call *malice afterthought*. It's as though they were surprised and alarmed at their own violence and realized they could get into deep trouble if found out, so they do their best to hide their crime and escape justice.[1] Their actions, that is, are not "purely" impulsive, such as we might see in the typical barroom brawl. Picture two strangers in a bar. One man might insult another; the second man breaks a chair over the first man's head—obviously with no malice aforethought: they didn't even know each other. And there are dozens of witnesses, so there's no way to drag the victim to a shallow grave and pretend innocence. In the absence of malice aforethought, what raises the specter of evil in the cases to be discussed here will be evil's other key ingredient: the *horror* evoked at the nature of the act—which will nearly always be one of violence. There is something wildly excessive, "over the top," about the violence described in this chapter. Often enough, our sense of shock will be a reaction to the gruesomeness of the violence, as, for example, in the dismemberment of a child. Occasionally, we will be shocked at the sheer number of victims (as in a mass murder case), even if each died a painless death via a bullet to the head. In still other cases, what we respond to is the innocence, the beauty, or the social importance of the victim, as in the murder of a nun, well-known actresses like Rebecca Schaeffer and Sharon Tate, or a prominent and revered figure like Martin Luther King Jr. The attempted murder of Pope John Paul II by hired gun Mehmet A ca in 1981 had the same effect.

Although the term *impulsive* captures the essence of these crimes, some authors prefer the term *reactive*;[2] they also speak of *proactive*, where we might prefer words like *premeditated*, *cold-blooded*, "*with malice aforethought*," or *instrumental*. All the latter seem preferable to *proactive*, which is usually reserved for positive actions, such as reading the state driver's manual before taking the written licensure test. Another distinguishing feature of the persons described in this chapter is that they are not career criminals, even though they have some antisocial traits. The crimes are "one-offs" (unique acts, that is, occurring once in the person's lifetime) that struck all those who knew them as totally out of character. Neighbors and acquaintances will be quoted in the media as saying, "I can't believe he did that," or "That isn't the person I've known all these years," as though *the evil that lurks in the minds of men*—a phrase we are fond of saying about those who repeatedly violate social norms—has no relevance to the kindly man next door who took an axe to his wife, or to the sweet, churchgoing adolescent cheerleader who one days shoots to death her whole family. I believe we say these things partly because it is truly bewildering that seemingly ordinary folk can in a moment of intolerable stress commit mayhem, mutilation, or murder—where Nature and all the rules we live by can be turned upside down in a millisecond.

The other reason we find these acts inexplicable is, I suspect, because we need to reassure ourselves that not even under the greatest imaginable stress could we descend to violence of that sort. And so with this reaction, we put an earth's diameter of distance, psychologically speaking, between ourselves and "those" people. In the sections that follow I will offer examples of these impulsive or "reactive" acts, acts that inspired many to pronounce them "evil"—where the underlying motives vary over a wide range: marital conflict, hate crimes, parental cruelty, school shooting, romantic rejection, and the like. In contrast to attacks on strangers, as in rape or serial sexual homicide, the bulk of the crimes in this chapter concern violence against known persons, especially intimates.

To find the stories that illustrate this theme of reactive violence in (primarily) antisocial persons, I have had to rely mostly on articles in newspapers and magazines. The short-tempered men and women depicted here are not evil enough long enough to have stimulated some true-crime author to delve deeply into their lives and make a book out of their nefarious exploits. Besides, the very impulsive nature of the violence in these cases usually coincided with carelessness, one might even say sloppiness, in any attempt at concealment. Either that, or the perpetrator simply made no attempt at concealment. Most were easily caught, so that there was little in the way of the laborious and ingenious detective work that lends itself to an absorbing book-length account, even if the crime itself was not so spectacular. Instead, these stories easily made the front pages of the tabloids, held the public's attention for three or four days, and then vanished from the press altogether, to be replaced by a still fresher horror story from the day before. As we would expect, the driving forces behind reactive violence are emotions carrying a short fuse: passion and hatred. Translated into the language of the Seven Deadly Sins, this means Lust and Anger. Pride and Envy can sometimes ignite anger intense enough to set off a violent impulse. In crimes of passion, Greed will only rarely be a motive.

There was an incident in March of 2008 where radical environmentalists calling themselves ELF (for Earth Liberation Front) torched three homes, burning them to the ground. Each home was valued at about two million dollars. Supposedly the homes were not sufficiently "green" (that is, environmentally friendly). Whether or not the radicals were aware of it, all of the newly constructed homes were built with all manner of heat-conserving and other environmentally respectful devices. As a psychiatrist, I cannot help thinking that the "green" problem here was being green with envy. If we could tap the innermost layers of these self-righteous torchbearers, I have a hunch that their ecoterrorism was covering up a secret desire to live in such beautiful (and environmentally friendly!) houses themselves. Luckily, the homes were not even occupied and no one was hurt, so the crime stopped short of being called "evil"; merely, "outrageous."[3]

In the next section I will give examples covering a broad range of impulsive/reactive crimes of violence. Because, as noted earlier, the material is derived more from the media than from full-length biographies, less is known about the early lives of the participants in these actions. Most appear not to have had previous encounters with the law. For these reasons it is not easy to assign them confidently to one or another category in the Gradations of Evil scale. The categories that seem relevant to the majority of these examples are 6 (impetuous hot-headed murderers, yet without marked psychopathic traits) through 10 (killers of people "in the way"; marked egocentricity). The adjectives *evil*, *depraved*, *heinous*, *and monstrous* were used by many of the journalists and reporters whose accounts I relied on for my information. Since a numerical grading is less reliable for these examples, it seemed more useful to present them alphabetically according to motive or type of crime.

ENVY

There are not so many examples of spur-of-the-moment murders prompted by envy, but one that stands out in my experience is that of a secretary in London who killed her employer. The secretary had emigrated from Canada to accept the position of administrative assistant. Cecile, a woman of no mean attractiveness herself, was thirty-three at the time and was considered "bewitching" by the reports, and able to "wrap men around her little finger." She was prettier than her employer, a woman in the banking industry who was seven years younger. But her advantages did not extend beyond her looks, for she had come from humble circumstances and was working for a wage she regarded as meager, whereas her employer had gone to the best schools, came from a prestigious family, and now had a very lucrative position. We know mostly Cecile's side of the story, but she is said to have been filled with "hatred and envy" toward the younger woman, her boss. The final confrontation, in the spring of 2003, was apparently sparked by a disagreement about her salary. Cecile felt she deserved a substantial raise; her boss firmly refused. Cecile then grabbed a heavy brass paperweight and bludgeoned her boss to death, fracturing her skull in several places. The younger woman had some broken fingers at autopsy, which were believed to be defensive wounds from trying to fend off the blows. Even the pathologist was moved to comment that the wounds were "monstrous." The large number of fracture sites, representing a kind of "overkill," suggests an attack precipitated by rage. The rage factor raised the question of possible "diminished responsibility" or "temporary insanity." By the time of her trial, however, Cecile was described as "ice cold" and in full possession of her senses. The absence of any previous brushes with the law, let alone outbursts of violence, was a mitigating circumstance.

Cecile's defense attorney succeeded in winning a reduction of the sentence to manslaughter partly because of her "clean record" in the past and also on the basis of "irresistible impulse." This type of defense is similar to that in certain US states in which the sentence falls short of an outright insanity plea and relies instead on an argument for "diminished responsibility" with the presumption that the impulse was impossible to control. In a famous 1994 case, Lorena Bobbitt was found not guilty after her defense attorney argued it was an irresistible impulse that led her, in June of 1993, to cut off her husband's penis. Lorena was able to marshal evidence that her husband had been unfaithful, as well as being physically, sexually, and emotionally abusive toward her, which meant that her violence had followed great provocation.[4] There was no indication Cecile had been so provoked, which made her a less sympathetic figure at trial. Granted that the attack was particularly brutal, the notoriety of the case and the readiness of the press to use the term *evil* (*depraved*, *monstrous*, *savage*) may have reflected in part the social prominence of the victim. Cecile belongs in Category 8 on the scale, showing "smoldering rage but without psychopathic personality."

FAMILICIDE

The murder of an entire family is more often a crime of impulse than of long premeditation; the motive will likely be a smoldering anger at one key member of the family that ignites into violence over some "last straw." Sometimes, the motive is to protect the perpetrator from some deep humiliation, such as the exposure of an embarrassing secret. The case of Eugene Simmons is an example. Simmons was a marine sergeant who killed twelve family members when the news surfaced of his having sired a child by his own daughter.[5] This puts Simmons in the category of 10 on the Gradations of Evil scale.

Rarer still is the motive of greed in a familial crime of passion, as in the case of Jeremy Bamber, the adopted son of a wealthy British family, who hoped to be the sole remaining legatee.[6] A more typical case is that of Brian Britton—an adolescent of sixteen, who in 1989 killed his parents and younger brother in upstate New York. The inciting incident seemed to have been a quarrel over his schoolwork. Brian had never been in trouble with the law, though he did have a reputation at school for his obsession with guns and death. He had written an essay about his summer vacation, mentioning that he shot a bird out of a tree and ran his bicycle over a cat. His girlfriend insisted he was a "nonviolent kid and didn't really like guns,"[7] but others remembered him differently. At one point, his parents had taken him to a psychologist. His father used to come home for lunch to make sure nothing was wrong with "Rambo"—the name Brian took for himself after watching Sylvester Stallone in the movie of that name, where Stallone played the part of a gun-toting tough guy.

An extraordinary, if not unique, case in the annals of familicide is that of Jean-Claude Romand. The only child of a couple from the Lyon area in France, Jean-Claude took great pains to conceal any bad news from his emotionally fragile mother. If he did poorly on an exam, he lied and said he did well. Somehow he got into medical school, but kept failing the third-year exam for ten years in a row, all the while making up fantastic excuses to the school authorities (that he had cancer, for example) and never actually finishing. He then lied to his parents, saying he had gotten his MD and now had a post across the border in Geneva with the World Health Organization. This was Act One in the bizarre tragedy of Romand's life.

Act Two: Now married, he told his wife he had a "top secret" job, such that she could not phone him at work. The money he brought home didn't come from work but rather from the money his parents gave him to invest for them—which he simply used for himself. He would drive off each morning as if to go to work, but he would park his car near the woods, read until the late afternoon, and then return at a time that would not arouse suspicion. By swindling money from his parents, in-laws, and friends to "invest," he kept the charade going for twenty years, with no one the wiser. All this came tumbling down when he began an affair with a woman in Paris. That set the stage for the third and final act.

Jean-Claude persuaded his mistress to let him take care of the proceeds from the sale of her property—money he instead used to buy a Mercedes and expensive baubles for her. When he eventually went broke, she worried something was amiss. She asked for her 900,000 francs, but he had gone through it all. He tried to strangle her, but she survived. Jean-Claude's wife began to realize he had lied to her about another matter. When his father-in-law demanded the money he had lent him, Jean-Claude pushed him down the stairs, killing him. He then got hold of his father's rifle and shot to death first his two children, then his wife, and finally his parents. After the impulse murders, the "malice afterthought" kicked in. He used accelerants to burn down his house to make it look as if his family had simply died in a fire. Curtain closed.

His imposture discovered, he made a half-hearted attempt at suicide by swallowing a few sleeping pills that were way beyond their shelf life. Sentenced to life without parole, Romand's earliest release date is 2015. Romand emerges as the consummate con artist, able to live the high life for two decades before his recklessness brought the curtain down. Never vicious until the end, he lived like the elegant jewel thieves in the movies of the 1930s: suave, charming, and, as far as his friends could tell, a good host, good husband, and good father.[8]

I put Romand's case under the heading of "familicide," but it was not easy to categorize, since it touched on so many other themes. The most appropriate category on the scale would be 10. From the Seven Deadly Sins alone, almost all were relevant: *Pride* (in maintaining a false front for twenty years), *Envy* (of those who really were capable of work), *Greed* (in swindling huge sums from everyone he knew), *Sloth* (never earning an honest franc in his life), *Lust* (the disastrous affair), and *Anger* (at the mistress and father-in-law demanding their money back). From what I read, he was innocent of *Gluttony*.

FELONY MURDER

Though murder is already a felony, a murder committed during the act of another crime (usually robbery) is often called "felony murder." Murders of this sort may earn the maximum sentence, including the death penalty. In November of 2006 actress Adrienne Shelley was found hanging in her Greenwich Village office in New York. Her death looked at first like a suicide, though there seemed to be no reason at all for this successful actress and mother to take her own life. The true story came to light within a few days. A nineteen-year-old illegal immigrant, Diego Pilco, had been renovating the apartment below Shelley's. He was making a lot of noise, which led to Shelley to come downstairs and complain. Pilco became panicky that she would complain to the police and he would be deported back to Ecuador.[9] Hot-tempered and in a fury he strangled Shelley and then staged the crime to make her death appear to be a suicide, hanging her body from a shower curtain rod. He confessed after police found Pilco's footprint in the victim's bathtub. The murder was clearly not premeditated: he never knew the woman existed until she came down to complain about the noise. But that act led to a spur-of-the-moment murder, followed by staging, as an afterthought. The murder became "high profile" because of the victim's fame, which in turn gave the murder an extra measure of shock, a greater appearance of evil. The appropriate category on the scale is 6.

HATE CRIME

The exclamation "evil!" will most readily be pronounced when the violence done *to* a celebrity or other highly respected figure[10] is done *by* a similarly well-known figure.[11] It is also used when there are many victims (as in the case of mass murder or serial homicide), or when the violence is extremely brutal, especially if the victim is a woman or a child. Hate crimes are similarly repugnant, perhaps because of the wide gulf that separates the malevolence of the perpetrator from the innocence of the victim, not to mention the total violation of our most cherished values of fairness and equality. Impulse is seldom a part of hate crimes, since premeditation and considerable planning are usually preludes to the final act. But occasionally a bigot with plenty of hatred built up over a long time hasn't really contemplated actual violence, until, that is, he (it is always a "he") is faced with an unanticipated event, at which point he swings into action.

Such appears to be the case with white supremacist Benjamin Smith,[12] whose rampage against Jews, blacks, Asians, gays, and other targets led to the murder of two and the wounding of a dozen others during the first days of July 1999—just two months after the Columbine, Colorado, school massacre.[13] Smith, who changed his name from Benjamin to August so as not to sound too "Jewish," was a follower of Matthew Hale, founder of the white supremacist hate group the World Church of the Creator. Hale allegedly preached nonviolence, though his incendiary "sermons" could easily serve as springboards to violence. But Smith, who came from a privileged (and nonabusive) background, had problems that preexisted his exposure to Matthew Hale. He got into trouble right away in college—for voyeurism and pot smoking; morbidly jealous of his girlfriend, he struck her and ended up with a restraining order against him. Smith finally quit college in January 1999, just as the administration was about to dismiss him. Somehow he got hold of a gun (because of the restraining order, he was unable to acquire one legally), but at first had no definite intention of shooting any "mud people"—the phrase of choice for the despicable "others," according to Hale and his followers. The stimulus for Smith's impulsive murders was the denial on July 2, 1999, of the Illinois State Bar Association to grant his hero, Hale, a law license on the grounds of moral deficiency.[14] Smith's rampage began that very day, with his shooting several Orthodox Jews (who survived), a black basketball coach (who died), and an Asian man (who survived). The next day he shot at several black people and a Chinese man. Then on July 4 he killed a Korean graduate student, finally putting his pistol under his chin and killing himself.

Mass murderers are a mysterious lot—all the more so in Smith's case, since, as far as we can tell, he came from a good family. Their usual fate is suicide just before capture or to be shot during a showdown with the police. Almost all have a paranoid personality, but how much of that is due to heredity and how much to adverse circumstances in early life can rarely be assessed properly. Smith's category on the scale is 13.

KIDNAP

The majority of kidnappings are not impulsive at all: the motive is greed, and the act is planned long in advance. Less common is kidnapping for sexual purposes, for example, abducting a child who may be raped and then murdered or in some cases kept alive as an unwilling sex mate for periods stretching up to a decade or more.[15] This latter variety always involves careful planning. Occasionally one hears of a lonely, childless woman snatching an infant from its pram outside a shopping mall or some other public place. This may at first seem impulsive, but she has likely thought for some time about abducting another woman's child and moves quickly into action when she finds a baby left briefly unattended. All these varieties of kidnapping are among the most detested of crimes, for which reason "kidnap" (the shorter name given to the crime in legal circles) shares with premeditated murder and treason top billing as a death penalty case wherever capital punishment is still enforced. These crimes smack of evil, even when they do not end in death.

A more "understandable" motive for *kidnap* (as I shall refer to it) is seen now and again in bitter custody cases, where one parent violates the custody agreement and takes a child away from the custodial parent. It is rare for the child to be killed in these situations. The abducting parent may claim that the child is being "rescued" from an unfavorable environment, though less than honorable motives are often at play—such as the wish to avoid child-support payments. Sheer spite often plays an important role as well. The needle on the evil meter doesn't swing so far in these cases, since the court can usually be relied upon to restore the child to the proper home and parent.

There are rare instances where kidnap in a custody battle reaches mythic proportions. Even in Greek mythology, when Hades kidnapped Demeter's beautiful daughter, Persephone, she was at least not his daughter: his aim was to marry her. But when in 1976 Eric Douglas

Nielsen kidnapped his twenty-one-month-old daughter, Genevieve—on Mother's Day—he promptly disappeared with her the day before the court was to make the mother's custodianship official.[16] The mother, Laura Gooder, was not to learn of her daughter's whereabouts until Mother's Day twenty-nine years later. We don't know what soured the relationship between these high school sweethearts who had married in 1970. We do know that Laura endured incalculable suffering when her daughter and ex-husband vanished. The kidnap appeared at first to be opportunistic and impulsive: Nielsen took Genevieve on what was supposed to be an overnight visit. But he then fled halfway across the country, changed his name—and his daughter's—and avoided using his Social Security number. He was thought to have had the help of his family in California; it is hard to imagine how he could have evaded detection all those years without assistance from someone.

Thanks to dogged detective work, Genevieve was finally located in Arizona, where her father was in prison on unrelated charges. Nielsen, to compound the evil of the decades-long disappearance, had told Genevieve that her mother had "died in a car accident," so she had no idea her mother was still alive. The case is a monument to selfishness: Nielsen was willing to deny a mother her infant child and to deny the child her mother. As to the crime of kidnap, the story is unique—the kind books are written about. But, to safeguard Genevieve's psychological well-being, no book should ever be written about her story, as she was already quite traumatized to discover she was not who she thought she was; indeed, that nothing about her life was as she thought it was, that her father was a liar and a criminal, and that her identity must now undergo a complete overhaul. It is difficult to find the appropriate place for this father in the Gradations scale, since it was developed primarily to deal with murder cases. But Category 14 is the most appropriate place for him: "ruthlessly self-centered psychopathic schemers," since he planned, for utterly selfish reasons, to take his child permanently away from her mother, at a time when she was still a baby and in great need of a mother's tender care.

MARITAL CONFLICT

Psychiatrists who study life events know that divorce and marital conflict rank near the top of all stressful situations, just below that of losing a child. Loss of a spouse or irresolvable marital conflict also create intense stress. The latter can be a breeding ground for violence, as every police officer knows when called upon to answer a 911 call about "domestic dispute." Furthermore, when violence breaks out, it is usually on impulse: a disagreement or a jealous accusation that leads to an argument, an argument that goes from words to lightning-fast action that is unplanned and unforeseen at the beginning. I include under this heading partners in an intimate relationship who are living together, whether married or not. The Australians have a nice term for nonmarried partners: "de facto"—meaning that the two are a couple in fact, though not in law (in other words, not "de jure"). Impulse murders in this group are seldom written up in books, because they do not elicit as much interest as do the more cunningly planned partner murders. This is especially so in cases where the murder is more "diabolical," more "evil" because, say, a hit man is hired or there is staging or some other form of pretended innocence by a partner who is "too clever by half" (and is ultimately caught anyway).

The New York City case of Herbert and Barbara Weinstein was clearly of the impulsive rather than the planned variety. In January of 1991 Barbara was found dead on the sidewalk by their posh East Side apartment—an apparent suicide. Herbert was sixty-five at the time, his wife, fifty-six.[17] This was a second marriage for both, and by all appearances, a happy one. No one who knew them saw any signs of discord, much less fighting. They were comfortably off, even with Herbert's love of gambling, which he was able to keep under control. There seemed to be no reason why Barbara would commit suicide. The autopsy confirmed what the police had suspected: she had been strangled first and was then thrown out the window of their twelfth-story apartment in her husband's effort to make the murder—to which he quickly confessed—look like suicide. Defenestration[18] to disguise murder is rare enough, but there was yet another intriguing aspect to the case. Perhaps because of his age and the "out-of-character" quality of the murder, Mr. Weinstein, at the advice of his defense attorneys, underwent brain examination by PET-scan (positron emission tomography). The scan showed a large brain cyst that encroached on the front and middle (fronto-temporal) sections of his brain on the left side. I will have more to say about the implications of such an abnormality in the section on neuroscience, but suffice it to say at this point that the damage in that area was believed capable of impairing his function, not to the level of legal insanity (not knowing right from wrong), but to the level of being less able to think properly and less able to retain self-control when irritated. A brain abnormality in that area likely shortened his fuse, which may even have remained otherwise unlit. This was a pretty controversial matter when the case was argued in 1991; the judge allowed the defense team to tell the jury about the cyst, but he could not tell them that it was associated with the violence. The prosecution, worried that the jury—even with that little knowledge—would not convict for murder, opted for a plea bargain down to manslaughter.[19] As for what triggered the murder in the first place, this remains a mystery. Because Mr. Weinstein was not psychopathic, his action would correspond most closely to Category 7 on the Gradations scale, granted that his brain abnormality would be a mitigating factor.

The case of Norman Harrell in Washington, DC, also arose out of marital conflict or, rather, conflict between a woman and her former "de facto" partner. The woman, Diane Hawkins, forty-two at the time of her death, was considered sweet and loving by all who knew her. She had six children: three by her first de facto, and one each by three other men, including Harrell's son, Rasheen. A truck driver with a steady job, Norman Harrell had a checkered past: two arrests for armed robbery in his youth and a rape charge that was later dropped. He was pathologically jealous, and as a man of six feet five (196 cm), he was an imposing and generally intimidating figure. Several of the women he had been with and who had borne his children had left him because of his physical abusiveness. He seemed allergic to the notion of child support, and when one of the women demanded a small sum for their daughter, she ultimately had to take him to court to have his wages garnished. A few years later, Diane found herself in the same situation. In May of 1993, the day before she was scheduled to take Harrell to court where he would be forced to make child support payments, he stopped by her house. A skilled hunter and a man familiar with knives (which he carried with him at all times), Harrell in a fit of rage stabbed Diane to death and then trussed her like a deer—

eviscerating her and carving the heart out of her chest cavity. One of Diane's daughters, twelve-year-old Katrina, was upstairs and aware of all the commotion in the living room. Harrell went up to the girl's room and killed her in the same fashion, later tossing her heart somewhere in the woods (it was never located). Though Harrell was immediately identified as the suspect, he denied any involvement. The prosecutor in the case, Kevil Flynn, became obsessed with the murders, in no small measure because of the horrifying way Harrell vented his rage and hatred.[20] DNA and blood-spatter analysis provided the proof that led to his conviction and a sixty-year sentence. Harrell professes innocence to this day. In his summary of the case, Flynn commented that "Norman Harrell didn't do these murders because he was evil; he was evil because he did them." Here Flynn wished to emphasize that Harrell was not "born" evil—no one is—but rather that Harrell became identified as someone whose *actions* were evil once the community became aware of their horrifying nature.[21] The category for this crime is 16.

PARENTAL CRUELTY

Many of the parental cruelty cases arise in homes where there is a stepparent. We know from studies of child murder that the risk of a child dying at the hands of a stepparent is many times higher than the risk of murder by a biological parent.[22] Worse still is the situation where a woman has a child by a previous union and now lives with a boyfriend (in a relationship not likely to lead to marriage). The boyfriend's chief interest is in pursuing a sexual relationship with the woman. The child is all too often just a nuisance he has to put up with in order to secure the woman's sexual favors. In this situation, too many of us behave not so differently from other social species. In lion prides, for example, if a new male takes over a pride, he may kill the cubs that had been sired by his predecessor and create a new family of cubs by mating with the various lionesses.[23] All the resulting cubs will then be his.[24] This is Nature's way. Parents are less likely to harm offspring that carry their DNA than that of strangers. The fairy tales about the wicked stepmother were not written to malign women who took on that role; the stories reflect the unfortunate likelihood that a child *will* receive worse treatment from a mother (or father) who is not the birth parent.[25] By the same token the risk for incest involving a female child is considerably greater (by a factor of 6 or 7)[26] when the adult is the child's stepfather with no blood tie to the girl.

It must be stressed that most couples who go through the steps of adopting a child have a sincere commitment to the welfare of that child and a strong predisposition to love the child as though it were their own biologically. But now and again there are exceptions where grievous harm is done to the foster or adopted child: harm that may be physical, sexual, psychological, or a combination of those. Here, under the heading of parental cruelty, we concentrate on cruelty meted out for some trivial failing or indiscretion on the child's part that would never result in such retaliation from a calmer parent. The methodically cruel parents who enslave or torture their children over prolonged periods without provocation will be discussed in a later chapter, dedicated to evil writ large.

The Zeigler Case

One of the more harrowing examples of impulsive parental cruelty is the case in Texas of a beautiful blonde toddler of two whose body washed ashore in Galveston Bay in late October of 2007. The little girl's body itself did not wash ashore as such; rather, it was the storage container in which her body had been placed that ended up on an uninhabited island within the bay. A fisherman chanced to find the bag—and the body within it; he then notified the authorities. The as yet unidentified body, bearing skull fractures in three places, was at first called "Baby Grace." A sketch was made of the girl, which was shown later to the paternal grandmother, Sheryl Sawyers, who lived in Ohio. She recognized the sketch as that of Riley Ann Sawyers, the girl her son, Robert Sawyers, had fathered two years before with Kimberly Trenor—then a girl of seventeen. After filing allegations of domestic violence against Robert, Kimberly, having gained custody, later moved with Riley Ann to Texas. Early in 2007, while still in Ohio, Kimberly had struck up an acquaintance with a twenty-four-year-old Texan, Royce Zeigler, whom she had met in cyberspace in an online game called *World of Warcraft*. He sent her expensive gifts while she was still living with Robert. It was on the strength of this budding relationship that Kim relocated to Texas, where in the late spring she married Royce, a technician in the oil industry. Come the summer of 2007 no one had seen Riley Ann; Kim told people, including her relatives, that a "social worker" had taken the girl, for reasons never specified, back to Ohio.

The real story was quite different. Unaccustomed to the norms of fatherly behavior toward a girl of two, Zeigler brought to this new assignment a mindset more appropriate to that of a marine sergeant burdened with the task of whipping into shape a rebellious troop of raw recruits. He demanded that Riley Ann answer him with "Yes, Sir" and "No, Sir"; she was always to preface any request with "Please." But as a girl of two, rather than a man of two-and-twenty, Riley Ann's responses sometimes fell short of her stepfather's orders, on which occasions Zeigler insisted that Kimberly spank the girl with a belt. It appears that Riley Ann's behavior, even after these belt-reinforced lessons, improved only marginally. Zeigler then took matters into his own hands—literally—and set about teaching her a lesson she'd never forget. Or, as it turns out, never survive. We will not likely ever learn what childish peccadillo of Riley Ann's pushed Zeigler over the edge. But on July 24, 2007, he gave the girl what one journalist described as a "savage beating with a leather belt that left welts and bruises,"[27] adding that, "as can be expected from a little girl being beaten by an evil step-father, she cried and cried." That got Zeigler even more furious with the girl. Things escalated. He then filled a tub with water and—perhaps with the mother's participation—held Riley Ann's head under the water until she nearly lost consciousness, then let her up briefly for air and dunked her again. When he finished "waterboarding" the girl, Zeigler lifted her up by the hair and threw her across the room. Riley Ann's head hit hard against the tile floor, fracturing her skull and killing her. Fury-driven *reaction*—the impulsive torture and murder of a two-year-old girl—now gave way to *planned action*. Realizing that the old biblical shibboleth "Spare the rod and spoil the child"[28] has its limits, and that they had rather exceeded those limits, the two now went to the local Wal-Mart to purchase a plastic tote bag. Placing the girl's body in the tote bag, they then stored it in a shed in their backyard—for two months. It was during this time, in the fall of 2007, that Riley Ann's disappearance attracted attention. At the end of that two-month period, the couple dumped the bag—and its contents—into Galveston Bay, where it was found on October 29. The rest, as they say, is history.

At the time of the discovery of Riley Ann, Zeigler, with a belated chivalry, attempted suicide, stating that "my wife is innocent of the sins that I committed."[29] As is customary in these cases, his attorney put the blame on Kimberly; her attorney, on Royce. The matter is purely academic, since both mother and stepfather were complicitous in the girl's death. Both face stiff sentences in a Texas court. Once these sentences begin, they will have a long time in which to contemplate how the moment of blind rage that took the life of Riley Ann caused them to throw away the entire span of their remaining years: about fifty in Royce's case; sixty, in Kimberly's.[30] To the extent that Riley Ann was a "nuisance" to Zeigler—someone "in the way" of his life—Zeigler's crime would ordinarily fall under Category 10, though we don't know whether he had ever shown such cruelty in the past. But the element of *torture* actually makes Category 18 more appropriate.

RAGE IN THE MENTALLY ILL

In people with severe mental illness—schizophrenia or mania, for example—outbursts of violence are more apt to be of the impulsive rather than of the planned type. Because they sometimes suffer from bizarre delusions, schizophrenic persons in particular will on occasion commit acts of a shocking and repellent nature—acts that have a surreal quality, something beyond one's imagination and beyond what one has ever heard of before. This is where the idea of "evil" comes into the picture—until, that is, the public is made aware that the person in question is psychotic (the word *crazy* will more often be used) and for that reason not responsible for what was done. We have already discussed a few cases of this sort. Here is another example of an impulsive murder, with bizarre characteristics, committed by a mentally ill man.

In 1996 Kenneth Lee Pierrot Jr. of Beaumont, Texas, bludgeoned to death his sister, who was confined to a wheelchair because of cerebral palsy. He was then sent to a forensic hospital after being diagnosed with paranoid schizophrenia. In addition he had been smoking marijuana that had been laced with embalming fluid. He was released four months later, having been treated with appropriate medications to the point where he was no longer in the grips of psychotic thinking. Unfortunately, he was not steadfast about taking his medication, and during a period when he was not on his medication, he killed the six-year-old son of his girlfriend. In April of 2004 he smothered the boy and stuffed his body in an oven. In his haste, he left the oven off, so there were no signs of burning. When caught shortly thereafter, Pierrot yelled at the police that he was "sanctified by the blood of Jesus Christ" and was noted to have a "glaze in his eyes and a smile on his face."[31] Pertinent to the standpoint of *motive* was the fact that Pierrot was the biological father of a son by his girlfriend and was angry at the attention she gave to her older son by another man. The comparison will not be lost on the reader between the "daddy" lion's elimination of cubs sired by a previous male lion and Pierrot's murder of his girlfriend's son by a previous partner. Cases of this sort strain the legal system to the maximum: the prosecution argued (correctly) that Pierrot knew what he was doing and knew it was wrong. He killed the boy when everyone was asleep and then in the "afterthought" of the impulsive murder, fled the scene. Therefore he was not legally insane. Yet he was a chronically schizophrenic man who had been "crazy" (1) to suppose that all his girlfriend's attention should be devoted to their son only, and none to her other son, and (2) to think that the older boy deserved to die. The real issue was not whether he belonged in prison (where he was sentenced to sixty years) or in a forensic hospital, but that his level of dangerousness (previous murder, chronic psychosis, noncompliance with treatment) was so high that he needed to be kept in one or the other type of facility for a very long time; *which* type really wouldn't make much difference.

RAMPAGE

The characteristics of a rampage are violence, frenzy, recklessness, and destructiveness. When such a scenario involves victims, the word is reserved for cases in which several people are hurt or killed, rather than just one. Overturning and setting fire to a dozen cars during a riot (as happened in Paris when two boys fleeing the police were electrocuted after falling on a subway rail in 2005) would be considered a rampage, but the public would not be likely to call that evil, since no people were killed in the ensuing violence.

A rampage where people were targeted occurred in New York in 2006, when a homeless man, Kenny Alexis, paranoid and high on drugs, went on a crime spree, stabbing four people: two men and two women tourists who refused his sexual advances (and whom he called "whores"). The police mentioned "there is a possibility of him being deranged."[32] There was a record of a psychiatric hospitalization at Bridgewater in Boston a few months earlier, after he had committed several assaults. The psychiatrists there had declared him "competent to stand trial," which merely means he was rational enough to be able to cooperate with his attorney. He was mentally ill, but how much his illness had to do with drug abuse and how much with his general mental state independent of any drugs is unclear. The nature and number of the stabbings Alexis had committed in New York were just the kind that inspires headlines with the word *evil*: in his case: "His Face Was Evil."[33] His were impulsive acts of violence with neither premeditation nor attempt to cover up his traces afterward. Because of his severe limitations in function and his mental illness (whether primary or aggravated by drug abuse), his place on the Gradations scale falls in Category 13: *Inadequate, rageful psychopaths, some committing murder*.

REJECTED LOVER

One of the shortest time spans between an anger-inducing event and a retaliatory murder was that of the Happy Land Nightclub massacre that occurred on March 25, 1990—the day of the Honduran equivalent of Mardi Gras. Julio Gonzalez, a thirty-seven-year-old Cuban immigrant and warehouse worker, formerly an army deserter and ex-convict, had been rejected earlier that evening, this time once and for all, by his girlfriend of six years, Lydia Feliciano. Lydia was a hatcheck girl at the Happy Land, a club in the Bronx filled on that evening mostly with Honduran immigrants. To make matters worse, Julio had just been fired from his job and was now broke. Gonzalez, fueled on alcohol and machismo, then went out and bought—for one dollar—a gallon of gasoline, poured it on the only staircase (all other exits being illegally blocked to prevent freeloaders from gaining access), and lit a match. In the ensuing inferno eighty-seven people died—pretty much everyone who'd been in the dance club—except his main target, Lydia Feliciano. She knew of a seldom-used door and managed to escape, along with a few other patrons.

The firefighters who came upon the scene minutes later—but already too late—felt as though they had stumbled upon a Nazi gas chamber. Standing across the street from the holocaust was Gonzalez himself, watching until the firefighters arrived. Apprehended half a day later, Gonzalez, still smelling of gasoline from his soaked clothes, told the police, "[I]t looks like the devil got into me." The evil of his act, depicted in the tabloid headlines as "Date with the Devil" and "The Monster,"[34] was due mainly to the huge number of victims. Mercifully, most died fairly quickly of smoke inhalation. It was the worst fire in New York since the famous Triangle Shirtwaist Factory fire that occurred seventy-nine years before, on the same day. Though Gonzalez walked back to his apartment after the fire, he made no effort to hide from the authorities and was remorseful when confronted—even more so as he imagined at first that he had killed Lydia. At his trial the next year Gonzalez was sentenced to 174 years in prison—a year for each victim and a year for depraved indifference toward each victim.[35] Gonzalez's crime is consistent with Category 15 on the Gradations scale: *spree or multiple murder*. This was mass murder, since the eighty-seven victims all died within minutes of one another during the same incident.

REJECTION OF FATHERHOOD

In many of the cases where a pregnant woman is murdered by the father of her child, the public's first guess is that the man's anger was directed primarily at the woman. This is seldom the correct guess. The underlying motive will usually turn out to be the man's dread over accepting the responsibility of fatherhood. This type of reaction is quite unacceptable to the man's ego, so he will offer some less embarrassing excuse ("I just know it wasn't my kid"; "I saw the bitch looking at another guy") or, if the man is also psychotic, he will claim that the devil made him do it or that a "voice" commanded him, and so on. Those "rationales" are also less embarrassing. How rare it is to hear a man openly acknowledge and say with words of contempt that he wanted that child dead. This is what makes the case of Brian Stewart so extraordinary. In February of 1992 he committed an act that defies belief and invoked the judgment of "evil" from every source. What he did on that occasion was the kind of act that moves ordinary people to say "I couldn't think of something like that in my wildest dreams" and "Even if I could imagine such a thing, I wouldn't do it to my worst enemy." Stewart's act of evil was to inject blood positive for HIV—not into his worst enemy—but into his five-year-old son.

To the extent that some planning was necessary, his was not a purely impulsive act, but by virtue of his being a hospital technician who gave injections (fancy title: phlebotomist) and who worked on a unit with many HIV patients, the opportunity and means were readily at hand. The mother of the boy had met Stewart in 1990 and gave birth to their son in 1991. She ended the relationship the next year and later sued for child support. He attempted to evade this obligation, claiming the boy "wasn't his." But paternity was proven in 1997, by which time the boy had become gravely ill with constant and serious illnesses, whose origin was mysterious. Stewart told the mother, "You won't need to look me up for child support, anyway, because your (notice: not "our") son's not going to live that long."[36] He further threatened her that he could have her "taken care of" and that no one would ever be able to trace it back to him. The court ordered him to pay $267 a month. Meanwhile, the boy was discovered first to be HIV-positive and eventually to suffer from full-blown AIDS. Stewart was imprisoned for "first-degree assault" that could be upgraded to murder if and when the child dies. At trial, prosecutor Ross Buehler spoke of Stewart as a "monster," adding that "[i]n the mind of an evil genius, HIV was the perfect disease to inject a death sentence into the child's veins."[37] In a related article on evil, psychologist Katherine Ramsland mentioned that the prosecution chose the assault charge "because it carries a penalty of up to life in prison, [whereas] attempted murder is limited in Missouri to 15 years.[38] The boy, now in his early teens, is too weak for a full school day or ordinary play and has nightmares that one day his father will get out of prison and kill his entire family. As a *ruthlessly self-centered psychopathic schemer*, Stewart belongs Category 14 on the scale.

RELIGIOUS ZEAL

We would like to think that religiously devout people, the truly God-fearing sort, would be at the furthest remove from evil. Then we rapidly make our descent from the ideal to the real and remember Pascal's cautionary note: "Men never do evil so completely and cheerfully as when they do it from religious conviction."[39] There is a cultural wrinkle here: certain practices that are sanctioned in one culture may easily strike those in other cultures as barbaric. I would like to think that the incident I am about to describe would be regarded, if not as evil, at least as repugnant —irrespective of culture. Alas, this is not the case.

On the night of November 6, 1989, listening devices that had been planted earlier by the FBI on the phone of Zein Isa, a St. Louis man who emigrated to the United States from Palestine, inadvertently picked up a family conversation. The three voices were those of Zein, his wife, and their sixteen-year-old daughter, Tina. Her name in itself is of interest. Her original name was Palestina, signifying their Muslim homeland. She Americanized it to Tina, which most would take as short for Christina, signifying perhaps a different religious background. That was already part of the problem: Tina was adopting different ways from those of her father. Worse yet, she was dating a non-Muslim; in fact, an African American boy, which, because of the father's prejudices, offended him in two ways instead of just one. In his interpretation of his culture, this called for an "honor killing," lest the girl disgrace the family by dating a man objectionable to the father. Never mind that he had married for the second time to a Christian woman from Brazil. Tina's defiance signed her death warrant, as we learn from the taped conversation:

> Zein: Here, listen, my dear daughter, do you know that this is the last day? Tonight you are going to die.
> Maria (the mother, after hearing Tina's shrieks, and holding the girl down): Keep still!
> Tina: Mother, please help me!
> Maria: Huh? What do you mean?
> Tina: Help! Help!
> Maria: Are you going to listen?
> Tina: Yes! Yes! Yes! I am! (coughing) No, please!
> Zein: Die! Die quickly! Die quickly!
> Tina: (moaning)
> Zein: Quiet, little one! Die my daughter! Die![40]

Zein stabbed his daughter six times with a boning knife, piercing heart, lung, and liver, killing her. This is what the FBI heard on their surveillance tapes, made because of Zein's participation in the terrorist Abu Nidal group. The autopsy on Tina was performed by Dr. Phillip Burch, who commented, "This was very evil justice."[41] Sgt. Guzy of the homicide squad had said earlier, "Zein was an evil son of a bitch." Assistant prosecutor Bob Craddick said, "It's worse than any movie, any film, anything I thought that I would ever hear in my life."[42] The Missouri court sentenced both Zein and Maria to death. Zein died of complications of diabetes in prison; Maria's sentence was altered to life without parole. Honor killings in radical Islam do occur. They are hopefully rare, but their numbers are not easily determined, since "killing your child because he or she is disrespectful is not open for discussion in any country."[43] Had the honor killing taken place in Zein's native country, nothing would have been said. But he was acculturated enough to realize that it would not go down well in America. So he and Maria pretended that their rebellious teenager had "attacked" them and that they had killed her in self-defense. It was this lie, easily shown in the court for what it was, that particularly enraged the jury, ensuring that they would hand down the maximum sentence.[44]

REVENGE

The theme of revenge runs through many of the accounts of impulsive violence we have touched on in this chapter. The case of Nathaniel Gale is one among hundreds we could have chosen to illustrate this topic. Gale's thirst for revenge grew out of his belief—an unrealistic, probably outright delusional belief—that a famous guitarist, along with the heavy metal band Pantera of which he was a member, had been trying to steal Gale's identity and the lyrics he had supposedly composed. For a long time Gale had been Pantera's number-one fan. At some point he snapped, and in December of 2004 Gale leaped onto the Columbus, Ohio, stage where Pantera had been performing, and shot to death guitarist Darrell "Dimebag" Abbott and three others, before Gale himself was killed by the police. Jeramie Brey, a former friend of Gale's, told the authorities that Gale seemed to have copied his lyrics from Pantera and then somehow imagined that he was the original author. At first he threatened to sue the band, but then he impulsively chose that evening to kill "Dimebag" and whoever was nearby. Not much is known about Gale, but his motive appears to have been revenge for what he considered "intellectual property theft." People described him as a tall and imposing "keep-to-yourself" type of person[45] who had become increasingly argumentative and paranoid. Andy Warhol once quipped that people will do anything for that "fifteen minutes of fame." That was true of another paranoid loner, Mark David Chapman, who killed John Lennon—a man much more famous than "Dimebag," and whose murder did earn fifteen minutes of fame for Chapman, and then some. But fame was not Gale's ambition. Still, the evil exhibited in the Pantera case related more to the murder of a celebrity—plus the number of "collateral" victims—than to with the way in which the victims were killed.[46]

SCHOOL SHOOTING

Though mercifully rare, school shootings by adolescent students gain enormous attention both because of the *number* of fatalities and because of the *nature* of the crime: children shooting to death other children, usually their own classmates. Sometimes teachers are targeted as well. These two aspects account for the public's reaction of horror and the response of "evil." This was very much the case in the massacre in April of 1999 at Columbine High School near Denver in Colorado, perpetrated by Eric Harris and Dylan Klebold. Before committing suicide, the two teenagers killed twelve students and one teacher, wounding twenty-one others. Although Eric Harris, the dominant figure in the Columbine massacre, was considered a psychopath, most school shooters are not. Instead, they are depressed young persons (like Klebold) or, more commonly, disgruntled students who are "loners," "misfits," or simply kids who don't fit in with the majority of students more adept at making friends. Some school shooters felt bullied and rejected by their classmates, either because they were indeed loners and misfits or because of other reasons: being part of a minority, being rude, or gay, or short, or obese, or ugly, or dumb, or awkward, or dishonest, or whatever else gets one marginalized by adolescents clamoring for acceptance by the respected "in-group." School shooters are in many ways like younger versions of adult mass murderers: paranoid, grudge-holding, alienated individuals who, before their one impulsive and final burst into violence, usually haven't had prior run-ins with the law.

This was certainly the case with Robert Steinhäuser, the nineteen-year-old school shooter in Germany who put Erfurt on the map a second time in history. Erfurt, located just east of Germany's geographical center, has a more treasured native son: Johann Sebastian Bach, whose father, violinist Johann Ambrosius Bach, and grandfather, court musician Christoph Bach, were both born in Erfurt. Like the other school shooters, Steinhäuser was a loner and a misfit, but he had several other strikes against him as well. He was considered lazy and slovenly, physically and socially awkward, described by those who knew him as "notably un-noteworthy."[47] He was caught cheating and forging excuse notes, and then got expelled before his final exams. He pretended to go to school so his parents would be none the wiser. This was shortly before that day in April, when, having legally acquired a Glock-17 pistol, he entered the school and singlehandedly shot to death seventeen people: thirteen teachers (his main target), one administrator, two students, and a policeman—before killing himself. As with their older counterparts, we know little about these young mass murderers because they usually die by their own hand or by police action. There is no court trial and little probing into their family life, mental health records, or situation at birth. The public's reaction of "evil" softens quickly in many instances because the killers are indeed children, sometimes mistreated or neglected children whom we do not hold to the same standard as we do the mass murderers who have reached adulthood. (As we shall explore in a later chapter, the brain in adolescence is still immature in many important ways; self-control is less efficient—and these are mitigating circumstances.)

STALKING

The obsessive, often secretive, pursuit of another person—an act we place under the heading of "stalking"—usually refers to people who are tied by some love relationship, whether real or imaginary, to the object of their longing. The term is borrowed from the habit of certain animals that sneak up quietly on their intended targets—as when a cat crawls slowly and silently toward its prey. The common motives behind stalking are thwarted or unobtainable love. There are other motives, such as anger at a boss after having been fired or the quest for sexual domination of a stranger, as in the case of a predatory "serial killer." (We will have occasion to look into those varieties in later chapters.)[48]

Once stalking is set in motion, there is considerable intention and planning. But the stage for this activity may be set and the impulse unleashed in an instant, following rejection in a love affair or the sudden collapse of a marriage. This is especially true when the stalker is of a possessive and morbidly jealous nature, convinced that the love object is "the only person in the world who matters" to him. In this case there is a life-or-death quality to the relationship: the stalker *must* have that person back—or else! It is easy to see how this morbid preoccupation can lead to the persecution of the former loved one or spouse; it may be a short step from persecution—to murder. Psychopathy is the order of the day in serial killers, but in the garden-variety thwarted lover, psychopathy is not part of the picture. Instead there are feelings of insecurity, self-centeredness, entitlement—the qualities, in a word, of the sore loser.

Pernell Jefferson fits the description of the rejected-lover-turned-stalker. Though he was physically strong and outstanding at sports, he abused anabolic steroids in his late teens to make himself even stronger. Already of a demanding, bossy, and controlling disposition, he was morbidly jealous; he actually fainted when his first major girlfriend left him. He had gotten her pregnant and they had a son, Pernell Jr., in 1982.[49] As with many athletes who abuse steroids, Jefferson became aggressive and assaultive. He acted violently toward his next two girlfriends, both of whom left him because of his anger and possessiveness. The second woman he later stalked, terrorized, abducted, and raped.

In 1984 he was about to try out for a position on a professional football team but was warned against steroid use. Stopping the drug abruptly, he fell into a depression and threw away his chance to be on the team. He took up with another woman, toward whom he was even more controlling and abusive than he had been with the others. She, too, left him and began seeing another man. Telling her, "If I can't have you, nobody's going to," Jefferson stalked her and found out wherever she was.

In 1989 he abducted her and shot her to death, and then buried her body with the help of one of his friends. Later the friend had a pang of conscience and told the police. Her body was located but could be identified only by forensic examination of tooth fragments. Although he was sadistically controlling of his girlfriends, Pernell was not psychopathic. He did not, for instance, have the extreme narcissistic traits of remorselessness, callousness, deceitfulness, and so on, that are the hallmark of psychopathy. Pernell's condition falls more within the realm of obsessive love.[50] Given a life sentence when eventually convicted, he became a model prisoner once the steroids were out of his system. Later on, he taught the other prisoners a course on how better to manage anger and aggression. The impulsive aggression and the evil acts of his late twenties were now behind him. Eligible for parole in 2011, it remains to be seen whether he will be able to put these tendencies behind him permanently—especially his jealousy and his overreaction to being rejected. Pernell's crime fits best in the Gradations scale at Category 7: *highly narcissistic persons who murdered loved ones.*

THEFT OF FETUS

There is something about the murder of a near-term pregnant woman, followed by the theft of her fetus, that raises the specter of evil more assuredly than most other crimes. The reasons are obvious. This is one of the few crimes committed *exclusively* by women, who are ordinarily much less prone to violence than men are. It is therefore all the more shocking when they do resort to violence. Then there is the murder of a *pregnant* woman, whose life and hopes are held sacred by people the world over. And finally, the kidnap—and since death is often the result—the murder of a baby, whose life and hopes are held equally sacred.

I have been able to locate nine such cases, all involving American women—five approaching menopause, and four of those coming from hamlets of very small population. The earliest case was in 1987: Darci Pierce, the youngest (age twenty) and the only one with distinct psychopathic features.[51] Darci had conned her boyfriend into marrying her by claiming she was pregnant. She then killed nine-months-pregnant Cindy Ray in a remote area near Albuquerque, slicing open her belly with a car key to extract the baby (who survived).

Another woman, Michelle Bica,[52] was pregnant at thirty-nine and in anticipation of the birth had decorated the baby's room, outfitting it with baby bottles and all the other paraphernalia for the newborn. But she miscarried. Announcing to her husband that she was pregnant again, she later presented him with a healthy baby boy in late September of 2000. Rather overweight anyway, she was easily able to fool her husband. There were two problems. She hadn't been pregnant this time, and she had killed a pregnant woman who lived a few blocks away—from whom she then removed the fetus. A week later it became clear to the police that Michelle had shot and killed the missing Theresa Andrews and that the baby had belonged to the Andrews couple. Michelle had buried Theresa in her garage. As she was about to be confronted, Michelle used the same gun to commit suicide. Oddly, her husband was a corrections officer. When evaluated by his superiors, he was called "simple-minded," "lacking in good judgment," and "gullible." Nor was this Michelle's sole foray into theft: Thomas Bica had met his wife in 1994 when she had been serving time for receiving stolen property.

Arguably the most well-known of the theft-of-fetus cases is that of Lisa Montgomery from the village of Melvern, Kansas (population 423).[53] Although she already had four children by her first marriage, she seems to have wanted to "solidify" her second marriage by having another child. This, although she had had her tubes tied at the end of her first marriage. With a husband as gullible as Mr. Bica, she went ahead and connived to meet pregnant Bobbi Jo Stinnett from the even smaller village of Skidmore, Missouri (population 342), under the guise of buying a puppy. The baby she stole after killing twenty-three-year-old Bobbi Jo survived. One would think that these women murderers, besides being unspeakably evil in the eyes of the public, were all psychotic. But none of them was. If anything, they seemed terminally naive, socially and psychologically "out of the loop," and of course massively self-centered—yet not crazy. There are plenty of small villages around the world, and no lack of women desperate to have a child. Why this fetus-snatching phenomenon is confined to America, I cannot answer, nor am I certain there are not other cases in other countries that have simply not as yet come to light. It is not easy to find appropriate spots for these women on the Gradations scale. Darci Pierce was psychopathic and therefore belongs most likely to Category 11: *killers of people who are "in the way"* (in her case, this was the real mother, whose baby Darci was intent on stealing). Michelle Bica had remorse (she committed suicide) and could be placed perhaps at number 5. Lisa Montgomery is not a full-blown psychopath, yet she killed the Stinnett woman in cold blood in order to steal her fetus. She acted like a *ruthless schemer* (14), though with only a few traits reminiscent of the psychopath.

THRILL-KILL

There are some impulse murders that seem not to fit into any common category. As far as anyone can tell, the murders are done purely "for the hell of it." Some refer to such incidents as thrill-kills; the perpetrators are usually adolescents or young adults. Presumably, there is a powerful "rush" associated with such murders—as great, perhaps greater, than one might get from cocaine or from high-risk, daredevil acts such as riding a motorcycle over a (not too wide!) chasm or riding a hot rod car in a "chicken race."[54] In Detroit, in November 2007, seventeen-year-old Jean-Pierre Orlewicz lured twenty-six-year-old Dan Sorenson, a bouncer, into the garage of the younger man's grandfather and stabbed him in the back, killing him. It seems that Jean-Pierre had made a deal with his friend, eighteen-year-old Alexander Letkemann, that Alexander would help clean up after the murder. As Alexander said in his statement later on to the police, "Me and JP hung out at his grandpa's house. . . . All I had to do was clean up. I would have no part in the actual act. He would call it even for the hundred dollars I owed him. I don't know why he had it out so bad for that guy."[55] The teens sawed off Sorenson's head and then burned his hands and feet with a blowtorch to hamper any attempts at identification. To make absolutely sure, they transported the torso to a remote spot, set it on fire, and then took the head and dumped it in a river fifteen miles away from the torso.

But with the stupidity and rashness that are the hallmarks of adolescent murder, Jean-Pierre asked yet another friend to help them haul the body. That friend notified the authorities, and the two were quickly caught. Even Dan's girlfriend knew he was going to the Orlewicz house to collect a debt. Unlike the murder of a stranger, which has the best chance of remaining unsolved, everyone who knew Dan could point to Jean-Pierre. The media and the Internet blogs were quick to pick up the case and enter it into their list of the "most evil people of the month" or create headlines like "Greater Evil: A Thrill-Kill in Michigan."[56] What shocked the public particularly was the absence of any discernible motive. Some people, grasping at straws, thought perhaps the teens looked down on Dan because he was a "registered sex offender"—assuming they even knew. But Dan's so-called offense was to have had sex with a fourteen-year-old girl when he was only seventeen. In the "Romeo-and-Juliet" laws of most states, that is not an offense at all. Jean-Pierre and Alexander may well have had the characteristics described recently under the heading of the *adolescent psychopath*.[57] They behaved like the persons of Category 11 (psychopathic killers of people "in the way"), though why they wanted their victim "out of the way" is unclear. The mutilation of the corpse was a postmortem act that is, for that reason, not sadistic (in the sense of causing great suffering to someone still alive), even though it is shocking and grotesque. As it is, the murder alone consigned both teens to mandatory life sentences, to which were added yet another ten years for mutilating a corpse.

Impulsive murder takes but a minute but can cost a lifetime.

Chapter Four

MURDER ON PURPOSE

The Psychopathic Schemers

Canto XXXI, ll. 55–57

Ché dove l'argomento de la mente	For where sharpness of mind is joined to evil will
s'aggiugne al mal volere e a la possa	and power, there is no defense
nessun riparo vi può far la gente.	people can make against them.

Many of the case histories from the last chapter hinged on sudden outbursts of destructive behavior, usually ending in murder. If the judgment of "evil" was ascribed to these outbursts, the reason for it had more to do with the act, in most examples, than with the perpetrator. If there was any planning ahead of time, the interval between thought and deed was brief; where there was intention, the intention was to *do* the act, not so much *how* to do it in such a way as to get away with it. Even that intention-to-do sometimes counted as "malice aforethought," but not to the degree of what I would call the more genuine and overt cases of malice aforethought, as we will confront in this chapter. Here we will encounter the real schemers, who, you might say, worked hard to earn the label of evil. They did so by conjuring up complicated plans and intrigues, long in advance of the act itself, and by resorting at times to the use of hit men, lovers, or other accomplices with the ultimate goal usually of getting rid of a spouse or lover or, in rarer instances, of killing a stranger for money. Almost all the people we will meet here had sterling reputations in the community until their acts became known. Because of this, the huge disparity between public image and private deed created much of the shock value that gave meaning to the label of evil. Almost all of them came from privileged social classes: some of great wealth, the majority from the upper-middle class. Only a few had ever had brushes with the law before the dramatic murder that turned them into notorious celebrities. These people did not languish for a few days in the inner pages of the tabloids; they all merited, if that is the right word, a full-length biography. There is another characteristic that sets them apart from the violent individuals we have encountered so far. Whereas the others had at most a few psychopathic traits from the traits mentioned earlier, here we are in the domain of psychopathy proper. To be more accurate, the persons in this chapter show chiefly the egocentric personality traits of psychopathy and fewer of the behavioral features present in the impulse killers. This is an important point, and to understand it more fully requires a bit of an explanation.

The most widely used measure of psychopathy today is an instrument questionnaire developed by Robert Hare called the Psychopathy Checklist (introduced in chapter 1). His scale is divided into two main factors: one for personality (and emotion), the other for behavior. The checklist was the outgrowth of thousands of interviews and records from persons in prisons and forensic hospitals. Many of these incarcerated people were habitual criminals with long rap sheets, often reflecting a wide variety of offenses. The majority came from socially disadvantaged backgrounds and were about as likely to show the behavioral qualities as the personality qualities. Many, that is, were con artists *and* had been juvenile delinquents; they were compulsive liars *and* they had poor behavioral controls. If they scored 30 or higher out of 40 on the scale (the maximum score and the number necessary for the label of full-blown psychopath), chances are the points were evenly divided between the two parts of the list.

But the persons in this chapter were not delinquent in their teens nor did they ever violate their parole—because they had never had any brush with the law in the first place. A few had done some outrageous things in their teens, but coming from affluent homes and indulgent parents, their acts were covered up. They might have been arrested once or twice, but they were never convicted, and they seldom stole even for drugs, because they had no need to. What these people had instead was the full menu of personality and emotional traits. As mentioned above, these traits were categorized by Hare into two factors:

Factor-I Traits

1. glibness and/or superficial charm
2. grandiose sense of self-worth
3. pathological lying
4. conning or manipulativeness
5. lack of remorse or guilt
6. shallow affect (shallowness of emotional display)
7. callousness, lack of empathy (also includes lack of compassion)
8. failure to accept responsibility for one's actions

The second factor concerns behavior and consists of nine qualities:

Factor-II Traits

1. parasitic lifestyle
2. poor behavioral controls
3. lack of realistic long-term goals
4. impulsivity
5. irresponsibility
6. juvenile delinquency
7. early behavioral problems
8. need for stimulations, boredom
9. revocation of conditional release (in the case of incarcerated persons)

There are three additional items that do not fit neatly into the two main factors:

1. sexual promiscuity
2. criminal versatility (by which is meant a history of committing a large variety of different types of crimes, such as assault, fraud, theft, escape, kidnap, vandalism, rape, etc.)
3. a history of many short-term marital (or "de facto") relationships.

But even if a person showed all eight of the Factor-I traits to the maximum, his score would be only 16—far from the 30 required for the psychopath label. Yet it so happens that these personality qualities (glibness, grandiosity, deceitfulness, manipulativeness, callousness, lack of remorse or empathy) are the ones least likely to change throughout one's life. Not only that, but if someone is callous, totally lacking in remorse or compassion, and is a habitual liar and a con artist, he (and it will much more often be a *he* than a *she*) is far less likely to outgrow his dangerousness over the years, in comparison with those who are impulsive and hot-tempered. Many outgrow those behavioral traits as they enter middle age. And if such traits were their only problem, they tend to stop acting in these "antisocial" ways.[1] For example, if alcohol fueled their bad behavior, they might join Alcoholics Anonymous and learn to stop drinking. In contrast, the personality qualities listed by Hare remain throughout one's life. This means that there are psychopaths in the community who never (or almost never) end up in jail, who score well under the radar for the Hare scale, and—if one relied *just* on that scale—would seem *not* to be psychopaths. Hare himself refers to some of these people as "white-collar" psychopaths; these people are known to us as crooked businessmen, corrupt politicians, and the like.[2] And some murder. The Factor-I traits, then, can best be pictured as the *essence* of psychopathy: the part, if present when you first get to know someone, that doesn't go away with time.

We are not dealing with embezzlers and graft takers here but with violent psychopaths, persons, that is, who usually made a good impression on their neighbors (because of the superficial charm), could fool people and talk their way out of tight spots (their glibness and calmness when lying), and lived, until caught, seemingly successful and morally upright lives. Theirs was a morality, however, that was only skin-deep, a camouflage. And when it suited them, violence was an acceptable option, even if the violence engulfed people in their closest, intimate life. Sometimes life circumstances—wealth, an indulgent family—can throw a protective cloak around the psychopath, who, unless pushed too far, manages to stay out of trouble. Even under the best of circumstances, the psychopath is incapable of meaningful and enduring relationships with others—especially love relationships. A predator at heart, he can say, "I love you," if it suits his purpose, but he can walk away in a heartbeat if something better, or someone more appealing, comes along. Here is an example.

A man in his midtwenties had not worked since dropping out of college after two years. He lived off an ample trust fund and had recently inherited an additional sum, a little under half a million dollars, from a grandfather. Within a year he had gone through the inheritance money by traveling back and forth every few weeks to Europe for parties with the "jet set." Quite reckless in his teen years, he had gotten in several drunk-driving accidents but managed to avoid serious consequences with the law, thanks to the influence of his family. At his high school graduation he was given a new car, which he promptly totaled three days later. Anxious to avoid punishment for his carelessness, he went to the dealer and purchased through his trust fund a new car of the same make and color. He guessed that his father, who was predictably in a cloudy state from drinking, would never notice the difference. He had carried on a few brief affairs with various women, sometimes several at once, whom he would charm with boasts of his prodigious, albeit make-believe, exploits. One of them urged him to get a job. He lacked any marketable skills but had no shortage of unrealistic pipe dreams: becoming a "top movie producer," or a "world-class tennis pro," and the like. A distant relative gave him a position in his real estate company. After only several weeks, he already boasted that he had sold a big commercial building in downtown New York for "a hundred million dollars." But this was pure fantasy. His job was really a both-feet-on-the-desk sinecure during which he mostly read the sports section of the paper and rarely ventured outside the office. This man had never been violent, so it seemed likely that he would not become so in the future. But if the course of his life were to take a drastic change for the worse, he might be more capable of a violent act than someone with solid scruples.

There is no telling whether people who have been nonviolent but who have displayed psychopathic tendencies would rise to the level of doing something evil. That depends on the coming together of many unforeseeable circumstances. The persons in this chapter did rise to that level. For most of them, we have enough pieces in the mosaic of their life to create a convincing portrait. This highlights the salient aspect of evil that represents "excess." Because we can begin to understand the *why* question—why did they end up doing what they did?—they will appear less as incomprehensible freaks of nature and more like twisted—very twisted—versions of you and me at our worst moments. This idea was captured well in the title of a book by an eminent forensic psychiatrist: *Bad Men Do What Good Men Dream.*[3]

Information about the persons described in the previous chapter was sometimes sparse, and it was not always easy to place them with any accuracy in the Gradation of Evil scale. Because this chapter is based on full-length biographies, assigning their acts to a particular category is easier. For that reason I have arranged the accounts according to what seemed the most appropriate category.

CATEGORY 9: JEALOUS LOVERS WITH MARKED PSYCHOPATHIC FEATURES

Richard Minns

When they met on the ski slopes of Aspen, Colorado, in 1977, Richard Minns was forty-seven, a successful and multimillionaire health-spa tycoon, and she, then known by her maiden name, Barbara Piotrowski, was a stunningly beautiful model of twenty-three. She was also a straight-A pre-med student at UCLA. Minns, obsessed with youth and masculine prowess, worked out fanatically at his own spas and made himself into as much of an Adonis as a man of forty-seven can be. He was smitten with her and begged her to come with him to Houston. Reluctant at first, she eventually accepted. They began a torrid affair, and she then moved in with him. Whatever he told her about his life, he omitted one detail: he was married and had four children. By and by he revealed that he "had been married" but was now separated. Not only was he still married to his wife of twenty-five years; she was his business partner. His wife, Mimi, eventually learned about the affair and sued for divorce. The impediment to marriage now removed, Barbara expected that Richard would propose to her. He was in no hurry to do so, though he put her up in a fashionable townhouse. They began to argue. Minns became increasingly possessive and jealous, though he still refused to marry her. He struck her on several occasions. Barbara had had enough and broke off the relationship. She remained in Houston and returned to her studies.

A short while later, in October of 1980, Barbara was at a doughnut shop when a man drove up beside her and shot her four times in the back. She was taken quickly to a hospital, where the doctors saved her life, though she was now paralyzed from the chest down. There were layers of hit men involved: Minns had hired A who then hired B to pay C and D to do the actual shooting. All (except Minns) were caught and sentenced. As for Minns, he was never formally charged and anyway escaped to Europe, where he went from one country to another (including Israel, where for a time he served in the army) and assumed at least five aliases and a collection of seven passports in different names. At one point he had been living in the Bahamas as "Richard O'Toole" and posing as a tax lawyer.[4] Always the real suspect, he was finally apprehended in 1994 as he tried to fly from Mexico to Vancouver via Dallas–Fort Worth, where he was arrested at the age of sixty-four under the name Harlan Allen Richardson. At that point he served a four-month sentence for fraud (the only crime for which the police had sufficient evidence at that time), and was then deported to Ireland where he had established residence.[5] Back in 1987, district judge William Elliott had ordered the court in a civil trial to accept that Minns was responsible for the shootings, and then charged him to pay $28.6 million to Barbara in damages.[6] By that time, she had changed her name to Janni Smith and had moved to California to avoid any more attempts on her life. She won another civil suit in 1991, in which the jury awarded her $32 million. She has yet to see penny one of these awards.

What you read in the last paragraph was based on the headlines of this case. To grasp what Richard Minns is all about, you need to read some of the fine print. Minns was brought up in a middle-class family in Texas in unremarkable circumstances. He had a sister, Janice, seven years younger. By age eight, he was already sadistic and violent—beyond his parents' control. He made his baby sister swallow a penny, which required a visit to the emergency room. When she was learning to crawl, he placed her near an open window, from which she fell out, as he stood by laughing. When Janice was two, he forced her finger against a movie-projector lightbulb "because he wanted to find out what skin smelled like when it burned."[7] At other times he tossed lit matches at her.[8] He boasted that when he was fourteen, he was booked for aggravated assault. The truth of this is uncertain, but it is in line with his emerging character that he saw fit to make such a boast. He emerged in his adult life as a supercharming but supervindictive man, bursting with energy, needing little sleep, hard-driving, and entrepreneurial, but dishonest, volatile, manipulative, and combative. On one occasion he broke the noses of his wife, Mimi, and his younger daughter, and, when things soured between him and Barbara, of Barbara herself. After he punched her, he said, "I didn't do it! Something came over me!"[9] Charismatic and thrill seeking, Minns was described by some as the flame next to whom others like to dance.[10]

Early in their relationship, when Barbara had become pregnant, he forced her to have an abortion against her will. She miscarried shortly afterward but still went on with their affair. Minns was also a bully in his business dealings and extremely litigious, suing anyone who dared to oppose or object to his numerous shady and unethical dealings. He was not above threatening his business associates with blackmail about their mistresses, if that's what it took to get his way.[11] He cajoled and threatened his wife when she moved to divorce him. She backed down for a while, but when she made another attempt, he tried to get a friend to swear in court that he had had an affair with Mimi. The man refused. Minns spoke of hiring someone to kill her, or else to blow up the plane on which Mimi and the children were flying to San Antonio. These things never happened, but his threats paint a lurid picture of how he thought and what he was capable of.

Minns had many of the qualities that come under the heading of "hypomanic," by which is meant a personality makeup just short of full-blown mania. It consists of traits reminiscent of mania, though in a less exaggerated form. He was, for example, socially extraverted, grandiose, hard driving, well beyond average in his sexual needs, risk taking, intense, arrogant, and boastful. Many of his other traits, however, were not hypomanic but were what one sees in the typical psychopath. He was a habitual liar, exploitative, unscrupulous, and dishonest to the extent of swindling his children out of their trust funds. He was totally opposed to divorce because he could not tolerate the idea of Mimi's ending up, under Texas law, with half their estate. When all his efforts to suborn witnesses and defame Mimi failed, the judge awarded her 60 percent of their assets; Minns, only 40 percent. This was his "Waterloo," after which he spiraled downhill, still refusing to marry Barbara even after he had divorced his first wife.

As he became increasingly cruel and controlling toward Barbara in the aftermath of his divorce, her love turned to contempt. She left him for good—and ended up at the wrong end of the hit men's guns. Minns, as was mentioned, hid behind three layers of intermediaries, like the Mafia don who decides to "whack" a rival, so he could claim what is quaintly called in the secret service "plausible deniability." We must credit him with a measure of success here, since the little justice Barbara has been able to garner has been only in civil, not in criminal, court. Minns, having been deported to Ireland, is perhaps still there living free, at age eighty as of this writing.

Later I will have more to say about what is known of situations that negatively affect the brain and that may contribute to violence. What is interesting about Minns is that, to the best of our knowledge, none of these conditions seem to have been operating in his case. There is no record of his having suffered head injury with unconsciousness in childhood. We don't know if his mother smoked or drank alcohol excessively when she was pregnant with him—either of which might have increased the risk for later antisocial (though not necessarily violent) behavior.[12] His parents never divorced. He was if anything much brighter than average. There is no evidence that Minns developed what has been called *acquired* sociopathy (or "pseudopsychopathy") from adverse conditions during pregnancy or in one's early years.[13] This leaves us with the more likely explanation that heredity played the major role. In other words, Minns was most likely born with a strong tendency to a driven, intense, and extremely self-centered personality, insensitive to the feelings of others, along with a need for "thrills"—to the point of risk taking and even sadism (as was present in his behavior toward his little sister when he was just eight or nine). Add his hypersexuality, possessiveness, and "midlife crisis" into the mix, and you have a recipe, not *inevitably* for murder, for murder is rare under these circumstances, but for a *much greater risk* for murder than exists in the average person. Minns was not a man who could admit or accept defeat (divorce, a judgment against him in divorce court, rejection by a lover, and so on). Once these events turned on his vengeance engine, there was no stopping until he could put the sources of these defeats out of the way, permanently. He had serious thoughts of killing Mimi. With Barbara there was no stopping him. But he was "cool" enough to work through hirelings and has escaped justice (apart from the brief stint for fraud in 1994) for almost thirty years. Now eighty, Minns will most likely die outside the United States, but also outside prison.

Ira Einhorn

The story of Ira Einhorn reads like a carbon copy of the Richard Minns story, almost as though he were Richard's eleven-years-younger brother. He, too, had a hypomanic temperament, needed little sleep, was hypersexual, egomaniacal, grandiose, charismatic, amoral, and given to explosive outbursts of aggression. Einhorn became a locally famous figure as an anti-Vietnam orator and hippie guru in Philadelphia during the 1970s. Before that, however, his dark side was already making its appearance. When he was twenty-two (in 1962), for example, he was carrying on a passionate romance with a dancer, Rita Siegel. She found him irresistible yet weird and frightening in the way he would expound grandiloquently on famous mavericks like Friedrich Nietzsche, D. H. Lawrence, and the Marquis de Sade.[14] He liked to torture cats by taking them into the shower and listening to them scream.[15]

What he wrote that year was equally frightening: "Sadism—sounds nice—run it over your tongue—contemplate with joy the pains of others as you expire with an excruciating satisfaction. . . . Beauty and innocence must be violated because they can't be possessed."[16] That July he strangled Rita until she passed out, and then wrote: "To kill what you love when you can't have it seems so natural that strangling Rita last night seemed so right."[17] Four years later in a *plus ça change, plus c'est la même chose* moment, he committed aggravated assault on another girlfriend, Judy Lewis, whom he attacked with a broken Coke bottle and then choked until she passed out. As with the first assault on Rita, Einhorn wriggled out with no more than a warning; neither girl pressed charges. Although Einhorn had turned violent only when a woman threatened to leave him, these incidents were just a foretaste of what was to come.[18]

In 1974 he met a beautiful woman seven years younger than he: Holly Maddux. Like her counterpart in the Minns case, Holly was as bright as she was stunning: class salutatorian as well as cheerleader at her Texas college. As with his other relationships, Einhorn was possessive, stifling, and, on several occasions, combative to the point where Holly's bruises were observed by friends. Finally, after three years she left him and went to New York, beginning a relationship with a new man. When Einhorn found out, he demanded she return to Philadelphia. Unfortunately she did and was never seen again. Einhorn murdered her and stuffed her body in a steamer trunk, which he then put in his closet. Neighbors complained about foul odors coming from his apartment—but not until two years later in 1979. Police investigated, found Holly's mummified body, and arrested Einhorn. Bail was set at $40,000 and was paid by a gullible supporter, Barbara Bronfman, who had married into the Seagram distillery family. Einhorn fled to Europe and settled for a time in Ireland under the name "Ben Moore." Once Irish authorities discovered who he was and were closing in for the capture, he fled to England and later to Sweden, where he changed his name once again and charmed a wealthy Swedish woman, Annika Flodin, into becoming his girlfriend. Still unaware of his identity, Annika left with Einhorn for France and later married him—a man then in his sixties whom she knew as "Eugene Mallon." By 1988, Barbara Bronfman had read Steven Levy's true-crime biography of Einhorn, learning of his cruelty to the other women and the facts about the steamer trunk. Disenchanted finally, she tipped off the police as to his whereabouts in Sweden—whereupon he and his Swedish inamorata abruptly left for France.

Finally, through laborious detective work and struggles with the French authorities, Einhorn was extradited back to the United States—after twenty years of freedom and high living. Time had changed many things about him: his beard was gone, his hair was gray, he had lost fifty pounds, but his fingerprints, alas, were the same.[19] He was sentenced in October of 2002 to life without parole for the murder of Holly Maddux. As with the Minns case, the Maddux family had won a pyrrhic victory in the courts a few years earlier, when Einhorn was convicted in absentia in civil court, yielding an award of some $907 million, not a penny of which the family will ever see. Einhorn continues to deny his guilt.

Among the many parallels between Minns and Einhorn—advantaged social class, high intelligence, pathological jealousy, Hare's Factor-I personality traits with very little of the Factor-II behavioral traits—is the act of killing during an act of impulsive violence. But then they cover up the crime with astonishing coolness and cleverness, even managing to win allies to their cause to bankroll them during their years of hiding from the law. Unlike Royce Zeigler (see chapter 3)—who acknowledged the "sins I have committed," marking him more antisocial than psychopathic—Minns and Einhorn lie and deny to their dying day. These psychopathic traits, especially the cold-bloodedness, the callousness, and the scheming, make the impression of "evil" more readily applicable than it was with the persons sketched in the earlier chapter.

CATEGORY 10: KILLERS (NOT TOTALLY PSYCHOPATHIC) OF PEOPLE "IN THE WAY"

Unlike the stories in the previous section, the following stories concern individuals who shocked the public with murderous acts that were *not* impulsive. We are dealing instead with violent acts that were carried out in a cold and methodical way from the beginning—followed by equally methodical ways of trying to escape justice. The same amorality and psychopathic personality traits (the "Factor-I" traits) were just as evident, but here they occur without the flashes of rage and intemperate behavior. Furthermore, the motive behind the scheming was quite different. Minns and Einhorn killed because the women they had once loved to distraction rejected them. Neither saw any other solution to his loss and wounded pride than to murder the woman who had hurt him. That each of these men had driven the woman away because of his abusiveness was clear to everyone else; they remained steadfastly blind to the obvious and thus felt "justified" in exacting revenge. In this next section, the killer's motive was to get rid of someone in order to be free to be with someone else, or to escape a deteriorating life situation. Certain people, as they saw it, were just "in the way."

John List

People somewhat familiar with the saga of John List connect his name with evil because of the emotionless way he went about killing his entire family, much as one might swat pesky flies in the kitchen. But there is more. List, with the palpably absurd excuses he later fashioned to explain away his actions, carried hypocrisy to heights even the most corrupt politician could not rival.

List was born in Michigan in 1925, the only child of a pious Lutheran family. His father was described as rigid, joyless, angry—the neighborhood crank and an ultraconservative religious zealot.[20] His mother, Alma, was alternately domineering and overprotective.[21] John himself was known in his early days as a priggish "mama's boy" and "neat freak," fastidious and obsessed with books about the military. Worried lest he get sick, Alma did not allow him to go out and play with the other children; "play" consisted instead of she and John reading the Bible together in the evening—a custom he maintained once she came to live with him and his family, until the very end.[22]

Though he saw no action during his stint in World War II, he did acquire a knowledge of guns, as well as some actual guns, which figure prominently in his life later on—especially an Austrian pistol he brought back from overseas. Outwardly moralistic, unspontaneous, and detail oriented, List was a caricature of the compulsive personality. He eventually obtained a degree in accounting, but because of his poor social skills and meager executive abilities, he lost many jobs—meantime becoming increasingly in debt. The debt became overwhelming once he moved to a huge eighteen-room mansion in Westfield, New Jersey, with his family, now consisting of his aging mother; his wife, Helen; and their three children. The house was way beyond his means, and the situation was compounded by his wife's progressive mental illness—the result of late-stage syphilis contracted from her first husband.[23] There was the added dissatisfaction with his teenage children, especially the eldest, sixteen-year-old Patricia—a fun-loving girl whom he called a "slut" when he had to go to the police one night after she and another girl had been innocently walking together in the late hours.

It was in this context that he carried out his meticulous plan on November 9, 1971. After kissing his mother a final time, he shot her in the back of the head, and then did the same to Helen. When two of his children, Patricia and Frederick, came home that afternoon from school, he shot them in the same way—all with the old Austrian pistol. The youngest, John Jr., had been playing soccer at school, so John drove over to watch his son in the game, brought him back home—and shot him to death too. For some reason John Jr. did not die immediately, so his father fired off nine more shots to complete his mission. After tucking the bodies of his wife and children in sleeping bags, he prayed over them—

and then departed. He had ample time to get to wherever he was going, since the family was not missed at first and their bodies not discovered for a month.

The hypocrisy machinery now moving into full gear, List wrote a letter to his pastor explaining the reasons for the murders. The 1970s were a sinful time, in his opinion, and his daughter was succumbing to temptation, given her interest in an acting career, which List saw as linked to Satan. By killing them all before they had renounced their faith, he had ensured their place in heaven. List changed his name to that of a student he once knew at college, Robert Clark. He began a new life, remarried, and lived free, first in Denver, then in Virginia—until his capture, which did not take place until eighteen years later. The arrest came about through the help of a forensic artist, Frank Bender, who created in clay a bust of what he imagined List would look like at age sixty-four. This image was shown on the television program *America's Most Wanted*. A week and a half later, someone recognized the face and called the police. List was arrested. On May 1, 1990, List was sentenced to life in prison on five counts of first-degree murder. Far from expressing any remorse for the murders, List was convinced he would rejoin his family in heaven—as he explained during a TV interview in 2002 with Connie Chung of ABC's show *Downtown*. She asked him why he didn't just kill himself when he saw his debts exceeding what he could ever hope to repay. As he patiently explained, suicide was a sin that would bar him from heaven and thus deny him access to his family. But if he murdered them and then sought forgiveness, they would have forgiven him—or else not even know that he had been the instrument of their deaths, so either way, they could all spend eternity as a family just as before. He also recounted to Chung how he cleaned up the blood from the room where he had shot his wife, and then, at the same table where she had been sitting, made himself lunch—because, as he told her, "I was hungry."

List's self-serving rationalizations had already moved into full swing long before the Chung interview: in 1995, during a radio interview, List was asking for a second trial because of what is sometimes facetiously called the "orphan's plea"; namely, that he was "suffering from post-traumatic stress disorder" as a result of "killing my family."

As I emphasize throughout this book, the label "evil" is an emotional reaction, and in a high-profile case like this one, a public reaction. In this light, the Gradations scale represents a method for acknowledging this reaction but then analyzing the case further as more information becomes available. There is the additional aim, as mentioned earlier, to look more closely at the resulting compartments—as a first step in learning whether there are particular background factors and causative elements that occur with special frequency among the persons grouped together in this or that category, or level.

For most people to consider List's act as evil, it would suffice that he had killed his (aging) mother, his (ailing) wife, and his (blameless) kids. But then there was the icy detachment in his twisting the words of the Holy Book in ways as yet unheard of—to justify getting rid of *people in the way*. In the manner of the CEO of a failing corporation who knows that you must either increase sales or decrease expenses, the easiest place to start is to cut down expenses. You do this by firing employees who bring in no income: the workers in the mailroom, the human resources personnel. List was not accountant enough to bring in more money—but he knew that one mouth to feed (his) was 83 percent cheaper than feeding six. Simply put: Five had to go.

Kristin Rossum

> And there she lulled me asleep
> And there I dreamed—Ah! Woe betide!—
> The latest dream I ever dreamt
> On the cold hillside.
>
> I saw pale kings and princes too,
> Pale warriors, death-pale were they all;
> They cried—'La Belle Dame sans Merci
> Hath thee in thrall!'
>
> —John Keats, *La Belle Dame Sans Merci*, 1819

The inspiration for Keats's famous poem is said to have been a hoax played on his brother Tom, who was deceived in a romantic liaison,[24] or perhaps Keats's own conflict over whether to marry a certain Fanny Brawne, of whom his friends disapproved.

Kristin Rossum fits the image of Keats's mistress well: a beautiful woman without compassion. She did not start out that way, so far as one can tell. The eldest of three children born to Professor Ralph Rossum and his wife, Constance, Kristin had the advantages of beauty, brightness, and balletic talent. After a triumph as the lead in the *Nutcracker*,[25] she seemed headed for a successful career in ballet—but she then sustained a leg injury and was no longer able to dance. This incident set in motion a disastrous sequence of events reminiscent of the old saying "For want of a nail, the kingdom is lost."[26]

As stated in her biography,[27] Kristin modeled as a child and excelled at school, but at sixteen she became depressed and disillusioned after the injury. A friend at her Los Angeles high school suggested she share in smoking some crystal methamphetamine. This gave Kristin a "high" in which, as she later explained,[28] she felt revved up and energetic and happy. Her personality deteriorated rapidly: she developed an eating disorder, scratched her face, and added cocaine to her drug abuse. Discovering her drug use (and her lying about it), her parents reprimanded her severely. They found their credit cards, personal checks, and camera missing—all used presumably to generate cash for illicit drugs. Kristin cut her wrists, became manipulative, and threatened suicide. She was sent to Narcotics Anonymous and for a time was clean, but she relapsed; she managed to finish high school, but was then expelled from college because of drug abuse. Reverting to crystal meth, she would drive over the Mexican border to Tijuana to get drugs from a dealer.

Kristin, still only eighteen in 1994, ran away from home and began using crystal meth every day—and became sexually promiscuous. During a chance encounter on a bridge to Tijuana, she dropped her jacket, which was retrieved by a young man from a good family: Gregory de Villers. It was love at first sight for Gregory, who vowed to help her kick the drug habit. For a time it seemed he had succeeded. Her feelings for him were mixed, yet the two remained together and, despite Kristin's wanting to cancel wedding plans at the last minute, they did marry in 1999. Meantime, she had returned to college and graduated cum laude in 1998. Ironically, or perhaps not so ironically, Kristin majored in toxicology and began work in a toxicology lab in San Diego. Her boss, Michael Robertson, was a toxicologist from Australia, older, handsome—and married. By 2000, Kristin was already feeling trapped in her marriage and had begun an affair with Michael, who in turn was cheating on Kristin with yet another woman. Kristin also reverted to her old drug habits and became once again dependent on methamphetamine—this time from the lab.

Greg found out about her infidelity, which she denied. Kristin and Michael exchanged numerous love letters via e-mail, one of which Greg came across and printed out. He became furious. Kristin shredded the letter, which Greg then tried to reconstruct. When Greg threatened to tell the lab higher-ups, Kristin misled him with protestations of "love," all the while still carrying on the affair with Michael. Finally she used her toxicological skills and access to drugs from the workplace to create a deadly cocktail—with which she poisoned Greg to death in November of 2000. One of the ingredients was fentanyl—an opioid analgesic eighty to one hundred times as potent as morphine, and capable in small amounts of causing death from profound respiratory depression. Kristin staged Greg's death to appear as a suicide, with their wedding picture near his pillow and some of her notes nearby in which she wrote of wanting to leave the marriage. These pieces of evidence led the police at first to conclude that Greg simply couldn't live without her.

But toxicologists from a different lab discovered in Greg's tissues fentanyl levels that were seven times the lethal dose. From this and other evidence accumulated by Greg's brothers two years later, Kristin was brought to trial, convicted, and sentenced to life without parole. She showed no remorse and continued to lie about the murder even while in prison. How her personality would have unfolded without the drug abuse is unknowable. For want of a ballet career—the lost nail in her case—she took to drug abuse, which led to deceitfulness, manipulativeness, promiscuity, absence of remorse, stealing drugs: altogether, the picture of "acquired psychopathy" in someone ultimately driven to murder in order to get her husband "out of the way." The descent into evil actions—such as murder or infanticide—under the impact of powerful drugs like crack cocaine or crystal meth is a story heard all too often by the police and in the courts. This happens more often among those who were neglected or abused as children,[29] but it can happen even in those who started out, like Kristin Rossum, with what seemed like every advantage.

CATEGORY 11: PSYCHOPATHIC KILLERS OF PEOPLE IN THE WAY

The distinction between Categories 10 and 11 lies not in the behaviors of persons in these groups but in the degree and origins of their psychopathic tendencies. Those in Category 11 are more "dyed-in-the-wool" psychopaths, showing signs of conduct disorder or marked antisocial behaviors consistently from age eight or nine all the way through adolescence and beyond. These are the people whom some call *early-onset* or *life-course persistent* antisocial offenders.[30] A proportion of them later on show the characteristics of full-blown psychopathy.

Christian Longo

The elder of two brothers raised originally in a Catholic family, Chris Longo's parents divorced when he was four. His mother, Joy, was a teenager when she divorced her first husband after he beat her over the abdomen in an effort to make her abort the child she was carrying. She remarried, this time to Joe Longo, and then converted to Jehovah's Witness when Chris was ten. Joy persuaded Joe to convert also. In this strict religious group parents often avoid contact with the "worldly people," and homeschool their children. Chris wet his bed until he was ten, which is often a sign of emotional instability. He started out in public school, but didn't do well, so he hacked illegally into the school computer in order to hoist his grades. It was at that point, as Chris was about to enter high school, that Joe and Joy pulled him out of that school and henceforth homeschooled him.[31]

Chris was not allowed to date even when he was turned eighteen. His reaction to that edict was to leave home the following week. Shortly after, he married Mary-Jane, also a Jehovah's Witness and seven years older than he. Chris had not graduated high school and had no good skills or prospects. He got a job in a jewelry store, from which he stole $108, resigning after he paid the money back. He was sued several times for nonpayment of other monies he owed. Chris wanted the best of everything—another sign of departure from the Jehovah's Witnesses, who emphasize austerity. He began using false names and stolen credit cards to maintain his lifestyle, and he once drove off in a test car and disappeared, using yet another alias. Forging $30,000 worth of checks to raise cash, he hastily moved his family from Michigan to Ohio. By then, he had three small children, all born between 1997 and 1999. At one point Mary-Jane discovered an e-mail between her husband and another woman. When confronted, Chris told Mary-Jane he had stopped loving her when she had all those children, and that she wasn't fun anymore.[32]

Mary-Jane, raised to be subservient to a husband no matter what, put up with his infidelity and his scams. Keeping a step ahead of the authorities, he stole a van and moved the family to Oregon, where he was only able to get a low-paying job—necessitating further thefts to feed the family. As the police were finally about to close in on him, he drowned Mary-Jane and the three children, dumping their bodies in different Oregon rivers, after which he fled to Cancun, Mexico. The body of his three-year-old daughter, Sadie, had been weighted down with a rock. Clearly he imagined their bodies would never be found, and he would be free to begin life over under a more favorable star. It was as though he taken to heart Joseph Stalin's famous quip (upon ridding himself of a rival): "No body, no problem."

Once in Cancun, he assumed the identity of another man, Michael Finkel, who wrote feature articles for the *New York Times*. He was arrested in Cancun a few weeks later, still in the guise of the well-known journalist, partying and enjoying his ersatz celebrity. His true identity soon uncovered, he was convicted and sentenced to death. He rationalized the murders as his way of sending his family to a "better place"—in keeping with his religious teaching.[33] Chris had the outward persona of a Prince Charming, convinced he could talk his way out of anything. One of his wife's sisters had a certain admiration for his talents at charm and deception, commenting that Chris was capable of conning anyone.

CATEGORY 14: RUTHLESSLY SELF-CENTERED PSYCHOPATHIC SCHEMERS[34]

Some of the persons included in Category 14 were, like those we have already met in this chapter, eager to get someone permanently out of the way, whether that person might be a parent, a wealthy stranger, or a spouse. Usually, however, it was a spouse. And because there are many more men willing to kill a wife than there are wives willing to kill a husband, uxoricides (the fancy term for wife killers) greatly outnumber husband killers. But there is something more diabolical, more glaringly premeditated and psychopathic—hence more evil—in the eyes of the public about this type of criminal than those described in the earlier sections. Many had longer criminal careers and a more checkered past than those in the lower categories. Among the six hundred biographies I have relied on for much of this book, the highest percentage of the individuals are found in Category 14—one person in seven. I will have more to say on the topic of wife murder at the end of this section, but at this point it is worth noting how often *staging* crops up in the stories of spousal murder when it occurs in the educated and the well-to-do. Relative to our focus on evil, there is not only the "regular" evil of murder, but the added evil of chutzpah: the brazen assumption by these killers that they are far more clever than the police and thus immune to prosecution. It is as though they believe that, paraphrasing the late Leona Helmsley, jail is for the little people.[35] *Staging* refers to the deliberate alteration of a murder scene to make it look like an accident. The use of a hired hit man—as we saw in the Minns case—is another way a spouse (more often a husband than a wife) may try to feign innocence and elude guilt by distancing himself from the crime. The case that follows illustrates this point.

Todd Garton

The younger of two sons from a northern California family of Irish American descent, Todd from his earliest days was addicted to risk and thrill seeking. He was a compulsive weaver of tall tales, embellishing his image with stories of derring-do and accomplishments that were all make-believe. Granted that the con artist has a keen nose for the gullible, Garton's virtuosity at deception put him in a class by himself. He got his friends to believe that when he was only twelve—or was it fifteen?—he was already a mercenary in Belfast for the Irish Republican Army, serving as a "sniper" before "returning" to his home in California. He boasted that he had killed two "bad guys" when he was sixteen and had thrown their bodies in the Columbia River. Garton was actually a fairly competent bass player and headed up a band that enjoyed some popularity in

Oregon and northern California—a band that was destined, according to his braggadocio, to become the "next Beatles." He became absorbed with the fantasy of organizing an assassination squad to be known as "The Company." To show that he meant business, Todd would shoot cats, as he walked along with a friend, Norman Daniels, whom he would later recruit into his plan for murder. To Daniels he said that the "Company" was headed by a mysterious Colonel Sean who was "out of Langley" (the headquarters of the CIA) and was into "cover-up stuff."[36] Todd also lined up another friend, Dale Gordon, to participate in "justified killings"—in which Todd would portray a certain Dean Noyes as a "scumbag" who "stole money from a hospital group and beat up his wife."[37] Dale later said: "I believed him because the stories were very real stories. He [Todd] would give you smells, sights, everything."[38]

When he was twenty-one, Todd married Carole Holman, though he had been having an affair with Lynn Noyes, who had been a "groupie" when Todd was still running his band. Having tired of Carole seven years later, he wanted to resume his relationship with Lynn on a full-time basis. As an added inconvenience, Carole was eight months pregnant. Revving up his gift of gab to the max, Todd convinced both Norman and Dale that Carole was an "evil woman from the IRA" who was threatening others, and that they needed to join his Company and assassinate Carole before she got the chance to kill them. Realizing there was a fee for such services, Todd took out insurance policies of $125,000 for himself and for Carole so each would have something in case the other died[39]—a sum that would more than cover the amounts he promised his hit men friends. Then, on May 16, 1998, Dale Gordon shot Carole to death (with one of the five shots directed at her abdomen, killing the eight-month-old fetus) as she lay asleep. Growing remorseful afterward, Dale confessed to the authorities. As the plot involved Dale, Norman, Todd, and Lynn, all four were arrested and ultimately convicted. Todd, as the mastermind and psychopath, was quickly converted from con man to convict, and was given the death penalty. He has never confessed. The prosecutor in the case, Greg Gaul, having read Robert Scott's account of the murder, warned the public: "Don't believe everything you hear," referring to Todd's flamboyant lies, and adding, "There are evil people out there . . . and Todd Garton was an evil person."[40] Given the *timing* of the murder (Carole was in her eighth month of pregnancy), there is good reason to suspect that the "why?" of this case has much to do with the utter refusal on Todd's part to accept the responsibilities of fatherhood.

Sante Kimes

Sante Kimes and her son Kenny Jr. achieved notoriety in the summer of 1998 for the murder and disappearance of a wealthy New York widow, Irene Silverman. This was but the last in a dizzying and lifelong career of theft, conning, escape, and murder, stretching back to Sante's childhood, and later, to her tutelage of her own son in the ways of crime.[41] Just to list the complete catalog of Sante's crimes and her many aliases would about double the length of this chapter. Readers with a fascination for the macabre may wish to read either Adrian Havill's book *The Mother, the Son, and the Socialite* or his shorter account featured on the Crime Library Web site.[42]

Sante was born in 1934 in Oklahoma, the third of four children. Her mother was Irish; her father, Rattan Singhrs, was from India. A few years later the family moved to California. The father deserted and the mother became a prostitute, the children ending up in orphanages or foster homes. For a time, Sante was a street child in Los Angeles, where she was arrested at age nine for stealing food. She had apparently also been sexually abused. This was her situation until a woman suggested to her sister and brother-in-law that they adopt her, which they eagerly did. Now as Sante Chambers, she was a high school student, who was known as a cheerleader and boy-crazy flirt. She also began shoplifting and using her stepfather's credit cards to steal. After high school she married, briefly, first to Lee Powers, and then to Ed Walker, by whom she had a son, Kent Walker. Attractive at that stage of her life, she was sometimes mistaken for Elizabeth Taylor. This proved a help in her scams and thefts, including an auto theft she carried off by conning a dealer into letting her test-drive a new Cadillac, alone. She simply drove off with it, and when she was eventually caught, she told the police she was "still testing it." For a time she worked as a prostitute in Los Angeles. Somehow, and stories differ on this, she met up with a self-made millionaire, Kenneth Kimes (Big Ken), in 1971. He was seventeen years older. Sante had a son by him, and she gave herself and the boy the Kimes name, even though they were not as yet married. Despite Kimes's wealth, Sante continued to steal and began teaching her son, Kenneth Kareem Kimes (Ken Jr.), the tricks of the trade.

Big Ken was no more weighted down with scruples than was Sante; the two now plotted to meet the great and near-great in Washington, DC. They touted themselves as "honorary ambassadors" and even crashed a party at the house of Vice President Gerald Ford. Although it was no longer necessary *economically* to steal, Sante stole for the *thrill* of it: at another gathering in DC she contrived to steal a mink coat lying on a chair, by donning first the mink and then over it her own coat. Arrested for that, she evaded trial for five years with one excuse after the other, and when declared guilty, she simply disappeared. Whenever ensconced in her luxurious La Jolla home with the two Kens, Sante hired maids from Mexico, whom she then enslaved in cruel ways—branding one with a hot iron, locking another in a closet, striking others for not cooking a meal the way Sante liked it. For these cruelties she was arrested and for the first time actually went to prison—for three years, until her release in 1989.

Apart from her abusiveness toward servants, Sante had so far confined her activities to property crimes. That was to change. Now, with the cooperation of Ken Jr., she embarked on a more ambitious career of conning—and killing—rich people. When a lawyer conspired with Sante and Ken Jr. to burn down one of their homes for insurance money, he boasted about it to strangers in a bar. The authorities learned of this and convinced him to be an informant. Sante and Ken invited him to join them on vacation in Central America—a trip from which she and her son returned, but not the lawyer. His body has never been found. In the Bahamas, they fooled and later killed banker Sayed Bilal Ahmed and then went on to make some real estate deals with David Kazdin, an old friend of Sante's now dead husband (who managed to die of natural causes). But when Kazdin didn't go along with Sante's scams and was about to inform against her, he ended up shot to death, his body then deposited unceremoniously in a dumpster.

Having heard about Irene Silverman, a wealthy Fifth Avenue widow, Sante and Ken moved to New York to launch a still more ambitious scheme: to rent a suite of rooms at her mansion, use their con artist abilities to get into the woman's good graces, forge a document that gave over the mansion to Sante and Ken, kill her, and then make the body "disappear." With Sante assiduously practicing Silverman's handwriting, they went through with the entire plan, lugging Irene's body out of the Fifth Avenue mansion boxed up in a big trunk, returning later with the forged document supposedly conveying the place to the Kimes. But Sante had made a careless phone call to a man she then invited to run the New York property. The FBI were onto him; he cooperated with the authorities, incriminating evidence was found (including paper on which Sante had practiced Irene's handwriting over and over), and Sante and Ken were arrested. Irene's body has never been found—a fact that Ken thought would shield them from the police. As Ken (perhaps another admirer of Stalin) told the court: No body, no crime. Both are now serving life sentences. I thought it might be interesting to interview Sante, since she is incarcerated in a women's prison just thirty miles north of my office. She answered my letter in a most gracious manner, giving me to believe that she had been the victim of false accusations. The interview never took place, nor do I think that, even if it did, her account of her story would bear the stamp of truth.

A COMMENT ON WIFE MURDERERS

I noted earlier that as we move up the Gradations of Evil scale, we move away from reactive or "impulsive" murders toward murders and other acts of violence that are more and more premeditated or "instrumental."

In America, spouse murders are, in general, committed twice as often by husbands as by wives.[43] In the numerous biographies I have surveyed, where spousal murders were often of the instrumental type, a comparable ratio existed: there were two and a half times as many husbands (114) who murdered their wives as there were wives (44) who murdered a husband. All but two of the men were white (there was a black physician and a black dentist). Impulsive wife murders accounted for only one case in nine. We have already mentioned three such men (Gingerich, Rowe, and Skiadopoulos) in earlier chapters. All the rest were "schemers." This is a much higher ratio than we would see in the whole population, where murder on impulse is the rule, even in the murder of a spouse.

Men are, in general, more aggressive than women: wife battering is common, husband battering is rare. This means that wives who kill their husbands have usually been provoked by physical abuse, though I also found in my series of "schemers" that the women in almost half the cases killed for insurance money. The motives of the men were occasionally to get insurance money (one in ten), but much more often they had to do with jealousy, anger at the wife for demanding a divorce, or wanting to be with a mistress. Those three motives accounted for three out of five of the cases. One man in ten killed to protect himself from public disgrace, as when the wife was aware of some sordid and illegal action and was about to tell the authorities. In one case the wife found out her husband, who claimed to be a medical student, was an imposter.[44] In another, the wife learned that her husband was a crooked attorney involved in get-rich schemes with illegal drugs.[45]

Homicide is the leading cause of death among pregnant women in the United States.[46] In this chapter we sketched the case of Todd Garton; there were three others in my series, including the more well-known case of Scott Peterson, who killed his wife, Laci, also when she was in her eighth month of pregnancy.[47] It was not the wife but the unborn child that pushed these men over the edge.

But of all the things I learned from looking at the histories of wife murderers, the most remarkable were these two points: the men hardly ever confessed, even when convicted, and they staged the wife's body to make it look like death was "accidental"—or used a hit man. These measures were the rule rather than the exception among the "schemers" (that is, the husbands who committed premeditated murder). Confession was common in the impulsive husbands (7 out of 10); only one in five among the "schemers" ever confessed. Both these qualities contribute to the aura of evil that surrounds these cases of wife murder. The vast majority of people are incapable of lying with anything like the poise and facility that the psychopath brings to this task. In contrast, the vast majority of people, though in their mind they may now and again plot to hurt or kill someone who has deeply offended them, have adequate inner controls that slam the brakes on these vengeful thoughts, which then whither and disappear.

Chapter Five

SPREE AND MASS MURDER

Evil by the Numbers

Canto XXVIII, ll. 1–6

Chi porta mai pur con parole sciolte
dicer del sangue e de le piaghe a pieno
ch'i' ora vidi, per narrar più volte?
Ogne lingua per certo verria meno
per lo nostro sermone e per la mente
c'hanno a tanto comprender poco seno.

Who could ever, even with unfettered tongue,
tell in full of the blood and wounds I now saw,
Though he should narrate them many times?
Every tongue would surely fail,
because our language and our memory
have little capacity to comprehend so much.

Most of the stories I've described have been about men and women who have killed just one other person. There were a few examples of "multiple" killers, mentioned to illustrate a particular point, usually about motive. Since we will be concentrating in this chapter on two different kinds of multiple murder, some definitions are in order by way of sidestepping the confusion that surrounds this term.

We speak of a *spree murder* when someone kills a number of people in spurts over a period of a few days or weeks; sometimes longer. The "someone" can even be a couple, as in the famous Depression-era case of Bonnie and Clyde.[1] Another famous couple were Charles Starkweather and his young girlfriend, Caril Fugate, who killed eleven people during their month-long shooting spree in Nebraska in 1958.[2]

Technically, *mass murder* refers to the killing of four or more persons at one point in time, all within one day[3]—as in the case of the Texas Tower murders by Charles Whitman at the University of Texas in Austin, August 1, 1966. The death toll in that case was fourteen plus Whitman's wife and mother, whom he had killed before ascending the tower. Sometimes the word *massacre* is used instead of *murder*—in the lay language and in the press—as in the St. Valentine's Day Massacre of seven men in Chicago, most of them members of the Bugs Moran gang, by four members of Al Capone's rival South Side gang in 1929. *Massacre* is a stronger term, conveying more sharply the shock and horror that people experience in hearing (or worse yet, witnessing) a mass murder. In my review of several hundred mass murders since 1900, three facts stand out. *First*, guns (whether rifles or pistols) are far and away the weapons most commonly used. It is very difficult to commit mass murder with a knife, since the killer can more easily be subdued by some of the intended victims. *Second*, the *average* number of victims in mass murder is about eight, although there are a few cases where dozens are killed. We saw one example earlier: the mass murder by arson of eighty-seven people at the Happy Land dancehall. The greatest death toll in a mass murder involving a gun is fifty-seven: Bum-Kon Woo was a Korean police officer in 1982. Disillusioned about his career and recently rejected by his fiancée, he went around a town near Seoul shooting everyone he could find, before using the gun on himself. Arson and bombs are rarer instruments of mass murder but obviously have much greater potential for destruction.

The *number of victims* is a key factor in the sense of evil surrounding mass murder, particularly because there is usually *nothing personal* about the crime: the object is merely to kill as many strangers as possible. This at least is the typical scenario. There are a few rare exceptions to the rule, as when a mass murder is committed as a byproduct of a lethal act directed at one specific person, with all the other victims ending up as, to use military jargon, "collateral damage." The most spectacular example of this phenomenon is that of Jack Gilbert Graham, to be discussed shortly.

The *third* fact: mass murder is almost without exception a man's crime. In the rare case where the perpetrator was a woman, several people were shot, but only one died—in what would have to be called *mass murder manqué*. The attempted mass murder failed, fortunately, most likely because the female perpetrator had less practice with firearms than her male counterparts. Women in general are less apt to become avid hunters, less likely to own guns and practice shooting than men. As an example, Jillian Robbins, a nineteen-year-old about to be discharged from the Army Reserves, walked onto the University of Pennsylvania campus in 1996 and began shooting at students. Despite her experience in the reserves, she apparently did not become a proficient marksman. As it turned out, she killed only one person and wounded another before she was tackled and subdued.[4]

One other term, *serial killing*, is too often used in an imprecise way that does not distinguish it from spree murder and does not make clear which of the various types of actual serial killing one is referring to. Serial killing encompasses those cases where murders are separated by fairly long periods of time, typically weeks or months. When people hear the phrase "serial killer," however, they usually think *serial sexual homicide*—a topic I will expand on in a later chapter. Although serial sexual homicide is rare, it is the most commonly encountered variety of "serial killing." A second variety comes under the heading of "Angel of Death." The Angel of Death in these cases is a medical professional—most commonly a doctor or a nurse who has easy access to lethal medicines. The usual victims are hospitalized patients, though in the notorious case of England's Dr. Harold Shipman, the victims were men and women, some in hospitals, some living at home, who were part of his patient roster.[5] He murdered several hundred patients (the exact number will never be known)—mostly with opiates.

Besides these two types, there are several other types of nonsexual serial killers. There are the mothers who smother to death one infant after another (usually with intervals of a year or more between each murder); misanthropic men who kill at intervals men, women, and children, out of their general hatred of humankind (and with no sexual motif); and a few one-of-a-kind types—which I will mention in the next chapter.

SPREE MURDER

One of the most humbling experiences in my exploration of evil was my meeting with the former spree killer Archibald McCafferty in the spring of 2007. Up until that time, what I knew of spree killers and mass murder came only from books. This put me at the mercy of the accuracy and, at times, the prejudices of the men and women who wrote these books. Since the killers had done terrible things—things the public, and the authors, regarded as loathsome, evil—those feelings filtered down into me as well. Because most spree killers and mass murderers die by suicide or police action, we often imagine that the way they were—in personality and behavior—at the time they died is the way they would always have been, had they survived. We could never know, for example, if Charles Starkweather might one day have overcome his antisocial ways had he lived into his fifties. He was all of twenty when he killed all those people in 1958, but even though he lived to face trial in court, the death penalty that was handed down came swiftly in those days: he died in the electric chair a year later, still basically a wild and vengeful adolescent.

I first became acquainted with McCafferty through a book ominously titled *Never to Be Released* by Paul Kidd.[6] The story was not encouraging. McCafferty was born in 1949 in Glasgow, Scotland. When he was eight or nine, people already thought of him as "trouble": trouble, in his case, consisted of truancy, theft, cutting girls' hair, strangling cats and dogs, burglary, vandalism, and tossing snakes and mice to scare people. His father, who was extremely abusive and physically punitive (in a fruitless effort to socialize his son) before and after Archie's early years, thought things would improve if the whole family moved to Australia to give Archie a new start. In Sydney, however, Archie was no different; at age ten he became an "incorrigible juvenile delinquent," doing the same property crimes as he had done back in Glasgow. He had been in and out of jail and reformatories many times and had thirty-five convictions by age twenty-four, some of which were for stealing cars and assault. He had an explosive temper, fueled in part by his abuse of alcohol and the whole menu of illicit drugs: LSD, angel dust, heroin, marijuana, amphetamines, and barbiturates. So far, not a very encouraging history! As Ovid knew, however, *amor omnia vincit*: Love conquers all. And for a time, it seemed as though love was the magic ingredient that was going to make Archie settle down into a peaceful life.

When Archie was twenty-three, he met, fell in love with, and married Janice Redington. His family hoped he would now give up his antisocial ways. For a few months he did seem different: he got a regular job, felt proud to be taking home an honest paycheck, and gave up his criminal activities. Unfortunately, the family's hopes went unrealized, for Archie was still abusing alcohol heavily; he began to cheat on Janice and was aggressive toward her. He became obsessed with ideas about killing her and even went to a psychiatric hospital voluntarily to see if he could get rid of his "evil thoughts." But when he was released, his thoughts and his behavior were the same. Still, Archie did love Janice, he told me, and he went a year without getting arrested. He felt even greater love for his infant son, Craig Archibald, who was born in February of 1973. Though still drinking and doing drugs, according to Janice, Archie was gradually settling into family life.[7]

Six weeks later, however, the baby died when (if the story is true) Janice rolled over him while she was fast asleep. Craig's death unhinged Archie. As he told me, "I went off the rails. I was taking LSD, Angel Dust, anything I could get my hands on, and I went to the cemetery and felt I could see a light; I saw a twenty-year-old version of Craig talking to me, saying, "Kill seven, Dad, and I'll come back to life!" Archie then gathered a small troupe of teenagers and set about killing strangers, hoping that when they'd killed the seventh, Craig would be resurrected. In a two-week period (this was the "spree") Archie and the gang had killed their third victim. He was arrested before he could finish his mission. In court he asked for the death penalty, saying, "It was the right thing to do." Instead he got three life sentences. In prison he was still convinced he needed to kill four more people and continued to be violent, so much so that he was placed in a special cell. He was nicknamed *Mad Dog McCafferty*. For a long time the prison authorities and the psychiatrists who consulted on his case agreed: Archie should never be set free.

His anger and violence continued for eight years. By chance he then met a woman—Amanda Queen, who'd been visiting another prisoner. There was something about Amanda that, as he put it, "reached my human side." He spoke of Mandy as "an angel: she showed me love and purity, visited me faithfully for sixteen years; with her I was a pussy-cat. I had no more vengeful fantasies." The prison recognized the profound change in Archie and began listening to his requests to be released. He was allowed to participate in work programs and showed himself to be rehabilitated. In 1997 a deal was made with Archie: he was granted release with the proviso he return to his native Scotland, where he could live as a free man. He and Mandy married, she accompanied him to Glasgow, and they eventually had two children. The tabloid press still painted him as the old Archie, printing such headlines as, when his first child was born, "*Mad Dog Has Pup.*" This relentless negative publicity, based on Archie's violent image from the past, made life intolerable for

Mandy. After a few years she returned to Australia with the children. His comment: "All she did was love a guy like me. I don't blame her. But I'm not 'Mad Dog' anymore." Archie, who is sixty now, has spent the past ten years living peaceably and inoffensively in Scotland—a changed person. As he put it: "I feel regret for the things I'd done, but not great remorse. I can't undo the past. I've been punished severely—those twenty-five years in jail, and the hounding by the press; I'm still angry at what the media put me through. I'm a better person today; I deserve a life."

Archibald McCafferty taught me that some men whom society dubs as evil and (once incarcerated) "never to be released" *are* capable ultimately—and in the face of everyone's worst fears—of rehabilitation and redemption. Despite all the minuses in his early life, there were some pluses. As we can sense from his years with Amanda, he had within him the ability to be part of a sustained and loving relationship. And from his brief time with Craig, we know he had the capacity to be a devoted and loving father. When in turmoil after the death of his son, and even before, he had the self-awareness to know he needed psychiatric help; once convicted, he felt guilty enough that he asked the judge for the death penalty. In the hours I spent with him, I found myself impressed by his candor and honesty—and his capacity for self-reflection. He had developed a workable philosophy of life—one that embodied the Serenity Prayer of Alcoholics Anonymous: "Grant me the serenity to accept the things I cannot change, courage to change the things I can, and the wisdom to know the difference." These are the qualities you see in certain people with "antisocial personality" who show signs of recovery in midlife and who can thenceforth live as respectable citizens in the community. These are emphatically *not* the qualities you see in the psychopath.

Compare Archie's life with that of Sante Kimes from the previous chapter. Sante is now a woman in her early seventies, yet she is still out to gull the public, still incapable of acknowledging what her life has been all about, still trying to pass herself off as the innocent victim of a "frame-up." The comparison of their two lives shows the power of the Factor-I traits in Hare's measure of psychopathy. With regard to Factor-II traits, both McCafferty and Kimes spent their early years as behavioral train wrecks. But lacking the extreme predatory traits of the full-blown psychopath, McCafferty was able, once the fires of youth burned less hotly, to walk away from lawlessness and violence. Kimes remains as she was.

If we look for answers to why these two people, scarcely distinguishable in their teens and twenties, took such different paths in their later years, one explanation, I believe, resides in *family*. McCafferty came from an intact family. His father, punitive though he was, cared enough about his wayward son to move ten thousand miles from home to give him a new chance. It didn't work, but at least some moral values got pounded into Archie that saved the day—even if it took thirty years. Kimes was abandoned by her father and then by her mother; she was left to survive by her wits in the streets of Los Angeles, first by theft, then by prostitution. She passed through her childhood without ever being the object of anyone's unconditional love. Heredity probably made a difference too: she may have started out with a risk to develop along psychopathic lines that was greater than McCafferty's. Spotting such distinctions in young persons who have begun to break the law—especially if they have been violent—is difficult, whether for psychiatrists or for jurists. It is even more difficult for people in ordinary life, who have little experience weighing these different factors. Understandably, they would rather be safe than sorry, like the people who crowded around McCafferty when he was released, objecting vehemently to his winning his freedom after all those murders. After reading Kidd's book, written four years before McCafferty's release and fourteen years before he and I spoke, I would have been opposed to his release too. I'm grateful for the chance to have met him and to have seen for myself that the evil some men do need not last a lifetime.

À propos my opportunity to meet with him, here is another odd twist to the history of Archie McCafferty. This one has to do with the idea of "sensitive dependence upon initial conditions," which James Gleick brought to our attention with his groundbreaking book *Chaos: Making a New Science*.[8] In this book he speaks about the well-known scenario of a butterfly flapping its wings in Brazil "causing" a tornado in Oklahoma, referring to the unpredictable impact of a minor disturbance bringing about a subtle change nearby that causes another change and that ends up as a profound change further down the line. Think of a small town with two mayoral candidates—one crooked, the other honest. They're tied 250 votes to 250—until a laggard citizen comes to the polls just before closing and casts his one vote. Without realizing it, he has cast the deciding ballot that determines whether the crook or the honest man gets elected.

The flapping butterfly in Archie's case was this: after he and his gang killed their first three people—on the way to the magic "seven" that in his LSD-besotted mind would revivify his dead son—they were on their way to kill Archie's wife Janice and her family, which they would surely have done, except that *the car ran out of gas*! Archie abandoned that plan and it was then that he got arrested. If not for that faltering fuel tank, Archie would have had his seven murders, and the court might have looked very differently upon a man who killed *seven* people, including his own wife. The public outcry against his ever being released (it was pretty shrill as it was, with three victims) would likely have been so great that he never would have been released . . . hence never be given the opportunity to show that he was capable of redemption. He would have been written off as the incurable psychopath that the detectives and doctors originally assumed he was, and he would have died in prison. I would have tended to agree with Paul Kidd that he should never have been released, and of course I would never have met him and seen the different Archie he later became. I believe there are people who, besides having committed evil acts at some point in their lives, are truly incurable.[9] But my experience with Archie McCafferty made me aware that we cannot rush to judgment about who these "truly incurable" people are.

Charles Manson

The spree murders engineered by Charles Manson in Los Angeles in 1969 are unique in that the person primarily responsible for the murders of Gary Hinman on July 31, actress Sharon Tate and four others at her house on August 9, and of the LaBianca couple a day later was Manson himself—in absentia. Manson didn't pull the trigger on any of those eight people. Instead, he amassed a group of followers blindly loyal to his depraved goals and to the cult he organized. His "family" was so loyal that several of them participated unhesitatingly in the executions he ordered them to carry out.

The spree murders of Manson are different from the more "ordinary" spree murders of Starkweather and McCafferty in another important respect. The motive behind the other two was rage at members of their own families: Starkweather's father and the parents of his girlfriend; McCafferty's wife. As mentioned in chapter 1, the motive behind the

Manson murders was terrorism. Self-aggrandizement was probably a secondary motive. Manson—taking a page from the Book of the Apocalypse (specifically chapter 9)—got his followers to believe he was God or Jesus Christ. He also convinced them that the "four angels" mentioned in that chapter were incarnated as the four members of the popular rock band The Beatles. The Beatles wrote a song called "Helter Skelter," which included the words: "Look out for helter skelter . . . She's coming down fast, yes she is." Manson purposely distorted these lyrics to fit in with his warped notion of Armageddon, which in his mind consisted of an uprising by the blacks to take over the world. It was when he noticed that this Armageddon wasn't happening all by itself that he decided to jump-start it in 1969 by getting a few of his most loyal, and (like himself) totally amoral, followers to murder some high-profile and noticeably wealthy people in the white community. We can assume Manson was bitten with a consuming envy of the well-to-do whites that made them no less a target of his hatred than the blacks, Jews, gays, and whomever else he hated. One can only marvel—or gasp—at the power of Manson's ability to mesmerize his followers, to infect them with his own hatred so thoroughly that they could no longer think with their brains, only with the brain of Manson. They became his malign robots.

If we compare the spree murders by McCafferty and those incited by Manson, we notice that the background factors are radically different. Manson was a psychopath and remains so at the age of seventy-five. His early years resemble those of Sante Kimes in certain ways; in other ways they were immeasurably worse. Like Kimes, Manson was abandoned by his mother and never knew his father. But he was never the object of anyone's even distant affection. His birth mother, Kathleen Maddox, was sixteen when he was born. She was either promiscuous or a prostitute or both, disappearing for days at a time and leaving Charlie with a grandmother or with his very strict aunt. Kathleen was later married briefly to a William Manson, whence the last name. His father may or may not have been a certain Kentuckian "Colonel Scott." When Manson was five, Kathleen was sent to prison for armed robbery. Upon release she was unwilling to accept responsibility for him and actually traded him for a glass of beer. Friendless, Manson stole and was sent at nine to a reformatory from which he escaped and spent the last part of his childhood and all of his adolescence in and out of jails and institutions. While incarcerated, he was sodomized, according to what Manson related, by men much larger than himself, many of them (also according to him) black—which moved blacks to the top of his hate list. Released at twenty-four, he pimped for a time but was rearrested a year later. He was not put back in prison until two years later—for rape, drug use, pimping, stealing, and fraud.[10] Manson stated some years later, when he was thirty-two and released from prison again, that he knew he could not adjust to the outside world, having spent all of his life locked up. One commentator added, "The prison guards ignored Manson and unleashed the evil man into society again."[11] Given what Manson later became, the term *evil* is applicable, but his premature release is hardly the fault of the prison guards, since they have no say as to whether a prisoner is given his freedom.

It was shortly after that, when he was thirty-four, that he became the Manson we know: the cult leader and supreme con artist of a group of gullible lost souls whom he corrupted into stealing and scavenging, meantime exercising sexual privileges with the young women whom he had persuaded to join. Admittedly, the formative years in Manson's life were so shorn of all humanizing influences that it is impossible to gauge to what extent heredity may have contributed to his early antisocial behavior and his lasting psychopathy. Put another way, the bad environment (absent father, absent and antisocial mother, violence endured in institutional settings) was enough to make many a young person into a "secondary" (that is, nonhereditary) psychopath. I suspect that these environmental calamities were nevertheless superimposed, in Manson's case, on a hereditary disadvantage—combining to create a picture of unalterable psychopathic traits of the Factor-I egocentric type (grandiosity, glibness, lying, callousness). McCafferty, in contrast, grew up in a family; it's true that his father was more punitive than the average, but it was a family all the same.

Manson has spent the past forty years in prison. One might think the world had forgotten about him—or at least had placed him on the back shelf of memory, alongside Al Capone, Leopold and Loeb, and Bruno Hauptmann of the Lindbergh kidnap (if indeed he was the kidnapper). But Manson retains his spot in the center of our memory as the embodiment of evil. Prosecutor and author Vincent Bugliosi speaks of our "continuing fascination with the case. The very name 'Manson' had become a metaphor for evil. . . . He has come to represent the dark and malignant side of humanity; and there is a side to human nature that is fascinated by pure, unalloyed evil."[12] Manson won this malignant fame through his ability to inspire the weak, the lost, the marginalized—not only to murder at his command but actually to glory in the unspeakable deeds his followers carried out in his name.

The analogy with Hitler is striking. If Hitler is evil with a capital E, Manson is Hitler with a small "h." Both got others to do the killing for them. Both targeted the victims of their blood-deep prejudices. Both rose from obscurity to celebrity through evil. Both were energized by hatred to seek a revolution that would turn the world upside-down. Instead of being "nothings" whom no one would notice, now they would become emperors, noticed and feared by all. Both ensured their fame through the murder of "high-profile" groups: for Hitler, the Jews; for Manson, the rich and the famous. And just as many Germans came to their senses fairly quickly after the death of Hitler, aghast at the horrors they took part in, many of the "Mansonites" were aghast and remorseful for what they had been a part of, once Manson was captured and put in prison. I can testify to this personally, having gotten to know two of the women who had once been in the Manson family. Neither was directly involved in the murders, and both have now been leading useful and blameless lives for forty years.

Having touched on the subject of *spree* murder, we turn our attention now to the larger subject of *mass* murder.

MASS MURDER

Of the crimes that move us to say "evil," mass murder is one of the most common. I thought it might be possible to put together from the Internet a complete list of mass murders in the twentieth century, but after the list grew to several hundred, I gave up. Three-fourths of the cases came from the United States, but it was clear that we just weren't hearing about the mass murders in Bulgaria, Pakistan, Zimbabwe, Burma, and a host of other countries where, apart from war, and granting that guns are not readily available everywhere as they are in the United States, mass murders are probably occurring with some regularity. Even in the countries where crime statistics are more carefully detailed, the full picture isn't available on the Internet, since only the more "noteworthy" cases from England, Canada, and Western Europe are publicized.

The sense of evil is mostly in the sheer number of victims, because the men committing the murders seldom survive their one explosion of violence. The mayhem makes the front pages but, except in the most spectacular cases, is soon forgotten. Many cases of mass murder are written up only in local newspapers; those that achieve national attention depend for their wide publicity on such special features as a very large number of victims, killers who are still adolescents (as in the school-shooter incidents of the late '90s), or predominantly child victims or college student victims, whose deaths stir up the greatest horror in the public and the greatest sympathy for the victims and their families. As it turns out, there have been almost a thousand mass murders (using the FBI's fairly strict definition of four or more victims killed in one brief incident) in the United States between 1900 and 1999,[13] with 495 occurring just in the years 1975 to 1996. No public mass shooting was committed by a woman during the whole of the twentieth century;[14] the only one known to me was committed by Jennifer Sanmarco, a postal worker in California, who killed six and then herself in 2006.[15]

Mass murderers do strike fear in the public, despite the fact that they often die at the scene—a fifth of these murderers die by their own hand.[16] In contrast to a serial killer still at large—an ever-present danger because he is still "out there"—the mass murderer makes people fear for their safety in public places, at work, in school, in the mall, and even in their own homes. The point being: somebody else, whom no one suspects could quite unpredictably do the same thing tomorrow or the next day. This type of fear became greatly magnified after Richard Speck's murder of eight nurses in Chicago and Charles Whitman's murder of fourteen in the University of Texas quadrangle—these acts occurred just two weeks apart in the summer of 1966.[17] And those dramatic murders came not so long after the 1959 murders of Herbert Clutter and his family—in their own home—as famously told by Truman Capote in his nonfiction novel *In Cold Blood*.[18] When it comes to safety and survival, our sense of statistics goes out the window. Never mind that mass murder is rare, that school shootings are particularly rare. The media blitz that accompanies all such crimes, especially the ones carried out by "crazy people" (like Jennifer Sanmarco, who was arrested once for public nudity and who used to argue with "voices" in front of her coworkers) or disgruntled workers (like James Huberty of the 1984 San Ysidro McDonald's massacre) magnifies the assailants as evil demons who target *anyone* and puts yellow highlighter under the message: This could happen to you!

Although it does appear that mass murder is on the rise since the 1960s, some of the increase is more apparent than real—and this is for at least two reasons. In the United States, for example, the population is more than twice what it was fifty years ago. This means that a number that seems twice as high may be proportionally (per million population) the same as before. Also, the more recent mass murderers are more prone to attack the public indiscriminately; those of the period between the two World Wars were largely mob-related (as in the St. Valentine's Day Massacre). As long as you weren't a mobster who confined his hit list to rival mobsters, you had no worries, and the newspapers (and now the TV) didn't force the public so vehemently to think that *you might be next*. This may help explain how it is that we tend to regard Al Capone and John Dillinger as "bad guys," but mass killers like Mark Lepine (who killed fourteen women at Montréal's École Polytechnique in 1989) or Patrick Purdy (who killed five Cambodian schoolchildren in California, also in 1989) as "evil." Lepine hated educated women; Purdy hated Asians. Understandably, we sympathize much more with women and children than we do with Bugs Moran's gangsters.

Among the different motives that lie behind mass murder, the public has come to put the "disgruntled worker" in first place, that is, the worker who has recently been fired or is threatened with losing his job. This idea, although only partially based on fact, has been fixed in the public mind thanks to the influence of the sensational press.[19] This sensationalism has given rise to the unfortunate phrase "going postal." The phrase gained popularity in the aftermath of the mass murder in Edmond, Oklahoma, August 20, 1986, when Patrick Sherrill, who was about to be fired from his post office job, brought a number of his many guns to the office and killed fourteen coworkers, before turning the gun on himself. What lifted this murder to national attention was the large number of victims. Sherrill was a friendless loner with no known family; no one even came to claim his body. His only earthly attachments were to the National Guard (of which he was a member) and to his gun collection. He boasted of having fought in Vietnam but was shown never to have seen active duty.[20] He gave the world nothing except a bad reputation to postal workers, and that only because he killed fourteen of his coworkers. Popular press aside, postal workers are actually *not* any more likely to commit a mass murder than are the employees of other large corporations.

That said, mass murderers, for the most part, do fall into one of a half dozen categories. The most common are indeed the disgruntled workers (more broadly known as *employment disputes* but also including self-employed men who have failed at their own ventures).[21] But the disgruntled workers make up only about 20 percent[22] of all the mass murderers. Also common: rejected lovers (including stalkers of persons with whom there is no real relationship) who comprise about 8 percent, hate crime killers (11 percent), and men committing some other felony. Less common are individuals who are obviously psychotic, the cornered cult leader, and, rarest of all, the man who commits a mass murder to hide the murder of just one targeted victim. Matters of definition enter into the equation here: about two out of five mass murders take place within the home, often with a father killing wife, children, and sometimes himself.[23] But some choose to call these acts "familicide" (my own preference), since they form such a special and important group—as highlighted by the case of John List in chapter 4.

All six of the female mass murderers known to me have been psychotic—either manic-depressive or schizophrenic.[24] This was true of Laurie Wasserman Dann, the *mass murderer manqué* alluded to earlier. She was the Illinois woman who tried to stab her ex-husband to death with an ice pick and later, in May of '88, after setting several fires, forced her way into a schoolroom in Winnetka, armed with three pistols, and proceeded to shoot at a class of second-grade pupils, killing one and wounding five others. When the police were closing in on her that evening, she killed herself with one of the guns.[25] A little earlier in her violent career she had seen a prominent psychopharmacologist, Dr. John Greist, presumably to treat her manic-depression. She brought him some Kool-Aid (shades of the Jonestown massacre in Guyana) laced with arsenic, however, rather than with cyanide. Dr. Greist wisely declined and thus lived to tell the story to those of us in attendance at a conference he gave at the hospital where I was working some years ago. It put me in mind of the line in Virgil's *Aeneid*: *Timeo Danaos et dona ferentes*—I fear the Greeks even when they bear gifts.[26]

Thomas Hamilton

The case I chose to exemplify disgruntlement is that of Thomas Hamilton of Glasgow. Born Thomas Watt in 1952, his surname was changed to Hamilton when at age four he was adopted by his maternal grandparents. As with many eventual mass murderers, Hamilton was a loner, a social misfit, a pariah, and a markedly paranoid person who would later send off letters to members of Parliament, even to Queen Elizabeth, complaining that the authorities were preventing him from engaging in youth work. Therein lay the rub, for Hamilton was a homosexual pedophile or (as others had said) a sexual psychopath. He became a Scout leader who ran gyms and camps for boys. He insisted the boys do their exercises clad only in bathing suits. He took numerous pictures of them, concentrating on their lower halves. At some point Hamilton embezzled £10,000 to buy camera equipment at a time when he was unemployed. In all fairness, there was no evidence that he actually had sexual contact with the boys. When his conduct came to the attention of the authorities, however, because of parents' objections, he offered the lame excuse that "it was necessary to identify what muscles were being used so that wrong movements could be corrected."[27] A failure at everything he undertook, he got heavily into debt, living off credit cards and social supplements.

An avid gun collector, he ended up owning at least six, boasting to the boys about his membership in a gun club. This is not the place to catalog the innumerable signs of trouble in the offing that were missed, ignored, or underestimated by the social workers, police, and scouting officials who were sent warnings about Hamilton (often enough from the parents of the boys in his camp). As is true with many histories of mass murderers, signs of impending disaster were glaring—in retrospect. We think of the title of a famous book by Gabriel García Márquez: *Chronicle of a Death Foretold*. Furious at the parents who voiced complaints about his treatment of their boys and down to his last three pence, Hamilton entered a schoolroom in Dunblane, Scotland, on March 13, 1966, armed with two Browning 9 mm automatics and two .357 Magnum revolvers, and killed the teacher and sixteen pupils, before finally turning one of the guns on himself.

Several prestigious mental health experts in Scotland offered their opinions about Hamilton after the tragedy. Those of forensic psychologist David Cooke from Glasgow are particularly apt. Cooke stated that "[t]here were major difficulties in Thomas Hamilton's life which threatened his self-esteem. He was in debt. . . . He was being refused access to premises to hold his boys clubs. . . . It may have been the case that, like many mass killers, he obtained feelings of power and mastery by fantasizing his revenge on those whom he perceived as persecuting him. . . . He believed that parents were spreading rumors that he was a pervert."[28] Hamilton seems to have figured, quite logically under the circumstances, that the "sweetest" revenge would be to kill not the parents but their children. He knew that would inflict upon his enemies a whole lifetime of suffering, rather than the few seconds of suffering that would be endured by the children. In choosing that alternative, he of course also ensured himself the enduring reputation of consummate evil. Dr. Baird, a forensic psychiatrist, felt that Hamilton's primary motive was suicide. I do not see this as an either-or situation. Hamilton wanted revenge, as Cooke mentioned; he wanted people to sit up and take notice; he wanted to rise from feeling unnoticed and ineffective to a position of power and affirmation.[29] To effect this change, while knowing he had run out of any hope to succeed in any other way, suicide beckoned. But it must be suicide with a flourish, with revenge and fame built into the final act, letting the world know without saying the words: *Après moi, le déluge*.

Examples from crime reports in the media are legion. In February 2008, for example, Steven Kazmierczak, a former Northern Illinois University student in his twenties, entered the campus and killed six, before killing himself.[30] He had been hospitalized for mental illness and was depressed, but he had refused to take his medications. He failed at various jobs and ventures, and finally—in an act of revenge-suicide—he "got back" at those whose lives appeared to be more successful than his, before then killing himself. In Japan, Tomohiro Katoh, a man of twenty-five, was apparently "tired of life" and ran his car into a crowd, then stabbing people who were nearby, killing ten people altogether, before committing suicide.[31] In a case where the motives are clearer, Richard Hawkins, an Oklahoma man of twenty, having been fired from his job and rejected by his girlfriend, killed eight people before turning his gun on himself.[32]

Richard Farley

The rejected lover is another popular "flavor" of mass murder. The psychology so often seen in mass murder: the socially awkward outcast and loner, grudge holding and paranoid, unable to succeed—yet unable to accept failure and move on—shows up about as often in matters of love as in matters of work. When Richard Farley was thirty-six, he met Laura Black; both had been employees of a California firm called Electromagnetic Systems Labs (ESL) in 1984. Laura did not accept his advances, at which point he began to stalk her. He did such things as attend her gym class, wait outside her house, and send her threatening letters. Two years later, undeterred, he threatened to kill her if she refused to date him. One can only marvel at how this otherwise intelligent man grew up so blind to social niceties as not to realize that this was not the way to a woman's heart. He managed somehow to get a set of her keys and left a duplicate set on the dashboard of her car, letting her understand he had access to her house. This got him fired, but it didn't end the stalking. Laura changed homes three times, got an unlisted phone number—all to no avail. She obtained an Order of Protection against him, which was about as effective as those documents usually are. Farley's rage now ignited to the flashpoint, he brought a few of his many weapons to ESL—two pistols and three rifles—and on February 16, 1988, shot to death seven employees. He tried to kill Laura, but she survived with a bullet wound to the shoulder. Rather than killing himself or committing "suicide by cop," Farley chose to surrender to a SWAT team. He was sentenced to death at his subsequent trial. This was a high-profile crime: both he and Laura were highly educated professionals; the crime came in the wake of several other notorious California stalking murders inadequately dealt with by the laws at the time. A movie was made of the case (*I Can Make You Love Me*), and California then passed its first anti-stalking law.

George Hennard

Mass murder triggered by hatred of one group or another is a common motif. In these cases there is often a mixture of reactions that become explosive only when suddenly combined, as when ammonium iodide crystals are ignited by (of all things!) water. A bigot, for example, may sit tight with his bigotry for years on end—until faced with romantic rejection or job loss or exam failure, which then becomes the catalyst to mass murder of people who belong to the hated group.

George Hennard had hated his mother (for reasons never made clear) and by extension women in general (whom he called "snakes"). He also hated Hispanics, blacks, and gays. Hennard's Swiss-born father was an army surgeon, and the family moved around a good deal when he was growing up. In school he was known as a withdrawn and sullen loner who never dated and never had friends. He joined the navy but got into trouble for smoking marijuana and for a racial argument, for which he had his seaman's papers suspended. He often made derogatory comments about women, especially after having a squabble with his mother.[33] By his midthirties he was working in a cement company in Texas; his behavior was becoming increasingly bizarre and menacing. A week before the incident, he quit his job—perhaps with the understanding that his life would soon be ending. On October 15, 1991, he reached his thirty-fifth birthday. That evening he watched a television program during the senate hearings about prospective Supreme Court justice Clarence Thomas, a black man, who had come under criticism for possible sexual harassment of an assistant, Anita Hill, also black. Hennard was heard to scream at the image of Anita Hill: "You dumb bitch! You bastards opened the door for all the women!" Woman hatred and bigotry now met in an explosive mix.

That combination seems to have been the trigger—that, plus the awareness that his biblical lifespan of "three-score and ten years" was about to be half over, with nothing to show for it. At all events, the next morning Hennard drove his truck through the glass wall of Luby's Cafeteria in (the ominously named) Killeen, Texas. With a pistol in each hand, he set about shooting to death everyone in sight—with the one exception of a woman and her four-year-old daughter, whom he allowed to leave, just after shooting her parents to death.[34] Yet, he yelled "Bitch!"

at another woman, before killing her. When it was all over, Hennard had killed twenty-two people, fourteen of them women (one of whom was a black grandmother and widow of a locally prominent official; the others were white), just before the police arrived; then he killed himself. Whether he sought to outdo James Huberty (who had killed twenty-one at the McDonald's restaurant in San Ysidro, California, seven years before) is unclear, as is most everything else about Hennard. His parents and three younger siblings were understandably reluctant to be questioned by the authorities. As with combative, paranoid, bigoted loners in general, we know little about Hennard other than that bare psychological fact. He did have a few drinking buddies, one of whom mentioned that Hennard "would talk crazy when he was drunk, but he's a nice guy when he's sober."[35]

Even though Hennard had many "risk factors" for mass murder: paranoid grudge holding and hatred of various groups, no friendships or sexual partners, substance abuse, gun ownership, poor work history, troubled relationship with a parent, being a male between the ages of eighteen and forty . . . all this made that final outburst "more likely" (than for some other young man in that town)—but not inevitable. People often say, "If only he could have gotten help." But there is a catch-22 here. It is no easy matter to compel a man with Hennard's personality to undergo psychiatric treatment; it is extremely unlikely that he would ever seek it voluntarily. It is also unlikely that such a man would benefit even if he were in treatment, especially if forced against his will. Hennard was not even psychopathic like Thomas Hamilton; he was belligerent, antisocial, and hot-tempered—but he would have more in common with men like Charles Whitman, who, despite the massive destruction they cause, belong on a lower rung of the Gradations of Evil scale: probably number 8, for murders (including mass murder) sparked by smoldering rage in someone without psychopathy. Hamilton, in contrast, having been a psychopath before he turned mass murderer, belongs in Category 16.

Dale Pierre

At the extreme other end of the Gradations scale is the story of the Hi-Fi Shop Murders in Ogden, Utah, which took place on April 22, 1974. This was Utah's worst murder to date. But I doubt if anything has rivaled it since, in terms of sheer sadism and in the degree of suffering inflicted upon the victims. The crime comes under the heading of "felony-murder," meaning: murder(s) committed during the course of some other felony—in this case, armed robbery.

Dale Pierre was born in 1953 in Tobago, West Indies, but then moved with his family to Trinidad. Both parents had respectable lives and jobs: his father was a carpenter, and his mother was a hospital worker. Dale was troublesome early on: disobedient, blaming a teacher for favoring another student, stealing flagrantly and often, and running away from home. He was expelled from school because of his behavior. Dale had grandiose dreams of fabulous wealth and prestige, driving in flashy cars so everyone would notice him. A loner with no friends, these dreams seemed far beyond his reach. In his midteens his family moved to Brooklyn, New York, where at first he did some menial jobs that offered no hope for realizing his lofty ambitions. At twenty-one, he decided to join the air force, but had no patience to spend the many years it would take to become a pilot; instead, he opted for a ground-crew job. He got stationed in Ogden, Utah, at the air force base north of Salt Lake City. His compulsive stealing continued, becoming even more brazen. Dale stole a car from a sergeant at the base and, when caught, murdered the sergeant, bayoneting him several times in the face. Dale was the prime suspect but the authorities were not at first able to gather enough evidence. When interrogated, Dale was unflinching in his lying and had the "thousand-yard stare" that intimidated everyone.

He then concocted a plot to rob a hi-fi store in order to steal its stereo equipment. Dale enlisted the aid of an accomplice, William Andrews, plus that of a third man who was to drive the getaway car. At the end of the workday, Dale and William entered the shop, where they held at gunpoint and tied up the four people inside. When sixteen-year-old Cortney Naisbitt failed to show up for dinner that evening, his mother got worried and insisted upon going out to look for him. Discovering his car parked outside the hi-fi shop, she too went inside—only to be captured and tied up with the others (two of whom were a father and son pair). Dale had watched a movie a few days before, in which the bad guys poured Drāno (a liquid drain cleaner) down the throat of a victim, who died immediately. This gave Dale the bright idea of making the captives in the shop do the same, not realizing that "dying " is far from the customary fate of someone forced to drink Drāno, which happens to be sodium hydroxide, or lye. He told the victims they were to drink this "vodka" and tried to get his accomplice to make them drink it—but William refused. So Dale took over and forced the Drāno down all the victims' throats, which caused immediate burning of the mouth and esophagus and excruciating pain. Dale took a brief "break" at this point to rape one of the employees even though she was vomiting from the effects of the Drāno. That done, he returned to the other victims, shooting each in the head. Three died immediately, including the mother who had come to fetch her son. One of the men seemed to move, so Dale shoved a ballpoint pen in his ear, kicking it in all the way until it came out of his throat. Remarkably, the man survived and was able to describe the assailants to the police. The two were arrested quickly as they were trying to escape. The air force, which had been trying to get rid of Dale via a dishonorable discharge now had more than enough evidence, once he and William were convicted of Utah's most heinous crime ever. Both were given the death penalty (not carried out until 1987 in Dale's case; 1992, in William's).[36]

The labels psychiatrists use to characterize someone like Dale Pierre—"lifelong-persistent antisocial," "psychopathic," "sadistic"—are all accurate in their way, but these are sterile, academic words that fall far short of conveying adequately the callousness of Dale's heart and the depravity of his actions. So the nonmedical phrase used by sociologist Jack Katz in describing the case—"primordial evil"—captures much better Pierre and the Hi-Fi Murders he committed.[37] As for the *sadistic* element, Dale's pushing the pen through the ear of one of the victims meant that he wanted to cause as much pain as possible, instead of simply firing a coup de grâce. Unlike the usual mass murderer who chooses a scapegoat group (as Hennard did), hoping to achieve a sense of power by killing as many of the scorned "others" as possible, Dale may have thought that, coming at closing time, he would encounter just the one clerk totting up the day's receipts. As a killer of one, he would not have made history, despite his cruelty.

Jack Gilbert Graham

The mass murder by Jack Graham was different from all the others mentioned thus far. His motive was not the usual one of revenge (as we saw with Hamilton, Farley, and Hennard). Nor was his motive to eliminate witnesses to a crime (as we saw with Dale Pierre). Graham's motive was unique: to create a mass murder in the hope that the intended victim, hidden in plain sight among all the other victims, would not be spotted by the authorities as the one true target of the (thus *never-to-be-identified!*) murderer. You can get a better idea of the scheme here if you think of the child's game Where's Waldo? A child is shown a picture book; one page has a large cartoon with dozens of people, all next to one another cheek by jowl. The task is to find Waldo, a particular individual nonetheless difficult to identify in the midst of all the other people. That was the task awaiting the detectives when United Airlines Flight 629, taking off from Denver on November 1, 1955, exploded in the sky, the wreckage raining down on the countryside some thirty miles from the airport. The laborious work performed by the airport officials and the FBI is a chapter in itself.

At the end of the day, after each of the forty-four victims were identified and profiled, it was discovered that one of the victims, Mrs. Daisie King, had keys to safety deposit boxes containing newspaper clippings about her son, Jack Gilbert Graham, who had been charged with forgery and was on the "most wanted" list of the Denver district attorney. Search of her home two weeks after the crash revealed an insurance policy of which her son was the beneficiary. He was also slated to inherit a substantial sum in the event of his mother's death. But Jack had recently wrecked a brand-new truck and was hoping to collect insurance from that "accident." Four years before the plane crash, he had been convicted on a forgery charge, though he was given a suspended sentence on the promise of making restitution. As the FBI delved further into the case, they learned that Jack had given his mother a bulky present gift-wrapped in Christmas paper just before her flight. He let his wife believe it was a "tool set" he had wanted to give his mother. With no one the wiser, he sneaked the present into her luggage. Still further probing unearthed copper wires and insulating materials at the Graham house of the sort used in detonating primer caps. From there the route to the true story was short: the present for his mom was not a tool box, but instead, twenty-five sticks of dynamite Graham had recently purchased, and a timing device set to go off shortly after takeoff. Graham finally admitted his guilt in making the bomb that killed his mother—the Where's Waldo in this drama—along with the forty-three "collaterals."[38]

Graham's half-sister later told the authorities that he had a penchant for violence: he had once knocked her down and broken her ribs; on another occasion, he had threatened to strike her with a hammer. He had also been physically abusive with his wife. Before his execution in the gas chamber fourteen months after his trial, Graham was questioned about his level of remorse. His response: "As far as feeling remorse for these people, I don't. I can't help it. Everybody pays their way and takes their chances. That's just the way it is."[39] He added that "the number of people to be killed made no difference to me; it could have been a thousand." There are many psychopaths who feel no remorse for the violence, mayhem, or murders they commit; Graham is one of the very few who shamelessly said as much out loud. In the annals of evil acts, this elevates him to a special perch high above the others. What he did not reveal, and what remains a mystery about this man, is: besides his obvious greed, why he felt such venomous hatred for his mother—a hatred so strong that her destruction and, as it turned out, his own, was a more compelling ambition than living out his life with his wife and two small children.

POSTSCRIPT

The forensic psychologist, Dr. Reid Meloy, brought several points to my attention. Adolescent mass murderers, in his experience, seldom commit suicide or die at the scene, in contrast to their adult counterparts. But because mass murder is a comparatively rare phenomenon, statistics may vary from one series to another. In my collection of sixty mass murderers from magazine and newspaper articles, for example, nineteen of the fifty-three adults committed suicide at the scene (36 percent), as did three of the admittedly small group of seven adolescents (42 percent). In Meloy's series of thirty adults and thirty-four adolescents, the suicide rate was 9 percent in the adolescents, in contrast to 53 percent in the adults. A second point concerns the intentions of mass murderer, Richard Farley.

In his evaluation, Dr. Meloy noted that Farley wanted only to *wound* Laura Black, ostensibly so that she would live to know the horror that (in Farley's warped mind) she had "caused." Had the bullet gone a centimeter this way or that, however, she could have bled out from an artery—and died. Farley's act still counts as attempted murder, and who is to say what was in his heart of hearts when he shot at her?

Chapter Six

THE PSYCHOPATH HARD AT WORK

Canto XI, ll. 37–39

Onde omicide e ciascun che mal fiere	Thus homicides and whoever wrongfully strikes,
guastotori e predon, tutti tormenta	spoilers and bandits, all are tormented
giron primo per diverse schiere.	in the first subcircle in different groups.

In the last chapter we concentrated on individuals who committed either *spree murder* or the much more common *mass murder*. Many were psychopaths, but a few proved in the long run not to be (Archie McCafferty) or were instead emotionally unbalanced men with towering rage (Patrick Sherrill). We can already begin to see that there is no neat formula for evil. Some of the risk factors are becoming more apparent, but so is the fact that many people, if we probed their background in great detail, would show half a dozen risk factors—and still lead socially inoffensive lives. Either that, or at some point in their lives, they'd commit a violent act or a profoundly humiliating act that falls short of what the community calls "evil." Charles Whitman, the Texas Tower shooter, had two important risk factors: a physically abusive father and a malignant brain tumor. We can never know whether, if he had only the *one* without the other, he would *not* have been a mass murderer. Whitman was not psychopathic and was not a "loner" or a social misfit; people didn't think of him as a "bad person." He seemed to have a good future. His IQ, at 138, was "genius level"; many careers would have been open to him. His final act bore the stamp of evil solely because so many lives were destroyed. If his anger took him only so far as to call his wife Kathy a "slut" (which she certainly wasn't) and to strike her in the face, she might have divorced him, but you and I would never have heard of him.

The people in this chapter had, for the most part, better success socially: they had spouses; a few had children. More than half had good jobs. But what sets them apart—certain notable exceptions aside—is that they spent most of their lives doing terrible things and getting in serious trouble with the law. The majority killed at least one person. Several killed on multiple occasions. Almost all were psychopaths; a few had personality traits that fell a bit short of "full-blown" psychopathy. Those who were psychopaths distinguished themselves by the grotesque and grievous ways in which they hurt or killed whoever stood in their way. Here "evil" had to do with the *nature* of their acts, not the *number of persons* they affected. The horror element was uppermost, which became apparent in the words people used, once the "news" came out: words like "fiendish," "revolting," "heinous," and (pretty regularly) "inhuman." This is how we distance ourselves from the acts in question, as if to say, "no human could do these things." We don't like to be reminded that *only* humans do these kinds of things, that evil is an exclusively human phenomenon. The only comfort we can take is that what we call evil is mercifully rare.

This chapter will also serve to remind us that evil is not a static concept. Since Dante's time, as we saw in chapter 1, the rapist, the child murderer, and the torturer occupy much higher berths in the hierarchy of evil than do heretics, traitors, and the murderers of a guest. The selling of indulgences by the church (simony) that so offended Dante is all but unknown in our day. But in his day, serial sexual homicide apparently didn't exist[1] and the medical profession didn't have the syringes and needles and drugs that allow a corrupt doctor or nurse to kill patients. In certain ways, evil has evolved. And our sensibilities have altered accordingly.

From the standpoint of the Gradations of Evil scale, many of the persons figured here belong in Category 16: psychopathic persons committing multiple vicious acts, including murder.

ANGELS OF DEATH

Kristen Gilbert

Born Kristen Strickland in 1967, she was the elder of two daughters. She was said to have undergone a change in personality after her sister Tara was born seven years later. Kristen became a habitual liar and stole things belonging to Tara. Outwardly sweet, she was considered manipulative and vindictive by school acquaintances. Toward boyfriends she was even physically abusive. She went to nursing school, where she met her future husband, Glenn Gilbert. They married when she was twenty-one. A month after the wedding she chased Glenn around the house with a butcher knife during an argument.[2] When she got her first nursing job at a VA hospital in Massachusetts, the number of deaths on her ward shot up precipitously. Her coworkers jokingly gave her the moniker "Angel of Death." In addition, she spiced up her days by staging bomb threats at the hospital or painting swastikas on Kleenex boxes to make it look like there were vandals roaming around the corridors. If she showed up late for work, she would make up fabulous lies such as, she came across a man in coma on the street and stopped to give him CPR. Things at home were not good either. She tried to poison Glenn with potassium, which sent his heart rate way up. Understandably, the marriage faltered and the couple divorced when Kristen was twenty-seven. She had already begun an affair with a married man who worked as a security guard at the hospital. During a phone conversation with him, she confessed to killing patients. Later, three nurses came forward with their concerns, and a police investigation was launched in 1996. Kristen was indicted a few months later and ultimately sentenced to four life terms without the possibility of parole. Though she gave some patients overdoses of insulin, she dispatched most of them with massive doses of the stimulant epinephrine (adrenalin).[3] Altogether, she was convicted of three counts of first-degree murder, and one count of second-degree murder—but she is thought to have killed as many as forty patients under her care.

Dr. Michael Swango

Swango was born in Tacoma, Washington, in 1954, to an army colonel who raised his three sons like recruits in boot camp. Michael's father was physically abusive to his brother Robert and his mother, Muriel, but not to him. The home atmosphere was said to be cold and inhospitable.[4] The family moved some sixteen times before Michael left for college. By that time, his father was barely involved with the family: he had a Vietnamese mistress and was essentially separated from Muriel.

Ever since childhood, Michael had collected articles about violent death and disaster. Later in college, he started a scrapbook of plane and car crashes, bloody military coups, savage sex crimes, arson, and riots. He even quipped that all this material would prove he was "mentally incompetent" in the event he ever killed someone and he would thus avoid prison. In between these activities, he found time to excel at school, graduating summa cum laude from college. In medical school, his performance was a little less stellar. He would fake write-ups of patients he never examined. He was contemptuous of his patients and of the deaths that followed in his wake. Still, he was allowed to graduate (in 1983) despite strong reservations on the part of the faculty, because only eight out of nine board members voted to expel him. Unanimity was required! He had been fired once before from an ambulance job, when he let a heart-attack victim walk to his car.

During Swango's internship at Ohio State, one doctor wanted to fail him because of his indifference to his patients, not to mention his preoccupation with the Nazis and his unprofessional manner. He was suspected of killing a certain patient with poison, and he lied that he had never been in that patient's room. Several more patients of his died for unexplained reasons. Swango also poisoned several colleagues with fried chicken laced with poison. They all became ill; he did not. Later, as an ambulance paramedic, he became very animated about violent events, such as Huberty's mass murder at the San Ysidro McDonald's in 1984; he also praised Henry Lee Lucas, the serial killer. In 1985 he poisoned four paramedic coworkers with arsenic. This time he was caught and sentenced to five years in prison; he served, however, only two.

Upon his release, he changed his name to David Adams, was married for a brief period, forged letters of recommendation on his own behalf, and got another job in a hospital. He even poisoned a girlfriend, Kristin, who later committed suicide. More patients unexpectedly died in Stony Brook hospital, where he was suspected and kicked out. In 1994, after being tracked to hospitals in the South, Swango vanished. He turned up in Southern Rhodesia (now Zimbabwe) where his past could be more easily papered over. In a rural hospital, Swango resumed his killings, extending them even to a new girlfriend and her four children. Caught in Africa, he escaped before trial. Trying to reenter the United States, he was arrested—at first only on fraud charges. Hard evidence was difficult to muster: nurses at his previous hospitals had tossed away the needles that would have shown traces of the curare-like drug he had used to kill various patients. Finally, in 2000 Swango admitted to three murders and was sentenced to life in prison without parole. But he is strongly suspected of having killed as many as sixty. One of the sad stories in the Swango case: a young woman, Cynthia Ann McGee, had been struck by a car when she was riding her bicycle. Admitted to Ohio State University Hospital—under the care of Swango—she died, though her injuries did not seem fatal. The driver of the car was convicted of "reckless homicide" and sentenced to thirty months probation. It is now suspected that her death came from potassium, injected by Swango, and not from her injuries.[5]

In the Angel of Death type of serial killing (a nonsexual variety of serial homicide), the killer's secretiveness is one of the most striking qualities. Psychopathy in these cases is predominantly of the Factor-I type; that is, showing extreme narcissistic traits—especially *grandiosity*. These nurses and doctors usually come from middle-class homes and show little behavioral abnormalities except perhaps an intense need for thrill seeking and stimulation. In their younger years, family life may not have been ideal, but it was not dreadful—as it so often is in cases of perpetrators of serial sexual homicide. It is not easy to explain how these Angels of Death developed as they did. It is said that Swango's father upbraided him when his son criticized the Vietnam War by calling him a "commie faggot." Yet Swango was his mother's favorite, and he had two brothers who did not get into trouble—evidence that his home life was not completely miserable. Still, one of the reasons for Swango's later acts might be revenge: getting back symbolically at the parents who "wronged" him during his early years. In addition, it's easy to see how the secret poisoning of patients can make one feel like God—who has the power of life and death over mortals. Perhaps this explains Swango's fascination with Hitler[6] and the Nazis; Swango was not alone in this fascination. Others include serial sexual killers Ian Brady and Jason Massey, serial poisoner Graham Young, and wife killer Glen Engleman—to mention a few. For the rest of us, the Nazis were fiends; for these folks, they were heroes. In some cases the trait of grandiosity took the form of showing the world how fantastically competent the nurse or doctor was by first poisoning and then "miraculously" rescuing a patient. This was the game plan of nurse Genene Jones, who gave a curare-like drug to newborns in the hospital nursery.[7] She would then prove herself a supernurse by reviving them, to the admiration of all. Unfortunately, a fair number of the babies died.

The psychopathic element in Michael Swango and Genene Jones was not evident during their adolescence. They had not been juvenile delinquents. Compared with the other individuals we will be discussing in this chapter, these two were the exceptions.

They would have been hard to spot as persons headed for trouble. Because of their slyness and cleverness, they were hard to spot even when, as adults, Swango and Jones had begun their careers as Angels of Death.

CHILD MURDER

In our culture children are cherished and protected, girls no less than boys; the community is quick to regard as evil anyone who kills a child of any age. Strangers who kill a child are regarded in a still worse light, especially if they kill a child who is still in the "innocent" years—roughly the preadolescent years—when it is highly unlikely that the child could have done anything so offensive as to warrant ill treatment, much less serious bodily harm or murder.

There is a kind of hierarchy of evil even in the realm of child murder. Judges tend to be more lenient with unmarried young women, often enough teenagers, who dispose of a newborn in a Dumpster. These mothers are usually not mentally ill; instead, they are usually poor and not prepared, emotionally or financially, to care for a baby. Mothers rarely kill a child older than age one; those that do are often found to be mentally ill.[8] Many of these mothers are scorned by the public as evil women—until the full story comes out that the mother was psychotic and thus not fully responsible for her actions. Where the idea of evil seems most apparent are the cases in which a parent or stepparent kills a child not only with malice aforethought but for some base motive such as greed (the parent would benefit from the child's insurance policy) or convenience (the parent would be free to enter a new relationship without the "burden" of a small child). Evil in its most uncontested form is associated with the torture of a child—as we saw with the Zeigler case in chapter 3—or the rape-murder of a child (which is much the same thing). The murder of children for spite (Hamilton, Dann) or out of hatred (Purdy) were confronted in the last chapter.

John Battaglia Jr.

As was mentioned in chapter 3, Zein Isa was the terrorist/zealot who killed his (to him) wayward daughter but who knew enough of American culture to pretend in court that he killed her in self-defense. John Battaglia was a home-grown terrorist who, to jump ahead a bit, left his defense attorney with no options at all. His grandfather was a mafioso who committed armed robbery; his father was a lieutenant colonel—a rigid and abusive disciplinarian, who once broke a guitar over his son's back. His mother, a depressed alcoholic, committed suicide when John was seventeen. He went downhill after that, becoming explosively violent, once pulling a pistol on one of his two brothers. He both dealt and abused cocaine, for which he was arrested.

He appeared to straighten out to the extent of joining the marines and later became a CPA. Marrying for the first time in 1985, he quickly showed a dark side, getting into murderous rages over trifles. He was physically abusive toward his wife, Michelle, who kicked him out. He stalked her and attacked her viciously, continuing to do so after she again kicked him out. After throwing a rock at her car, John spent eight days in jail, but in general he earned the reputation of being the "Teflon Man," always managing to wriggle out of probable arrests. He bugged Michelle's phone, which allowed him to listen to her conversations and thus anticipate her next move, thereby dodging whatever charges she tried to bring against him.

John then met another woman, Mary Pearle, whose family he envied because of their much higher social status and wealth. Ignoring the warning signs of his past abuse charges, she married him—only to discover that he was still abusive and menacing. Mary threw him out because of his threats. By this time they had two small girls. Still abusing cocaine, he entered the house despite Mary's order of protection and assaulted her severely. Eventually they separated and lived apart.

Two years later, in 2001, John insisted on visitation rights with his daughters—at his place. When they arrived, he phoned Mary, and while the phone line was open, he shot both girls to death so that their mother couldn't help but hear their screams and the gunshots.

Right before his inevitable arrest, he went to a tattoo parlor, where, in a gesture of unaccustomed delicacy, he had images of the two just-murdered daughters made, one on each arm.

At his trial, the defense attorney, struggling to find some extenuating circumstance in this ridiculously open-and-shut case, tried to argue "bipolar manic disorder" as the "illness" that drove his client to commit such a depraved act. The jury was unmoved, and John was convicted of first-degree murder. If indeed he had any "highs" at all, they were in response to his abuse of amphetamines and cocaine, not to an unsubstantiated mental disorder. He showed no remorse at trial—in keeping with the extreme narcissistic traits that are intrinsic to his psychopathy.[9]

Latasha Pulliam

The sad case of six-year-old Shenosha Richards, a kindergarten pupil at the Sexton Elementary School on Chicago's South Side, began when she came home from school the afternoon of March 21, 1991. She was led away by an acquaintance of her mother, Dwight Jordan (known as Tank) and his girlfriend, twenty-year-old Latasha Pulliam. Only the day before, Latasha had taken the girl to a children's park. Shenosha mentioned this to her mother that evening, adding that she "had a nice time." Her mother warned her not to go anywhere with strangers. Probably the girl no longer regarded Latasha as a stranger; in any case she was willing to go that next afternoon with Tank and Latasha to her apartment nearby, with promises of a snack and a movie.

What happened next is depressingly clear, although who did what to the girl is partly obscured by self-serving statements from the two abductors. The girl was left alone at first with Tank, an ex-convict in his forties, while Latasha went elsewhere to take cocaine. She returned to find Tank trying unsuccessfully, so she said, to rape Shenosha. According to Latasha, he then took a bottle of shoe polish, in a kind of rape by other means, inserting it in and out of the girl's rectum amid her crying and her promises she wouldn't tell anyone.

When I spoke recently with Dr. Paul Fauteck, however, who had conducted a forensic evaluation with Latasha before her 1991 trial, he told me that she had not been coerced by Tank into hurting the girl. Instead, she had acted on her own. It was she who inserted the bottle. Dr. Fauteck found that she met the full criteria for psychopathy, according to Hare's checklist. It was when Latasha got Shenosha to acknowledge that she would indeed tell her mother that Latasha killed her, somehow hoping to escape being found out. Minutes before that, when the girl was screaming (after the assault on her body), Latasha led her into an empty apartment down the hall, where she proceeded to strangle the girl with an electrical cord, tightening and relaxing the cord by turns to frighten her. Finding a piece of wood with a protruding nail, Latasha shoved it into the girl's chest, puncturing her lungs in two places. Shenosha pleaded with her: 'Don't hurt me, I love you!" Latasha then pulled the cord tighter for several minutes, which led to the girl's death. To make sure, she next struck the girl's head with the metal part of the hammer, fracturing the skull. After tossing the girl's sneakers out the window, Latasha placed her body in a garbage can, covering it as best she could, and then ran off (as Tank had already done a while before). Later that afternoon, Mrs. Richards discovered her daughter's body in the garbage can, mistaking it at first for a doll. As she later told the court: "That doll was my baby."[10]

Latasha and Tank were quickly arrested. At trial he was sentenced to life without parole; she, to death. Appeals were mounted on the grounds that Latasha herself had been tortured and sexually abused throughout her childhood by an alcoholic mother who also forced her into prostitution. At fifteen she was made pregnant by one of her mother's boyfriends. What the defense assumed was a more compelling point was: Latasha was "mentally retarded," with an IQ of 69, and thus not "death-eligible" by statute. This argument fell flat because previous tests showed IQs in the 70s, besides which, everyone who spoke with her noted how her vocabulary was much too sophisticated for a "retarded" person."[11] In addition, the abuse Latasha suffered at the hands of her mother failed to win the sympathy of the jury, owing to similar abuses (burning with cigarettes, scalding) that she was known to have inflicted on her own two daughters, who were at the time five and two.

When I interviewed Latasha some fifteen years later, she was by then remorseful and tearful when recounting the torture-murder of the little girl. Calm and cooperative in recent years, she had been assaultive when first in the prison, and had even forced another prisoner to have oral sex with her. In 2003 Governor George Ryan of Illinois rescinded all death penalties (to the consternation of the victims' families), before which time Latasha would pretend to hear voices—as if to plead mental illness as a mitigating factor when the other appeals were overturned. It was this feigned illness that led Dr. Fauteck to diagnose her as a malingerer,[12] though how "abnormal" such behavior is in a person awaiting execution is an open question. Even to this day, Latasha denies taking such an active role in torturing the girl, insisting that Tank had forced her to confess to things done mostly by him—or else he would kill her younger daughter, Patrice.

This appalling murder has some of the elements of *Rashomon*, the famous Japanese story of a murder retold in four different versions by four different witnesses.[13] Was Tank really the main culprit? Or was Latasha? Going over the evidence again, I must conclude that Latasha bore the major responsibility. Tank was not even in the room where Shenosha was strangled, stabbed, struck, and killed. In many murders committed by two persons, each finds it convenient to shift the blame onto the other, which in turn contributes to a crime more violent and heinous—more evil, if you will—than either participant would have felt comfortable doing on his own.

There would be no reason for Mrs. Richards to feel sympathy for Latasha, even at this late date. I did feel a measure of sympathy when I took into account the well-documented torture she had suffered once her parents split, leaving Renee, her mother, as the sole "caregiver." We know that violence breeds violence, and extreme violence often breeds the same in the next generation. What Renee committed was "soul murder"[14] for which the law is rarely able to prosecute to the extent it merits. What Latasha committed was actual murder, which the law finds easier to deal with. Was it inevitable that Latasha, violated and dehumanized as she was, would grow up to be a murderer? No. Was it far more likely that she would injure or kill a child than would a woman not exposed to such a malefic environment? Certainly. So what we have here is the transmission of evil down the generations—not from genes so much as from parental cruelty and sadism.

As I will show in the section "Parents from Hell" (chapter 8), some children do escape. But those reared in broken homes and in poverty, and who have limited intellectual resources, have few escape routes. Referring to Latasha's background, one of the prosecutors asked the rhetorical question "Is that an excuse for what she did to Shenosha Richards? Wouldn't an abused person know the pain that you go through when you get abused?"[15] Naively, we might think so. What is nearer the truth, however, is that parental cruelty often rewires the brain itself, augmenting the desire for revenge (to be taken out on others, who, like Shenosha, are as weak and helpless as the formerly abused child—and future abuser, Latasha—had been years earlier). This limits the menu of responses to stress down to one that was learned all too well before, greatly increasing the likelihood that one will in the future *resort* to violence rather than *shun* violence. Latasha has now spent half her life outside and half her life in prison. Having been raised in what can only be called a manufactory of evil, the only sympathetic humanity she has come to experience has been, ironically, at Illinois' Dwight Correctional Center, the only home she will ever know and the only one where she has known kindness.

KIDNAP

In earlier times, before the public attitude toward the death penalty began to change, kidnap, along with murder, treason, and killing an officer of the law, were all viewed categorically as meriting the death penalty. In the case of kidnap (the legal term for the *act* of kidnapping), it was the agony of the family members, as well as of the kidnap victim not knowing what was going to happen next, that added up to the kind of extreme psychological torture for which the death penalty was seen as appropriate. Formerly the bulk of kidnaps were motivated by greed: payment of a ransom was the quid pro quo for the return of a loved one, who more often than not was a child. We have become familiar with other types of kidnap over the past decades, to say nothing of the wholesale use of kidnap by ruthless political regimes. In my visits to Haiti during "Papa Doc" Duvalier's rule in the 1960s, I learned of many people among the well-to-do who were abducted by the Tonton Macoute[16] in the middle of the night, never to return. Then there were the political dissidents—the *desaparecidos* or "disappeared ones"—in Argentina. Space does not permit a complete list of such atrocities.

In recent times, we have become familiar with kidnaps motivated by factors other than greed. There is kidnap for the purpose of rape (almost invariably ending in murder) and kidnap in order to secure, and to keep indefinitely, an unwilling sexual partner. Cases of the latter sort involve a pedophile and his (it is always a "his") child victim. The pedophile is not interested in ransom but in the unlawful imprisonment of the child, usually for sexual purposes, for months or for years; the agony of the parents is thus magnified a thousandfold, incalculable really, and well into the realm where one speaks of evil.

In 2006 the story of Natascha Kampusch came to light. She had been abducted and held captive in an underground bunker for eight years by an Austrian pedophile, Wolfgang Priklopil, until at age eighteen she was able to break away and return to her family.[17] One is usually declared legally dead after being missing for seven years, so her parents must have assumed she had been killed by her abductor, even though parents "hope against hope," no matter what. A similar case happened in Long Island in 1993, when John Esposito, the forty-three-year-old bachelor friend of twelve-year-old Katie Beers and her family, abducted her and kept her in a secret underground room beneath his garage. Access to that room, which Esposito, like Priklopil, had constructed himself, was guarded by a two-hundred-pound slab of concrete; her little room was ventilated and equipped with a bathroom and a TV. Clearly Esposito meant this to be a long-term residence. But having abducted a twelve-year-old boy some years earlier, he was immediately a suspect. He broke down after intense police surveillance, with the happy result that he confessed sixteen days after Katie's disappearance.[18] From a psychological standpoint these two men had less than the full panel of psychopathic traits. Deceitfulness was, however, certainly part of Esposito's repertoire: before he finally confessed, he managed to shed tears during a public interview for the "missing little girl." These two men might better be characterized as introverted, socially awkward pedophiles with some of the narcissistic (Factor-I) traits, especially exploitativeness and lying. In the more flagrant examples of psychopathy, there were plenty of warning signs early on unfortunately ignored until great damage was done . . . as the following case will illustrate.

Kenneth Parnell

Parnell was born in 1931 in Texas to a mother who was a religious fanatic. She made life intolerable for his father, who divorced and abandoned the family when Kenneth was five. At thirteen he was sexually molested by a boarder at his mother's place. Following this he set a fire, for which he was incarcerated for a year. Upon his release he stole a car, which landed him in a reformatory for two years.[19] By age twenty he was arrested for sodomizing a boy and for impersonating a police officer with a fake deputy badge.[20] He was remanded to a hospital in California, escaping when still in his twenties, only to be recaptured again and to escape again. This led to his spending three and a half years in San Quentin, after which he violated parole and was arrested yet again. Parnell had two brief marriages in the mid-1950s and had a daughter by each; he was technically bisexual, but predominantly homosexual. In the 1960s he graduated to armed robbery, for which he spent six years in a Utah prison. The crime that brought him notoriety happened a bit later—in 1972. That was the year he kidnapped seven-year-old Steven Stayner in Ukiah, California. Besides forcing the boy to perform oral sex and to submit to (quite painful) anal sex, Parnell conned the boy into thinking that his parents "couldn't afford to keep him anymore," and that a judge had awarded Parnell with custody. Furthermore, his new name was to be "Dennis." Steven was kept for over seven years—to the point where he no longer recalled his last name. It was when Parnell abducted yet another boy (a five-year-old, this time) that Steven, now fifteen, ran away while Parnell was at his job. He carried the boy on his back and went to a police station, where the truth gradually emerged and Steven's true name was finally recognized. Pedophilia and nonfatal kidnap were not viewed with the seriousness they deserved in the California courts of that era, so Parnell was sentenced only to seven years. In 2003 at age seventy-one he actually tried to purchase a four-year-old boy, with the stipulation that the boy have a "clean rectum"—a request that raised a lot of red flags to the person he was dealing with. For this attempt at child molestation he was arrested; he spent his remaining years in prison, dying at age seventy-six in 2008.

À propos psychopathy, in my experience with prisoners and forensic patients, those who show what Hare has called "criminal versatility"—being *arrested for six or more different varieties of crime*—tend almost invariably to meet the full criteria for psychopathy. You hardly need to look at the rest of the record. As a "career criminal," Parnell's arrests touched on the following: armed robbery, sex offenses, escape, kidnap, theft, arson, and fraud (impersonating a police officer)—for a total of seven. Parnell was one of those comparatively rare persons who scarcely lets a day go by without doing something bad; many of those actions (sex offenses, kidnap, arson) were also of the sort that evoke the reaction "evil."

Gary Steven Krist

The inspiration for kidnap in this case was greed. Krist, born in the Northwest in 1945, had a checkered past already by the time he was twenty: drug abuse, assault, theft, weapons possession, time in reformatories, and escape. The more striking of his psychopathic traits were grandiosity and superficial charm. Some said he could be incredibly charming; others, that he "had an ego as big as my office."[21] The grandiosity came through in some of his comments, such as: "I didn't want to lead a mediocre life; I wanted to make an impact on the world . . . be remembered"; or on another occasion: "I think I am a different species; I don't think scientists have genetically classified me."[22] Krist might have had a point in a way: with an IQ measured at 160, he was brighter than most people with so-called genius-level (that is, above 135 IQ) intelligence. When he was twenty-four, he thought up a scheme to kidnap a young woman from a prominent family and then followed through with it. Once abducted, the woman, Barbara Mackle, was buried in a wooden box a foot and a half underground in rural Georgia, where she was given water, candy, blankets, and tubes to breathe through. She was held here pending the payment of a half-million-dollar ransom by her father. Kidnap was the sixth variety of crime Krist had committed, which put him in the "criminal versatility" category—the same as in the Parnell case. The ransom was paid, and Barbara was rescued after three and a half days in the underground box. The circumstances of the kidnap —the elaborate outfitting of the box, the prominence of the victim— made it a high-profile crime with the aura of evil surrounding it. Though sentenced to life in prison, Krist was paroled ten years later.

In his forties, Krist entertained hopes of becoming a physician, but when his old record was unearthed, he was denied this possibility, despite his charm and intelligence. Years went by, and Krist surfaced again in a way that brings to mind the French saying *plus ça change, plus c'est la même chose*: the more things change, the more they stay the same. The "same" in this case is the penchant for the underground. Krist was arrested in 2006 when a lab was discovered under the ground, beneath a shed at his home. The lab, outfitted with water, light, electricity, and an escape tunnel, was used for processing a million dollars worth of cocaine. The setup showed an ingenuity similar to what he devised in the Mackle kidnap.

Richard Allen Davis

The idea of kidnap as a prelude to rape and murder was imprinted upon the public mind with especial force following the murder of Polly Klaas in 1993 by ex-convict and career-criminal Richard Allen Davis. The middle of five children from a working-class family in California's Bay Area, Davis was raised by a number of stepmothers and his grandmother after his parents divorced when he was eleven. He grew furious at his mother when she brought home various boyfriends, ostensibly for sex, which led him to regard her as a "whore." It did not enhance her image in his eyes that she once burned his hand because he smoked. She was punitive in other ways as well. Living with his father for a time after the divorce did not improve the situation; his equally punitive father once broke his jaw. In 1969 Davis's father turned him and his older brother in to the authorities for incorrigibility.[23] A juvenile delinquent at least since age twelve, Davis stole and committed burglaries and forgeries. He always carried knives. Acquaintances spoke of his having "evil eyes." He took delight in dousing cats and dogs in gasoline and setting them afire; once he even cut up a live cow. He entered the army at seventeen but was discharged a year later because of fighting with knives. He also abused drugs: marijuana, cocaine, and heroin.

By age twenty-one, in 1975, he had accumulated twenty arrests for a variety of crimes, including auto theft, for which he was jailed briefly. The next year he attempted a rape at knifepoint, but this was foiled by a police officer. Later, in jail, he faked a suicide attempt, was sent to a psychiatric ward—and escaped. In 1977 he was given a long sentence for attempted kidnap; he was labeled a psychopath at that time. Released in 1982, he kidnapped again and was sentenced in 1985, this time for sixteen years, only to be released prematurely in 1993. It was in October of that year that he sneaked into the home of twelve-year-old Polly Klaas, carried her off, raped and then killed her. The crime was given national attention. When Davis was caught two months later, his case led to California's "three strikes and you're out" law in which felons are sentenced automatically to life without parole after their third felony conviction.[24] Sentenced to death in San Jose's Superior Court in 1996, Davis's final beau geste (besides giving the finger to the judge) was to say that Polly's father had sexually molested her—a lie aimed apparently at "leveling the playing field," psychologically speaking, as though he were no worse than her dad. After handing down the death penalty, Judge Hastings had the last, and best, word, when he said: "Mr. Davis, this is always a traumatic and emotional decision for a judge. You made it very easy today by your conduct."[25]

RAPE

Most rapes of strangers are committed by men fairly low down in the social order, with poor social skills and strong contempt for women. When men from privileged backgrounds, with good looks and good manners, rape, and do so repeatedly, we are more apt to apply the term *evil*—probably because we expect better behavior from men who have enjoyed every privilege, and experience greater shock and disgust (key ingredients in the "evil" response) when such men indulge in sexual violence. There is a dispute nowadays, sometimes acrimonious, as to whether rape should be viewed primarily as a sexual crime or as a crime primarily involved with a quest for power by means of violence. Like the rabbi's answer to some "either-or" conundrum—*Is it this? Or is it that?*—to which he says "Yes," the correct answer here is "Yes," meaning that rape is both a sexual crime and a violent crime. What is *not* the same, admittedly, in every case, is the balance between these two motivating forces. Some men are raised in families where the mother's behavior fosters a contempt for women, either because of her cruelty or (as in the case of Richard Davis) her flaunted promiscuity. Yet other rapists have grown up in families that were intact and not notably troubled, or at least not abusive, and where there had been, in addition, no history of either mental illness or head injury. Somehow these men became predators anyway, sometimes even psychopaths, with a sense of entitlement: women were theirs for the taking. One always suspects heredity in such cases—some innate tendency to the narcissistic part of the psychopathic picture. Here is an example.

Fred Coe

In the absence of abuse, neglect, or any of the other known "risk factors" for violence or psychopathy, there is no ready explanation as to what turned Fred Coe into a multiple rapist. He was born in 1947 into a prominent household in Spokane, Washington. His father was the managing editor of the local paper. His mother, Ruth Coe, an attractive woman, was obsessed nevertheless with appearances: she pushed Fred and his sister into having cosmetic surgery they didn't need, since they, too, were very attractive. Ruth was extraordinarily overattached to her son; both lacked moral scruples in a way quite out of keeping with their status in the community. A B student in high school, he would break into the teacher's desk and change the record to give himself A's. He lied artfully when threatened with expulsion, ascribing the "error" to "an administrative mistake." When he married, he was broke most of the time, and he would instruct his wife how to skip restaurants without paying, explaining to her, with the self-serving philosophy of the psychopath, that a person without money had an "ethical right to steal."[26]

Fred imagined himself a famous writer—the "next Hemingway or Shakespeare"—but was utterly without talent; his prose was overblown, filled with cutesy puns ("cuntree, Amareeka, unWashedington, Catlicks, Proudestunts") of the sort we associate with manic patients. He lived a parasitic life, cadging money from his parents on into his thirties, earning nothing at a real estate job he held only briefly. He was fired for paying his basic expenses with bounced checks, all the while boasting he would become first the top salesman in the firm and that he would one day be "one of the richest men in the world."[27] Typical of his grandiosity, he went out and bought a whole fancy wardrobe with money he didn't have before starting the job. This, despite his wife admonishing him: "Fred, just go to work. Sell a house. *Then* buy your clothes!"[28]

He committed his first documented rape in 1978 when he was thirty-one; this was followed by as many as forty more, though the exact figure will never be known. The influence of his family, the shameless loyalty of his mother, combined with the failure of the police over the next three years to make the needed connections between the various rapes occurring in Spokane's South Hill section delayed his being brought to justice. And when in August 1981 he was finally sentenced to seventy-five years in prison—as a sexual psychopath and rapist—his mother, outraged that her "boy" could be accused and convicted—went and hired a hit man for $4,000 to kill the judge. The hit man was a police undercover agent, whose testimony got her sentenced as well—albeit to a much briefer stay. Fred Coe claims innocence to this day. The rape victims, one of whom came close to suicide, would have had no trouble recognizing the evil and cunning that lay behind the suave and handsome mask of this man. Many other were fooled. As one person put it during the trial: "Mr. Coe is no ordinary criminal. He is . . . a pathological liar and a consummate actor whose quickness of mind cannot be disputed. Like most psychopaths . . . he has spent his entire lifetime outwitting others. . . . We, his potential victims, have reason to worry now that Mr. Coe will be clever enough in the end to outwit even the most intelligent members of the community, persuading them he is safe to be at large."[29]

The best clue we have in trying to unlock the mystery of Coe's psychopathy lies not so much in the pampering and misplaced loyalty of his mother as in the mother herself. When testifying on her behalf at court, Coe's father mentioned that his wife had undergone a change of personality after several operations and later, after menopause, when she went first into a severe depression. Treated with various medications by a psychiatrist, she went into a manic phase, buying all sorts of expensive things that she didn't need, until her condition was brought under control with lithium. It is quite likely that Fred's extreme grandiosity and his impulsivity, even his penchant for foul language (evident in his writings), were a milder version of his mother's manic illness. There are of course many grandiose psychopaths with no tendencies to mania; the vast majority of manic persons are not psychopathic. But there is an overlap. Added to this factor (which I feel is the decisive one in Coe's case) was his mother's blind loyalty and amorality: he could do no wrong in her eyes. Fred had no internal brakes. Had both parents consistently supplied external brakes by making him adhere to proper social standards, he might have grown up the supersalesman he fancied himself, or an engaging master of ceremonies, instead of the egomaniacal fraud and repeat-rapist that he became.

SADISTIC MURDER

In any discourse on evil, we will inevitably make frequent reference to the kindred concept of *sadism*, as touched on in chapter 1. Twenty years ago, "Sadistic Personality" made a brief appearance in the official manual of diagnosis used by the American Psychiatric Association.[30] The term was dropped in subsequent editions, largely under political pressure from feminist groups. They worried that defense attorneys in cases of wife bashing and the like would try to get their clients off the hook, making it look as though these men "suffered" from sadistic personality and (supposedly) couldn't help doing what they did. Obviously the sadist does not "suffer" from this disorder; *others* suffer from it. I believe the disorder belongs in the manual because, after all, it exists, and there are many who suffer—terribly—from what sadists do to them. But given the chicanery defense attorneys will sometimes resort to—blaming the death of Jennifer Levin at the hands (indeed, *the hands*, for she was strangled) of Robert Chambers as though it were just "rough sex"—it is easy to sympathize with the objections that the feminists were voicing.[31] "Sadistic Personality" was described as having eight different characteristics, of which one needed to exhibit any four (or more) of them to qualify. Included were using cruelty or violence to establish dominance, humiliating someone in the presence of others, intimidation, limiting another person's freedom, and *taking pleasure in the suffering of others*. This last, italicized item is the key one. Some of the stories mentioned so far in this chapter had to do with persons who intimidated or humiliated or cruelly dominated—but didn't necessarily get a thrill out of the pain they were inflicting on someone. They showed sadism—but not the *quintessence* of sadism: relishing the pain they forced others to experience. This is the very quality that was front and center in the persons sketched in the paragraphs below.

The Hate Crime in Jasper, Texas

In early June 1998, three drunk men—John William King, Shawn Berry, and Lawrence Brewer—kidnapped a black man, James Byrd Jr., who was hoping for a ride home after the bars closed. The three men "offered" Byrd a ride but first clubbed him to near unconsciousness and then hitched him to the back of their pickup truck. They dragged him, still conscious and undoubtedly suffering incredible pain, for some three miles, until they drove past a sewage drain where Byrd's head and right arm were pulled off. Their deed done, the three men then dumped Byrd's mutilated remains in a cemetery where black people were buried and set off for a barbecue. All three men were avowed white supremacists who had met while in prison. Among his tattoos King had one depicting a black man hanging, though to be fair, King was an equal-opportunity bigot: his murderous hatred extended to Jews, Asians, and gays as well. King had been adopted into a family of people who were not racist and who found him uncontrollable as an adolescent. This points in all probability to a genetic factor from a source, however, that we know nothing about. Having left many traces of their despicable act, the three were arrested the next day. At their trial the jury was made up of eleven whites and one black. King, proud of his act, (along with unrepentant Brewer) received the death penalty; Berry, life in prison. One can gauge King's level of remorse from his reply to a reporter who asked him, "What do you have to say to the Byrd family?"—to which King said, "Suck my dick."[32] This was the first time in Texas history that a white man received the death penalty for killing a black man. One reporter wrote of how the townspeople, black and white, showed a "stunning display of racial unity," adding that "in the face of naked evil, a community comes together."[33]

Phillip Skipper

When people see patterns of behavior repeating down the generations, they like to say, "The apple doesn't fall far from the tree." We saw an example of this with Ruth Coe and her son, Fred. It's not always clear, of course, how much these patterns reflect heredity or how much the children's mimicry of their parents. As I've mentioned, the worse the environment while growing up, the harder it is to detect what heredity may have added to the picture. But it probably means something that the father of Phil Skipper was sent to prison for life in Louisiana for rape, aggravated sodomy, and murder. One of Phil's two sisters died of a drug overdose; the other, Lisa, was married to John Hoyt. Phil and his wife took a teenager, Johnny Baillio, under their wing, and all five lived close together in a rural area near the border with Mississippi. The two men and young Johnny were part of a small gang, led by Phil, of racist thugs, modeling themselves after the Ku Klux Klan. They were all poor, lived in trailers, and had arrest records for assault and battery, drug dealing, and, later on, for murder and grave robbing. Lisa was a cocaine addict. It is a testimony to the way a dependent child will often cling to an abusive parent figure to note how Baillio, when he first moved in, put up with Phil's torture. Phil would tie Johnny to a tree and burn him with a cigar, he made the boy submit to fellatio at knifepoint, and beat him with his fists or a garden hose. Yet Johnny remained loyal to Phil and readily joined in when Phil popped the suggestion, "Let's go out and kill a nigger."[34]

Their intended victim happened to be Phil's next-door neighbor, a black woman of forty-two, Jane Nora Guillory (known by her friends as Genore), who, unlike Phil and his gang, was a highly respected member of the community, had a good job in Baton Rouge, was loved by all, and was known for being "generous to a fault."[35] Genore lived alone in much better circumstances than Phil and his family, and not only gave the Skippers food for Phil and his wife's baby, as well as diapers and money for other necessities, she even included them in her will—and made them aware of that. Despite her generosity, Phil got angry at Genore when Phil's dog (cared for temporarily by Genore) ate his pet goat. That was the "trigger." Phil, in the company of his sister, Hoyt, and Johnny, barged into Genore's house and proceeded to stab, shoot, and bludgeon her to death—to the point of rendering her face unrecognizable. The men also raped Genore's corpse, careful to use condoms, so as to leave no DNA. Though illiterate, Phil had the fiendish cleverness to pay a black man to ejaculate into a cup, so Phil could then toss the semen over Genore's body, by way of making the police assume the killer had been a black. Phil and his crew then returned to their "profession" of robbing graves for jewelry and gold, which they melted down to obscure its origins. Justice was delayed because of their scheme to use another man's semen, but eventually Johnny, still a juvenile, was persuaded to turn state's evidence in exchange for a lighter sentence. Phil, Hoyt, and Lisa all received life sentences. Sheriff Talmadge Bunch, involved with the case, said of Lisa, "That's an evil, evil girl . . . she comes from an evil family,"[36] a sentiment shared by the prosecutor, Sam D'Aquilla: "Those are some evil people." Even in the next chapter, devoted to serial sexual homicide and torture, we will not encounter many examples of atrocities in peacetime that match the murder of Genore Guillory.

Jeff Lundgren

In chapter 1 I gave a brief account of Jeff Lundgren, the leader of a self-styled Mormon cult and self-professed Prophet of God. His sadism was a thing apart from his murders: when the Avery family became disenchanted with Lundgren, he shot them one at a time in the back of the head—a painless death for each. Sadism exists quite independent of murder. The emphasis on murder cases in this section (and in this whole book) has to do with the fact that murder, compared with other acts of violence or purely psychological torture, is usually more fully documented. As for Lundgren, he cannot lay claim to being the outstanding con artist/cult leader. Jim Jones in Guyana and even David Koresh in Waco, Texas, both megalomaniacs like Lundgren, gathered larger flocks of the gullible. But none outdid Lundgren in sadism. In a way, the Averys got off easy. Before killing them in that relatively painless way, he told his "faithful" that he had "searched the Scriptures" and had found the proper punishment for the disobedient: the men were to be cut in two; the women, to be slit across the abdomen with a sword so their organs spilled out; the children, to be swung by their heels and smashed against a wall so their brains spilled out.[37]

Like his more successful "rogue messiahs,"[38] he felt he was entitled to have sex with, or to make into supplementary wives, whichever women in his flock struck his fancy. This was later to prove his undoing, but not until he committed the ultimate act of sadism—one perhaps unparalleled in the literature. After fleeing Ohio after killing the Averys, Jeff and some of his members camped in Missouri. He had by this time taken a second wife, Kathryn, who was already married to one of his followers. Prettier than Jeff's dowdy wife, Alice, and already pregnant by him, she aroused Alice's jealousy to the point of Alice having a nervous breakdown. She made a suicide gesture with some pills washed down with beer. Jeff's punishment for Alice's intolerance of the new wife: he forced Alice to rub his feces around his genitals and then to perform oral sex, swallowing some of the feces in the process.[39] Ironically, Lundgren was executed in October of 2006 for murdering the Averys, not for the crime of subjecting a fully conscious person, his own wife, to that degradation[40]—to many people's way of thinking a worse crime. The authors of his biography mention that Jeff could not have killed the Averys without the cooperation of his followers, but as prosecutor Ken LaTourette said at the trial, none was as "completely evil as Jeff."[41] Further on, in their commentary on the death penalty meted out to Lundgren, the authors wrote five years before his execution: "Jeff Lundgren has never shown any evidence of a broken heart or a contrite spirit. More, he is dangerous, and he is evil, and no civilized society that is obliged to protect itself from evil should allow him to survive."[42]

PSYCHOPATHY AND SPOUSAL MURDER

The spousal murders we have looked at so far were mostly done on impulse. The main actors in the dramas were often jealous partners, battered wives, and the like. But the malice aforethought and too-clever planning that so readily strike the public as "evil" are more apt to be seen in husbands or wives with prominent psychopathic traits. Sometimes the plot is so bizarre that horror author Stephen King wouldn't touch it . . . only it isn't a novel, it's real. The murders are often staged with such inventiveness, originality, and care that the police (so the killer thinks) will never even figure out that there was a murder, let alone put their finger on the "who" of the "whodunit." Until they do. Here are two examples.

Richard Crafts

In the fall of 1986, Helle Helsner Crafts—a former Danish stewardess, then married to an American pilot and the mother of their three children—went missing. Her husband, Richard Crafts, at age fifty a good bit older than Helle, had begun to have a series of affairs. Helle was making serious plans to divorce him. Her friends began to worry when Richard told them different stories (she went to Denmark; she went to Africa), and he was known for his aggressiveness. Helle had told her friends, "If something happens to me, don't think it was an accident."[43] Someone eventually notified the police that on the last night Helle was seen, a man had been spotted with a wood chipper, standing on a bridge over a lake in Connecticut. Other facts came to light: Richard had, in the recent days, rented not only the wood chipper (used to reduce logs to tiny fragments) but also a chain saw and a freezer. Little by little the police were able to piece together (the emphasis being on "piece") the whole story. By the lake they were able to find pieces of human hair (of Helle's blonde shade), fingernails, and tooth fragments, along with some blood of her (admittedly common) type, "O." Crafts had presumably bludgeoned his wife with a blunt instrument, severed her body into manageable pieces with the chain saw, frozen them until hard in the freezer, and then transported them to the lake—there to be reduced to little pieces by the rented wood chipper. Helle would thus disappear, and Crafts could circumvent the law, according to the maxim "no body, no problem." The tooth fragments, however, matched Helle's dental records. Crafts's first trial ended in a hung jury, but at the second he was convicted and sentenced to life in prison.

Susan Grund

Violence begets violence, which may be part of the reason for the acts perpetrated by Susan Grund. Sue Ann, before she changed her name to a classier-sounding Susan, was from a large, blue-collar family in Indiana. Her alcoholic father was said to have beaten her almost to death when he was drunk, leaving her with scars. She grew up to be a domineering, seductive, embittered woman with no remorse for the cruel things she did to others in her turn. Acquaintances spoke of her as being manipulative and a habitual liar as well. She married four times altogether, becoming Susan Sanders Lovell Campbell Whited Grund. The first marriage was when she was seventeen. Three years later, she married Gary Campbell by whom she had a son, Jacob. She stole money from Gary and stabbed him with a scissors during sex. She struck Jacob furiously, injuring him. She cheated on Gary with Tom Whited, whom she later married and who had a son, Tommy, by a prior marriage. Susan once beat Tommy so hard for not obeying her "command" that he throw away a certain toy that he developed a blood clot on the brain, which left him permanently retarded and unable to care for himself. On another occasion she left Tommy tied to a stake in hot weather till he got a severe burn; another time she gave him a burn directly—with a cigarette against his leg. For those cruelties she was given a mere five-year suspended sentence. Not surprisingly, Tom divorced her, though she was then pregnant with his child—a daughter, Tanelle, who was born when Susan was now living alone and penniless.

Not one to stay down for long, she returned to her family's home in northern Indiana, dressed in her customary see-through, slinky attire, where she attracted the attention of a lawyer, Jim Grund. She was still only twenty-five. Grund had a teenage son, David, by his first wife. Socially, this was a big step up for Susan, who nevertheless cheated on her new husband with his accountant. Greed was as important to her as adventure; at one point, she was strongly suspected of having burned down a boutique Jim had set her up in and for which she collected insurance money. She staged a break-in of their home and received another hefty sum from the insurance company. By the 1990s, she appears to have begun an affair with her stepson (denied by him in court but attested to by others). In the summer of 1992, Jim was murdered in his bed with a gunshot to the eye—from a gun that belonged to his son. Susan acknowledged to one of her sisters, Darlene, that she killed Jim, though even Darlene felt uncertain, since, as she said in court, she didn't know whether to believe her sister Susan: "She's always been a liar." Susan was sentenced to forty-four years in prison (plus twenty more for aggravating circumstances). Her restlessness in trading sex for status seemed never to have abated: rumor had it among the people in her town that Susan had had her eye on a certain senator, who would have represented a still higher rung on the social ladder than the one to which she had already ascended. As is the norm in spousal murder, Susan continues to profess her innocence.[44] Like many of the persons featured in this chapter, Susan Grund belongs in Category 16. After I learned of Jeff Lundgren's torture and degradation of his wife, I felt, because of the extreme degree of suffering he inflicted on her, the more appropriate category for him was 22.

STRANGER MURDER—BY A WOMAN

When women murder, the victim is usually someone close to them: a child, a parent, a lover, or a spouse, occasionally a rival. The killing of a stranger, especially the serial killing of one victim after another with intervals of time in between, is almost entirely a male preserve. But there are exceptions. Some of the exceptions are women who work as accomplices with a man, as in the Bonnie and Clyde bank robber team, or (rarer still) women who act as lures for men committing serial sexual homicide. We will meet a few of these women in the next chapter. In the meantime, here is a woman who became a serial killer of strangers, all by herself.

Dorothy Puente

Born Dorothea Helen Gray, she eventually became Dorothy Helen Gray McFaul Johannson Puente Montalvo, but she settled for using the name of her third husband, Puente. In 1929 she was brought into the world—one would hesitate to say "raised"—by one Trudie Yates, an alcoholic and abusive prostitute who put Dorothy in an orphanage with two of the younger of her five siblings. Dorothy was four at the time, her father having died shortly before. In the orphanage she was molested by some of the men there; later, by an older brother. To get away from this unhealthy environment, she married at sixteen to a man named McFaul, having run away from school and turned to prostitution. She soon had two daughters, whom she abandoned. At eighteen she was arrested for theft, but skipped parole, meanwhile inventing fantastical names and occupations—claiming to be a nurse, a doctor, even a surgeon. Marrying again at twenty-three, she emerged as a psychopath with a gift for lying and self-promotion; in a word, a world-class con artist. She set up a rooming house in Sacramento for elderly recipients of Social Security checks—many of which mysteriously ended up in Dorothy's bank account. Her skills failing her temporarily, she did a three-year stint in a California prison for stealing some three dozen checks from her tenants. Some suspected her of homicide as well, but this was not proven. Her downfall came as she neared sixty, when in 1988 a concerned social worker, unable to locate a chronically ill man she'd placed with Puente, suspected foul play. Police eventually checked out the grounds around the rooming house and turned up a human leg bone in the backyard, followed by the remains of seven bodies. It was then discovered that another twenty-five of her boarders were then shown to have gone missing. It turned out Dorothy had killed them with overdoses of sedatives, and then continued to cash their welfare checks. Her sweet-old-lady façade still served her to some advantage: at her trial the jury was hung on the issue of the death penalty, so she was given a life term instead.

The lives of Susan Grund and Dorothy Puente have much in common. Both married early to escape bad homes. Both had four husbands. Both seem like female versions of the mythical Sweeney Todd. In the story, Todd was born in the worst slums of London, left to survive by his wits when barely in his teens, jailed for theft, befriended by a barber there who taught him the barber's trade when they're released. Todd then seeks to satisfy his greed and take revenge upon more fortunate persons through clever murders for which he is not caught until after many years later. Grund and Puente were born into deplorable circumstances— bad enough to nudge them toward "secondary" psychopathy (based, as far as one can tell, mostly on an adverse environment, that is, rather than on genetic factors). They both personified a combination of greed and revenge in a life dedicated to doing anything to get ahead and to "show them" (all those who had hurt them early on), even if it took murder.

TERRORISM

In times of war or group conflict, terrorism usually refers to techniques used by the (militarily) weak to stand up against the strong. Suicide bombers are an example. In peacetime the situation is often reversed: a bully uses violence and intimidation to force the weak to do his will. Rape comes under this heading, though we ordinarily reserve the word *terrorism* for cases where threats and violence are used repeatedly and where more than just one person is affected. One of the most widely publicized examples of terrorism—one man terrorizing a whole town—took place in the same tiny town where, a quarter century later and only a few blocks away, another crime made national headlines.[45] That crime was the murder of Bobbi Jo Stinnett by Lisa Montgomery (mentioned in chapter 3) in her attempt to steal Bobbie Jo's near-term fetus. The town is Skidmore in northwest Missouri; the terrorist was Ken McElroy.

Ken McElroy

Said to have been the fifteenth of sixteen children from a two-room farm family near the meeting point of Kansas, Nebraska, Iowa, and Missouri, McElroy had little schooling but great talent for activities across the whole spectrum of crime. He rustled livestock and was arrested numerous times for theft, assault and battery, stalking, arson, pedophilia, rape, and intimidation; later on, for attempted murder. He made fast friends with a lawyer who matched Ken's talent for crime, in twisting the legal system to get Ken off the hook, no matter the offense. Although he earned a reputation for evil among the townspeople for harassment, robbery, and assault, Ken nevertheless professed to love children. But his "love" was decidedly morbid. He craved sex with pubescent girls and married and raped a total of six young girls over the years, one of whom was only thirteen. Her parents (not to mention the laws of Missouri) understandably disapproved of that union, but Ken shot their dog, burned their house down, and forced their consent—a move that also made it impossible for his new wife to testify against him in the rape charge. McElroy seemed fond of the ten children that four of the girls bore him, but he beat all six wives and "de factos" literally into submission, many of whom stood by him no matter what he did, possibly because of the "Stockholm Syndrome," where the abused begin to identify with and show loyalty to their abusers. If anyone dared challenge him, Ken might drive past that person's house over and over, brandishing a rifle—combining stalking and intimidation in one maneuver.[46]

Having beaten twenty-two arrests, thanks to his well-paid lawyer, McElroy became an invincible tyrant, the despotic king of all he surveyed. Until, that is, some of Ken's children stopped in the grocery store owned by Bo and Lois Bowenkamp to buy candy. One began to walk out with some candy that hadn't been paid for. A clerk yelled at the girl, and her older sister took the candy and tossed it back to the store. Another older sister got wind of what happened, and shouted, "Nobody accuses my little sister of stealing!" Ken learned of the dispute and, enraged that anyone should cast aspersions on his daughter (even though no one actually had), fired at Bo Bowenkamp a few days later with a sawed-off shotgun. The owner survived, but the town had had enough—especially when the timid police and judge ordered Ken released for the attempted murder "pending an appeal." The next time Ken showed up in town—July 10, 1981—several of the citizens shot him to death as he sat in his car. Though some decried the vigilantism that substituted for the law in Skidmore—a lesser evil that put paid to a greater evil—no one talked, nor was anyone ever prosecuted.[47]

Chapter Seven

SERIAL KILLERS AND TORTURERS

Canto XXXII, ll. 133–35

"O tu che mostri per sì bestial segno odio sovra colui che tu ti mangi dimmi 'l perchè," diss' io . . .	"O you who show by such a bestial sign hatred over him you are eating, tell me why," I said . . .

Most of the persons described in the last chapter belong to Category 16 on the Gradations of Evil scale; a few, however, to levels a few steps below. In the case of Jeff Lundgren, his public acts (the murder of the Avery family) were consistent with that level, yet his private acts (the degradation of his wife in the most repugnant fashion) belonged to the worst level: 22, reserved for murders involving prolonged torture. Lundgren is one of those people who does not fit neatly into just one pigeonhole. Many of the acts the public is least hesitant about condemning as evil do not involve murder at all, as it turns out. We saw this with Lundgren and, ironically, even with Dale Pierre—two of whose victims managed, I suspect somewhat to their regret, to survive their suffering. By surviving, their suffering—both physical and psychological—extended for days and years beyond the few minutes after they were compelled at gunpoint to swallow the Drāno. Here we will confront the extremes: the serial killers (including those who seemingly made a profession out of torture), along with a few individuals whose physical torture of their victims was never meant to have ended in their death. To begin, we need to clarify what is meant by the phrase "serial killer."

SOME DEFINITIONS

Aficionados of movies, television, and contemporary "airport" fiction will have noticed that the theme running through so many of the programs and books is, with almost monotonous regularity, serial killers. Perhaps because we in America no longer have a frontier, serial killers have replaced cowboys as objects of popular fascination. There is even a secret admiration, since these are men who do as they please, whereas the rest of us are obliged to rein in our more violent impulses.

Not all serial killers are cut from the same cloth; as a result, the phrase is used in confusing ways. There are three major varieties. The serial murders of patients by unscrupulous nurses and doctors—a few of whom we encountered in chapter 6—make up one of the less common varieties: one in which a sexual motif is lacking. A second variety concerns murders with fairly long intervals in between of random strangers, irrespective of age or gender. These killers are misanthropic men who simply hate people; again, there is no sexual motif. This is also the rarest type. Finally, there is the largest (albeit still uncommon) group: men committing serial sexual homicide. When people speak of "serial killers," this is the type they usually mean. The sexual element is central to the type, since the scenario is one of rape followed by murder (more common) or else murder followed by sex with the corpse (this necrophilic type is less common).

We could even speak of yet another variety of serial killing with a sexual overtone but without rape. If we were to make this into a fourth type, it would truly be the rarest of all the varieties: serial homicide committed by women who are seeking vengeance symbolically for sexual wrongs done to them (incest, usually). But I prefer to categorize this scenario as an uncommon variant of serial sexual homicide—one in which more attention is paid to the motive than to the overt act. The men (and the rare women) in this category belong to the higher levels of the scale: Categories 17 to 22.

There are not many persons who devote themselves single-mindedly to torture *in peacetime* that do not show at the same time a perverse sexual preoccupation. In times of war or group conflict, there is no lack of torturers who serve as functionaries of the state: men (and a few women) who would not be recognized by their friends and neighbors as sadists or as otherwise abnormal people. They are just doing a nasty job that (according to what they have been made to believe by the leader or some other higher-up) just "has to be done." After the conflict is over, most such persons return to their ordinary lives and their ordinary families, continuing to pursue their ordinary work. I in no way mean to place them outside the realm of evil; but theirs is a different kind of evil than the one we are focusing on in this book. For brevity, in this chapter "serial killer"—unless otherwise specified—will refer only to men who have committed serial sexual homicide. The FBI prefers to limit the phrase to men who have killed at least three persons, even though a pattern strongly suggestive of serial killing may emerge after only two murders (because of similarities in method and choice of victim). The reason for this definition is to allay anxiety in the public. There are more occurrences of two similar rape-murders than of three. If the media began writing scare-headlines after every instance of two such murders within a short time span in the same area, terror and hysteria would be rampant in the community, which might interfere with the painstaking detective work needed to catch the killer.[1]

DIVERSITY IN THE RANKS

When I began to study serial killers some twenty years ago, I knew of only a dozen or so. My main interest was to find peculiarities in their backgrounds that might help explain why they did what they did. The personality of serial killers was of special interest to me, since personality disorder was the area of my research and very little had been written about the topic at that time. As a psychiatrist and psychoanalyst trained during the 1960s, I had been taught that psychiatric conditions, even the most serious ones like schizophrenia, were caused by bad environment—which usually meant bad parents, which in turn usually meant bad mothers. Heredity was given short shrift, since it seemed that if you were born with a certain condition there was no point in trying to cure it: this was an affront to our American optimism that said you could cure anything (provided you weren't born with it). Only after I finished my training did I come to the realization that "nature" was of great importance in understanding psychiatric conditions; not only that, but that nature and nurture were inextricably bound up with one another, each interacting with the other in often complex and poorly understood ways.

I made a spreadsheet that contained a list of each serial killer with as many "variables" as I could think of that might help me understand the similarities and differences among serial killers (as well as among murderers of other types). For "nature" variables, I looked at the close relatives of each man: which relatives were mentally ill, which had committed crimes (especially crimes of violence). For "nurture" variables, I looked at the makeup of the family: Were the parents known to be caring and consistent? Had either been abusive to the future serial killer—either physically, verbally, or sexually? Which men came from intact homes, which from families where the parents divorced early on? Which ones came from fragmented families where the parents had so many divorces and remarriages that the family tree was a crazy quilt—where no one seemed to know who belonged to whom and no "caretaker" seemed much concerned with any of the children, stepchildren, foster children, half-siblings, and in general the chaotic mishmash that substituted for "family life"? How many of the men had been adopted, and what, if anything, did we know about their natural parents: Were they mentally stable? Had either been arrested for crimes? And what were the adoptive parents like—kind and devoted or neglectful and exploitative?

I realized that nature and nurture weren't the whole story: some of the men developed epilepsy or meningitis or some other disease of the brain that might have an effect on future behavior. Others met with serious head injuries that caused long periods of unconsciousness and damaged key areas of the brain that were important in governing behavior. Sometimes these injuries were just plain bad luck. But sometimes bad parenting helped to create this bad luck: a neglectful parent might ignore a rambunctious son whose wild behavior leads to a head injury. Then there is the occasional parent who, to turn the phrase around, added injury to insult by smashing a boy's head with a wooden plank. This was but one of the indignities visited upon Henry Lee Lucas by his mother.[2]

Before these men became serial killers, a great many of them engaged during their adolescence in what some have called "rehearsal" behaviors: assaults on family members or strangers, armed robbery, arson, and animal torture. They graduated over time from these types of (juvenile) delinquent acts to the sex-murders by which they would later become identified. Material of this sort went into my spreadsheet as well. Another item of great importance is drug abuse. Alcohol and many of the street drugs like cocaine, marijuana, methamphetamine, and angel dust[3] have the effect of priming the pump toward action (murderous action, in this case) by drastically lowering inhibitions and by clouding judgment. Here again, nature and nurture are often intertwined: some of the serial killers had alcoholic parents who either passed on their genetic tendency to alcoholism or at least taught their sons—by example—the charms of liquor.

When I started out and knew only of those dozen or so serial killers, I couldn't make any generalizations about drug abuse. But now, twenty years and 130 serial killers later, it's clear that a third of the men had one or both parents who were alcoholic. Albert DeSalvo, the Boston Strangler; John Wayne Gacy; and Peter Sutcliffe, England's Yorkshire Ripper (nicknames being the norm rather than the exception among these men) all had alcoholic fathers. Tommy Lynn Sells and Mike DeBardeleben had alcoholic mothers. In the families of Gary Heidnick and Henry Lee Lucas, both parents were alcoholic. With some of the men, alcohol was both a nature *and* a nurture factor: before Gary Heidnick grew up to become Philadelphia's Cellar of Horrors killer (chaining black women to his cellar wall, raping, and then killing them), his alcoholic father used to get into a rage when four-year-old Gary was crying—and would then suspend his son outside a fourth-floor window by his feet, threatening to drop him if he didn't stop crying.[4]

One of the problems I encountered in my search for the causes of serial killing stemmed from having to rely mostly on biographies, since I was able to interview personally only a small number of men. The biographies told me a great deal about the personalities of these men and something about their immediate families and past criminal records. But little mention was made about certain aspects of their past that we now know are very important tip-offs to later antisocial or even violent behavior. One such tip-off that got a lot of attention forty years ago—its accuracy has been debated back and forth since then—is the triad of childhood fire setting, bed-wetting, and animal torture.[5] Children whose behavior included this triad were considered at high risk for committing crimes (that might include sexual crimes) as they became adults. Since arson is a crime, it is likely to come to the attention of the authorities. Animal torture may not get much attention at first, but that part of a serial killer's history comes to the surface after he is arrested, thanks to all the investigative work that surrounds the arrest and trial. But bed-wetting is no crime, so it is often ignored. From the biographies, I found that about one serial killer in twenty was known to show the whole triad. There were just as many who were known to have set fires *and* tortured animals (usually cats) but whose bed-wetting (or, more medically, *enuresis*) history was unknown. David Berkowitz, known to most of us as the "Son of Sam" for his lover's lane murders of 1976, recorded the number of fires he set in his teen years: 1,488.[6] He also tortured animals. Did he also have enuresis? We don't know. In any case, animal torture is a much more important indicator of possible violence in the future, because a boy setting a cat on fire or hurling rocks at a dog means that he has no compassion for living creatures, is indifferent to their pain, and is in all likelihood getting vengeance vicariously for being treated outrageously by one or another parent. There are many serial killers, such as Albert DeSalvo (the Boston Strangler), Ed Kemper, Gary Ridgway (the Green River Killer), and Arthur Shawcross, who were brutalized by a parent and who also tortured animals.

Attention-deficit disorder in children and adolescents (exhibited as inability to concentrate and tendency to be fidgety, restless, and irritable) is another risk factor for later antisocial behaviors.[7] ADD, as it is usually abbreviated, is more common in boys than in girls; the tendency is often passed from father to son. Many serial killers probably had this condition in their younger years, but it is seldom mentioned in their biographies. An exception is Richard Ramirez, the Los Angeles Night Stalker, who, as we now know, had ADD as a child.[8]

Looking at all of these and similar risk factors made one thing clear, however: *there is no one-size-fits-all profile for serial killers*. Instead, there is a complicated mix of nature and nurture adversities, on top of which are still other highly unpredictable situations, such as being born "funny-looking," which leads to being mocked by classmates. Coming from a poor or even a working-class family adds to the chances for aggressive behavior,[9] as does coming from a culture of machismo, where it is common for men not only to control women but to use physical force to exercise that control. Or, there may be a seduction by a close relative early in one's life that suddenly and drastically creates an obsession, an idea that one can never get out of one's mind and that shapes forever the pattern of one's behavior. The pattern—here, an addiction really—may be one of violent revenge that one must carry out again and again on all who resemble those who mistreated him in adolescence. I will give an example of a serial killer transformed and transfixed by such an experience in his midteens. But before that, I would like to provide a "menu" of characteristics and occurrences before and after birth that we see more or less frequently in the ranks of serial killers: attributes that contribute importantly to the development of a serial killer, granted that no serial killer shows all of them, and a few show almost none.

THE MENU

From the *Nature* Side

- Mental Illness (severe, with psychosis)
- Schizophrenia
- Manic-Depression (especially the manic type)
- Autism or Asperger's Syndrome
- Delusional Disorder

Psychiatric Conditions (less severe, without psychosis)

- Attention Deficit Disorder (with or without hyperactivity)
- Alcoholism (of the familial/inheritable type)
- Epilepsy (such as temporal-lobe epilepsy)
- Inordinate sexual drive (in the absence of overstimulation in early life; may be related in some men to *very high innately determined testosterone levels*)

Personality Disorders (inheritance accounts for about half the disorder)

- Antisocial (more common in males)
- Psychopathic (more common in males)
- Schizoid (chief characteristic: aloofness; more common in males)
- Sadistic (more common in males)
- Paranoid
- Impulsive-Aggressive/Intermittent Explosive

From the *Nurture* Side

- Parental (*any* primary caretaker) cruelty/physical abuse
- Severe parental neglect/abandonment
- Severe parental verbal abuse/humiliation
- Death of a parent
- Growing up without a father
- Parents divorce before child is sixteen
- Being adopted
- Family with low socioeconomic status
- Parental sexual abuse/seduction, with subsequent hypersexuality. (This may include the repetitive *witnessing* of parental overt sexuality/promiscuity, sexual misuse of a sibling, and the like)
- Brain disease or damage—especially head injury to frontal lobe(s)
- Immersion in violent television—in psychologically vulnerable children

Of Mixed or Uncertain Origin

- Paraphilia (voyeurism, sexual sadism, bondage, exhibitionism, etc.)
- Early "after-effects" of adverse nature-nurture events
- Juvenile delinquency
- Substance abuse (especially cocaine, methamphetamine, angel dust)
- Alcoholism (if not primarily on a genetic basis)
- Conduct disorder in childhood (can reflect nature: ADD or early signs of manic illness, or nurture: parental cruelty)
- Animal torture and/or fire setting
- Rape or other sexual offenses committed in adolescence

As one can see from this list, these characteristics could be assigned to a simple set of categories: Bad Genes, Bad Parents, Bad Luck (head injury, for example), Bad Drugs, and "Raging Hormones."[10] This menu, or "schema" can be understood as a collection of ingredients from which a prescription for *violence in general* may be written. The murderers and rapists sketched in previous chapters showed either a few or many items from this menu. What nudges some men who have a number of these characteristics to go in the direction of *serial killing* cannot easily be predicted just from knowing their particular attributes from the menu. There must in addition be either abnormalities of a *sexual* nature that account for the difference or an exaggerated thrill seeking that can be satisfied only by intense sexual experiences.

SEDUCTION AS A KEY ELEMENT IN A SERIAL KILLER

I became acquainted through my work in a prison with a man in his forties who had, in the context of sexual encounters, strangled four men over a period of about two years. He had been married and divorced but was predominantly homosexual. His pattern was to meet a man in a gay bar, promise an evening of sex back at his place, and then, after he had gotten quite drunk, take the man to a secluded spot, engage in sex, and immediately afterward strangle the man to death with the image in his mind that the victim was actually his mother. This man had grown up as one of five brothers, among whom he had the misfortune to be his mother's "favorite." The father was a policeman; the mother, a security guard. A bulky, tough-as-nails woman, his mother was a formidable figure at home; she was the chief disciplinarian, and she used her guard's baton to exact the same measure of obedience and submissiveness in her children as she did with the miscreants she collared during her workday. The man I had gotten to know in the prison had been beaten often and severely by his mother (sometimes to the point of bleeding)—a punishment also meted out to his brothers. But because he was her favorite, she enticed him at age fourteen into having intercourse with her on a regular basis. From that point on, there seemed to be an oscillation between the two activities: beating one day, sex the next, beating the third day, sex the day after, until he finally left home at nineteen. He developed a blistering hatred for his mother, which he said was 70 percent because of the beatings and 30 percent because he knew her seducing him was wrong. In his alcohol-besotted state he was killing his mother over and over again. In addition he had strong psychopathic traits: he was an inveterate liar and con man, full of charm and glib speech.

From the standpoint of the Gradations scale, this man would be placed in Category 17 for serial sexual murder without torture. One might not think of him as an "evil" person; the evil resided in his habitual act when overcome by the urge to find and murder a potential victim in a bar. He was psychopathic but not sadistic; he was not a loner; in fact, he was extraverted, charming, and good-humored in ways that could have made him a supersalesman, were it not for his penchant for murder. He was also physically strong and athletically built, qualities that enabled him to overpower his prey. I believe it was the mother-son incest that created the pattern of sexual crime, but for which he may have either committed no crimes at all or only property crimes.

To show you something more about the diversity among serial killers, I'd like to take you now on a journey into the lower depths of serial murder and torture. If this were Dante, we'd have to dig a good bit deeper than his (lowest) Ninth Circle, because there were no people he described even at hell's "bottom" that did anything like the people you'll meet in this chapter. Throughout our journey, I will introduce people who exhibit most of the characteristics on the "menu" in the areas of nature, nurture, and what might be called misadventure (head injury, being raped while in a reformatory). These people will illustrate the various degrees on the Gradations scale—from 17 to 22.

MENTAL ILLNESS; PSYCHIATRIC DISORDERS

Because of the common belief that anyone who would do the things serial killers do must be "crazy," many would conclude they must all be "mentally ill." Granted that "mentally ill" is a vague phrase, psychiatric circles still use it to refer to persons who suffer from an inborn major psychosis, such as schizophrenia, delusional disorder, and manic-depressive psychosis. Heavy abuse of LSD, angel dust, cocaine, methamphetamine, and, in vulnerable persons (adolescents, especially), marijuana can also create a lasting state of "craziness" that resembles schizophrenia. To make matters more complex, some people who start out with a psychotic condition also abuse some of these drugs, ending up with an aggravated psychosis: their original inborn illness is now made considerably worse by drug abuse. Within the ranks of serial killers, though, very few started out with a mental illness where hallucinations, bizarre ideas, and delusions—that is, a psychosis—were present *independent* of drug abuse. What is extremely common among serial killers is a (less severe) psychiatric disorder of some kind, particularly a personality disorder. It wouldn't be incorrect to assume that they *all* have a personality disorder—such as narcissistic, antisocial, psychopathic, sadistic, irritable/explosive, schizoid, or various combinations of several of these. It is not always so easy to make a correct diagnosis of mental illness in serial killers once they are on trial for their crimes, since a few feign psychosis in hopes of receiving a less severe sentence via an insanity defense. In the end, however, these attempts almost invariably fall flat.

PSYCHOSIS

Two of the most clear-cut cases of psychosis in a serial killer are those of Richard Chase and Joseph Kallinger. Both have been termed, I believe correctly, schizophrenic.

Richard Chase was born in 1950 in Sacramento into a working-class family where the parents bickered a great deal. His father was a strict disciplinarian and critical, but he was not really abusive. Richard showed peculiarities early on: he liked to set fires and torture animals while in elementary school. He used to bury the cats he'd killed in the backyard. In his teens he began to show signs of "weirdness": whereas he was popular at first, his personality underwent drastic changes as he began to date girls. He was impotent on several occasions and began to abuse LSD, alcohol, and marijuana. A psychiatrist whom he saw briefly thought he had a "major mental illness" but did not suggest hospitalization. His behavior became more bizarre, and he became disheveled. He would nail his closet shut in the belief that people were "invading his space" from within the closet. Once he took himself to an emergency room complaining that someone had stolen his pulmonary artery. On another occasion he claimed that bones were coming out through the back of his head or else that his heart had stopped beating. He was diagnosed as "paranoid schizophrenic" at this point, with the added note that hallucinogenic drugs were making his illness, whatever it was, a great deal worse. When his parents divorced, he lived with his mother but said he was being "poisoned."

Apparently on the assumption that his impotence was caused by lack of blood, Richard became preoccupied with killing animals and drinking their blood and smearing himself with their blood. He would catch rabbits and tear their organs out, eating their entrails raw. Once he actually injected himself with rabbit blood—and, of course, became violently ill because of the blood incompatibility. He caught and tortured cats, dogs, even a cow. In his twenties he graduated to killing and disemboweling humans: a man, then two women, and three children, drinking their blood in the same vain hopes of curing his sexual dysfunction. With one of the women he committed his most depraved act after he killed her: carving off a nipple and stuffing animal feces in the mouth of her corpse. When he was finally caught in 1978, he was considered a "disorganized" type of serial killer, since his acts were accompanied by rage (one sign of which was multiple stab wounds) and because he made no attempt to hide the evidence of what he had done.[11] He once even called the family of a dog he'd mutilated and told them that he was responsible.

Chase committed suicide in prison with antidepressant tablets he had saved up. Though considered mentally ill at trial, he did not win an insanity defense because he knew what he had done was wrong. *Insanity* is now simply a legal term signifying that an offender did not understand the nature of his act nor that it was wrong. One might quibble that *serial sexual homicide* was not the right term for Chase's crimes because he didn't always have sex with the victims, or if he did, it was only after (in several cases) they were dead; in other words, Chase performed necrophilic acts with some of his victims. But his motivation was certainly sexual in nature. Because of these variations, Chase does not fit neatly into any one of the categories of the scale. The fact that he shot some of his victims and stabbed others—without torture—is consistent with category 17. But the gruesomeness of his acts suggests that he belongs to the extreme end of the scale: Number 22. Mutilation after death can no longer be felt by the victim, however, so it is not considered "torture," nor does it represent the kind of extreme sadism or torture that would place him at the far end of the scale.

Joseph Kallinger, in contrast, did torture his victims. Kallinger was adopted by a punitive couple in Philadelphia, who, besides beating him, also taunted him when he was an adolescent that his "bird" (that is, his penis) would never get hard. Although he later married and had several children, he always was obsessed with fears about his penis; in his late thirties he claimed God spoke to him, telling him to kill young boys and to cut off their penises. He eventually killed one of his sons (who had accused him of abuse), a young boy, and a nurse, whom he had sexually assaulted. Kallinger said at one point that he was 961 years old and had been a butterfly. There is some question whether Kallinger faked some of these bizarre responses or else exaggerated what he really felt in order to win an insanity plea. Psychiatrist Dr. John Hume, with whom I spoke and who had testified at the trial in October 1976, thought Kallinger had an antisocial personality and was otherwise malingering. The jury agreed and waved aside the insanity defense, consigning Kallinger to life in prison (where he died in 1996). Some experts felt Kallinger was "schizotypal" in personality: eccentric, with odd and magical beliefs but short of full-blown schizophrenia. One author who wrote up the case thought he was schizophrenic,[12] but the truth of his mental state may elude us as to where acting crazy ends and being crazy begins. As far as is known, Kallinger did not abuse drugs, so, unlike Chase, whatever his mental state—mad, malingered, or a combination—drugs had not worsened it.

ATTENTION DEFICIT DISORDER

Richard Ramirez, who earned a measure of celebrity in the mid-1980s as the Los Angeles "Night Stalker," had many more strikes against him than just Attention Deficit Disorder with hyperactivity (often abbreviated to ADD/H). I include him under this heading because he is one of the few serial killers whose history makes explicit mention of the condition. He grew up in El Paso, Texas, as the youngest of five children in a Mexican American family. Richard's great-grandfather, grandfather, and father had all been extremely abusive physically toward their sons down the generations as a means of instilling discipline. Two of Richard's three brothers had gotten in trouble with the law for heroin addiction. Richard suffered at least two bouts of unconsciousness after head injuries: once, when a dresser he had been climbing fell over on him; another time, when a playground swing struck him. After the head injuries he began to have seizures, both grand mal (causing unconsciousness) and temporal lobe (causing strange visions or automatic movements but without unconsciousness). In the wake of these experiences, he also became hypersexual, aggressive, and prone to "visions" of monsters. In his midteens he began to abuse a host of hallucinogenic drugs: mescaline, LSD, angel dust, and cocaine.

Richard had a cousin, Mike Ramirez, who had served with the army in Vietnam. Mike boasted about his exploits there: rapes and beheadings of Vietnamese women, stealth killings, and the like, all of which made Mike a hero in Richard's eyes. Mike settled in Los Angeles (after being released for the murder of his wife, committed in full view of Richard) where Richard later joined him. By then, Richard had become reclusive, suspicious, and totally depraved. He began to sneak into the houses of people, mostly women, whom he would kill or rape. On one occasion he cut out the eyes of a victim and took them with him. Ramirez entertained grandiose fantasies of becoming more famous than Jack the Ripper.[13] Arrested after his fourteenth murder, he told the authorities with his characteristic callousness: "You don't understand me . . . you are not capable of it. I am beyond good and evil," and "I love to kill people. I love to watch them die. I would shoot them in the head and they would wiggle and squirm. . . . I love all that blood."[14]

One of the qualities that characterizes Ramirez as an "evil" person—as opposed to someone who has now and then done evil acts—is his lifelong inability to make a lasting and harmonious attachment to anyone. Unlike a number of the married serial killers who have led double lives—being thoughtful and attentive to their wives and families while brutal to their victims—Ramirez appeared to spend each of his waking hours in a state of hatred toward people in general, continually planning for his next sadistic act. In this respect he resembles the next person we will discuss, whose case is an example of (among other things) hypersexuality—the need, that is, for excessively frequent sexual release.

HYPERSEXUALITY

Leonard Fraser, born in 1951 in northern Australia, had been a compulsive liar and a loner from early childhood—a childhood that was punctuated by frequent tantrums and rages. In all fairness, his father aggravated Leonard's aggressive tendencies by beating his son "black and blue" with his belt—not realizing (as few parents do) that abusively punishing a fearless child who is utterly unresponsive to such treatment is absolutely ineffective and only makes a bad situation worse. Violent and destructive in school, Leonard was markedly hypersexual (heterosexual more than homosexual), defiant, and uncontrollable. The degree to which hypersexuality can be ascribed to heredity rather than to sexual overstimulation in the early years is not always an easy equation to solve. But in Leonard's case, at least, hypersexuality was evident even before he was subjected to forced sex by the bigger boys in the reformatory to which he was later sent. In turn, he raped the boys smaller than himself and, when released at seventeen, he set about raping women in large numbers.

Typical of serial killers, he also tortured animals, boiling cats alive. He abused alcohol and drugs, stole a car, and at one point raped and killed a French tourist. He went on in this way until he was arrested for rape when he was twenty-three. Sentenced to twenty-one years, he was nevertheless released after seven by a parole board that paid no attention to his having been diagnosed as a psychopath by the prison psychiatrists. Arrested again for rape right after his release, he was sentenced to only two months in jail. After a few more trips in and out of prison, he raped some sixteen women in an area around Brisbane and later raped, killed, and performed necrophilic acts on three more women and a nine-year-old girl. He continued to torture cats and also engaged in bestiality—sex with animals, in his case, with dogs. He kept a woman locked up in a room, insisting on having sex with her six times a day, before finally being arrested once again, this time diagnosed as an "incurable sexual sadist." As a predator, Fraser performed acts that others call evil. He did so seemingly from morning till night, concentrating his efforts on waiflike women whom he would stalk and rape. The police characterized him as "alarmingly evil."[15]

PERSONALITY DISORDERS

Of the various personality disorders in serial killers, psychopathy is arguably the most common. This disorder was present in 87 percent of 145 serial killers in my biographical records. Psychopathy is common as well in other persons who become known for evil actions (apart from serial sexual homicide), such as Charles Manson, who showed all the behavioral tendencies and the narcissistic personality traits in about equal measure. In such a crowded field it seems quite arbitrary to single out any one particular serial killer as the example for psychopathy. Serial killers in general are predators who, by their very nature, are indifferent to their victims and are self-centered to the utmost. These men are narcissistic at the least. Most go the extra mile and show the special traits of callousness, lack of remorse, glibness, and deceitfulness that put them at the outer edge of narcissism—that is, in the category of the psychopath. Perhaps it is their total *lack of compassion* for their victims that is their most important characteristic, even in those serial killers who, like Gary Ridgway or Herman Mudgett, led double lives and retained a measure of compassion for their wives.

PSYCHOPATHY

Paul Bernardo grew up in an Ontario family. His mother was a frumpy and undemonstrative woman; his father, an ill-tempered man who was also a Peeping Tom. As a child, Paul was a teaser and a bully who, once in his teens, got involved in various scams and rip-offs to make money. Very much the braggart, he was cocky and, as he began to date girls, possessive. His mother informed him when he was about sixteen that her husband was not his biological father. After this revelation about being a "half-adoptee," he turned abusive and rebellious toward his mother. He developed into a con artist and supersalesman of no mean aptitude. A string of girlfriends followed. Paul was jealous and abusive, calling one girl a whore and beating her savagely because she'd gone to a bar with a girlfriend. To another girl he made obscene phone calls and was slapped with a restraining order. He became obsessed with rape, anal sex, and power fantasies.[16] A man without scruples or morals, he became all the more immersed in get-rich-quick schemes, relying on his considerable charm.

At twenty-three, he met Karla Homolka, whom he mesmerized to the point of making her his willing sexual slave and eventually his wife. After the flowers and candy came the bondage and the criticisms of her being "ugly"—all with the effect of subjugating her to his will.[17] Ultimately Paul engaged in many acts of voyeurism, pedophilia, kidnap, and murder and was responsible for the deaths of three women.

His first victim was his sister-in-law, Tammy. Paul convinced Karla, who worked in a veterinarian facility, to anesthetize her fifteen-year-old sister so Paul could have sex with her. Upon awakening, Tammy vomited and aspirated some of the stomach contents into her lungs—and died. This was not planned, but Paul and Karla made it seem accidental, so they were not charged with any crime. Paul did rape and murder two young women, however, around the time that he and Karla married in 1991.

To exert maximal control over Karla, Paul made videotapes of her in sexually compromising situations to use as blackmail, should she ever feel like squealing on her husband. Finally he went a bit too far, punching Karla and giving her two black eyes. She turned state's evidence, and Paul was sent to prison for life without parole. She herself was given a lengthy sentence but was released in 2006. As for Paul's *sadistic* traits (with which psychopathy in serial killers is often mingled), one story tells all: Karla had a pet iguana, which bit Paul when he incautiously put his hand in its cage. For "retribution" Paul cut its head off and made Karla cook the iguana and eat it.

George Schaefer was a psychopathic serial killer who was less outwardly charming than Paul Bernardo and whose sadistic traits were, if anything, even more repugnant. He was raised in an upper-class family in the South. His father was alcoholic and abusive toward his wife, at times beating her and calling her a whore. George was tormented during his teens by violent sexual fantasies. His attitudes toward sex swung wildly between craving it and vilifying girls who wore revealing clothes—condemning them as "sluts." He became a deputy cop, and in that guise lured women by pretending they had committed a driving offense, then handcuffing, raping, and strangling them. His "signature" act was to frighten the women to such an extent that they would lose control of their bowels. Handsome and charming, but also hypersexual and ghoulish, he boasted of killing over eighty women, though the actual number remains uncertain. Once arrested and imprisoned, he penned stories of his crimes (either actual crimes or ones he aspired to), adding nauseating and sadistic details. Considered an "organized" type of serial killer by the venerated former FBI profiler Robert Ressler, Schaefer was depicted as one of the most evil and sadistic.[18] Schaefer, while serving his life sentence, was killed by another inmate in 1995.

SCHIZOID PERSONALITY

The hallmark of a schizoid personality is aloofness. Unlike *avoidant* persons, who simultaneously crave connectedness with others yet are too fearful to reach out for it, *schizoid* persons are predominantly hermit-like and live as loners—unattached and not keen on becoming intimate with others. There are some types that don't fall into either of these categories: loners who do experience loneliness and like the idea of being close with someone yet run from such relationships, fearing they would not be accepted. Or, perhaps they lack the social skills to keep a relationship going. Among serial killers this personality type is unusually common: about half the men are schizoid or at best loners with mostly schizoid traits, though some of them do yearn for an attachment they are psychologically unable to negotiate.

Another prominent quality of schizoid persons is a kind of eerie *detachment.* This is made worse over the years because of the lack of "feedback" from exchanges with other people, which leaves the schizoid person more enveloped in his own world, increasingly more strange or peculiar. Among serial killers, some of the most gruesome murders are committed by the schizoid killer, who can mutilate and carve up bodies with no disturbance of emotion, much as though he were a child whittling wood or taking apart a clock to see what's inside. It is this detachment, side by side with the bodily mutilation, that unfailingly elicits the reaction of "evil" in ordinary people. The fact that the killer may not have been cruel in his interactions with coworkers and acquaintances does not change that label. Under the umbrella of schizoid personality we find serial killers who—apart from their murders—seem decent, even likable. Yet we find others who are habitually cruel, outlandishly so, arousing in us no feeling of their being "human" at all: men whom people formerly, and more delicately, called "sports of nature"—who might now be considered freaks or mutants.

Dennis Nilsen is an example of a schizoid man who nevertheless was tormented by loneliness and hungered for closeness. He is as well known in England as Jeffrey Dahmer is in America, and for the same reason: both were lonely, schizoid men, homosexual, unable to form lasting attachments but hoping against hope to create fantasied (and necessarily short-term) friendships with men whom they then strangled and preserved for as long as they could within their apartments. The corpses, albeit no longer available for conversation, were at least guaranteed of "being there" for a while as companions for these lonely loners. They were also available for necrophilic sex, for however many days it took before the bodies became rank.

Dennis was the son of an English woman—a distant relative of the famous novelist Virginia Woolf—and a Norwegian soldier who had served in World War II. Theirs was a stormy marriage that ended when Dennis was four. The one relative he was close to was his maternal grandfather, and he was sent to live with him after his parents divorced. The grandfather died when Dennis was six, after which he felt bereft and alone in the world. Unlike many serial killers, he enjoyed pets and owned both a dog and a cat. He never suffered abuse of any kind and later held responsible jobs. He served for eleven years in the British Army where he learned to cook; later he served briefly as a police officer. In his early thirties, back in London, he fell into the habit of picking up men in bars, some gay, others not, and inviting them back to his apartment. Before developing this routine, however, Dennis had had a roommate, David Gallichan, with whom he lived for about two years in what was apparently a nonsexual relationship. When they parted ways, Dennis began to drink to excess, felt unbearably lonely—and went to bars to pick up men.

Dennis committed his first murder in 1978, when he was thirty-three. After strangling his invited guest, he kept the body for a time under the floorboards of his flat. For a time, he would pry up the floorboards and have sex with the corpse—until the body was in too great a state of decomposition and had to be disposed of. Altogether, Nilsen killed fifteen men, though there were others he released unharmed. It was when, in 1983, he tried to dismember his current victim and flush some of the remains down the toilet, that the plumbing got stopped up and neighbors complained of bad odors. When the authorities came to look into the matter, he confessed in detail and made no plea for compassion, nor did he show remorse.[19]

At trial he was evaluated by psychiatrists from both the defense and prosecution sides. The defense concluded that Nilsen had an impaired sense of identity and was able to depersonalize to the point where he felt hardly anything about his murderous activities (this depersonalization is akin to the extreme detachment mentioned above). The prosecution asserted that he had a "mental abnormality," though not a "mental disorder"[20]—perhaps a distinction without a difference. Be that as it may, he was clearly not psychotic. A distinguishing feature of Nilsen, compared with the majority of other serial killers, is that he did not seem dominated psychically by hatred. This is not to say that there wasn't any deeper skein in his psyche, somewhere beneath ready availability to consciousness, where hatred resided. Perhaps he felt hatred toward his mother, whose attention was diverted elsewhere when she remarried and had other children, or hatred toward the father who left the family after a few years of an alcohol-fueled stormy marriage.

Nilsen seemed curiously attached, if one can speak of such a thing, to the men-made-into-corpses whom he invited home. Were they symbolically connected with the beloved but now dead grandfather? Probably, but we cannot know. He does not strike us, at all events, as the typical serial killer, suffused with hatred for the family members of whom his victims were the unwitting representatives. Nilsen bore no animosity toward his victims. Another oddity about Nilsen: he was remarkably intelligent and even self-reflective. This came through in a letter he sent me when I had requested permission from him for a face-to-face interview. This is what he wrote:

> Dear Michael: Thank you for your letter dated October 24 which I received yesterday [on All Soul's Day] . . . on Halloween—this inappropriate meeting of magic and superstition with science and knowledge. I see your letter is replete with stock phrases from the True Crime genre: "genesis of various violent crimes," "the origins of criminal behavior" . . . I think when one begins to pre-package humanity into neat dark boxes indelibly labeled "criminal" and "murderer" . . . then you begin to stray from knowing the full picture of dysfunction as being a primarily human one . . . a dysfunction that precedes any artificiality of the deflecting label.

He went on to tell me that he was willing nonetheless to meet with me, but that the authorities where he is incarcerated would not permit this. (Nilsen was sentenced to a minimum of twenty-five years.) Unbeknownst to Nilsen, the letter he received was a stock letter sent him by an agency helping me to set up possible interviews; it was not written by me, personally. I am in total agreement with him about how such phrases tend to rob the recipient of the humanity he surely possesses, regardless of his criminal acts. That is, of course, doubly true of such a sentient and reflective person as Nilsen is—in spite of all that he has done.

Edmund Emil Kemper III stands in stark contrast to Dennis Nilsen. Like Ramirez and Kallinger, hatred was the driving force behind Kemper's serial murders. A giant when he reached his adult height of six foot nine (206 cm), at the age of fifteen Kemper had already shot both his paternal grandparents to death—with a gun the grandfather had given him as a present. His response to the "why" question when he was interrogated: "I just wanted to see what it felt like to kill Grandma and Grandpa."[21] Kemper had already killed a cat by burying it alive, when he was just ten. At thirteen he shot a boy's dog to death and beheaded another cat. Between 1972 and 1973 Kemper picked up hitchhiking college girls in the Santa Cruz area in California; he would stab or shoot them, then dismember the bodies after conveying them to his apartment—where he would have sex with the dismembered corpses. He later dispatched his extremely abusive and domineering mother (the prime source of his hatred) in a similar fashion, with the added touch of using her severed head as a dartboard. Kemper, currently serving a life sentence, is on record as having mused: "When I see a pretty girl walking down the street, I think two things: One part of me wants to take her home, be real nice and treat her right; the other part wonders what her head would look like on a stick."[22]

Kemper was clearly a schizoid psychopath, but there is one similarity with Nilsen: neither was able to form a sustained intimate relationship with anyone. This led Kemper to comment that women, while alive, were unavailable to him, whereas dead they were "his."[23] It may say something about his inability to inspire warm sentiments in others to add that my late cousin, Dr. Bruce Danto, a forensic psychiatrist in California, once interviewed Kemper and had come away with the feeling that, albeit vigorously opposed to the death penalty in general, he would have had no hesitation in "pulling the switch" on Kemper.

SADISTIC PERSONALITY

In some respects the Gradations of Evil scale could be reinterpreted as a Gradations of Sadism scale. The crimes and offenses that are the most likely to earn the label of "evil" are also the ones where sadistic traits are the most pervasive. If we look just at the men in my true-crime biographies (who are more likely to be sadistic than the women), 70 percent of male murderers are sadistic.[24] But the higher one goes on the scale, the higher the percentage of men who are sadistic: in Categories 2 through 11, 25 percent are sadistic, but in the large remainder (12 through 22) 70 percent are sadistic. Limiting the search to the last four categories (19–22) all 81 are sadistic. The great majority in the higher categories (16 or higher) are also psychopathic at the same time, so the phrase "sadistic psychopath" would be an accurate characterization of these men: serial killers making up the largest group.

Some of the sadistic traits are stronger indicators than others. *Enjoying the suffering of others* is the key trait, but lying (deceiving) to others in order to inflict pain (tricking the victim into going to some remote or secret place where the sadist can do his work without detection) is another important trait. A third important quality is the intimidation of others by threats and cruelty. There are several serial killers whose obsession with torture—*prolonged* torture, at that—is so pronounced that the word *evil* would spring to the lips of just about everyone who heard what these men had inflicted on their victims.

It so happens that some of the torturers have committed acts the full extent of which even the police and crime scene investigators can't fully discover. The children whom David Paul Brown (aka Nathaniel Bar-Jonah) is suspected of torturing, for example, have simply disappeared but for a few bone fragments underneath his apartment. Had they been tortured just a bit? For hours or days? Hardly at all? We will never know. So his place along the scale is uncertain. But there are other serial killers who not only reveled in torturing their victims, but were also compulsive record keepers of their repugnant deeds—deeds that struck the public as fiendish beyond anyone's worst nightmare or exercise of imagination. Such men serve as examples of the worst of the worst—and it has now become obvious to me, having looked at the records of over seventy such men, that had I known when I first created the scale in the late 1980s what I know now, I would have extended it to a few still-higher levels.

As I expressed in chapter 1, I had also wondered whether such men perhaps didn't exist in Dante's time—is there something new under the sun, after all? Or did Dante know of such men but then blushed at the thought of shocking his readers with such gruesome details, for which his elegant poetry would scarcely seem the proper vehicle? What follows are a few examples of "sadistic personality" of such a nature that I cannot convey to you their enormity without apologizing in advance for putting such material on the printed page. But my pen stops well short of putting the full horror of these men's sadism before your view in the same way that soldiers returning from the front lines who have seen mutilation share their memories either not at all or only with other veterans—and then only on rare occasions and in hushed tones.

David Parker Ray appears to be the most cruel and sadistic of all the serial killers, indeed, of all the murderers I have known or studied. I say "appears" because there could be another sadistic killer somewhere who tortured his victims even more than Ray did, but who left no records of his crimes. Of Ray we can once again paraphrase Dr. Simon's book title,[25] "Bad men do what good men dream." David Ray did what the Marquis de Sade only dreamed of. Dr. Simon, a distinguished forensic psychiatrist, knows full well what psychiatrists in general know: many people (men much more so than women) from time to time, especially after suffering insults, rejections, reverses, assaults, and the like, do have moments of murderous fantasies. The mental images may even include torture of those who have wronged or hurt them. This is what Dr. Simon meant by his book title. You may consider this a deplorable aspect of human nature, but it is a part of human nature all the same. But here is the important point: the vast majority of us—probably 97 percent of men and 99 percent of women—never assault, let alone torture anyone. Is this because the rest of us are so free of "impure" and murderous thoughts? Hardly. It is because most of us, besides having better genetic underpinnings, have had the good fortune to be well socialized by caring and nurturing parents or by other benevolent interactions with those close to us, with the result that we are more predisposed to love than to hatred. Likewise, our brains have more reliable mechanisms in place that instruct us: "But of course you must not *do* any of those nasty, retaliatory things you were thinking of!" And we don't. Even the Marquis de Sade didn't, though he committed some cruel acts (but no murders) in his younger days. His reputation is built mostly around his sadistic (I don't know what else to call them) fantasies, which he consecrated voluminously to paper (my editions run to about three thousand pages) but never carried out on a person. But to return to David Parker Ray . . .

Ray was a mechanic of uncommon skills, a superlative draftsman, a meticulous recorder of his fantasies, and a diabolically clever inventor of torture devices. Ray was no less clever in the methods of escaping justice. And like the notorious Dr. Mengele of Auschwitz, Ray was able to live as two persons in one: a Jekyll and Hyde who could be sociable and pleasant to coworkers and to his children (though not so much to his wives), then switching in an instant into a callous executioner, experiencing a greater high or adrenaline rush from torture than the addict's high from cocaine (which Ray never used).

Ray was born in rural New Mexico in 1939 some thirty miles southeast of Albuquerque. Below is a sketch of his family tree. Cecil, Ray's father, was an alcoholic with a violent temper, of whom a childhood friend of Ray's said, "I heard some things about [Ray's] dad, but I don't want to repeat them."[26] Ray's parents divorced when he was ten, at which point Nettie, his mother, sent him and his sister, Peggy, to live with their paternal grandparents. The grandfather was a strict disciplinarian who insisted on a dress code for David that got him mocked by his more casual classmates. David and Peggy almost never saw their father, and their mother seldom visited. David was known as a loner. When he was about thirteen, bondage fantasies began percolating through his brain, and it was not long before he put them into action—tying a woman to a tree while he

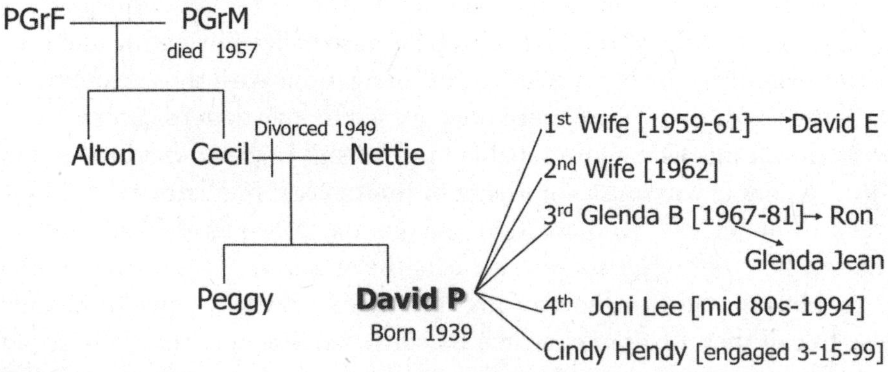

Figure 7.1

was in his midteens and torturing her to death.[27] It is characteristic of men who become serial killers that they relish the sense of godlike power over others, the moment of a victim's death establishing as "factual" this power. This can go a long way to paper over what are usually shameful feelings of worthlessness and inferiority in the pre-murderous phase of the killer's personal life. The "serial" part can best be understood as stemming from the addiction to this morbidly fulfilling "high"—where the *petite morte* (as the French sometimes call an orgasm: the little death!) comes at the moment of someone else's *grande morte*. Lust and addiction by definition are acts that must be repeated—calmness, buildup of the craving to the tipping point, satisfaction of the craving, calm—in an endless cycle. Once the brain becomes wired for this cycle, it is like flowers pressed in Lucite—stamped eternally and unmodifiable.

A meager performer academically, Ray soon showed a remarkable talent for mechanical things. Outwardly, he came across as a pleasant, affable man; he went from one job to another over the years but acquitted himself well at each: gas station attendant, railroad-track repairer, and, in the later years, park ranger in a town south of Albuquerque called (after the old radio show) Truth Or Consequences (original name: Hot Springs). It is not clear when precisely he turned "professional" as a sadist, but by the early 1990s he had already begun building a torture chamber consisting of a double-wide mobile home situated in nearby, and very isolated, Elephant Butte, close to the lake of the same name. Ray outfitted the large trailer—which he dubbed, with his morbid humor, the Toy Box—with all manner of soundproofing, pulleys, chains, gynecological devices, nail-encrusted dildoes, bondage and stretching devices, stun-guns, cameras and TV monitors, cattle prods, syringes, chemicals, and fortified walls and doors. Ray's macabre paraphernalia were every bit as horrifying as the worst contraptions of the Spanish Inquisition, Hitler's death camps, and Moscow's Lyubyanka prison—the difference being merely one of focus. Ray's primary interest was not in breaking bones, burning, or cutting, but in tortures that concentrated on the organs of sex.

For much of his adult life and apparently even in his teens, Ray's bondage fantasies grew increasingly grotesque, until, in his thirties, he could reach orgasm only by masturbating with the fantasy of murdering a woman. In his forties he began kidnapping and torturing women, subjecting them to painful and degrading sex, with the emphasis on anal sex so typical of sexual sadists of heterosexual orientation—as with Paul Bernardo, mentioned above.

By 1993 he had created what he called an Introductory Tape—a lengthy commentary and description (sixteen pages, single-spaced when transcribed) that his victims were forced to listen to right after they had been lured from bars back to Ray's "home," thrust into the Toy Box, and immobilized—suspended from the ceiling via the pulleys and chains.

We do not know how many years Ray operated as a professional sadist, nor how many victims he ultimately killed and disposed of. Because he was so shrewd at eliminating all evidence of bodily remains—either in the abundant New Mexico desert or in Elephant Butte Lake—no bodies were ever located. His accomplice and fiancée, Cindy Hendy, estimated that Ray had killed over a dozen, perhaps several dozen women following their torture—but she can give no accurate estimate.[28]

In writing this book about evil I was aware from the outset that the most convincing examples of evil acts would be the ones hardest to convey to the reader, without descending to the pornographic and the sensational. It may be, of course, that I am simply preaching to the converted and that you already agree with me that *evil* is the appropriate word to use when we hear of, say, the child murders of Royce Zeigler and Zein Isa or the depravity of Jeff Lundgren. But if you remain uncomfortable with the concept of evil as presented thus far and would say "amen" only upon hearing—or seeing—the torture evidence of David Parker Ray, then I am handicapped. I cannot show you the worst of Ray's hideous but artistically crafted drawings. I cannot reprint here more than a few sentences of the Introductory Tape. I *can* share with you my own experience when trying to read the transcription of the tape: Though I have been studying murderers and their personalities for over twenty years, I could not bring myself to read past the first of its sixteen pages. When I told this to a close friend—a preeminent psychiatrist and former chairman of a prestigious psychiatry department—he said: "Oh, c'mon, Stone, you have to be kidding." But when he started reading, though he did get through most of it, he readily understood my reluctance. Just as hearing (or reading) Ray's words makes one want to turn away, viewing the Toy Box makes one want to look away so as not to dwell beyond one's tolerance upon the suffering Ray's victims had to endure. When a local locksmith, Bill King, was summoned after the arrest to open up the Toy Box, this was his reaction: "I could feel an evil presence in there. It was like something floating in the air, and I didn't want to be there. I'd seen enough."[29] In a like vein, several TV shows reporting on the case titled their programs *The Evil in Elephant Butte*.[30] Here is a brief excerpt from the Introductory Tape:

> My lady friend and I have been keeping sex slaves for years. We both have kinky hang-ups involving rape, dungeon-games, etc. . . . Our fetishes and hang-ups include stringent bondage, a little sadism. . . . You're gonna be here a month or two, or maybe three, if you keep us turned on. If it's up to my lady, we'd keep you indefinitely. She says it's just as much fun and less risky. But personally I like variety.[31]

Reading this brief excerpt, as uncomfortable as it is, can in no way compare to the emotions of a woman immobilized, limbs bound tightly, mouth covered with duct tape, her body hoisted by chains toward the ceiling of the Toy Box, a captive audience to Ray's voice coming from a loudspeaker—announcing what is about to happen to her.

In the dossier accumulated on Ray after his arrest is a file titled "Copies of Drawings Illustrating Women Being Subjected to Sexual Torture," which runs to forty-seven pages.[32] In the least repellent of these pictures, none of which will be shown here, a woman is portrayed tied to a table, bound by a variety of tightening winches and chains, in preparation for electric shocks and whatever other tortures Ray and his accomplice were in the mood for. Oddly, the picture is not pornographic in the sense of arousing one sexually—unless one happens to be a sexual sadist. Instead the picture is at once sickening and clinical—a measure of Ray's utter detachment from the suffering of which his "blueprint" is the harbinger. How can we begin to understand the origins of sexual sadism in men like David Parker Ray or Robert Berdella, Leonard Lake, and Dennis Rader?[33]

All we know at this time is that there are many factors that play a role, some more common and perhaps more significant than others: genetic risk for psychopathy (and certain of its components like thrill seeking and callousness or lack of compassion), parental brutality, father absence, maternal neglect, sexual molestation, low socioeconomic status, mental illness, and so on.[34] But there is no factor that is present across the board in all sexual sadists, and no "crucial" factor without which one never sees sexual sadism. That is, no analogy can be made with the tuberculosis bacillus without which one doesn't get TB. A better analogy is to Persian carpets. Each is made of interwoven strands of different color and thickness (these are the various "factors"), each ends up a Persian rug—but no two are the same; each has its own pattern of colors and shapes. Some are quite similar; they are woven in the same city: Tabriz, Isfahan, Shiraz, and experts can tell which city they came from. In Ray's case, he had a violent father who abandoned the family, a mother who left him in the care of grandparents and saw little of him afterward. There is no suggestion of sexual molestation, yet in his early teens he was already obsessed with bondage and divided the world of women into ladies and whores, the latter as disposable after use as dinner napkins.

Leonard Lake, whom we will discuss a bit further on, was abandoned by his mother when he was a toddler. Robert Berdella had a violent and abusive father. Dennis Rader, whom most know as "BTK," came from a rather normal middle-class home where his mother occasionally spanked him on his backside for naughtiness—which seems to have stirred up sexual excitement. How many millions of boys experienced a similar life at home, or worse, and never became violent, let alone sexual sadists?

I think of a patient I once treated years ago who came from the same town as Jeffrey Dahmer. My patient had been sodomized by his father when he was nine; his older brother used to throw lit matches at him and force his hand onto a hot radiator. He grew up to be a loner: angry, embittered, suspicious, but also a gifted student of languages who hated most people but never laid a hand on anyone. Dahmer's father was a kindly man who did not abuse his son sexually or otherwise; the family was better off economically than was my patient's family. Dahmer's mother seems not to have been very available emotionally. My patient had more "reasons" to be a violent person; Dahmer had fewer of the popular "reasons." Genetic factors probably account for much of the difference—and I will say more about this in the chapter on neuroscience—but these are as yet too ill defined or else hard to detect for us to be able to claim *in advance*: this man is going to be a sadist or a serial killer (or whatever else we are looking for). In any case, the genetic factors account for no more than a tendency, a predisposition that can either be muted by a protective environment later on or else brought to the point of aggressive outbursts by exposure to a harsh environment. We can be fairly certain, at all events, that once the pattern of excitement through sexual cruelty got established in Ray during his teens, the pattern became fixed. There was no going back.

PARENTAL ACTS OF OMISSION AND COMMISSION

What turns that innocent baby boy in the obstetrics ward into a serial killer? Many people seek the answer in bad family circumstances, as if those alone can account for such a drastic detour from the normal path of development. There are two main reasons for this tempting but not very accurate conclusion. First of all, it is rare to find a serial killer who was raised in a family that was even a close approximation of "normal." A family, that is, where mother and father remained together as a harmonious couple, gentle and devoted to their children—whose punishment for "naughtiness" was mild, effective, and fair. Secondly, the departure from this ideal, in the families of serial killers, was often radical—so destructive as to cry out for intervention by the Child Protective Services. A more realistic view would give heredity its due, since any coherent explanation of serial killing lies in the interaction of circumstances both before and after birth. Admittedly, the worse the family environment, the harder it is to see what (if any) genetic factors or problems during pregnancy may also have played a role. This is because a horrific environment can lead all by itself to future violence, including the extreme kinds of violence that we label as evil. This may paper over, as it were, whatever unfavorable prebirth influences that may lie hidden underneath. We will look more closely at these interactions in the chapter on neuroscience, but for now, we will examine four different destructive family influences, using vignettes of serial killers whose early lives were marred by one of these four factors.

Parental Cruelty

James Mitchell ("Mike") DeBardeleben is one of the schizoid psychopaths who swell the ranks of serial killers.[35] He was the middle child in an upper-middle-class family. His father was a lieutenant colonel in the army and was known for his punitiveness toward his sons. When Mike was five, for example, his father would thrust his head underwater as a punishment for various childhood peccadilloes. He also beat Mike on many occasions.[36] His mother was a chronic alcoholic, at times violent in her punishment of Mike for his stubbornness.[37] She was promiscuous, picking up men in bars, especially when her husband was stationed away. Mike was the most rebellious of the children and thus drew the most fire from his parents.

In DeBardeleben's case, parental cruelty (coupled with his mother's promiscuity) merged with what is almost certainly a genetic tendency to psychopathy, as suggested by his rebelliousness.[38] His brother, Ralph, with what may have been a different set of genetic givens, later committed suicide.

Like David Parker Ray, DeBardeleben aspired to create a torture chamber (though he never carried this out). Unlike Ray, he did not have a pleasant social exterior. At his very best, Mike was mean, nasty, and brutal toward his five wives—blackmailing some with pornographic pictures he had them pose for, so they would be too afraid to expose him. He was unspeakably cruel to the twenty or so victims of his serial murders—some of whom he tortured to the point where (as he recorded on tape) they pleaded with him to either stop or kill them.[39] True-crime writer Stephen Michaud saw DeBardeleben not only lacking in the merest trace of decency toward anyone, but "so evil, so unspeakably bad" that he found it difficult to tell his story: "It was too bloody horrible, sustained horror."[40]

DeBardeleben's hatred—demonization would be a better word—of women surely stemmed from his hatred of his mother. He viewed women as whores and sluts, worthy only of being reduced to nullities via rape and murder. In the classification of sexual sadists developed by former FBI profiler, Roy Hazelwood, DeBardeleben was of the "anger-excitation" type that punishes women for supposedly being "evil" and "powerful." Men of this stripe are animated by the urge to eliminate that power.[41] Gary Ridgway, the Green River Killer, also hated his seductive and punitive mother; both he and DeBardeleben can be understood as committing "serial matricide": killing, symbolically, their mothers over and over again. DeBardeleben was much crueler than Ridgway, becoming in his eighteen-year-long career of serial murder a black hole of narcissism, sucking in and destroying any woman who came near. For all that, DeBardeleben was curiously more "philosophic"—if one dare apply that word to a serial killer—in that he penned a psychologically accurate account of what sadism is all about:

> The central impulse [of sadism] is to have complete mastery over another person—to make her the helpless object of our will, to become the absolute ruler over her, to become her god . . . and the most radical aim is to make her suffer, since there is no greater power over another person than that of inflicting pain on her.[42]

Given that purposely causing intense suffering is the heart of what evil is all about, DeBardeleben comes across as a kind of high priest and spokesman among the practitioners of evil. And since serial killers commit the acts we define as evil—routinely and habitually—it is not surprising that evil's high priest should arise from within the ranks of serial killers, rather than the ranks of those who dip into evil just once or twice in their lives, like the wife killers and mass murderers.

Parental Neglect

Since a third of serial killers experienced parental neglect, there are many examples to choose from to demonstrate its effect. Neglect by the mother is more damaging in the first few years of life than neglect by the father, though father absence becomes a serious matter in the lives of boys in their preteen and teenage years.[43] To grow up without a mother's love and without any compensating maternal influences from other sources altogether will tend to rob the child of the qualities we lump together as "human." A boy in these circumstances is at risk to grow up like one of Harry Harlow's monkeys—the ones raised next to a substitute "monkey" made of wire rather than one made of cloth.[44] The monkeys with the wire mothers were deficient in every social and sexual sphere.

Maternally deprived boys and girls grow up handicapped in the same ways. As for the boys, many tend to be filled with envy and hatred of normal people. If they are, in addition, beaten by foster parents or other caretakers, they are more likely than others to lash out violently and to treat other people as though they are no more than inanimate objects to be smashed or carved up at will.

Leonard Lake was a California man born in 1945 to Elgin and Gloria Lake. Elgin abandoned the family after the birth of Leonard's younger brother. Gloria later tried to reunite with him, taking along the two younger children and leaving Leonard in the care of her parents. He was never reunited with his mother even after she divorced and remarried when Leonard was nine.[45] What contact he did have with his mother was far from perfect: she encouraged him to take nude photos of girls, including his sister and cousins—as if to develop pride in the body—but with the effect of his developing instead a preoccupation with pornography and, later, a penchant for having sex with his sister. Like David Parker Ray, he was intact enough to sandwich in two marriages before he teamed up with an illegal immigrant, Charles Ng, to create a torture-bunker in a remote area, where they captured and tortured some two dozen people (mostly women), reducing their remains to ashes in an adjoining crematorium. Of some of their victims they made "snuff films"—films that depict the victim's murder. Lake's second marriage went aground when his wife discovered he been making amateur pornographic films featuring bondage acts.[46] Lake was devastated for a time after the divorce, yet he then felt free to do anything he wanted, commenting, "Society is powerless against one who is not afraid to die." What makes Lake noteworthy, placing him, along with Ray and DeBardeleben, at the end of the Gradations scale, was his compulsive diary keeping, where his extreme acts of sadism were faithfully recorded for posterity. Like the monkey reared with the wire mother, Lake couldn't make normal connections. He spoke of his envy of beautiful women and rich men who always end up getting the best of life and of whom Lake said, "I live to correct this."[47] As for Lake's participation in evil, this is best grasped by viewing one of his filmed scenes. He and Ng captured a young mother, Brenda O'Connor. They had already killed her baby, but she didn't know this. When she begged for her baby, Lake engaged in the following dialogue:

Lake: Brenda, you have a choice. We'll give it to you right now.

Brenda: What?

Lake: You can cooperate with us . . . that means you will stay here as our prisoner. You will work for us, you will wash for us, you will fuck for us. Or you can say, "No, I don't want to do that," in which case we'll tie you to the bed, we'll rape you, and then we'll take you outside and shoot you. Your choice.[48]

Later, when arrested—ironically, for theft, by a policeman who knew nothing of the torture-murders—Lake committed suicide, swallowing two cyanide pills. Looking back on the crimes of Lake and his younger accomplice, I feel compelled to add a footnote to my definition of evil. Beyond the world where we can say *tout comprendre c'est tout pardonner*—to understand all is to forgive all—lies a world where we can understand, but not forgive. The bondage and enslavement of Lake's women victims were Lake's antidote to the abandonment and neglect by his mother: Lake's women were immobilized and held captive. And taking a page from DeBardeleben, his torture of a woman showed that he had (godlike) power over them, rather than the woman/mother having power over Lake. But his fury at his mother's abandonment made him go the extra step and kill them. So much for my "psychoanalysis" of Leonard Lake. But what he did to these women takes him to a world where there is no forgiveness. When people speak of evil, this is the world they are talking about.

Parental Humiliation

About two serial killers out of three suffered humiliation from one or both parents. There are certain kinds of put-downs that are hard for young boys or adolescents to shake off, especially hurtful remarks about sexuality, lack of manliness, stupidity at school, or odd physical features (including being grossly overweight). Humiliation, if severe enough and prolonged, can create a vicious circle, undermining the boy's self-esteem, making him more hurt or more angry and argumentative with the overly critical parent, who retaliates by further humiliation, and so on. The serial killers who were humiliated usually endured other negative experiences as well, but sometimes this particular misery seemed to be the one that overshadowed all the others.

Gerald Gallego, for example, was raised by his mother and a stepfather; he never knew his birth father. Like many serial killers, bed-wetting was a problem for much longer than is usually the case—and for this he got taunted by his stepfather, who dubbed him "pissy-pants." Of course there's more to the story with Gallego. It came out at his trial, after he was arrested for killing women and dumping them by the side of the road. Apparently his birth father had killed two policemen—and had dumped their bodies by the side of the road (for which the elder Gallego was executed).[49] I'm sure there are no genes for dumping bodies by the side of the road—but the son may have inherited some genes (genes that relate to *aggression*, for example) that, when mixed with the humiliation, heightened the risk for violence.

Jerry Brudos, a serial killer of some dozen or more women in Oregon, liked to wear his mother's shoes when he was a boy of five.[50] A strict, puritanical woman, she grabbed and destroyed the shoes, shaming him that what he had done was "wicked."[51] But a pattern got established, no doubt fixed for all time, by his mother's making such an issue of his boyhood experimentation. By his teen years, he was collecting and hiding shoes and women's underwear; touching these articles of clothing was both soothing and sexually exciting. His activities passed a line in the sand when he was seventeen: he became violent, demanding at knifepoint that a girl of his age strip naked. When caught, he was sent for a psychiatric evaluation; the conclusion was that he had a hatred toward his mother, which then gave rise to a thirst for revenge against women in general. In his late twenties he progressed to serial sexual murders, violating the bodies of his victims usually after they were dead, not only having sex with the corpses but in some instances removing a breast—and using it as a mold for a paperweight.

Brudos was a psychopath: utterly callous and without remorse, not all of which, I think, can be laid at his mother's doorstep. There are plenty of little boys whose mothers made them feel emasculated for trying on their shoes who never grow up to do the things that Jerry Brudos did. So he may have come into the world with some of the genetic low cards as well. As for the "no remorse" factor, a journalist once asked Brudos when he was languishing in prison for the serial murders, "Jerry, now that you've been here a while and can look back on your life, do you have any different thoughts about those women you killed?" Whereupon Brudos rolled up a little piece of paper into a wad, flicked it onto the floor, and said, "I care about those women as much as I care about that paper-wad."

Parental Seduction

Not all serial killers had been seduced by a mother or sodomized by a father. Some were sexually molested in their early years by a foster parent. This kind of premature introduction to the sexual life often has the effect, through its overstimulation, of making the child both preoccupied with sex and "hypersexual." A boy born with genetic risk for violence who is then exposed to such an erotically "turned-on" environment may steer his course toward sexual crimes rather than, say, embezzlement or bank robbing. I chose for my example here a man, Tommy Lynn Sells, I had interviewed on death row in Texas, not so much because he was one of the few who was seduced by a foster parent, but because he could talk about it with unusual candor. Most murderers and men on death row claim innocence and lie about their crimes, especially if the victim(s) were family members (think of Scott Peterson and his pregnant wife, Laci).[52]

Tommy Lynn Sells was born, along with his twin sister, Tammy Jean, in 1964 in California of uncertain paternity. They both came down with meningitis when they were a year and a half old; Tammy Jean died. His mother was poor and was overwhelmed with trying to care for the other children and sent Tommy to an aunt, but when he was about eight, he was sent to live with a man who gave him food and shelter—but at a price. The man was a pedophile and made Tommy give him oral sex.[53] Sells did poorly in school, was mocked by the other students because he spoke differently and had fewer possessions than they did, but he learned to "level the playing field" through violence. He had to fend for himself in his teens and became a drifter, going from state to state (in the South mostly), doing crimes of theft to put food in his mouth and crimes of violence to get even with those he hated: the women who had abandoned him and the pedophile who seduced him. Even his mother shifted at times between seductiveness and rejection. Sells began murdering in his teens: first, men who crossed his path, but later on, women and even children. By the time he was caught, he had killed, according to his reckoning—whose accuracy is hard to verify—some seventy people. What led to his arrest was the attempted murder of a young girl whose throat he had slit after sneaking into the trailer where she and a friend were sleeping. The friend died, but the other girl was able to walk, bleeding profusely, to a neighbor, and also gave the police a description of her assailant.

Many of Sells's murders were horrific, including that of the Dardeen family in 1987 in Illinois. After being invited to a meal with the family, he shot the husband, beat the wife and their three-year-old son to death. During the beating, the pregnant wife spontaneously delivered a baby girl whom he also beat to death.[54]

Yet, Sells had the kind of charm that Ray and Lake also had: he married several times and had two children, in among all the slaughter.

When I had the opportunity to interview Sells on death row in Texas, my reaction—before I actually met him—was that I would like to kill him for all the atrocious rapes and murders he had committed. Death row interviews are always conducted in special cubicles where three inches of glass separate the visitor from the inmate. My opening comment was: "Well, Tommy, I guess they got these three inches of glass so I don't kill you and you don't kill me!" He laughed and said, with a broad Texan twang: "You got that rahht!" But then he told me with remarkable candor about the man who violated him when he was a boy of eight and nine, and about the hatred this (and everything else that had happened to him) filled his mind with ever after.[55] Tommy spoke to me about the "adrenaline rush" he got when he slit the throat of a victim and saw the blood rushing out. "That settled down my anger for a couple weeks," he told me, until, that is, the hatred built up again, and he craved another murderous "fix." He was also forthright enough to acknowledge to me that were he to feel full remorse, instead of just a little bit, he'd have to go kill himself for all the terrible things he'd done. This was the voice of a conscience, however meager and beaten down. And within the vast desert of damage and depravity that surrounded his life, there was this oasis of humanity, miniature though it was, that allowed me to feel a measure of compassion for this man.

All but a few of the murderers I have interviewed in prisons and forensic hospitals have lied and denied—and in so doing, have earned a contempt that is by no means easily overcome. This does not mean that the public was wrong in considering the serial murders of Tommy Lynn

Sells as "evil." Far from it. It suggests, however, that in some people evil can coexist with a few human qualities one would scarcely imagine were there underneath. Sells has indicated that what launched him on his career as a murderer was his having witnessed, inadvertently, during the Peeping Tom days of his adolescence, a neighbor who had his son perform oral sex on him. This reminded him, so he told me, of his male caretaker of a few years before. But this may be a self-serving memory of dubious authenticity. So what earned my measure of compassion was not his honesty, for that was not unimpeachable; it was not his remorse, for that was meager. It was rather his candor about what had happened to him during his early years, and about the destructive (and ultimately self-destructive) path of vengeance he then pursued.

I am often asked by friends who knew I had been going around the country interviewing serial killers: Was I ever frightened, or even a bit anxious, as I faced these men? I *was* anxious, as it turned out, before the first such interview, wondering what it would be like to sit across from a man who had killed people by the dozen—and not even in combat or when ordered to partake in "ethnic cleansing" but in peacetime, and just because killing was what he liked to do. My first interview was with Arthur Shawcross, who had killed a dozen prostitutes in Rochester, New York. There were, of course, guards all around, and Arthur himself is disarmingly jovial. My anxiety quickly dissipated. By the time I interviewed Tommy Lynn Sells, I felt like an old hand at it and wasn't anxious at all. Not consciously anyway. But there must have been something about his "adrenaline rush" at slitting the throats of all those young girls that left its imprint on my brain despite my nonchalance during the interview, for that night I had the following dream:

> *I am in the reception room where a receiving line has formed to congratulate Hitler on his reelection to some office. Hitler is in military uniform, shaking everyone's hand as each one has his turn. It is 1954—nine years after Hitler's suicide, but I am not aware of this in the dream. I am about tenth in line, and as I approach, I feel ill at ease, thinking: Shake the hand of Hitler? I want to kill him! But would killing Hitler be a crime? Would it be murder? My mentor, Dr. Kernberg, is standing off to one side, so I go up to him and ask: "Otto, I feel I should kill Hitler. But would that be murder?" He ponders a moment, but then tells me: "Well, in the case of Hitler, no, it would not be murder; it would be all right."*

The meaning was pretty clear to me. My feelings toward Sells were very divided. It was as though he were two people scrunched together into one enormous person, as he had indeed become after years of prison-fare carbohydrates: one man who was disarmingly jovial, like Shawcross, but who could talk with candor about his past and about his deeds. And a second man, who inspired fear and loathing for the murders of all those women and children. Before I met him, I felt like killing him. After I met him, I felt respect for Sells—for his acknowledging openly what he had done, and for the small seeds of remorse that were beginning to sprout in this man. Confronting the half-human, half-demon "split-self" that Sells had become evoked the same sort of split in me: half-homicidally contemptuous, half-compassionate. Small wonder that I summoned Otto Kernberg as my adviser in the dream: When he was a boy, he had once seen Hitler during the first days of the 1938 Austrian *Anschluss*, and had then escaped with his family. And he went on to become the world's leading authority on the psychological defense mechanism of splitting, which takes place when we try to grapple with totally disparate, oil-and-water emotions, usually of love and hate, that we cannot comfortably integrate.

OTHER FACTORS

Among the many threads that make up the tapestry of serial murder, some are common, detectable in almost every case; others are rare yet very noticeable when present. In the closing sections of this chapter I will touch on several of the more important of these as-yet-unexamined threads.

Adoption

Adoptees make up about 2 percent of the population in the United States. The vast majority are adopted into homes with loving and devoted parents; the adopted children, however curious they may be about their birth parents, grow up as reasonably well-adjusted people, leading constructive, gratifying lives. But if we look at crime statistics, especially in the tiny arena of serial killers, the story is not so optimistic.

The FBI, reporting on 500 serial killers, found that 16 percent had been adoptees.[56] In my study of 145 serial killers, 15.8 percent were adoptees —basically the same conclusion.[57]

Being an adoptee can create problems in several ways. Since we're talking about serial killers here, I am focusing only on boys. The boy might, for example, resent having been given up by his birth mother, becoming, even though he is happy with his adoptive mother, an embittered, angry person. This was the case with David Berkowitz, the "Son of Sam." He had been adopted by middle-class parents who were loving, consistently there for him, and not at all abusive. A social misfit and loner, he went downhill after the death of his adoptive mother. In his teens he set fires and tortured animals. He pictured his birth mother as promiscuous and indifferent; he earned his celebrity status by shooting to death girls (and a few young men) who were making out in lovers' lanes around town—equating the girls with the kind of promiscuous, unmotherly woman his birth mother seemed to have been. Since there are thousands of adopted boys in similar circumstances—who never commit crimes, let alone serial murder—there has to be something else wrong with this picture. Did Berkowitz have a violent birth father? Did the birth mother abuse alcohol in the first months of pregnancy? We don't know. But we are pretty sure his life *after* he was adopted did not contribute to his later violence.

Joel Rifkin, the serial killer of seventeen or so prostitutes in Long Island, was also raised by adoptive parents who were caring, devoted, and well-to-do.[58] Here again, the less we can find wrong with his life once he was born, the more we have to assume there were troubles in the genes or in the mother's pregnancy. These factors we examine further in the chapter on neuroscience.

Charles Schmid presents a more complicated picture: adopted at birth, he was raised by parents who were generous and indulgent in the main, though his father and he got into frequent arguments and sometimes his father was physically abusive. Schmid was clearly psychopathic: charming, glib, grandiose, dishonest (to impress women he rigged a guitar with tapes of famous guitar players), and thrill seeking (he liked to do parachute jumps, not pulling the opening cord until the last second). So the evil, as defined by his serial murders, seemed to come from three parts nature and one part nurture. Perhaps more injurious than his father's beatings was the response of his birth mother after Schmid tracked her down during his adolescence. She said, "I didn't want you when you were born, and I don't want you now. Get out!"[59]

The situation with Gerald Stano was even more complicated and raises the question whether good adoptive parents can make up for truly horrendous circumstances that were limited to the first few months of life. Stano was adopted as a one-year-old (having been given up for adoption at six months) from a promiscuous, alcoholic mother who neglected him to such an extent that he was considered unadoptable by the doctors in upstate New York. The neglect was such that he was found eating his own feces in order to survive.[60] Eugene Stano was the manager of a large corporation; his wife was a social worker. They were devoted parents who provided all the comforts of upper-middle-class life. But Gerald began stealing early on and progressed to worse behaviors later: he bribed schoolmates (with money he stole from his father) to let him win races so he would look successful in his parents' eyes, he abused drugs, and was violent with women, including the wife he was briefly married to when he was twenty-four (in 1975). Well before that, he committed his first murder, when he was eighteen. Eleven years later he was in prison for the murders of forty-one women, though the total may have been even greater. He claimed to experience sexual arousal from the slow strangulation of his victims. Stano was executed in 1998 when he was forty-six. Raymond Neal, whose sister had been murdered by Stano, was present at the execution. For him, Stano was an evil man, a monster, and Neal felt relief when Stano was pronounced dead.[61]

There is a tendency in modern societies to view vengeance as a barbarity; ditto, the death penalty. These issues go beyond the scope of this book. Suffice it to say that the desire for vengeance when one has been grievously wronged answers to something deep within us. This is illustrated beautifully in a recent article in the *New Yorker* about life among the tribes in New Guinea, the subtitle of which is, "What can tribal societies tell us about the need to get even?"[62] The author argues persuasively that the "thirst for vengeance is among the strongest of human emotions," adding (on the last page) that "[w]e grow up being taught that such feelings are primitive, something to be ashamed of, and to transcend." My only point here is that transcendence comes hard when your sister has been strangled by a serial killer.

Head Injury

One in four serial killers suffered during their early years either a head injury or (more rarely) a condition affecting the brain—such as meningitis or a very high fever. A good deal depends on just which part of the brain was damaged. But if the "right" regions were damaged, such damage could have serious consequences on self-control, on sizing up social situations correctly, tuning in to other people empathically, resonating with them compassionately, and so forth. The effects of such head injuries are hardly limited to serial killers but are important as precursors to crimes of all sorts. Usually when head injury is part of a killer's history, it is interwoven with other negative circumstances: having been beaten as a child (including on the head, as in the case of serial killer Henry Lee Lucas[63]), being mentally ill, or being at risk for psychopathic personality. But sometimes serious head injury seems to be the only background factor even in a serial killer.

Richard Starrett came from a well-to-do family in Georgia. The parents were good people and spared him the kind of physical or verbal abuse or the neglect that was part of the picture in the lives of so many other serial killers. He suffered a head injury when he was a toddler and an even more severe one when he was seven. On that occasion he had been hanging upside down on a jungle-gym in the playground and fell onto the asphalt, unconscious. His mother rushed him to the hospital, but doctors found nothing seriously wrong at that time.[64] Shortly afterward, however, Starrett began to have headaches, dizzy spells, blackouts, and moments of collapsing. He loved animals yet became intrigued with sadistic magazines that emphasized bondage. He became a Peeping Tom in adolescence, and by the time he went to college, he was hearing internal voices and had headaches that were triggered by violence or sex magazines. Rather than finish college, he dropped out and went to California because of uncontrollable urges to stalk women. Yet he was able to marry when he was twenty-three and have a daughter, though he still suffered blackouts, headaches, and "absences." Back in Georgia for a time, he had a love affair with another woman, but when she discovered he was married, "something happened." He said he removed a gun from a drawer so she wouldn't see it—and it accidentally went off, killing her. Maybe. I think a betting man would put more money on murder. It was after that, at all events, that Starrett began to meet and overpower women for sex: he would then indulge in bondage and torture, killing about ten women before he was arrested. Now serving a life sentence, he himself figured his head injuries were the main reason he ended up with damaged brain function and an abnormal electroencephalogram, along with the paraphilia (as defined below) of bondage. All these led ultimately, in Starrett's case, to the serial murders. Starrett even felt remorse for his crimes, which is unusual in a serial killer. This suggests that he was not a psychopath—certainly not from birth—but rather someone whose behavior was shunted way out of line by brain damage in key areas. Which areas those are I will outline in detail in the chapter on neuroscience.

Paraphilias

Sexual urges directed at nonhuman objects (including animals) or the infliction of suffering and humiliation on a sexual partner or children are viewed together under the heading of "paraphilia." In hearing about a person with a paraphilia (almost all such persons are men), the public may react with bewilderment or disgust if the paraphilia is not very harmful. The Peeping Tom (voyeurism) or the "flasher" (exhibitionism)—even the man who rubs against a woman on trains or subways (frotteurism) will seldom be called "evil." Public opinion becomes much more severe where harm is involved or when the degree of depravity is extreme. Men who engage in or force sex on children (pedophilia), or who eat a victim's flesh (cannibalism), or who have sex with a corpse (necrophilia) are far more likely to be labeled evil by ordinary people or by the media. This goes double for men who rely on murder for sexual arousal (sexual sadism), which is the case with many serial killers: at least 30 percent. Tying up and immobilizing a victim (bondage) is often a prelude to the more harmful (and lethal) paraphilias, since once immobilized, the victim is under the total control of a man who is free to do exactly as he pleases.

Just how a man develops a paraphilia is not well understood. Both genes and family environment appear to play a role. The subject will be treated more fully in the chapter on neuroscience, but it does appear that many men with one or more paraphilias have either witnessed inappropriate sexual encounters during childhood, or were themselves sexually molested in some way. But this is not always the case: some men seem to be born with brain differences in certain areas that incline them to develop a paraphilia, even in the absence of childhood maltreatment. Sexual sadism in a man like Tommy Lynn Sells, who as a child was maltreated in every way we can imagine, is less surprising as an outcome. But that same paraphilia—the hallmark of serial killing—is quite surprising in a man whose childhood seems reasonably normal . . . and to that extent, all the more intriguing from the standpoint of a possible heredity factor.

Dennis Rader, who baffled the Kansas authorities for the better part of two decades when he embarked on his career as a serial killer, gave himself the nickname BTK—for bind-torture-kill.[65] By the time he was finally caught, he had killed ten people. The long interval between the first murder and the arrest had partly to do with his cleverness and partly with his leading a double life—the other half of which was that of an ordinary married father of two, well dressed in a business suit, and president of his local church. His double life extended down to his being able to juggle sadistic sex with his victims and "vanilla" sex with his wife, who had no idea of his other self.

We know little about his early life, apart from the fact that when he was spanked by his mother, he used to have erections. Already by age eight or nine, he developed sadistic sexual fantasies, though in other respects his façade to the outside world was unremarkable. The progression from fantasy to paraphilia was not long in coming: he had a whole menu of paraphilias, most of them the dangerous ones. Besides dressing in women's clothes (transvestism—a nonharmful variety), there were also pedophilia, bondage, sexual sadism, and yet another, characterized by hanging oneself briefly so as to experience a stronger orgasm when masturbating (called "autoerotic asphyxiophilia"). As for the sexual sadism, during the Otero murders, which he committed at age twenty-nine in 1974, he had an orgasm when he killed the eleven-year-old Josie Otero, marking this as a distinctly a sexual crime. A hint that his perversions arose from genetic peculiarities (or possibly birth complications) is the fact that Rader had three brothers who are apparently normal. Because a complex personality trait depends on the interaction of many genes, and on their subsequent interaction with the environment, it is not to be expected that even relatives as close as his three brothers would develop the same abnormality.[66]

What is particularly chilling about Dennis Rader as a serial killer is this: here is a church president in (what looks like) a Brooks Brothers suit, well mannered, articulate, suave, forthright, telling the judge about strangling this or that woman with no more inflection in his voice than you or I would have were we to read to a friend a newspaper ad for lawn chairs or a travel clock. This is a man who took an intermission from murder so that, like any good dad, he could attend his kids' athletic games.[67] The point being: he was more like you or me than any other of the serial killers, meaning that—outwardly—we are not so different from Dennis Rader. Perhaps this is why Phil Kline, the attorney general, told people at Rader's trial: "In a few minutes you will look face-to-face with pure evil. . . . Victims whose voices were brutally silenced by the evil of one man."[68] In Rader's case, evil resides not only in what he did, but in the distance required for the rest of us to reassure ourselves that, well, at the end of the day, *on the inside at least, we're not at all like Rader*! Perhaps this kind of distancing helps account for the public's fascination with Ted Bundy, charming, handsome, smart—not so different from us. Whereas, when it comes to a ghoulish freak like Ed Gein or Richard Chase, "evil" appears to reside not just in the grotesqueness of their acts but in their bizarre thoughts and attire. We already feel pretty secure that we could never be like them. Their evil strikes us, comfortably, as totally "alien" to ourselves.

The Triad

As mentioned earlier, boys who set fires, torture animals, and wet the bed long past the age when other children gain bladder control are known to be at risk for behaving in violent ways as they grow older. Killing or torturing the kinds of animals that children usually cherish as pets—cats, dogs, and rabbits—is probably the key element here, since these animals are the closest, in the child's mind, to people. So it is not surprising that serial killers were much more likely, in their early days, to have tortured animals than were the men who killed their wives.[69] Boys who are on the path to becoming serial killers and who have an underlying hatred of women will often resort to killing cats as a kind of rehearsal for murdering women. It is easy to see why, given that, apart from the ears, cats look like beautiful women in miniature: heart-shaped face, high cheekbones, big eyes, small nose, demure mouth, coy expression. Animal torture when combined with one of the dangerous paraphilias like bondage or sexual sadism makes for an even greater predictor of repeated sexual crimes. Men who kill their wives rarely show these types of predilection. It is for reasons of this sort that those who end up being called "evil" (as defined by the extreme of depravity and victim suffering that characterize their acts) are likely to have exhibited such destructive behaviors as bondage, fire setting, and animal torture. Within the realm of serial killers, this childhood "triad" is a significant tip-off to future violence against humans.[70]

Gary Ridgway, who was later to achieve notoriety as Washington State's Green River Killer, ultimately killed, by his own inexact reckoning, about seventy women. He targeted prostitutes, though some of his victims were not. Unlike most of the well-known serial killers whose IQs tend to be well above average, Gary's IQ was below normal (82), but this was no impediment to his career as a serial killer—a career that spanned as many years as that of Dennis Rader. Gary's mother was apparently very attractive but equally cruel. When he wet his bed, his mother would parade him naked in front of his two half-brothers and make him stand in a tub of cold water, while she herself was half-naked, staring at his genitals.[71] His mother's alternating cruelty and seductiveness got transformed in Gary's mind into violent fantasies of killing her and, later, other women with a knife. During his teen years he killed cats and birds and also set fires. Gary began his serial killing in earnest after he learned that his first wife had cheated on him—which made her into a "whore" in his mind. Though psychopathic, he could be a friendly and helpful neighbor. Gary read the Bible, went to church, and encouraged neighbors to take God more fully into their lives.[72]

He seemed genuinely in love with Judith, his third wife. I happened to meet Judith when she and I were guests on the Montel Williams TV show in 2007 (and Gary was already in prison). She told the audience that during the years they were together, the frequency of his killing declined appreciably, as though he were finally happy enough, once he was with a good woman, that the destructive urge was no longer so strong. Of course, she only learned this after Gary's arrest. During their marriage, she knew nothing of his secret activities. When first arrested and interviewed by the police and by the FBI, Gary was for the most part amiable and calm. But when asked why he dumped by the river the bodies of the women he strangled, he suddenly grew angry and said,

"The women were garbage!" The general feeling was that Gary had been committing a kind of serial matricide, killing his sexy but hated mother again and again.[73]

Substance Abuse

Abuse of alcohol or other drugs is common in serial killers: almost half (45 percent) drank alcohol to excess, and another 7 percent used other drugs, such as marijuana, cocaine, or methamphetamine. The larger group that abused alcohol could be divided into a somewhat bigger half (of men that used alcohol exclusively) and a smaller group where the men relied on multiple substances: alcohol *plus* cocaine or LSD or whatever. But people who commit violent crimes (whether or not they reach the level of evil) often abuse drugs to work up the nerve, in many cases, to do what they're itching to do.[74] This is true for serial killers as well. It would be no exaggeration to say that serial killers are addicted to serial killing the way cocaine addicts are addicted to cocaine. As we saw with Tommy Lynn Sells, murder gave him both sexual release and at the same time, release of the pent-up rage he felt against the world.

The ordinary and rhythmic build-up of sexual tension in men[75]—which in general demands release with greater urgency in men than in women—gets intertwined with the periodic need in serial killers to seek victims and to rape and kill them. And for a good half or more of them, alcohol (or whatever is the killer's drug of choice) is the fuel that gets the engine going. How alcohol affects the brain, acting as a catalyst to violence, will be shown in more detail in the chapter on neuroscience. The short explanation is that (as almost everyone has had a chance to witness at some time or other) alcohol (or cocaine or meth) lowers inhibition; the drugs take one's foot off the brakes, making it easier to *do* what one merely *felt like doing* before guzzling the beer or the whiskey or doing the line of cocaine.

Jack Unterweger was born a few years after World War II in Vienna. His mother was a barmaid (whom Jack later characterized, probably incorrectly, as a prostitute); his father was an American GI whose identity remains uncertain. Raised partly by his maternal grandfather in rural Austria, Jack began abusing alcohol by age twelve. This was followed by a period of juvenile delinquency: he committed theft, fraud, burglary, and robbery. He committed his first murder when he was twenty-four. By this time, he had grown into a highly intelligent and boyishly handsome charmer—a kind of Middle European counterpart to America's Ted Bundy. Initially sentenced to life in prison, his stay was downgraded—with a softness in sentencing that has come to typify postwar European courts—to fifteen years.

While in prison, Jack wrote an autobiography called *Purgatory, or the Life in Prison*, which, unbeknownst to the public, was filled with self-serving lies and distortions.[76] The book won Unterweger many ardent supporters from the leftist and counterculture press. He was even able to con various psychiatrists, who convinced themselves and the public that he was a changed man, remorseful and cured of his hostility toward women. This helped accelerate his release in May of 1990. It wasn't long afterward that Unterweger used his considerable charm both to acquire girlfriends and supporters (who succeeded in launching a movie about his book)—as well as female victims, whom he sodomized, bound with ligatures, strangled, and murdered in the Vienna woods. He even managed to go to Los Angeles, ostensibly to "study" prostitutes in that city, and murdered three prostitutes in the same fashion as the female victims back home.

Like many serial killers, Jack had a "signature" killing method: he strangled his victims with their own bras. A classic sexual sadist, he experienced orgasm at the moment of strangling the women to death. When he was finally arrested, his former supporters were dumbstruck at how they had been conned and betrayed. When rearrested and put back in prison in 1994, he showed his loyalty to the choking method, twisting the strings in his prison clothing into a noose—and hanging himself. There is yet a final twist. Because he died before he could appeal the verdict for his eleven murders, the verdict—according to the peculiarities of Austrian law—is not valid. So in Austrian eyes, he is still, officially at least, "innocent."[77]

There are eerie similarities between the Unterweger case and that of another accomplished psychopath, Jack Henry Abbott. Born to an American soldier and a Chinese prostitute in 1944, he was in and out of foster homes, became a juvenile delinquent, and served time in Utah for forgery. His stay there was extended after he stabbed a fellow inmate to death. Inspired by Norman Mailer's book about Gary Gilmore's murder and eventual execution, Abbott wrote *In the Belly of the Beast*. Thanks to Mailer's support (but despite the misgivings of the prison officials), Abbott won release on parole in 1981. A scant six weeks after winning his freedom, Abbott, lunching in a small New York City café, argued with the aspiring playwright Richard Adan, son-in-law of the owner, and stabbed him to death.[78] Back in prison, he wrote another book—but this one was unsuccessful. He came up for possible parole in 2001 but was turned down because he expressed no remorse for the murder. A year later, fashioning a noose with shoelaces and bedsheets, Abbott hanged himself.[79]

Chapter Eight

THE FAMILY AT ITS WORST

Canto XI, ll. 25–27

Ma perché frode è de l'uom proprio male, più spiace a Dio; e però stan di sotto li frodolente, e più dolor li assale.	But because fraud is an evil proper to man it is more displeasing to God, and therefore the fraudulent have a lower place, and greater pain assails them.

The serial killers whose backgrounds and deeds we analyzed in the last chapter could easily be labeled as evil: all of them murdered repeatedly, and half of them subjected their victims to prolonged torture. Predictably, the word *evil* was used in the courtroom, in the media, and in the comments by the public when describing either the pain these victims were made to suffer or the men who had inflicted this cruelty. The victims of serial killers are almost invariably strangers; when their deaths are discovered, law enforcement and crime scene investigators become involved, headlines get written, and the community is alerted (and understandably frightened). This is public evil. But there are similar acts that take place within the family—and that often go undetected for long periods because the family is a sacrosanct unit not readily invaded by those outside.

English law is particularly famous for advancing the thesis that a man's home is his castle. This was underlined in a famous murder case in the English midlands in 1860, when a three-year-old boy, Saville Kent, was murdered and mutilated by one of the inhabitants in an upper-middle-class manor house. The local police were loath to examine the family, let alone to point the finger at one of its members. With great reluctance a Detective Wicher from London was finally summoned to investigate, even though this meant "violating a sacred space."[1] One of the local papers had this to say: "Unlike the tenant of a foreign domicile, the occupier of an English house, whether it be mansion or cottage, possesses the indisputable title against every kind of aggression upon his threshold. . . . It is this that converts the moorside cottage into a castle."[2] Thanks to Detective Wicher's unwanted intrusions, he was able to piece together who was the responsible party and why it was that the sleeping boy's throat was slit in the middle of the night, his body unceremoniously dumped in the family cesspool. It was not the butler. It was his sixteen-year-old half sister Constance, who had become morbidly jealous of the attention bestowed upon the little boy by her stepmother—her own mother having died, insane, when Constance was eight. What Wicher had the misfortune to uncover had been hidden behind a "mesh of deception and concealment."[3] His detective work earned him the opprobrium of the townspeople, who now had to confront the fact that "one of their own"—from the highly respectable family of Road Hill House—had murdered the boy. Just as in detective stories and murder mysteries—which the Road Hill House case actually inspired[4]—many family members were initially suspects, and each had something to hide, which led them to lie, dissimulate, and refuse to cooperate with the police, even if they were innocent.

Fast-forward 150 years, and the family is still the sanctuary and safe house it is—under ideal circumstances—supposed to be and usually is. But sometimes terrible things can go on inside the home that none on the outside are at all aware of. Similarly, when murder, mutilation, torture, crushing humiliation, and other forms of inhumane treatment within the family are eventually brought to light, we are as quick to respond with the term *evil* as our instant reaction—just as though the same kind of crime were committed by a stranger. Often our reaction is even stronger, because we inherently assume that parents, for example, would be far less likely to commit such an outrage against their own flesh and blood.

I had planned at first to title this chapter *Parents from Hell*, but I had to acknowledge that terrible crimes, including torture, may have their source in family members other than the biological parents: spouses, for instance, or siblings, surrogate parents and caretakers, and even children. Some of the examples here come from newspapers and magazines rather than from full biographies. From these briefer sources, we get to know more about the *who* and the *how* than about the *why*. Since this is a book that explores the "why" question, I apologize in advance for not being able to share as much about the underlying causes as you and I would like to know.

PARENTS FROM HELL

Recently in Austria, an incident came to light (literally) that is unparalleled in the annals of crime. Josef Fritzl, a seventy-three-year-old engineer in the southern Austrian town of Amstetten,[5] fathered seven children by his wife Rosemarie. In 1977 he imprisoned one of his daughters, Elizabeth, age eighteen, in a bunker he had carefully constructed underneath his house (a project begun several years before her imprisonment). He first drugged her with ether, then dragged her into the bunker, handcuffing her at first to a metal pole—there either to be raped and fed, or not raped and starved. We can hear the words of Leonard Lake echoing in the walls: "Your choice!" She "chose" incest. In that dark cellar, Fritzl fathered yet another seven children through incest with Elizabeth. His daughter and her children did not see the light of day until twenty-four years later, when Elizabeth was let out for the first time, at age forty-two, because her first-born (then nineteen) had become gravely ill and was obviously medically unattended. The story came out when the girl was hospitalized.

This was not the first of Fritzl's offenses. Earlier, he had tossed one of Elizabeth's babies, allegedly a stillborn, into the furnace.[6] He had once been in prison for rape years before. A woman from Linz came forward after the children had been freed accusing Fritzl of having raped her years ago.

We know very little about Fritzl's early life, other than that he grew up in the Nazi era and had a "domineering mother whom he loved desperately."[7] During his adult life, he had also been domineering, insisting on total obedience. He was good at lying, too—telling his wife that Elizabeth had "run away to join a Satanic cult" when she disappeared (to the cellar bunker just below where his wife was standing!) in 1977. Fritzl had apparently turned away from his wife when he felt the bloom was off the rose regarding her looks; she had also become good and tired of his bullying. Elizabeth at eighteen was prettier and, once a captive, left her father free from any worries that she would leave him.[8] As for Elizabeth's children, they had spent their entire lives like the imaginary prisoners in Plato's *Republic*, chained in such a way that they could only see shadow-images in two dimensions cast by a fire in back of them like puppets between the fire and the prisoners.[9] They had hitherto glimpsed the outside world only on the two-dimensional screen of the television and were dumbfounded when, released to the light of the day, they saw real three-dimensional cars and houses and, most astonishing of all, the sun. Equally astonishing to those of us familiar with American law, sex offenses older than ten years are wiped off the slate in Austria, and even Fritzl's crime carries a sentence no longer than fifteen years. So we are left with the "why" question.

Aside from Fritzl's boundless narcissism and psychopathy and his contemptuous disregard for the well-being of his fourteen children (Elizabeth, the six now shamed by their father's scandal, and the seven children born of incest and burdened not only with that shame but also with their enforced ignorance of the real world), was he also hoping to create a new race of people, all with blood-loyalty to Papa Fritzl? There is some precedent for this. In Philadelphia during the mid-1980s, self-styled preacher Gary Heidnick chained a number of black women to the wall of his cellar, where he tried to impregnate them with the goal of creating a race of people loyal to Papa Heidnick.[10] The experiment was a flop: the tortured women didn't conceive, and Heidnick killed and dismembered them, burying their remains in the backyard. Heidnick committed suicide in prison, whereas Fritzl, in his post-capture photos, and although called "evil" in the press, appears gleeful.[11]

I can't help interjecting a note about *evolutionary psychiatry* at this point. It has to do with the idea of "fitness." Fitness, from the standpoint of evolution, is a measure of how many offspring an animal leaves into the next generation. In the case of humans, this means how many living children you have—even if you've been a dreadful parent. An antisocial man killed in a barroom brawl at age thirty-three but who has fathered four kids he doesn't even know about shows more "fitness" than an eighty-year-old, law-abiding parent of two children. So Papa Fritzl, with his fourteen children (well, half of whom are also his grandchildren) showed greater "fitness"—more strands of his DNA into the next generation—

Plate 1. SUSAN WRIGHT

A traumatized, desperate person who killed a relative (her husband) but had remorse (Gradation #5). (AP Photo/Pat Sullivan.)

Plate 2. CLARA HARRIS

A jealousy murderer (Gradation #6). (AP Photo/Pat Sullivan, Pool.)

Plate 3. CHARLES WHITMAN

A mass murderer sparked by smoldering rage (Gradation #8). (AP Photo.)

Plate 4. IRA EINHORN

A jealous lover with strong psychopathic traits (Gradation #9). (AP Photo/Bob Edme.)

Plate 5. JOHN LIST

A killer of people "in the way"; extreme egocentricity (Gradation #10). (AP Photo.)

Plate 6. NEIL ENTWISTLE

A killer of people “in the way”; full-blown psychopathy (Gradation #11). (AP Photo/Allan Jung, Pool.)

Plate 7. RICHARD SPECK

An inadequate, rageful psychopath who committed a multiple murder (Gradation #13). (AP Photo/Charles Harrity.)

Plate 8. JUSTIN BARBER

A ruthlessly self-centered psychopathic schemer (Gradation #14). (AP Photo/Daron Dean, Pool.)

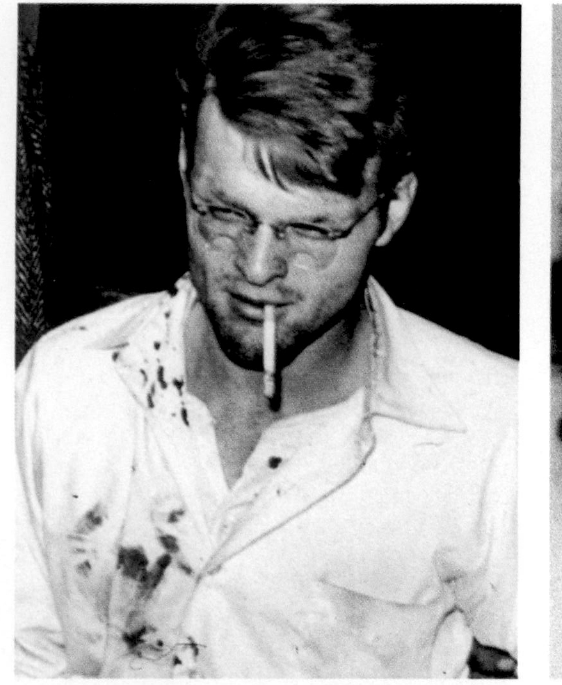

Plate 9. CHARLES STARKWEATHER

A psychopath on a cold-blooded spree or a multiple murderer (Gradation #15). (AP Photo/Don Ultang.)

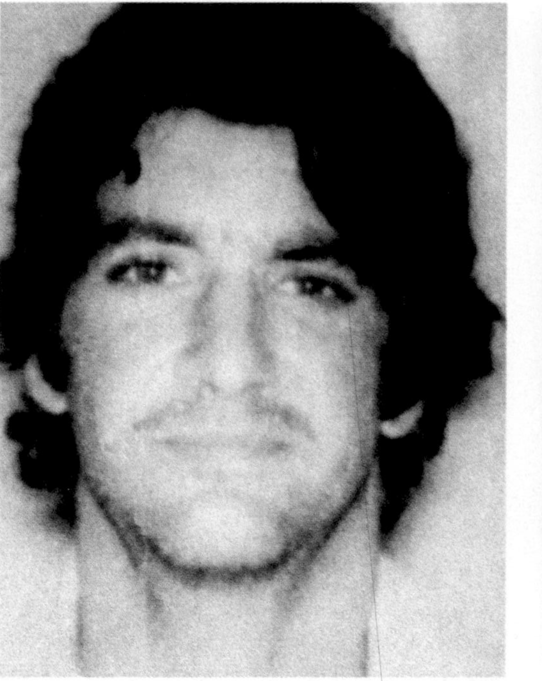

Plate 10. GEORGE HENNARD

A psychopathic person committing multiple vicious acts, including murder (Gradation #16). (AP Photo.)

Plate 11. TED BUNDY

A sexually perverse serial killer; murder aimed at escaping detection; torture not a primary element (Gradation #17). (AP Photo.)

Plate 12. DAVID PAUL BROWN AKA BAR JONAH

A torturer-murderer; torture not prolonged (in Brown's case the degree and length of torture could not be decisively evaluated because of lack of evidence) (Gradation #18). (AP Photo/ *Great Falls Tribune*, Wayne Arnst.)

Plate 13. CAMERON HOOKER

A psychopath committing extreme torture but not known to have killed (Gradation #21). (AP Photo/Paul Sakuma.)

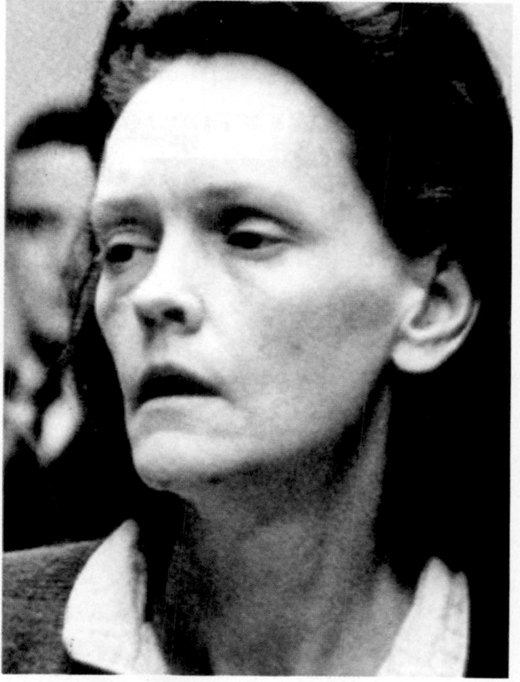

Plate 14. GERTRUDE BANISZEWSKI

A psychopathic torturer-murderer; torture—the primary motive (Gradation #22). (AP Photo/ *The Indianapolis Star*.)

PLATE 15. LEONARD LAKE

A psychopathic torturer-murderer; torture—the primary motive (in Lake's case, the crime was also sexual in nature) (Gradation #22).

PLATE 16. DAVID PARKER RAY

Psychopathic torturer-murderer; torture—the primary motive (in Ray's case, the crime was also sexual in nature) (Gradation #22). (AP Photo/ Judd Bradley.)

Key Brain Areas

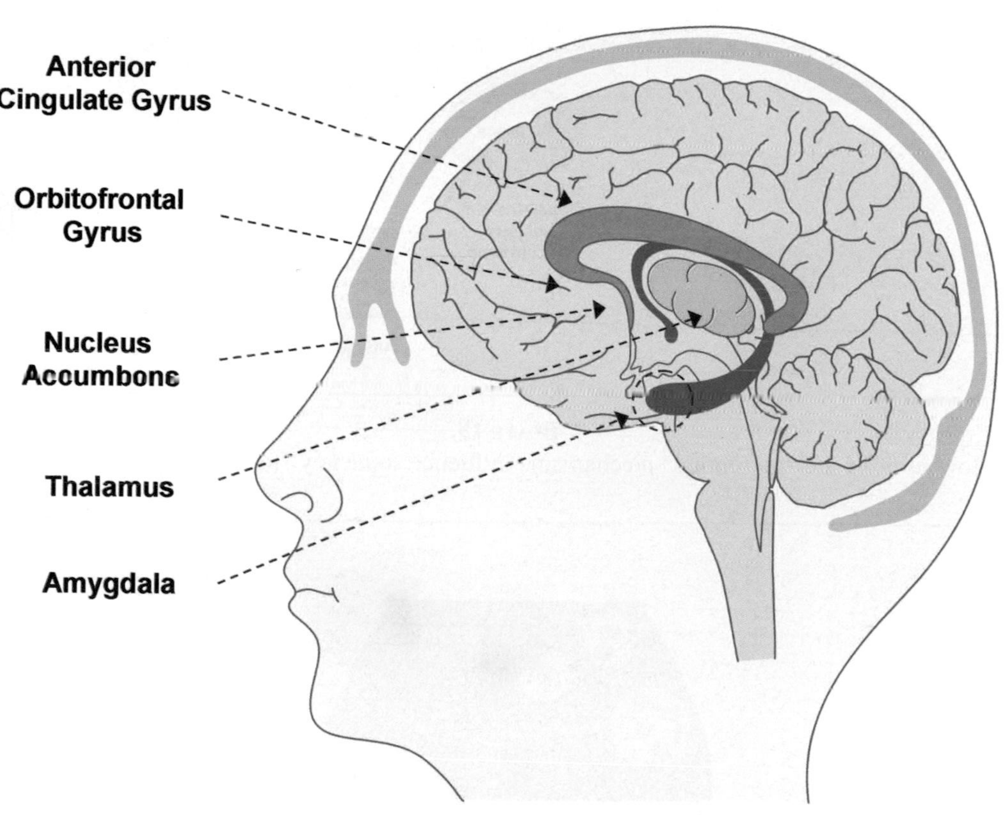

Plate 17. Areas of the brain that deal with our basic drives.

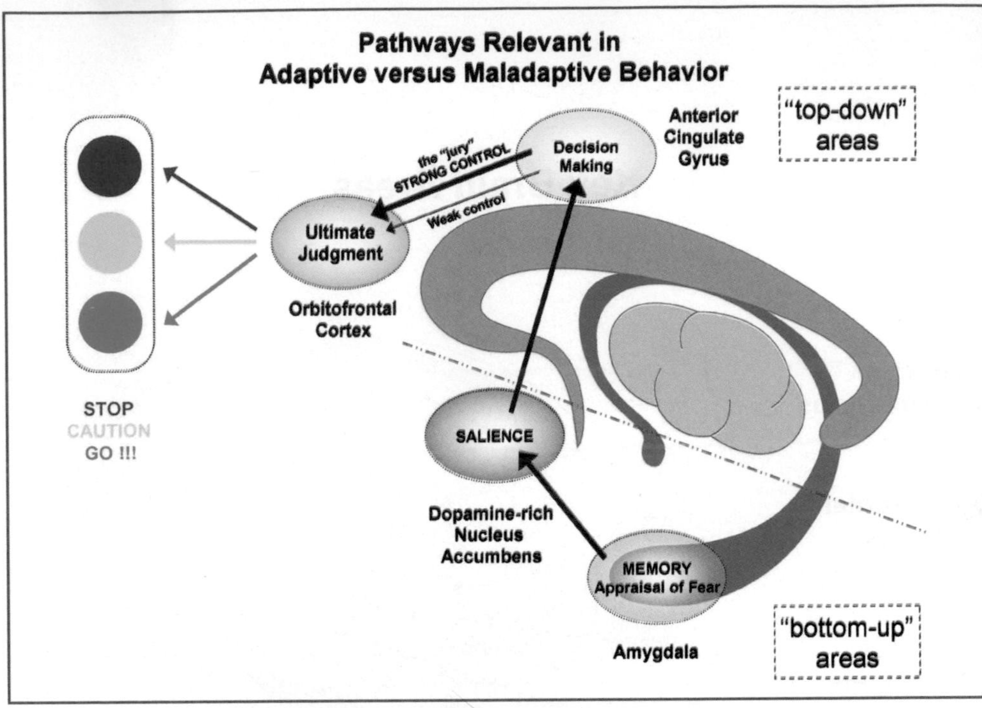

PLATE 18.

How some of the "bottom-up" mechanisms influence some key "top-down" mechanisms.

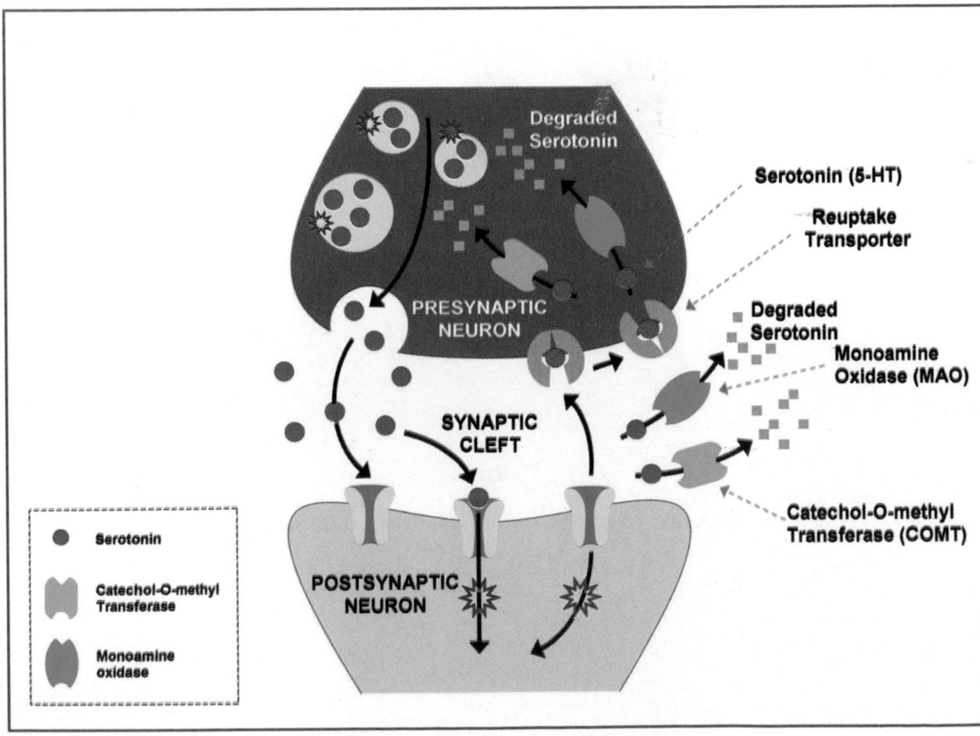

PLATE 19. Nerve Communication.

than I with my two sons or you, the reader, with however many children you may have, which is probably a good deal fewer than fourteen. This helps explain why there is always a fair percentage of antisocial and psychopathic persons in the community. The less extreme examples manage to be successful: conning and swindling their way through life, doing things that fall a bit short of what we would call "evil." Their number never dwindles; their "type" does not die out.[12]

When it comes to harming children, and even more so, to the killing of children, the measure of evil becomes almost meaningless. Nothing seems worse, so there are hardly any gradations. Still, some people—not all—tend to react more strongly when they hear of an older child being harmed than a newborn, because toddlers or young children have already begun to establish themselves as persons and to develop distinct personalities. Likewise, it seems futile to argue whether a parent harming or killing a child is worse than a stranger doing so—or vice versa. When parents kill a child, the act is a transgression of the most sacred bond: *evil* writ in the largest letters possible. Yet the ripple effect may be smaller, like a pebble tossed into a small pond, compared with a stranger killing a child, where the ripples spread out over a larger lake. For when a stranger kills a child, besides whatever suffering the child may have endured, there is then, added to the picture, the incalculable suffering of the parents and all the other relatives and family friends. Killing one's own child strikes us as monstrous precisely because it was a parent that did it. Killing someone else's child strikes us as monstrous because of the widespread "collateral" suffering by the family members, over and above whatever happened to the child.

It is the mark of the psychopath that Josef Fritzl, once his story came out, objected to being called a "monster" (as he was by the press and just about everybody else except the defense attorney) and pretended instead to be "crazy." As for the monstrosity of his long imprisonment of his daughter, the incest, the imprisonment of her children, their being cut off from access to the outside world, here physical torture and psychological torture are combined. The horror of torturing of someone else's child has already been confronted in chapter 6.[13] Because torturing a child seems like the lowest depth to which a human being can sink (I say "seems," since there is always a depth still lower than any you can imagine), torturing one's *own* child may be, for most of us, evil's bottom-most layer—well below the lowest layer that Dante dared to envision in the Ninth Circle of his *Inferno*. This brings us to Theresa Knorr.

Theresa Jimmie Francine Cross Sanders Knorr Pulliam Harris, more conveniently known as Theresa Knorr (after her second husband), was born in California in 1946, the younger of two sisters (plus two older half-siblings by their mother's earlier marriage).[14] She was jealous of her sister, even though she was the favorite of their mother, Swannie Cross. But when Theresa was fifteen, her mother collapsed and died in her arms, after which Theresa went into a deep depression.[15] Her father became ill a few years later, which spurred Theresa to marry the first man who proposed to her. At eighteen she became Mrs. Clifford Sanders. They quickly had a son, Howard, but Theresa was inordinately possessive of Cliff and accused him of infidelity. On July 6, 1964 (the day after Cliff's birthday), Cliff decided to leave the marriage. As he was just about out the door, Theresa shot him in the back with a rifle, killing him. Already pregnant with their second child, she persuaded the court this was in "self-defense," and she won an acquittal from Judge Charles Johnson. She and the judge were to meet several more times.

Theresa began to drink heavily, giving birth to a daughter, Sheila, in 1965. A year later she met a marine, Robert Knorr, got pregnant again, and discussed marriage. She gave birth to another daughter, Suesan, two months after she and Robert married. A son, Robert, came the next year in 1967. The marriage was failing because Robert's job took him away frequently. Theresa now became abusive toward the children: she would slap them for not being completely still and would lock them in the closet. At twenty-three she divorced for a second time and remarried two years later, this time to Ron Pulliam. That marriage lasted all of a year, as he resented her making him a "babysitter" for the three children while she went out partying, drinking, and, eventually, cheating on him—with Bill Bullington. Alcohol became her main consolation until she met yet another man willing to marry her: Chet Harris, who married her three days after they met and divorced her three months later. Judge Johnson presided over both the latter two divorces.

It is not recorded whether the judge was beginning to have second thoughts about the trustworthiness of Theresa's "self-defense" plea after she killed husband number 1. Stuck now with six children and no husband, Theresa began drinking more heavily than ever and became more

The Family of Theresa Knorr

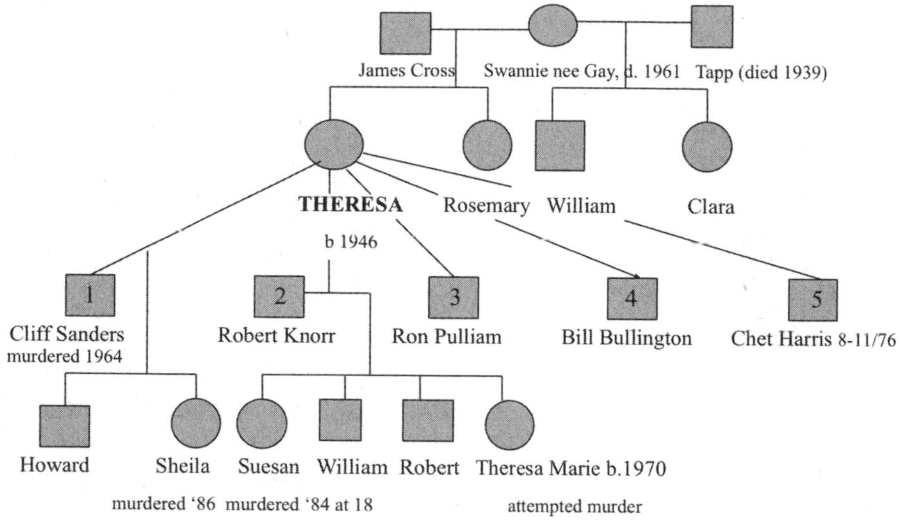

James Cross Swannie nee Gay, d. 1961 Tapp (died 1939)

THERESA b 1946 Rosemary William Clara

1 Cliff Sanders murdered 1964

2 Robert Knorr

3 Ron Pulliam

4 Bill Bullington

5 Chet Harris 8-11/76

Howard Sheila Suesan William Robert Theresa Marie b.1970

murdered '86 murdered '84 at 18 attempted murder

Figure 8.1

abusive with her brood. At this point, there were more players in her life than in the average Shakespearean play. I have tried to make it easier for the reader to follow via a family diagram (see figure 8.1). Unfortunately, the children could do no right by their mother: if they said they loved her, she felt they were trying to appease her; if they failed to say so, she regarded them as evil.[16] She beat them, punched the girls repeatedly, and threw knives at them, especially when Suesan ran away for a brief spell. Picked up by a truant officer, Suesan tried to tell the authorities about her mother's abusiveness, but Theresa said the girl was lying, and she was returned to her mother's tender mercies. By now Theresa, grossly overweight and no longer so attractive, became crazily jealous of her pretty daughters and began to force-feed them with macaroni and cheese so they would be fat and unattractive too. She would burn Suesan with cigarettes and claim the girl had "VD" and was a "witch."

In 1984, when Suesan was eighteen, Theresa and her son Robert took Suesan to a remote spot in California's Sierra Mountains, where Theresa had Robert douse his sister with an accelerant (probably gasoline), setting her afire. Suesan's body was charred beyond recognition;

Robert was warned he would be "next" if he ever told. Two years later, it was Sheila's turn: Theresa locked her in a closet and bound her limbs to a metal pole until she confessed that she had "VD." The girl confessed, despite her innocence, but that won her only a brief reprieve. Theresa locked her in the closet again, this time leaving her to starve to death. The youngest daughter, Terry, had run away and was supporting herself by prostitution; when she tried to tell the police what went on in her home, she was not at first believed. Theresa was at last brought to trial and convicted in 1993 and sentenced to life in prison for the torture-killings that the judge called "callous beyond belief."[17] Because Suesan's body could not at first be identified, and because of the enforced secrecy and deceptiveness about Sheila's death, Theresa got away with murder for about seven years. At the time of her arrest she was working as a paid companion of an elderly woman.

There are many child murders as horrifying as Theresa's, their grotesqueness triggering the reaction of "evil." Two morbidly religious mothers in Texas, for example, shocked the public—one with the murder of her two children by smashing their skulls with rocks; the other, by severing the arms of her ten-month-old daughter, intoning the words "Thank you Jesus, thank you Lord," when the police came to take her away.[18] But those mothers were certifiably insane. The level of evil becomes reduced when we take into consideration the mitigating circumstance of their madness. Like other psychotic mothers who murder very small children, the explanation (from a psychiatrist's point of view) for such behavior can lie in the overwhelming tasks of motherhood, coupled with the inability to let this difficulty register in one's consciousness (because of the psychosis). *Hence the formation of a face-saving delusion*: "I must consign these children to God," or "This child is the devil and must be destroyed in order to save the world." But Theresa Knorr was not insane. Twisted, paranoid, afire with jealousy . . . all of that, but not insane. As a cold and cruel torturer of her own daughters (and corrupter of her sons), Knorr belongs to the extreme end of the Gradations of Evil scale, where those who torture in a prolonged fashion reside, whether or not the end result is death.

The Knorr case is reminiscent of another case of child burning in 1983. A career criminal, Charles Rothenberg, when involved in a custody dispute with his ex-wife, decided to kill his six-year-old son, David, and himself. To that end, he gave the boy a sleeping pill, poured kerosene over his body in their motel room, kissed him good-bye, and set him on fire. Rescued by another guest, David suffered third-degree burns over 90 percent of his body, losing fingers, ears, nose, and genitals during the attack.[19] Because the child survived (to which end thirty-five skin grafts were needed), Rothenberg received only a thirteen-year sentence for *attempted*—as opposed to completed—murder. As all too often happens in these "murder-suicide" cases, the parent loses his nerve; Rothenberg did not kill himself. But he at least confessed to what was called at the time "one of the most unforgettable crimes ever committed against a child"[20] (this was a full year before Theresa Knorr swung into action). When he was released after seven years, Rothenberg said in a letter, "Do I deserve to be set free? No! It's an unforgivable act."[21]

Terribly disfigured at first, David Rothenberg has made an amazingly good adjustment: after completing a film course at the University of California, he now hopes to pursue a directing career.[22] He commented, "Charles is an evil man, and I feel that he should just take responsibility, because no one else lit the match."[23] That his father was able to confess and express remorse—and had not engaged in systematic torture on any previous occasions—does at least place him on a wider island of humanity than the one occupied by Theresa Knorr. Also the "why" question is a little less elusive in Rothenberg's case. Rothenberg had a worse background than Knorr's: his mother was a prostitute and he was raised in an orphanage. On the other hand, Knorr is the proverbial mystery wrapped in an enigma within a conundrum. There's no straight line one can draw from her mother's sudden death when Theresa was fifteen to the calculated torture of her daughters twenty years later. Rosemary, her sister, turned out well, as did her half-siblings. Alcohol certainly played a role—that was the "accelerant" Theresa used—but she drank to quell demons that were already circulating in her brain: loneliness, jealousy, paranoid thoughts. Perhaps there was some genetic flaw that lay behind her egocentricity that made her daughters, after her fourth husband left her (fifth, if you count her "de facto," Bill Bullington), hated rivals instead of the solace of her lonely days. But we can only guess.

Perhaps because the concept of evil is so bound up with what is shocking and horrifying, we usually reserve the term for cases that are unlike anything we have ever heard of before. They are unique.

Shooting a spouse caught in bed with a lover is murder, but it hardly passes the "uniqueness" test. Having seven children by one's own daughter and keeping them all locked up underground for twenty-four years is unique. A mother torturing her daughters for years on end, finally killing two, is unique.

Another, and more subtle, feature commonly found in families devastated by abysmal parenting is what I have called the Cat's Cradle Family Tree. The lines of relationship are so complex: so many marriages, divorces, children born of casual encounters, siblings, half-siblings, step-siblings, incest children, and the like, that there is no way to draw the family tree neatly on a piece of paper. The lines that go every which way—crisscrossing and overlapping—reflect the chaos and instability of these families. Often there is no set of values and rules that guides people's behavior and morals. If incest is "right," then what is "wrong"? Murder is not "wrong."

I once worked with a young woman in therapy whose father shot her mother to death in front of her and then told her, "What you saw didn't happen, and if you tell anyone, I'll kill you too!" The Cat's Cradle Family scenario shows up in the lives of many murderers, not just in cases of "Parents from Hell." Other examples of complex family trees include Sante Kimes and Scott Peterson (chapter 4), Charles Manson (chapter 5), Ken McElroy and Tommy Lynn Sells (chapter 6), and David Ray and Leonard Lake (chapter 7). In the case of Sells, for example, who was Tommy's mother? His birth mother? The aunt his mother gave him to? The pedophile his aunt gave him to? And who was his father? Perhaps several of his "caretakers" read to him from the Bible, told him the right things to do. But children learn more from parental example than from words. Absent enduring, socially proper examples from loving parents, a child (especially a son) may grow up with little trust, great hatred, and no inner restraints. Anything is possible. Robert Knorr, the son Theresa Knorr ordered to burn his sister to death, later murdered a bartender.

The next Parents from Hell case has these same chaotic features: unique cruelties and a twisted family tree. Figure 8.2 shows my best attempt to draw the undrawable.

Ed Sexton, born in 1942, was raised in the coal mining area of West Virginia. He was one of nine children, though there was an unknown

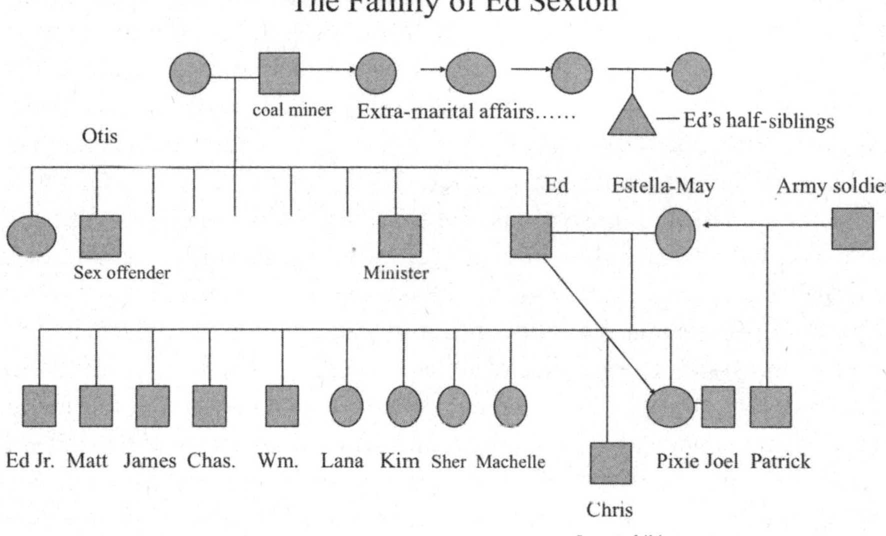

Figure 8.2

number of half-siblings from his father's affairs with perhaps four other women. When he was ten, he set fires and killed cats and dogs. We don't know if he had the whole "triad" that included bed-wetting.

A juvenile delinquent, Ed was involved in thefts and robberies for which he spent some time in prison. Briefly in the army, he was given a dishonorable discharge for bad conduct.[24] Once out of prison at twenty-nine, he married Estella May. They had a large number of children, as shown in Figure 8.2, but one was Estella May's by a soldier she met while he was en route to Vietnam, and another was fathered by Ed via incest. This daughter, Pixie, was forced to marry a man her age, so it would appear that her son was by her husband rather than by her father. Incest was rife in rural West Virginia, so it was said, and Ed tried to impregnate another daughter, Machelle, whom he raped when she was thirteen or fourteen—apparently without success (that is, without her conceiving).

Machelle may have tried to intervene when Ed went after her two younger sisters, Kim and Lana. Ed punished Machelle so severely, she had to be hospitalized. He had warned her: "You get the belt till you're sixteen, then my fist." Actually, all the children got whipped and beaten regularly, as did Estella May, who gave as good as she got: she beat her sons continuously as well. She also held the girls down when they were being raped. Ed would beat his son Charles until he bled, making him stand naked in front of the whole family, and did the same with the other children. Ed himself ran around the house naked and encouraged the children to have sex with one another.

Another of Ed's punishments was to lock the children in a closet and spray roach-killer into the closet space. Now and then there would be a complaint, and inspectors from the health department would come over. Ed would then fake a disability, like multiple sclerosis or muscular dystrophy, and perch in his wheelchair as though unable to walk until the inspector left. Another of Ed's punishments was to tie the children up; some of them ended up lying in their own waste. He threatened to kill any of the children who dared talk to people on the outside. Ed smoked marijuana, and he was not stingy with the whiskey. He killed cats and dogs and, in the case of his daughter Sherri, he killed her pet rabbit—and then forced her to eat it. Ultimately he killed Pixie's husband, Joel, and she in turn killed the incest-child she had been made to pretend was Joel's.

One of the girls became a snitch. The news finally got out as to what was happening in the family, and both parents were arrested. In court, Ed was given a death sentence; Estella-May, life in prison.

As we saw in chapter 7, blame for an "evil" outcome is at times laid at the doorstep of foster parents or stepparents. On closer look, the stepparents might have been uncommonly caring and supportive, yet were still unable to stem the tide of adverse genetic factors (as with Gerald Stano). But sometimes stepparents really did seem to have been the main destructive force in a killer's early life (as with Charles Schmid). The wicked stepmother of the fairy tales is a figure born of real-life circumstances. Despite how kind and loving most stepparents are, there remains a small proportion—greater, nevertheless, than is true of birth parents—who kill[25] or who psychologically ruin their stepchildren. The expression *blood is thicker than water* comes to life with particular vividness in homes where the natural children are treated with tenderness and the stepchildren with a cruelty beyond the imagination even of Hans Christian Andersen or the Brothers Grimm.

Jessica Schwarz, a truck driver in Florida, had two daughters: one by her first marriage, and another by her second husband, David Schwarz, also a truck driver. David brought to the marriage a son, Andrew, from a previous marriage to Ilene Logan.[26] Ilene had been a go-go dancer who abused drugs and alcohol—and sometimes abused Andrew: she once, so it was alleged,[27] hit him in the ear with a frying pan, leaving him deaf in one ear. She had various lovers, one of whom beat Andrew so badly that he had to be hospitalized. Those were the good times.

The bad times began when Andrew moved into his new home, with Jessica as stepmother. By all accounts, Jessica took good care of her two daughters, who slept in a well-appointed and well-kept bedroom. Andrew was stuck in a messy, closet-sized room—with a lock on the outside, so Jessica could, in effect, imprison him in his bedroom. Beyond that, the things Jessica did to Andrew, when added together, create a veritable textbook of sadism. She would yell at him, "I hate you," or "I'm gonna tie you up and run you over." She threatened to kill Andrew if he wanted to see his real mother, Ilene. She took to calling him "Jeffrey Dahmer" as though he were some monstrous younger version of the serial killer. She also called him "bastard," "crackhead," "bastard's baby," and "fuck-face." While she gave hardly any responsibilities to her daughters, Andrew was made to do most of the chores and usually with a sadistic twist: she made him clip the hedges of the lawn with a small scissors and clean his father's car with a toothbrush. She drove her daughters to school but made Andrew walk even in the rain, and she allowed no neighbors to take him in their cars. Andrew was made to stand in the yard and repeat over and over, "I'm no good, I'm a liar." Jessica once made him wear a T-shirt at home on which was written "I'm a worthless piece of shit, don't talk to me." The babysitter who was there offered to give him a sweater to put over the T-shirt so he would not have to admit to Jessica later that he had taken it off. Jessica once hit Andrew so hard he ended up with two black eyes and a broken nose, but she made him tell the school he had "fallen off his bike."

The egregious failure of the local authorities to figure out the actual cause of his injuries and to take proper steps is whole other story. Jessica was once punished and made to do community service—picking up used soda cans—but she made Andrew do that work for her, forcing him to skip school on Thursdays in order to collect the cans. At times she would make the boy run down the street naked and would put tape over his mouth so that he couldn't speak to the neighbor children.

Jessica was intimidating toward her neighbors, most of whom were too frightened to warn the authorities what went on in the Schwarz household. One girl that did manage to speak to a detective about possible child abuse charges mentioned that Jessica would make Andrew sit at the dinner table with his mouth taped shut, while his sisters ate their dinner. Other neighborhood children spoke of Jessica setting a timer, and if Andrew didn't finish his supper in five minutes, she would put the dish on the floor next to the kitty litter box, making him eat it there like an animal.[28]

But what I found most shocking, and what would have brought tears to the eyes of the Marquis de Sade, was Jessica's forcing Andrew, if he failed to clean the kitchen to her satisfaction, to eat a roach. That alone would have earned her the seventy years in prison to which she was eventually sentenced—but she would have escaped justice altogether had she not gone the full distance and drowned Andrew in the family pool when he was ten. This is what the prosecuting attorney, Scott Cupp, had to say when Jessica was finally brought to trial: "I may not be able to define evil for you—not as a black-and-white statement lifted from the pages of a dictionary—but I can say without equivocation that I know it when I see it, and Jessica Schwarz will forever personify it in my eyes."[29]

Recently, the author of Jessica's true-crime biography sent me some photographs from her teenage days, when she was Jessica L. Woods at Glen Cove High School in Long Island. The transformation from the sweet face in her high school yearbook to the tough-looking woman in her prison photo twenty-five years later seems at first astonishing, inexplicable. Her parents related in court, for example, that there was "no drug abuse or alcoholism in the family," and that she had not herself been abused.[30] But from collaterals we learn that there was indeed alcoholism in the family and that Jessica and her friends "dropped acid" (LSD) while in high school. Jessica moved in a social circle of "tough" young men and was herself known as "tough." The picture that emerges is one that makes her transition into the sadistic bully she became not so inexplicable after all.

What is particularly poignant about the fate of Andrew Schwarz is that he was singled out for barbarous treatment, while Jessica Schwarz's own daughters, as Andrew could see for himself, were grossly favored. This situation is quite a contrast from the children of Fritzl, Knorr, and Sexton, who lived in what amounted to mini-concentration camps, all treated with equal savagery, almost all denied access to the outside world. They at least did not have to endure the added indignity of radical unfairness. But all these children suffered ego-crushing experiences—Andrew's lot simply being the worst, because Jessica reduced his status to that of a despised animal—not even a human animal—while her own daughters flourished. From a psychological standpoint, the lot of these children was in some respects worse than that of the victims in the Nazi camps—for those people usually came from loving families and knew that there were good people in the world. Many of those who survived made fairly good adjustments once they were liberated.[31] The camp victims knew that the evil afflicting them came from the Nazis: a malignant group *outside*. For the children of Fritzl, Knorr, and Sexton, evil came in the form of one's own flesh-and-blood "protectors"—the parents. And those parents were their entire world. How could they later entrust themselves, as did Tennessee Williams's heroine in *A Streetcar Named Desire*—to the "kindness of strangers"?

When children are subjected to physical suffering at the hands of their parents,[32] they tend to develop in one of two directions. Most are up to their necks in anger and hatred; some become violent toward others (this happens with boys more than with girls), while others take these strong emotions out on themselves and become depressed or even suicidal (this happens more with girls than with boys). Parental violence meted out to boys is a pretty reliable recipe for violence done later on *by* those boys. Just how reliable a recipe this is comes out clearly in a beautifully written book by criminology professor Lonnie Athens.[33] Athens describes stages through which the battered child may go. First, the child is "brutalized": severely beaten and humiliated or made to witness other family members enduring such treatment, or just encouraged by a parent to injure or kill anyone who "messes" with you. After "brutalization" comes "belligerency." The idea of lashing out at others becomes absorbed into one's personality; it seems the appropriate philosophy for dealing with life's stresses. The next step is "violent performances." At this stage—reached now in adolescence or early adult life—one progresses from violent thoughts to repeated violent acts against anyone who presses even lightly on one's sensitive buttons. At the end, we may see "virulence." For Athens, this is a stage, mercifully not the inevitable consequence of parental violence, where some young persons go on to violence as a way of life by now so entrenched, so much a part of their nature, that there is no going back, no corrective treatment still available. The violence will surface as retaliation for the wrongs suffered. One cannot easily predict in advance whether the target will be the offending parent or, as is much more often the case, others on the outside who remind one of that parent. We saw this with Tommy Lynn Sells, when I asked him if he ever felt like killing his mother, given all the troubles he had after she abandoned him. Tommy said, startled that I could even think such a thought: "Anyone touch a hair of her head, he wouldn't last a minute; ya only got one mum!"

Sometimes, of course, even a daughter subjected to enough neglect and torture can pass through Athens's stages, though seldom as far as "virulence," but certainly as far as "violent performances." This was true in a famous British case of a girl who also "only had one mum" and who took out her hatred on others. She was widely regarded as an evil child, someone on the dark side of celebrity—so much so that everyone seemed oblivious to the primary evil in her case: the violence and sadism of her mother.

Mary Bell was born in Newcastle-upon-Tyne in northeast England, not far from the Scottish border. Betty, her mother, was a prostitute who gave birth to her when she was only sixteen. Betty was a professional dominatrix whose specialty was to whip her clients. This was a kind of controlled sadism from which she earned her keep. Her sadism was not confined to those men, however. She tried on many occasions to kill Mary before she even reached her first birthday. When Mary got a little older, she was pressed into service herself: her mother forced her to give fellatio to her "johns," after which she would vomit the ejaculate. The men were invited to insert objects into Mary's rectum, a practice in which Betty also took part. On various occasions Betty would whip her daughter or try to drown her by pushing her head underwater. What few moments of respite Mary had from these atrocious acts were during the times Betty was in a psychiatric hospital. Some time after Mary was born, Betty began living with a de facto, Billy Bell, from whom Mary took her last name, though he was not her father. Betty never told Mary who her father was, nor is it at all likely she knew herself.[34] Billy was a habitual criminal, arrested for armed robbery at some point, yet he treated Mary with gentleness and devotion: he was perhaps the only person in Mary's early life who did so.[35] Betty, in contrast, would threaten her with dire consequences if she ever told what went on in the house. Hence the sexual abuse went undetected.

Her road paved with these jagged stones, it is not surprising that Mary turned to violence herself. She killed birds and cats. There is no indication that she set fires, though she did have one other element of the "triad": she was enuretic and would often urinate on the floor on purpose, and then run away. When Mary was ten she gave the community a foretaste of what was to come: she threw her three-year-old cousin over an embankment. The boy survived, and her act was written off by the police as a childish prank.[36] She then tried to strangle some little girls in a play area. But in May of 1968 she strangled to death a four-year-old boy, Martin Brown. Two months later—this time with a friend, Norma Bell (no relation) participating—the victim was Brian Howe, age three. Mary tried (unsuccessfully) to castrate Brian, apparently in revenge for the despicable sexual offenses that she had to endure. She even returned later to Brian's body and carved an "M" on his belly. As the story unfolded, it became known that Betty had tried on several occasions to throttle Mary into unconsciousness, so the murders Mary committed could be understood as reenactments of what had happened to her. And since Mary had survived these attempts, the line between unconsciousness and death was not neatly drawn in her mind—if indeed she grasped the finality of death at all at her age. She used to say that she liked hurting things that couldn't fight back.[37]

Both girls were soon apprehended. Norma showed some remorse; Mary did not. The court and the public regarded her for that reason as a vicious psychopath, "evil incarnate," and as an example of Bad Seed. Because of her age, Mary was convicted of manslaughter due to diminished responsibility, rather than murder.[38] For ten years she was consigned to a reformatory, then to two years in prison. Though sentenced originally to be detained at Her Majesty's Pleasure (which could amount to an indefinite period of incarceration), she appeared to have shown enough improvement after the twelve years to warrant release. As with the Archie McCafferty case (chapter 5), the public was outraged, all the more so when Mary was granted anonymity and a changed name.

Mary eventually married and had a daughter (in 1984). Her life story—ultimately one of rehabilitation and redemption—was portrayed with sympathy and psychological astuteness by Gitta Sereny, whose earlier writings had focused on evils of a different kind: the Nazi atrocities and Hitler's henchmen. She summed up: "Children are brought to the breaking point, and it is not their fault, but ours." At first Mary herself was perplexed by the way her life had unfolded; she asked: "What made me what I am? What made me capable of evil?" Through Sereny's gentle but persistent efforts, Mary got back in touch with the sexual violation she endured, which she had for so long repressed. And it was when she became a mother herself that she could begin to grasp the enormity of her crime.[39]

The most likely paths she could have taken, given her history, were suicide and prostitution. That she became at first violent most likely is a reflection of some genetic influences (perhaps helped along by adverse factors during Betty's pregnancy) that made her impulsive and irritable. That she later became capable of redemption is related most likely to other and more favorable genetic influences that left her with a good capacity for compassion and reflection: these, then, interacted with what little she knew of kindness from her stepfather. Such a mixture of positive and negative influences is not rare. What is not easy to explain is why in Mary's case the good finally triumphed, despite the fact that she came from one of the worst homes imaginable, while in Jessica Schwarz's case, despite coming from a merely bad (though outwardly more ordinary) home, evil triumphed.

Mary's case also teaches us that, just as with mental illness, youth itself is a mitigating circumstance. And she was not an example of Bad Seed for two reasons: she was subjected to the unspeakable evil of her mother right up until the murders (which, paradoxically, rescued her: the court took her away from Betty and put her in the much more humane environment of the reformatory), and she did not become and remain a true psychopath, inclined to evil actions 24/7 like Jessica. There *are* cases that warrant the appellation of Bad Seed (as we shall see in the next chapter), but it is meaningless to apply such a label unless the home environment was uniformly favorable, the emerging personality clearly psychopathic, and there were no other factors present to explain it—not even complications during pregnancy—just the genes. Such cases are rare indeed.

The Mary Bell case illustrates another paradox: the noble principle that each man's house, be it mansion or cottage, is a sacred and inviolable space will now and again be set upside down by the Law of Unintended Consequences. Terrible things may go on in those mansions or cottages—whether the manor house of Saville Kent or the much humbler abode of Betty Bell—that remain unsuspected and undetected. This is because of the difficulty in learning what goes on in some of these "inviolable spaces" and the reluctance of the police to cross these sacred boundaries even when strong evidence comes to light. The transient evil of Mary Bell cost her twelve years of incarceration. This was fully justified by the circumstances. The perpetual evil of Betty Bell was left unpunished. She should have been sent to prison and had all parental rights terminated. Instead, and in a manner of speaking, she got away with murder. The law that safeguards the good majority protects, unintentionally, the Betty Bells as well.

Compared with birth parents, adoptive parents and foster parents are more at risk for mistreating the children under their care, just as stepparents are, and for the same reason: the lack of a blood tie to the children. Some of the most outrageous situations arise from households in which a young mother with an out-of-wedlock child—whose birth father may not even be known—now lives with an on-again off-again boyfriend. The boyfriend is sometimes referred to as the "stepfather," but, to judge from his behavior, he is not a father in any meaningful sense of the word. His interest is in maintaining a sexual relationship with the young woman. The child in these real-life scenarios is an encumbrance in the path of the boyfriend's sexual ambitions, the more so if the child cries, soils itself, or misbehaves. This is a prescription for disaster. The risk for violent forms of child abuse skyrocket, but when and if the violence reaches the level of evil is unpredictable. We are all familiar with how much difference a half-inch makes in a gunshot case. A person shot in the mid-thigh is on crutches for six weeks with a broken femur. A person struck a half-inch toward the groin bleeds out from a severed femoral artery and dies.[40] As with James Gleick's comments on chaos, small differences can make a big difference. If Jessica Schwarz made her stepson swallow some castor oil for misbehaving—and that was all—no one would have said "evil!" But she made him swallow a roach. Suddenly we are in the realm of evil. The next two cases are mansion-and-cottage versions of the same depressing story. Stepparents from Hell, Non-Blood-Parents from Hell, shielded by our noble legal system from the prying eyes of neighbors—and from the local Child Protective Services—until the day after tragedy strikes.

THE "COTTAGE" CASE

Cesar Rodriguez became the last of Nixzaliz Santiago's lovers and was the father of her two youngest children—both boys born twelve months apart. She lived with Cesar in a two-bedroom apartment in a poor section of Brooklyn, but she had been born in Puerto Rico in 1979, the same year Cesar was born. By the time she was twenty-seven, she had had six children by four different lovers—and almost a seventh, but the last pregnancy ended in a miscarriage in November 2005.[41] What raised this couple from obscurity to nationwide public attention was the torture-murder of Nixzaliz's seven-year-old daughter, Nixzmary Brown, on January 10, 2006. Her mother did not know the father's full name; this was learned only at the subsequent trial. The family tree and its bewildering complexity are shown in figure 8.3, drawn to the best of my ability and with as much information as I could gather.

The biological father played no role whatever in the girl's life. She took her name (and not much else) from yet another of her mother's lovers, Edward Brown, by whom Nixzaliz had two other children. Nixzmary, who weighed only thirty-six pounds at her death—half what a

Nixzaliz Santiago

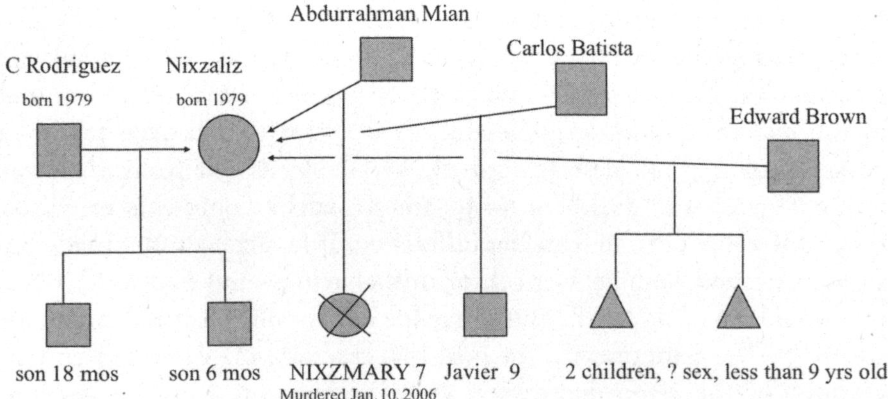

The six out-of-wedlock children of Nixzaliz by various men

Figure 8.3

normal seven-year-old girl should weigh—had tried to get some yogurt from the refrigerator one night. This was for the obvious reason: having been systematically starved by her "caretakers," she was hungry. She also inadvertently jammed Cesar's computer printer with some of her toys. Enraged at her "badness," Cesar stripped the child, plunged her head into cold water in the bathtub, and hit her head against the faucet. The latter blow gave her a hematoma (a pocket of bleeding in the brain) from which she died the following morning.

Poverty was not the reason Cesar and Nixzaliz reacted so strongly to the girl's attempt to take some food; the refrigerator was full. It was rather that they had not allowed her to eat a proper amount of food. In addition to not getting enough food, Nizmary was often locked in her room with only a litter box for a toilet. Earlier, Cesar had been in the habit of punishing Nixzmary on a daily basis by strapping her to a chair with duct tape, rope and bungee cords—and beating her. Her bruises were noticed by her teachers at school, who notified the ACS (Administration for Child Services). The ACS made no meaningful contact with the family; worse yet, the caseworker assigned to look into the family after hours, on January 10, decided to wait until the next morning. By that time, the girl was dead. Nixmary's body bore bruises all over, as well as "ugly cuts."[42]

Cesar was tried first in court, and, as is customary in such cases, each adult blamed the other for inflicting the decisive wounds. It is much more likely that Cesar did the bulk of the damage, for which he was convicted only of first-degree manslaughter. The jury could not agree about the more serious possible charge of second-degree murder. It makes an interesting comment on the special semantics—just plain *antics* would be a better word—so often heard on the defense side in these cases. Cesar acknowledged in court that he slapped, spanked, and whipped Nixzmary with a belt, but "he didn't do it with intent to hurt."[43] No comment is necessary. By the time Nixzaliz and Cesar put in a call for medical help, the girl had already been dead for at least seven hours, so the mother, too, has much to answer for. As for the backgrounds of either adult, we know very little, so we cannot begin to answer the "why" question. Given the degree to which violence breeds violence, we can speculate that gentleness was not the main characteristic of their upbringing either. This seems like a good guess, because Cesar spoke as though Nixzmary was a wildly naughty child for whom the (as we experience it) monstrous punishments to which he subjected her were somehow normal, par for the course. At the murder trial of the mother, who blamed her daughter for her miscarriage and had called her a "devil," Nixzaliz was convicted in October 2008 of manslaughter.

THE "MANSION" CASE

John and Linda Dollar's latest home (they changed residences many times) was in a small community some seventy miles north of Tampa, Florida. A spacious 3,800-square-foot abode with a three-car garage and a pool in the backyard, it was worlds away from the poor Brooklyn setting of Nixzaliz and Cesar. By the time the Dollars came to the world's attention, John was fifty-seven, an affluent real estate appraiser; his wife of fifty-one, a former businesswoman with a master's degree in education.[44] Unable to have children of their own, they began adopting and ended up with eight children, mostly during the 1990s. The first, a daughter, was grown and out of the house by the time, in January 2005, the "troubles" came to the surface regarding the remaining seven kids.

The Dollars had started out in Tennessee, where they ran a private Christian school: the Mountain View Christian Academy in Strawberry Plains, a village of seven hundred some twenty miles northeast of Knoxville. They attended a nearby church but had a falling out with the pastor when he disagreed with their conviction that the world was coming to an end in the year 2000.[45] If that were their only manifestation of religious fanaticism, the Dollars would have continued to live out their lives (even beyond 2000) in obscurity. But they had seriously twisted notions of how best to discipline children—though even these notions seem destined to remain unexposed, for they were in the habit of home-schooling their children and of confining them to the house—beyond the ken even of their neighbors, let alone any schoolteachers or caseworkers from Child Protective Services.

Of the seven children still in the Florida home, all were adolescents between twelve and seventeen. Two were the favorites of their adoptive parents and were treated well. The other five were treated quite differently. This would not have come to light but for the sixteen-year-old boy requiring the services of the local emergency room because of a head wound. He also had red marks around his neck. In addition, he was extremely underweight—and this sparked an investigation by the Citrus County sheriff's office.[46] Meantime, the Dollars fled to a remote part of Utah in their SUV, only to be apprehended, thanks to their having made calls on their cell phone. They were apparently unaware that these gadgets also serve as global-positioning devices.

The authorities then discovered that all five of the less-favored adolescents were more than underweight: they were near death's door from being deliberately starved by the Dollars. Twin boys of fourteen, for example, had weights of thirty-six and thirty-eight pounds—eighty pounds less than they should have weighed, but quite in keeping with the standards of Auschwitz and Treblinka. Besides starving the children, and to ensure obedience, the Dollars took to torturing them with electric cattle prods, chains, bondage equipment, and hammers. They ripped out the toenails of one of the children with pliers, which made John Dollar's protestation in court that "it was not intentional that they be harmed in any way"[47] doubly horrifying: once, because it simply is; and once again, because the Dollars, out of their morbid religious fanaticism, actually believed what they said. They were not liars.

The Dollars hit the feet of the five children with rubber mallets and canes and made them sleep in a closet with (shades of Jessica Schwarz) a lock on the outside. Or they affixed wind chimes to the bedroom door, so that if any of the unlucky five dared to sneak out in the middle of the night to garner a few extra calories from the refrigerator, the Dollars would be alerted and would swing into action. As for the boy whose condition called for emergency room intervention, investigators believed that John Dollar had grabbed the boy by the neck, raised him in the air, and then dropped him, such that he struck his head on the fireplace, sustaining a laceration.[48]

What it was about the three boys and two girls that made them fall out of favor with the Dollars was not made clear. At their trial the Dollars argued that they were merely carrying out their religious convictions. As John put it, "We are firm believers in the God almighty . . . and because of those principles, we were led to do certain things."[49] For their aggravated child abuse/torture of five children, the Dollars were each sentenced to fifteen years in prison. Linda Dollar informed the court that she had left home at sixteen because of her abusive and alcoholic father, and that her first marriage had ended because of (an unspecified) abuse.[50] Given the millions of people whose early histories are replete with such conditions and worse, this cannot be the full explanation for Linda's behavior. Detective Lisa Wall sounded the right note on this matter when she said, "I will always remember the children, but will never understand what led the parents to such abuses."[51]

As for the Dollars invoking God's name to justify their evil acts (what else can we call them?), one would like to think that religion-based, self-serving rationalizations about improving people by killing and torturing them have become a bit tiresome, especially after 9/11. But this is not so. I will burden you with one more example. In the West Yorkshire city of Bradford, the Crown Court found a Nigerian couple guilty of unlawful wounding and cruelty to their two sons.[52] Their father had put pins through their tongues and lips, as well as pressing the tongue of one son with a pliers until the tongue swelled. The boys' mouths had been cut with scalpel blades; both had also been bound and beaten. They were kept at home during school holidays so their wounds would not be seen. The father was a fanatical Christian preacher; his wife, also a religious extremist, would watch while her husband inflicted the injuries. He did so, he told the court, because, according to his reading of the Bible, God had had his tongue cut out. The judge, no more able than you or I to find any such passage in the Good Book, told the man: "You are calculated, determined, persistent, and cruel in the extreme. . . . You have sadistic tendencies and took pleasure in inflicting pain on your children. To all right-minded persons, in particular parents, the idea of causing injury to children is almost beyond belief."[53] Amen.

The parents described in the above vignettes all subjected their children or stepchildren to prolonged torture, meriting placement at the extreme end of the Gradations scale: Category 22. That category includes the act of physical torture, so the Fritzl case is atypical. Fritzl subjected Elizabeth to some physical torture in the beginning, but what followed was a predominantly psychological torture: imprisonment in a cellar for over half of her forty-two years, as well as the imprisonment of her children. We don't even know if he added, over and above the sexual torture of rape, a little nonsexual physical torture along the way, but the complete ruination of Elizabeth and the seven children surely puts him at the extreme end, regardless.

CHILDREN FROM HELL

The relationship between parents and children is a two-way street. So far we've seen some extreme examples of how parents' acts can push their children to violence, but there are also children with genetic disadvantages, birth defects, or brain damage during pregnancy whose behavior is difficult, at times uncontrollable, and who have a very negative impact on their parents. The parents may become too punitive in response to a child's "wildness" or disobedience, resorting to harsh measures that only make things worse. A vicious cycle gets started, and one or the other—parent or child—may spin out of control, with tragic consequences. In still other families, the parents may remain in good control, consistently kind and understanding, with a disruptive child who goes on to become antisocial, even murderous. There are, in other words, a few "children from hell," with whom the parents have done nothing out of the ordinary. These are children whose behavior, nevertheless, may even reach the level of "evil" because of some shocking act of manipulativeness or violence. Such an outcome is seen most clearly when an adopted child with many prenatal disadvantages is raised from day one by loving parents who manage not to lose control no matter what the child does. But this can certainly happen in families where the children are brought up by their birth parents. One of the examples I have chosen here concerns children raised by their birth parents; the other is about an adopted child.

THE MENENDEZ BROTHERS

> E fu nomato Sassol Mascheroni
> Se Tosco se', ben sai omai chi fu.
>
> And his name was Sassol Mascheroni
> If you are Tuscan, you know who he was.
>
> —Dante, *Divine Comedy: Inferno*[54]

The mansion-and-cottage analogy I used for the last two parent examples was a bit figurative. Nixzaliz and Cesar didn't live in anything as commodious as a cottage; the Dollars' spacious home was a little short of a mansion. More literally, Lyle Menendez and his three-years-younger brother, Eric, murdered their parents in their twenty-three-room nothing-short-of-a-mansion mansion in the posh Beverly Hills section of Los Angeles. This was in August of 1989, when Lyle was twenty-one and Eric not quite eighteen. Their father, José, was forty-four; his attractive wife, Kitty, forty-seven. Their boys killed them execution style, using a 12-gauge Mossberg shotgun. They shot José first, then turned to Kitty, who found herself spattered by her husband's blood and brain tissue, before she, too, was dispatched with ten shots to various parts of her body. Mindful of the details required of a "perfect crime," one of the sons then fired shots at the left knee of each parent, so that the murders would take on the appearance of a Mafia hit man at work.[55] These touches did throw the police off the scent, who were reluctant to implicate the sons in this gruesome murder. The truth emerged only slowly over the ensuing months.

The Menendez parents were not perfect: José, a refugee from Castro's Cuba, was an ambitious, self-made millionaire who expected his sons to succeed at the best schools. He was as demanding of his sons as he was of his subordinates at work, which gave him the reputation of being a boss from hell. Kitty, American-born, supported her husband in these demands and contributed to the pressure that the boys felt to meet their parents' high standards. Both parents helped the boys more than was appropriate with their homework; teachers noticed that the work they handed in from home was much better than what they were able to do in class. In their early teens, the brothers tried, unsuccessfully, to rape one of their young female cousins.

Lyle managed to get into Princeton, thanks to his father's influence, but he plagiarized a paper and was suspended for a year.[56] Then, while working for his father, Lyle alienated people and was considered "nasty, arrogant, and self-centered." Back at Princeton, Lyle got a friend to write papers for him, so he wouldn't fail. Kitty, meanwhile, was busy completing much of Eric's homework. Eric, too, was acquiring the reputation of being arrogant, loud, and rebellious. The year before the murders, the brothers began burglarizing homes in the exclusive area where their parents lived. The full recitation of their criminal actions would be too long to recite here; suffice it to say that José and Kitty were now threatening to write their sons out of their will, by way of convincing them how seriously they took their behavior. Kitty had learned from a therapist she had been seeing that her sons were "sociopaths," lacking in conscience, and narcissistic. This was just a month before the murders. In retrospect it becomes clear that with the threat of disinheritance, the parents had signed their own death warrant.

Since the brothers were not at first considered guilty, they did inherit—and lost little time (four days to be precise) in engaging in a major spending spree, buying new cars, Rolex watches, jewelry, and . . . shotguns. Eric eventually confided in his therapist that "we did it," adding that they took care to create the "perfect crime." He mentioned that they were reluctant to kill their mother, but had to, since she was resting on his shoulder the night of the murder—and besides, he noted, with uncharacteristic compassion—she would be devastated with her husband gone. Eric's confession sounds disingenuous: after all, unless both parents were killed, the brothers would not have inherited everything. There was a long path between the murders, the realization by the police that the sons were the guilty parties, and the lengthy trials. The first trial actually ended in a mistrial, owing to the unfounded assertion of the defense attorney that the brothers had been violated sexually by their father.[57] It was only at the second trial that both brothers were given life sentences. Since the Menendez parents were nothing at all like the Sextons, the Dollars, Betty Bell, or Jessica Schwarz, the "evil" in this case resides squarely in the sons. This was a case prompted by greed; specifically, what I call "accelerated inheritance," such as Dante alludes to in the above passage regarding Sassol Mascheroni. There is no justified parricide (murder of a close relative) here, as there was in the case of Richard Jahnke Jr. (chapter 1).

"JOLLY JANE"

Though never formally adopted, Jane Toppan took the last name of Anne Toppan, the woman to whom she became an indentured servant around the time she was eight. Originally she was Honora Kelley, born in 1857, the younger of two daughters (there may have been other siblings) to Peter Kelley in Boston. Her father was a violent man and a severe alcoholic, who gave the two girls to an orphanage when Honora was six, their mother Bridgett having died of tuberculosis some years before. Ensconced two years later with the Toppans, Honora changed her first name also—to Jane. Both her father and her sister, Delia, died "insane," which in that era meant some kind of psychosis, whose precise nature we do not know. Though Jane herself was not mentally ill until the end of her life, she began showing unmistakable psychopathic traits while at school. She was a pathological liar who spread nasty rumors about her classmates and told tall tales of a grandiose nature to the effect that, for example, her (nonexistent?) brother was a hero at Gettysburg singled out for honor by Lincoln, and that her (insane) sister was a legendary beauty affianced to an English lord.[58] Released from her indentured status at eighteen, she trained as a nurse but was dismissed from nursing school for the same kinds of reasons that marred her reputation at grammar school: malicious gossip, compulsive lying—and perhaps also thievery. That dismissal was one of what seems in retrospect two turning points in her life at roughly the same time. She was also jilted by a prospective fiancé, following which, she became depressed and made several suicide gestures.

It was from this imperfect chrysalis that Jane emerged as the serial poisoner that we know today: responsible for the deaths of at least thirty-one persons, perhaps as many as a hundred. Most of these murders came in the course of her work as a private-duty nurse who, though never licensed in her profession, did manage to learn a thing or two about morphine, atropine, and arsenic. She killed almost exclusively those whom she knew. Her victims included her landlord (she then moved in with his widow) and her foster sister (whom Jane envied and hated), Elizabeth Toppan, who was at that time married to a Mr. Brigham. Later described as a pyromaniac, Jane set fires to several of the houses where she had worked. It was only after she had killed, one by one, the entire Davis family (with whom she had moved in with earlier), that suspicions were aroused enough to exhume the bodies. Though not mentally deranged at that time (she was forty-four), she was declared not guilty by reason of insanity, and was sent for life to an institution for the criminally insane in Taunton, Massachusetts.[59]

People at the time of her trial felt that nothing short of insanity could account for evildoing on such an appalling scale.[60] A remarkable feature of her murders was that she experienced orgasm when her victims were dying from her poisons. In this respect she resembles Countess Erzsébet

Báthory (mentioned in chapter 1), the only other woman I know of who can be described as a *female* serial *sexual* killer. As Jane rounded the turn of fifty, she showed paranoid traits, fearing that the hospital staff were, of all things, trying to poison her. Even toward the end of her long life (she died in the hospital in 1938), she would sometimes beckon to one of the nurses, urging her to "get the morphine, dearie, and we'll go out into the ward. You and I will have lots of fun seeing them die."[61] On the topic of evil, and comparing Jane with men who have committed serial sexual homicide, her biographer estimated that "though degrees of evil are difficult to gauge, the sheer malignancy she embodied was equal to that of her better known male counterparts."[62]

In a book that attempts to rank the hundred most evil people ever to have lived, Jane is assigned the fiftieth spot, well below Hitler, Ivan the Terrible, and the Countess Báthory, but well above Leonard Lake, Ian Brady, and the Marquis de Sade.[63] Though the Toppan name is no longer that well known among the public, Jane lives on secretly as the inspiration for the novel *The Bad Seed* by William March. This was later turned into a play and movie about a sociopathic child, who, despite having normal parents, became a serial poisoner at a young age.[64] The real Jane Toppan may have been something of a Bad Seed, inheriting some unfavorable genes from her father, but as we have seen, there were many other negative forces acting on her *after* her birth: the untimely loss of her mother and her years as an orphan and then maidservant to the Toppans.

JEREMY BAMBER

> Heredis flētus sub persona risus est.
> An heir's grief is laughter under the mask.
> —Publilius Syrus[65]

Coincidence or fate? On the very day I was writing this page about the murders of the Bamber family in a farmhouse northeast of London in August 1985, I thought it a good idea to check with Google about Jeremy Bamber's current fate. It had just been posted earlier that day, May 16, 2008, that Justice Tugendhat had declared, "These murders were exceptionally serious," and added, "In my judgment, you ought to spend the whole of the rest of your life in prison, and I so order."[66]

Jeremy, one of two children adopted by wealthy English landowners in Essex, was convicted of killing his adoptive parents, Neville and June Bamber, his adoptive sister Sheila, and her twin six-year-old boys, Dan and Nick Caffel by her ex-husband, Colin Caffel. The instrument was a rifle with a silencer. Jeremy was twenty-four at the time, and with all other heirs to the Bamber estate now dead, Jeremy was due to inherit their £400,000 estate. Both Jeremy and Sheila (twenty-seven at her death) had been adopted when they were about six months old from people who were considered normal and reputable. His birth father, for example, had been comptroller of stores at Buckingham Palace. Sheila had several nervous breakdowns after the twins were born and was felt to be a "paranoid schizophrenic," though the illness may have been a post-partum psychosis of some sort. Earlier, she had enjoyed a modest success as a model in London. After a threat that she might have to give the boys into fosterage, she reacted with a flare-up of her illness.

Jeremy, at all events, insisted he was innocent, claiming that the killer was his "nutter" of a sister, who killed the other four and then turned the rifle on herself. Evidence gathered at the time suggested otherwise, and as there were no others in the house besides the family (including Jeremy), the only possible assailant was Jeremy himself.[67] That is the way the Crown saw it, anyway, and Jeremy was sentenced to twenty-five years in prison—the sentence extended just now to life without parole.

The judge at the original trial said that Jeremy represented "evil almost beyond belief."[68] If Jeremy, who has protested his innocence all these years, is indeed guilty, he would be a better example of Bad Seed than Jane Toppan. By his own acknowledgement, he had enjoyed a secure and comfortable childhood, free of any neglect or abuse; his childhood memories were happy ones.[69] And since he was not mentally ill, his psychopathic traits presumably must have stemmed from inherited or other prenatal sources. Some students of this famous crime currently favor Jeremy's claim and put the blame on the (allegedly) suicidal and mentally disturbed sister.[70] Sheila, who also had a happy childhood, could not be considered a Bad Seed because she was not at all psychopathic. Her "inheritance" was simply a tendency to mental illness. So either Jeremy really is innocent after all, or he almost managed to stage the "perfect murder."

We see a picture of him (readily available on the Internet) looking appropriately sad at the funeral. Was this feigned grief (as suggested by the Latin maxim above)? Or is the judge wrong all these years later, calling Jeremy "evil," when he may not be? If Jeremy is ever released, albeit truly guilty, we can invoke another maxim by the same Latin author: *Judex damnatur ubi nocens absolvitur*—The judge is condemned when the guilty is absolved. Until such time as we know the truth, we at least know that in this case the only two possible suspects did what they did based solely on factors (psychopathy or psychosis) already in place the day they were born. To drop yet another Latin phrase used often at trials: *Cui bono*? Who benefits? If Sheila were truly suicidal at the prospect of losing her boys, she might have killed herself and maybe even the boys.[71] But why the parents? No benefit to her there, even psychologically. But Jeremy almost got his hands on that £400,000. That's a lot of money even today; it was a lot more in 1985.

PATTIE COLUMBO AND THE VICIOUS CIRCLE

In what seemed at first to be a Bad Seed case—a young woman of nineteen raised in an excellent family, then conspiring with her lover to kill that family—on closer look doesn't appear so simple. Pattie Columbo was the elder of two children in a working-class Chicago family. Her father, Frank, was of Italian American and Catholic background; the mother, Mary, of English, Irish and Baptist background. When Pattie was seven her parents had a son, Michael. The parents were loving, generous, and indulgent but also strict and unyielding when it came to moral standards. The latter qualities didn't really come into the picture until Pattie reached puberty when she was ten or eleven. Like her mother, Pattie had terrible cramps before her period. She began to have nightmares in which her favorite dog fell into a roaring fireplace. Her formerly sweet behavior underwent a change: she became wildly aggressive—once smashing a hair dryer over the head of one of her girlfriends. Already at twelve she wore a lot of makeup and dressed in a vampish way. A doctor suggested birth control pills to her mother as a means of controlling Pattie's premenstrual pains, but her mother refused, thinking this would legitimize Pattie's premature experimentation with sex. Her father would make her change into more demure attire before going to school. Pattie rebelled, packing a miniskirt and low-cut blouse in her backpack, changing into her sexy clothes the minute she arrived.

A real head-turner, Pattie was statuesque, looked older than her age, was sultry and tough in front view; quite beautiful in profile. At sixteen she had a boyfriend, with whom she was at once seductive and moralistic. She refused sex and was vehemently opposed to his using pot or other drugs. For a time he dated another girl, which excited jealousy in Pattie to the point that she threatened to beat that girl up. She grew resentful when her parents would ask her to babysit for her brother. Her mother had to undergo an operation for colon cancer; when she returned home, Pattie was asked to help out around the house with chores. She refused, and her father became so angry he slapped her hard in the face. Feeling that she was no longer "Daddy's girl" and that he loved Michael more than her, she threatened to call the police. This was the beginning of the vicious circle. She made her erstwhile gentle father furious, his slap made her enraged and defiant, which made him even more furious, the whole situation spiraling out of control.

Pattie worked as a waitress at a restaurant next door to a Walgreen's drugstore, where she met the manager, Frank DeLuca, who was forty years old and married with five children. It was love, or at least lust, at first sight. They became inseparable. He taught her things about sex she never knew; she was the beautiful young girl he had hitherto only dreamed about. Pattie dropped out of high school a few months before graduation, much to the consternation of her parents, who were becoming aware of her infatuation with DeLuca.[72] At eighteen Pattie moved in with DeLuca and his family. She and DeLuca would have sex in the marital bed while his wife, Marilyn, was out in the yard playing with the children. Pattie's father was so enraged at his daughter's immoral conduct and betrayal of his values that he charged over to Walgreen's with a rifle and threatened to kill DeLuca. Stopping just short of that, he swung the rifle at DeLuca, knocking out one of his teeth. Pattie retaliated by signing a warrant against her father for aggravated battery. The vicious circle was getting wider.

Finally, on May 4, 1976, Pattie and DeLuca, who by then had moved into an apartment of their own, went over to Pattie's parents' home and shot to death her parents and thirteen-year-old brother. Michael was also stabbed ninety-seven times, apparently by Pattie. The shooting was probably done by DeLuca. The scene was amateurishly staged to look like a burglary gone bad. The police know that overkill of that sort indicates rage and hatred; professional criminals kill when they feel they have to, using much neater and more efficient means.

Pattie and DeLuca feigned innocence but were eventually arrested and tried in court. Both were convicted of triple murder and sentenced to two hundred to three hundred years in prison. The prosecution contended, "She killed her father and she killed her mother, and she killed her brother, which is the hat-trick of evil."[73] The judge told Pattie's relatives after the sentencing: "You're going to want to figure this out. Don't. Don't even try to understand the criminal mind. You can't understand it. Only criminals understand it."[74] Yet we do have to try to understand it. When Pattie's father once asked his priest, "What did we do wrong?" the priest told him: "Nothing. It could just be Bad Seed."[75] I don't think so. Maybe Pattie inherited some of her father's volatile temperament, which would have made the "raging hormones" of puberty more inflammatory than in a calmer girl. Then there was the vicious circle of parents and daughter each offending the sensibilities of the other, each handling the stronger stresses by *physical* means rather than by reaching accommodations through talking things out. Add to all this the important element of *synergy*: two impetuous lovers acting together in a way neither would have acted alone, and the path to murder becomes not so incomprehensible after all.[76]

In the thirty intervening years, Pattie has had a long time to cool down. Ensconced in Illinois' Dwight Prison for Women, she has now completed college and spends her time fashioning study guide computer courses for some inmates and teaching other inmates to read. Dwight Prison lacks only a moat and a drawbridge to resemble a medieval castle. When I visited it, I noted that it was also uncommonly (for a prison) pretty on the inside. Pattie, it is said, still shows little remorse (and thus fails her chances at parole), but is popular among the women housed there: she is the queen of her new castle.

SPOUSES FROM HELL

In previous examples of husbands and wives whose spousal murders gained wide attention—and whose stories raised the specter of evil—we see people who were able to live for a time, if not in harmony, then at least in a kind of fragile truce. Nothing terrible happened until some event shook the marriage to its foundation and inspired murder. Discovery of infidelity was the triggering event for Clara Harris (chapter 2), whose behavior at work and at home was otherwise exemplary. Exposure of a reputation-shattering fraud was the turning point in the lives of Jean-Claude Romand (chapter 3) and Mark Hacking (chapter 4, note 44), neither of whom was quite the physician he made himself out to be. The desire for escape from a marriage gone stale into the excitement of an illicit affair, as it reached the boiling point and then some, propelled Kristin Rossum (chapter 4) and Jonathan Nyce (chapter 2) over the edge. It was debt that turned the moralistic crank John List (chapter 4) into a murderous crank. When he was finally identified eighteen years later, List's new wife swore that he had been a decent, honorable husband.

Besides these more celebrated cases, there is a much greater number of "spouses from hell" unsung and unnoticed, except by their unfortunate partners. In my forensic work I have dealt with several wives caught up in ugly divorces—"gaslighted" (that is, tricked into thinking they were going crazy) by their husbands—who spoke of these men as "evil." Two of these men were pedophiles: one molested a daughter; the other, a son. The men, knowing that a good offense is the best defense, used their considerable wealth to get their wives labeled "paranoid" or "delusional," since there was not a shred of evidence that they were psychologically disturbed. Manipulating the courts to their advantage, the men won out: bad fathers got custody; good mothers lost it. Several wives, equally manipulative and unscrupulous, were able to gain custody by tarring their husbands with the incest brush—claiming that their husbands had molested a daughter when there was not the slightest evidence to support such an accusation. The courts are not well equipped to ferret out the truth in many of these situations, with the result that Oliver Wendell Holmes's prayer, "May justice triumph over law!" went unanswered.[77]

One of the major impediments to justice in spousal cases, as we saw in the previous chapters, is the general reluctance to tell the truth whenever the victim of one's abuse or violence is a loved one or one's child. Most psychopaths will go to any length to avoid the public condemnation awaiting them if they admit to killing a family member. The aptly named Jimmy Ray Slaughter, for example, cheated on his third wife with four mistresses at the same time, one of whom (Melody Wuertz) refused to abort a pregnancy and gave birth to his daughter Jessica (proven his by DNA). Infuriated when she sued for child support, Slaughter shot to death Melody and their one-year-old daughter. After his conviction, far from confessing to the double murder, he sent out a notice from his Oklahoma death row cell in hopes of attracting the attention of some sympathetic woman. He wrote:

> My name is Jimmy Ray Slaughter. I've been accused of murder and it's not true. It was a lie from the beginning. You people will know it's true some day. May god [*sic*] have mercy on your souls. . . . I have an incurable romantic heart. I need to communicate with a warmhearted lady who also desires something extra special in life and beyond. I am a realist and have a story to tell, capable of shattering anyone's belief in the present justice system.[78]

Men like Jimmy Ray know better than anyone how easy it is to con others into believing their story. As we have seen in previous chapters, some are convincing enough to win an ill-advised release and with it the freedom to do again what they did before.

The main stories I have chosen for this section are about spouses who were impossible to live with throughout the length and breadth of the marriage. They created a hell so dreadful and suffering so excruciating that they converted the "real" hell, as depicted by Dante or Hieronymus Bosch, into a refuge devoutly to be wished for.

GENEROSA AMMON

Generosa took her name from her birth father, Generoso, an Italian sailor with whom her mother had had an affair. Her mother, who had once contemplated entering a convent, made a 180-degree switch, and became instead a wild party girl. Before giving birth to Generosa, she had two children by her first marriage and a daughter by her second. Generosa, besides being the one out-of-wedlock child, was also sexually abused by a man (possibly an uncle) who warned her to tell no one. Her mother died of breast cancer when Generosa was nine. She then learned of her illegitimate birth, after which she became insolent, irritable, and demanding.[79] She was expelled from school because of her incorrigible behavior and developed a ferocious temper, much of it directed at one of her half-sisters. She eventually completed college and moved to New York, where she hoped to work in the field of art and design.

In New York she met and married Ted Ammon, who became a multimillionaire in the finance industry. Wealth often serves as an emollient to an abrasive temperament—but not in Generosa's case. Quite the opposite, she became a snobbish bully, arrogant, insufferable, and with a talent for alienating everyone she came in contact with—especially people she hired for various tasks. She flew into blinding rages at any criticism or opposition. When she and Ted bought a large house in the swanky Hamptons of Long Island, she threw out thousands of tulips the gardeners had planted because they were "the wrong shade of yellow," then demanded thousands of replacements of the "right" shade. Unable to have children following an ectopic pregnancy, she and Ted adopted two fraternal twins from the Ukraine. The simplest word to describe her brand of mothering would be *sadistic*. When, for example, her adopted daughter ate a cookie before dinner, Generosa forced the rest of the cookies down her throat. With the marriage deteriorating like a bear market before a crash, Ted could take no more of her and began an affair. Generosa began meddling in Ted's business and made verbal threats to have him killed.

In 2000 she filed for divorce, and, besides poisoning the children's minds against their father, she had Ted surveilled via secret video devices planted throughout the Long Island house, in hopes of catching him "in flagrante" with his mistress. This scheme was not entirely unsuccessful: the camera did indeed yield some footage of Ted in bed—with their puppy. Generosa now started her own affair—with an ex- (and future) con, named Dan Pelosi. In yet another outburst of rage she, with Dan's help, went to the Hamptons and tossed thousands of dollars' worth of antique furniture out the window, then set fire to it all. Finally she hired Dan to kill Ted. Dan carried out that job, using a blunt-force instrument.

Their perfect crime was a flop in two ways: Dan was caught and convicted, and she died soon thereafter of breast cancer—a disease she had neglected just as her mother had. So any plans she had for a life with Ted's money but no Ted went unrealized. From the standpoint of character aberrations, she had, to an intense degree, the traits of paranoid, borderline, narcissistic, and sadistic personalities, along with the callousness, lack of remorse, and manipulativeness of the psychopath.

JOHN RAY WEBER

The story of John Ray Weber is chilling beyond words. Even if there are words adequate to tell the full story, they would be too graphic for a book aimed merely at explaining evil, while avoiding the obscene.[80] I faced this same dilemma in the previous chapter when trying to describe the tortures inflicted by David Parker Ray. One writer, in reviewing a book about Weber, commented: "There is no other word for John Ray Weber except evil," adding that "it could be argued that the word describes what Weber did, not what he is. The other side of the argument, however, is that John Ray Weber started doing evil things from the time he could walk, almost as if it were an inborn capability."[81] A similar sentiment is expressed in yet another book about Weber: the killer taunts his wife, Emily, whom he tortured and nearly murdered, with the remark, "Oh, you didn't know I killed [his wife's sister] Carla, did you?" Until that moment, "Emily had never realized how evil John was."[82]

I spoke of David Parker Ray as *appearing* to be the most cruel and sadistic of the serial killers, barring the existence of another whose tortures exceeded those that took place in Ray's Toy Box. Granted that there is no accurate yardstick for gauging the extreme ends of suffering, we cannot readily compare Ray with Weber, because much of what Ray did to his victims in the Toy Box remains unknown. The bodies of his victims have not been found; we assume he killed many, but we do not know precisely how. We do know that the suffering of Ray's victims was protracted. What Weber did to his sister-in-law and wife was, I think it is fair to say, worse than what we *know* Ray did—but not necessarily worse than what Ray *may have done* to his victims before each woman was finally murdered.[83]

Weber grew up in Phillips, Wisconsin, a working-class town of 1,500 people some fifty miles from Lake Superior. He had an older sister, Cathy, and five half-siblings from his mother's first marriage. His mother, Marguerite, had suffered two nervous breakdowns of an unknown type. By age four, Weber was already setting fires in his house and in his aunt's house. Bed-wetting remained a problem until he was fifteen, and later, he strangled a dog. Thus he showed the whole "triad" of behaviors considered to be a predictor of future violence.

At the ages of ten and sixteen, he suffered head injuries—the first in a car accident—though we do not know how serious these were. By age ten he was hearing voices, experiencing nightmares of drowning in blood, and assaulting his friend's sister in the vaginal area. He also began to have fantasies of eating a girl who lived next door. A misfit at school, at age twelve he wrote down various sadistic fantasies and placed them on his teacher's desk. She is said to have left town afterward. Weber cross-dressed in his sister Cathy's clothing and became consumed with morbid sexual obsessions. These thoughts related to bondage, pornography, cannibalism, torture, burning people, shocking people with electricity, shoving needles or even wheelbarrow handles into their body parts, and squeezing other body parts with pliers. He used to mutilate his sisters' dolls in what would be their "sexual" areas.

At thirteen he struck Cathy with a beer bottle; three years later he threatened to kill her with a .22 rifle—this prompted the first of two psychiatric hospitalizations; his parents now realizing that there was something "not right" with John. A psychologist who had examined John presciently predicted that he would "commit a hostile act against a woman by the time he was eighteen."[84] Before that, at perhaps fourteen, he would attempt sexual acts during the night with Cathy, with whom he was infatuated. She would awaken and discover that "things were done to her." He stole panties and bras from Cathy, and money as well, including large sums from the family's store where he worked for a time. This was actually his grandmother's store, which later went bankrupt. He once smeared his grandmother's dresses with feces. Cathy was terrified of him and moved away to live with relatives. But when she returned home after graduating high school, he attacked her again, which brought about his second hospitalization. Weber then went into the army in 1981. During his three-year stint he stayed out of trouble, though he did begin to use alcohol and LSD and, eventually, marijuana and angel dust as well. He primed himself with alcohol before the sexual crimes he was later to commit.

In 1986, when he was twenty-three, he married Emily Lenz and worked as a laborer. His bed-wetting resumed, and he was impotent with his wife. Weber became preoccupied with her younger sister, Carla. Three months into his marriage he abducted Carla at gunpoint, tortured her, and then killed and buried her in the woods. Her body was not found until he confessed to the crime two years later. He seems to have put the blame for his impotence on Emily, since he later exclaimed that "women are nothing. . . . They flaunt their bodies and think they can get anything by being a cock-tease."

Picturing himself a "star," he boasted at his 1989 trial, "I'll bet they make a TV movie out of this." The trial came only after he had tried, two years later, to murder Emily in the same fashion as Carla. It came out at the trial that he had taken Emily to the same secluded area in the woods, had tortured and beaten her, cut her with a knife, and raped her with a wheelbarrow handle—just as he had done with her sister. John had also forced his wife to write and sign letters, postdated some months ahead and addressed to her family, which he planned to send later on as if to substantiate the claim he would make that she had simply run off and abandoned him.

Emily, though she barely survived, had gotten off easy: she was unable to open her eyes when she was found, had serious internal injuries, and was black and blue over her entire body. Carla had suffered all the tortures Emily had, but in addition suffered more extreme tortures, including being burned in her sexual areas and having needles inserted in her breasts. At first John put duct tape over her face so she could neither see nor speak. But at the end, he ripped off the tape, forcing her to see what he was going to do to her next: he severed part of her breast tissue with a knife and cut part of her left leg. He then suffocated her with his foot and buried her in the woods. Responding to the accusation of cannibalism, he claimed and later denied that he ate the tissues he had cut off. So whether Weber's depravity reached the level of cannibalism remains somewhat in doubt. What is not in doubt is the degree of his lifelong obsession with sadistic fantasies, about which he said, in a manner typical of sexual sadists, "The act is never as good as the anticipation."[85] No matter how excruciating and savage the tortures, that is, they always fall short of the scene that the sadist, like a failed artist whose canvases never measure up to his inner vision, had hoped to "create."

Currently serving a life sentence in Wisconsin's Green Bay Correctional Institution, Weber—his six-feet-six-inch frame just a few inches short of Ed Kemper's six-feet-nine—is as docile in prison as he was intimidating on the outside.[86] Though declared mentally ill by his defense attorneys—partly on the strength of his previous hospitalizations—Weber is not psychotic. As proof, he is able to write in a terse but logical fashion.

For me, one of the strangest facts of the Weber case concerns the criminal complaint by the Wisconsin Circuit Court, issued against him after the attempted murder of his wife. In an eerie and of course totally unintentional coincidence with David Parker Ray's sixteen-page single-spaced message to his victims—cited in the last chapter as being too repugnant to read—the Wisconsin complaint also consists of a sixteen-page single-spaced document. It is written by the police in graphic vernacular terms that render their account of the tortures also too repugnant to read.[87] In another similarity with Ray, Weber had made a cassette tape that set forth in detail just how he had killed Carla Lenz, who was reported as missing on November 12, 1986. The tape had been prepared with the intention of Emily being forced to listen to it, just as was the case with the victims of David Parker Ray.

The extraordinary depravity of the Weber case is in many ways a carbon copy of the David Parker Ray case, albeit worse, primarily because we *know* he committed a murder of the most degrading sort, while we only suspect Ray did likewise (and much more often). For some, the Weber case raised the question whether the evil embodied in his actions lay so far outside the human domain that a supernatural explanation was required—as though the ancient religious writers were correct after all.[88] Only if some malefic god of evil—Satan perhaps—had infiltrated the soul of John Weber could he have harbored such evil ideas from merest childhood, finally putting them fully into action during his twenties. Would that it were so. This would get John Weber and the rest of humanity off the hook; he was just a puppet on the devil's strings. Unfortunately, human beings are capable of actions just as devilish and demonic as those of Weber.

Despite the similarities of the actions of Ray and Weber in their extreme sexual tortures announced by sadistic taped messages, the two men differed in important ways. David Parker Ray was a loner but not a social misfit; he married, fathered children, was a reliable and steady worker and, of course, an all-too-skilled mechanic. He was in no sense crazy. John Weber had everything going against him: a mentally ill mother, head injuries, parental physical abuse, alcohol and drug abuse, as well as bondage and torture fantasies from early childhood. Like Richard Chase, Weber may have made his psychological state worse by drug and alcohol abuse, but he appears neither schizophrenic, as Chase was, nor as coldly rational as Ray. He was, rather, somewhere in between. He could also be considered a serial killer of the "disorganized" type (careless, for example, in letting his wife survive) and therefore more readily caught. We would have to say he was a serial killer manqué, since he had all the psychological features of a serial killer but killed only one person that we know of, another that we suspect, and his wife, who survived—all of which falls short of the FBI's standard of a minimum of three murder victims. How the various risk factors interacted in Weber to twist him into becoming a serial killer is the topic we will discuss in greater detail in the next chapter. Meantime, we must acknowledge that it is this interplay of adverse factors that answers—as much as can be answered—the "why" question about Weber's evil. Curiously, in his youth, Weber had an imaginary friend with whom he conversed in his head and whom he called *Natas*—"Satan," that is, spelled backwards. That seems to have been his explanation for his evil mind, but it should not be ours. We do not need to invoke Satan.

Chapter Nine

SCIENCE LOOKS AT EVIL

Canto III, ll. 72–78

"Maestro, or mi concedi	"Master, now grant
ch'i' sappia quali sono, e qual costume	that I may know who those are, and what
le fa di trapassar parer sì pronte,	disposition makes them seem so ready to cross over,
com' I' discerno per lo fioco lume."	as I can discern despite the weak light."
Ed elli a me: "Le cose ti fier conte	And he to me: "These things will be made known to you
quando noi fermerem li nostri passi	when we stay our steps
su la trista riviera d' Acheronte."	on the gloomy shore of Acheron."

It should be clear by now, from reading the vignettes of the various men and women whose actions were considered evil, that there is no common route they all traveled to reach the place they did. Even among the men who became serial killers—the group most likely to garner the appellation of "evil"—their histories are quite dissimilar. Tommy Lynn Sells and the serial killer manqué John Ray Weber both had many different risk factors: Sells had an abysmal childhood full of abuse and abandonment; Weber's childhood included physical abuse, head injury, a mentally ill mother, and what are called "risk genes" for some sort of mental illness. Here the phrase *risk genes* is a technical term meaning genes that are believed to increase the risk for developing a particular condition (in Weber's case, the risk for a serious mental illness such as schizophrenia).

But Richard Starrett and Dennis Rader both came from what appears to have been rather ordinary, nontraumatic home environments. Head injury seemed to be the only factor in Starrett's case, whereas none of the common risk factors was present in Rader.

For an act to reach the level of evil—whether violent or murderous or simply humiliating or sadistic in the extreme, though without violence—an intense *narcissism* is almost always part of the personality makeup: the red thread that runs through all the persons we have encountered earlier. This characteristic stands out unmistakably, for example, in the men who "stage" the murders of their wives, hoping to make the murder appear as an accident or as the act of some other assailant. These men do not always show the full picture of psychopathy (as was sketched in chapter 1).

Given that the pathways to what we call evil are so diverse, we are moved to ask: Can modern research provide any useful clues, let alone firm answers, as to what factors count the most as precursors to evil actions? How much, and in which cases, are heredity (of mental illness and unfavorable temperament), maternal drug abuse, fetal distress, and low birth weight the prime culprits? How much, and in which cases, are maternal neglect, parental brutality, sexual abuse, head injury, alcoholism and drug abuse, and hormones the main culprits? Some factors span both heredity and environment: personality is said to be half related to genetic influences, half to "non-shared" environment.[1] Being male or female makes a big difference: males are far more likely to commit violent, including "evil," acts. Gender is something we inherit, but once we start out in life as a male or a female, expectations and experiences begin to differ—to a significant degree because of the sex we were born into.

If we want to look at evil from a scientific perspective, we need to take another factor into consideration. This is because the actions we call evil are usually not very different from degrading or murderous actions in general—yet we don't call all of them "evil." When we look at evil actions, or at those few people who strike us as evil personified, we begin to realize there is a cultural or, in other situations, a sociological element in the equation that we often overlook. Actions that are unpleasant or even outright criminal—but that don't wound anyone physically or emotionally—are seldom spoken of as evil. This goes for embezzlement, selling fake watches, stock manipulation, even most instances of corporate skullduggery. Perhaps the many employees who lost their pensions because of the higher-ups at Enron, whose manipulations caused the whole firm to go under, regard those men as evil. I wouldn't argue with them. But "evil" is not the term customarily applied to those men. Arrogant, greedy, rapacious, unscrupulous, Ponzi-scheming fraudsters . . . all that. But not evil. To rank as evil, something else is required: the element of shock and horror that touches the public in a special way. There are two broad categories we need to look at. One is the nature of the act. The other is the nature of the victim.

Here are some crimes and other acts likely to be regarded as evil:

- Rape of a stranger
- Serial sexual murder
- Serial murder of patients in a hospital
- Mass murder[2]
- Torture, especially of a child
- Kidnap, especially of a child[3]
- Murder with malice aforethought, especially of a wife, with such motives as greed (Justin Barber, who killed his wife, April, for insurance money[4]); to avoid the responsibilities of fatherhood (Scott Peterson); or to avoid fatherhood and be free to be with a mistress (Charles Stuart, who shot his pregnant wife to death, then himself—superficially—and pretended they had been accosted by a (nonexistent) black man in Boston[5])
- Mutilation of the body, especially of a live victim (e.g., John Ray Weber)
- Horrific crime with mutilation by a mentally ill person[6]
- Jealousy murders of a spectacular (hence unusual) sort[7]
- Certain revenge-inspired acts even in the absence of violence[8]

"Evil" will likely be the reaction if the victim fits any of these categories:

- Beautiful women[9]
- Celebrities (performers, famous politicians)[10]
- Child/children[11]
- Elderly persons
- Physically disabled persons
- Persons in an "honorable" profession: judges, doctors, teachers, priests (or other religious figure: nuns, ministers, rabbis)[12]
- Victims of a terroristic crime[13] (this will include the wife whose husband engages in "gaslighting" in hopes of driving her into submission or even suicide)

- Victims of a hate crime[14]
- The victim is an iconic and widely revered art object[15]

To get a sense of the difference that fame and social class of the victim make in our view of evil, let us contrast the hate-crime murder mentioned in chapter 1, in which a bigoted Vietnam vet stabbed a homeless black man (in his belief that the "blacks were taking over"), with the Matthew Shepard case. Shepard was a (white) student from a good family, who was murdered in a novel and spectacular fashion by two bigoted men. The Shepard case came to national attention both because of the shocking manner of the murder and the fact that Matthew was a well-liked and talented young man with whom people (irrespective of their sexual orientation) could sympathize and identify. Both murders had the quality of evil, but most people had heard only about the Matthew Shepard case. The public knows evil when it sees it. My purpose here, and throughout these pages, is to look for the nuances of evil and to refine that search.

For these reasons, when science holds the magnifying glass to evil, it is looking at the same set of motives that apply to bad actions in general: actions motivated by the usual suspects of jealousy, greed, lust, revenge, hatred, and the desire to avoid public humiliation. There will be no key that opens all doors to the mystery of evil: no "evil gene," no specific type of parental brutality that underlies all cases we label evil and that can be understood as a causative factor *guaranteed* to produce evil. Instead, we will see only a complex menu of "risk factors": a vegetable soup, if you will, of factors from which, if the soup simmers long enough, and if some of the special ingredients we listed above are mixed in, evil may eventually rise to the surface. There will, in addition, be many crimes we designate as evil but where the deciding factor was accidental. For example, a fifteen-year-old girl was recently killed in New York by a stray bullet fired by a drug dealer aiming at a rival dealer. Because the girl happened to be pregnant, the media understandably dealt with this crime much more harshly. In a like vein, a serial killer caught after the fourth murder may be cut from the same biological cloth as another who has killed dozens, but "evil" will be applied more readily to the latter, because he has wreaked so much more damage and tragedy.

Some of the stories from the previous chapters have already made clear what is crucial to our discussion of scientific aspects—that it is not so much this or that single factor but instead a *pathway*, peculiar to each person, leading from before birth to the moment of the evil action. The risk factors may be very few in number, though *multiple* factors are the norm, with the "menu" varying from one person to the next. And we must always keep in mind that there still remain many "x's"—many unknowns—in the algebra of evil. One of the most important of these is the number of people who have just as many negative factors as a multiple murderer or a serial killer, but who have led an innocent life as a bank clerk, a nurse, an engineer, a dressmaker—and who have never harmed anyone. Gary Gilmore (mentioned briefly in chapter 7), for example, was a violent, sadistic man who tyrannized his girlfriends and ultimately shot a gas station attendant to death for the $24 that was in the cash register. Gary, the "evil" brother in his family, was executed in Utah by firing squad and was then immortalized (if that is the right word) by Norman Mailer in his book *The Executioner's Song*.[16] Gary had three brothers. All four were beaten and abused by their alcoholic father, but Gary got the worst of it, because he was the rebellious one (owing to genetic influences, I suspect) and thus drew more punishment from his father. Gary's rebelliousness is consistent with what would also be called *childhood conduct disorder*, which is known to have a strong hereditary component and to be closely linked with future antisocial behavior.[17]

The other three brothers were never in trouble. One of them, Mikal Gilmore, became a distinguished writer. Mikal wrote a book about his brother—a much better (and mercifully shorter) one than Mailer's, in my opinion.[18] So right there is one person among millions—and a blood relative, to boot—who suffered parental brutality and did not end up becoming a violent criminal.

As we survey the findings from research into human violence, mental illness, personality aberrations, and the like, we will find that the material will be pertinent to our discussion of evil as well. We just need to keep in mind that, although brain and background among murderers may be very similar, the evil/not evil distinction will usually depend on the unpredictable nuances mentioned above: *Who was the victim?* and *What was done to the victim?*

SOME BASIC BRAIN MECHANISMS

People who do acts of violence (or who subject others to physical or emotional suffering of a sort that falls short of violence) have presumably made a choice. They could have acted otherwise. Even among those whose acts were impulsive, made too abruptly to have been preceded by anything much in the way of conscious thought, there was a life history that led up to the hurtful or evil event. Had they often been exposed to violence? Had they been taught (as had the young persons Lonnie Athens wrote about) that lashing out quickly was the right way to handle stressful encounters? Had they so meager a repertoire of responses that they simply behaved in a knee-jerk fashion to whatever bothered them? As far as the brain is concerned, their action still can be understood as the final pathway—the final "solution," no matter how dreadful and inappropriate—of a complex process going on in the relevant centers within the brain.

Before we look at the anatomy of the brain itself, it will be useful to consider an analogy from a different world: that of the automobile. The human brain, with its hundred billion neurons and quadrillion (a million billion) interconnections, has rightly been called the most complex thing in the known universe.[19] The car is much simpler. There are, to be sure, a lot of parts and pieces under the hood, but once the car is turned on, it responds basically to what we do with the accelerator, and what we do with the brake pedal. The steering wheel guides us to our destination. Think of the accelerator (along with the steering wheel) as the representatives of our wishes, desires, preferences, impulses, or to use a psychological word, our *drives* (driving and "drives" make a good comparison here). The brakes can be compared to the brain mechanisms we summon (only a few of which will ever be fully *conscious*) to *inhibit* our drives.

Translating this imagery back into the workings of the brain, we find that there are areas of the brain that deal with our basic drives, including our basic emotions. These areas are found primarily in the more primitive brain centers that are attuned to grasping what is good and what is threatening in the environment. These centers also call forth immediate, and what are considered life-saving, reactions: where quick response rather than deliberate, slow reflection is what will save the day. Neuroscientists lump these brain regions and their responses under the heading of "bottom-up" mechanisms, since they are related directly to elemental needs and drives, with little or no modification from the higher centers. The analogy here is to the car's accelerator. The higher centers involve our gray matter, the cerebrum, with its four main areas of lobes—frontal, temporal, parietal, and occipital—on each side. The frontal lobes are much more developed in humans than in other animals. These frontal centers act as if weighing and measuring which of various possible responses to the outside world may be in our best interest and which ones would be bad for us—or even disastrous. These centers are lumped together under the heading of "top-down" mechanisms. They correspond to the car's brake system.

Moving from the simple car analogy to a somewhat more complex analogy involving the brain itself, we can look at how some of the bottom-up mechanisms influence, and may in turn be influenced by, some of the key top-down mechanisms. A useful comparison to the behavior of violent persons is the behavior of the drug addict, particularly, the person addicted to cocaine. Some of the more significant brain regions in the pathway operating in cocaine addicts have been worked out by Dr. Nora Volkow, director of the National Institute on Drug Abuse, and her colleagues.[20] Four of the important areas are shown in a side ("sagittal") view through the middle of the brain (please refer to color plate 17). These are the amygdala, the nucleus accumbens, the anterior cingulate gyrus, and the orbitofrontal cortex. The first two belong to the bottom-up mechanisms; the last two, to the top-down mechanisms. In the next diagram, these areas are shown in a schematic way (please refer to color plate 18).

The *amygdala* is a small twin organ (on either side of the middle temporal lobe) that serves a number of functions, such as learning and storing information about emotional memory. Emotional memory is primarily "implicit," or unconscious, in contrast to the function of the nearby hippocampus, involved in storing declarative (conscious) memory.[21] Recent research has focused on the processing of fear by the amygdala, though the organ deals with other emotions as well. In general the amygdala weighs the emotional significance of stimuli from the environment. Damage to the amygdala interferes with developing the appropriate conditioning to stimuli that would normally inspire fear.[22]

The *nucleus accumbens* is also a twin organ: one at the lower part of each frontal lobe. This region plays an integral role in laughter, pleasure, addiction, and fear. The nucleus accumbens is also the site of action of highly addictive drugs such as cocaine and amphetamine, which, as with most recreational drugs, increases the levels of dopamine (a transmitter chemical associated with pleasure sensation) in this already dopamine-sensitive organ.[23] A term often associated with the function of this nucleus is *salience*. What this amounts to is the degree of desirability of the various potential choices we might make in any given situation—in effect, our priorities.

The *anterior cingulate* is associated with executive functions and has connections with the frontal, temporal, and parietal lobes but also with the amygdala. The anterior cingulate serves, as one of its important functions, the brain's error-prevention system, detecting conflicts and helping to control strategic processes. Putting those processes into action, however, is not the task of the anterior cingulate. Instead, it relays its "suggestions" for the resolution of conflicts to the prefrontal cortex for the actual setting in motion (implementation) of the appropriate behavior. "Appropriate" here does not always mean the most socially adaptive behavior but rather the behavior the brain "decides" is in its best interests at the moment (even if the behavior turns out upon subsequent reflection to have been unwise or dreadful).[24] In this sense the anterior cingulate acts as a jury, giving its recommendation to a "higher authority"—one that is capable of actually carrying out the recommendation.

The *orbitofrontal cortex*, also located in the lower portion of the frontal lobes at the level of the eyes, is part of the prefrontal cortex. The orbitofrontal cortex is involved with thought processes and decision making. As such, this region regulates planning behaviors associated with reward and punishment.[25] The portion of the orbitofrontal cortex nearer the brain's midline (the "medial" portion) is occupied particularly with monitoring, learning, and also with memory of the reward value of various incoming messages from other parts of the brain. The lateral portion is involved with the evaluation of punishment warnings, which, if heeded, may lead to changes in behavior.[26] Damage to this area of the brain may result in such unwanted behaviors as excessive swearing, hypersexuality, poor social interaction, compulsive gambling, abuse of alcohol and drugs, and an impaired ability to tune in correctly to the emotions of other people (that is, lowered *empathy*).

THE FOUR REGIONS AND THE COCAINE ADDICT

In a lecture given by Dr. Nora Volkow, she outlined how these four regions might interact in the case of a cocaine addict, using imagery of the traffic lights that drivers are supposed to obey.[27] In the scenario typical of the addict, the bottom-up regions show a strong drive to use cocaine. The fear that the amygdala might ordinarily register in relation to the expected bad consequences of such use is muted in the addict. As a result, instead of sending warning signals, *favorable* signals are sent to the nucleus accumbens, where it turns out that the salience menu is drastically abbreviated. A normal person, faced with the prospect of an evening with nothing to do, might choose from a variety of possible pleasures: calling a friend or sweetheart, going to a movie, reading a mystery novel . . . the list will be quite long. For the user of cocaine (or possibly the equally dangerous methamphetamine), only cocaine has salience. If the anterior cingulate declares "that is not a good idea" —but in too weak a voice—the orbitofrontal cortex, as final arbiter, may conclude: "All things considered, I'll reach for the cocaine." The drug then gets the green light in Dr. Volkow's schema. If, as a result of a rehabilitation program, the drive for cocaine remains strong but the top-down centers are now also strong enough to veto the plan, the person may be able to avoid the temptation to use cocaine and may opt for a wiser choice. This relatively simple example prepares us to look at the more gnarled and difficult situations that certain people face as they contemplate an action that has socially terrible consequences or even the overtones of evil.

I have taken for an example that of the wife killer Justin Barber and his unfortunate wife, April.[28] What prompted the murder in the case of this highly narcissistic man was a combination of mounting debts, compulsive womanizing, and increasing irritation at his model-pretty but (to Justin) oppressively sensible and reasonable wife. April was moderation-in-all-things. Justin, though a midlevel executive earning a good salary, was grandiose and reckless. To acquire the fanciest cars he resorted to risky day trading on the stock market, with the result that he owed large sums both to his broker and his car dealer. He needed, as fast as practicable, a change of fate and a change of mate. April had been keeping up her payments on a two-million-dollar insurance policy of which her husband was the beneficiary. He had already let lapse the similar policy on his life. Justin evolved a plan for a "perfect crime": the murder of his heavily insured wife artfully constructed to appear as the work of a mysterious assailant. After tapping into the Internet for guidelines about where to shoot oneself so as not to sustain any real damage, Justin lured April to a secluded Florida beach, where, a few days short of their third anniversary, he shot April to death (with one bullet) and shot himself in the hands and right chest (with four bullets). He told the police they had both been attacked by a man whose features he couldn't clearly make out because it was a dark night. If we try to grasp the "reasoning" of the husband according to the model of these four brain regions, we come up with a scenario that could have unfolded in this fashion:

The amygdala (rather than reacting with *fear* at the prospect of committing murder and the likelihood of getting caught, justifies the action): "There's some risk, sure, but I've been in tough situations before and I always got away with it; I've got it all figured out, foolproof, and I have nothing to worry about."

The nucleus accumbens (waving aside an accommodation with the bank, divorce, declaring bankruptcy, etc.): "Wow! With that two million, I'll pay off the debt, and have enough left over to live off the interest in the Bahamas . . ."

The anterior cingulate (acting as jury instead of shouting down such an absurd plan): "Well, I guess cops are stupid and you can fool them, though maybe they *could* figure out there was no third person; so I don't know. . . . That'd mean a long sentence. . . . I'd vote against it" (but the voice of the jury is weak and vacillating).

The orbitofrontal cortex (the final judge—paying more attention here to the strong drives than to the weak conscience): "I've listened to the arguments on both sides. We're too smart for the police, and that two million can solve a lot of problems. Do it!"

April had been dead only a few days before the detectives began to suspect that there was no mysterious assailant after all and that the killer was the husband himself. The police found it unusually difficult to gather enough evidence to bring the husband to trial where he was eventually found guilty and sentenced to life in prison. As is common in cases of planned murder of a wife, Justin never confessed to the crime and showed no remorse. His self-confidence (that he could literally get away with murder) and determination to go ahead with his plan (remaining deaf to the voice of conscience) are typical of men and women who do commit serious acts of violence.

Apart from a few persons who have either spoken or written candidly about their crimes, we are seldom granted a window into their conscious minds.[29] As to the kind of cross-talk between the four brain centers mentioned above, we can only speculate about the kinds of (unconscious) communication that goes on among them. But it is fair to assume, given that they have all crossed the line from intention to action, that the voice of the Will was ultimately stronger than the voice of Conscience. From a neurophysiological point of view, the inhibitory brain centers, and the pools of neurons within them, could not stem the tide of violent desire. It is worth emphasizing once more that the physiology of violence (and here I include the nonphysical forms of extreme humiliation and subjugation, as well) and the physiology of evil are fundamentally the same. In either case we are dealing with acts that are criminal specifically because, as Émile Durkheim reminds us, they shock the "collective conscience" of society.[30] Those deemed *evil* by this collective conscience (the voice of the public, as I have referred to it throughout this book) happened to have shocked this conscience a step further—by the nature of the act, the nature of the victim, or both.

Contemporary psychiatric research now includes many important contributions, in addition to those of Dr. Volkow, supportive of the analogy I have been making about a failure of the brain's "braking mechanism." Dr. Larry Siever, for example, in his masterful review of the neurobiology of aggression and violence, has advanced the view that the "aggressive diathesis [or tendency] can be conceptualized in terms of an imbalance between the 'top-down' control or 'brakes' provided by the orbital frontal cortex and anterior cingulate cortex . . . and excessive 'bottom-up' drives triggered or signaled by the limbic regions, such as the amygdala and insula."[31]

The analogy of the "conversation" among brain centers applies not just to cases such as Justin Barber's murder of his wife but to the majority of the cases we have been considering. The serial killer, for example, whose accumbens-related salience system has forsworn all the simple pleasures in favor of rape-murder—the only thrill that will satisfy his "reward centers"—is not to be deterred by any *fear* messages from the amygdala: he assumes he could get away with disposing of his victims. And the more apparent success he has, the more emboldened he becomes. Gary Ridgway, though one of the least intelligent serial killers (looking only at his IQ), went eighteen years undetected for the seventy or so women that he killed. The higher centers that regulate our level of empathic concern for others (often called *compassion*) were also seriously compromised in Gary's case: he referred to the women as "garbage." But Gary Ridgway was not mentally ill: he was not schizophrenic, not manic, not delusional because of drug abuse, not brain-injured, not "crazy" in any other way. The balance between drives and inhibitions in Gary's case was disrupted primarily by an abnormality of *personality*. In general, this balance can be overturned in any of a variety of other ways as well, as, for example, by mental illness. Keeping in mind that an imbalance in the mental forces we have been discussing can come about in many different ways—insufficient fear of punishment, drives that are overpowering, weak or faulty sense of right and wrong, skewed or enfeebled judgment—we are now in a better position to understand from a neuroscience perspective some of the more common ways this can occur.

PRIMARY MENTAL ILLNESS

The Major Psychoses

Mental illness is generally "multifactorial," meaning that genetic as well as environmental factors have interacted to produce the clinical picture we see. In the so-called major psychoses—schizophrenia and manic-depressive psychosis—the genetic factor is of crucial importance. The so-called risks genes for these conditions are going to be present, though in some people the combined effects of these various genes are not enough to make the condition clinically recognizable. This may be because the genetic contribution was not so powerful or because there were other favorable ("modifying," or *protective*) genetic influences that softened the effects of the abnormal genes. At the moment, our focus is on the primarily genetic forms of mental illness.

Briefly put, the phrase "mental illness" ordinarily refers to conditions where one's reality testing is gravely impaired. By reality testing I am referring to having a good grasp on one's identity and on the natures of the people in one's everyday life. A more subtle aspect of reality testing relates to ideas about what is happening in the world and to estimates about the likelihood of notions about cause and effect. To think, for example, that there is a radio implanted in one's teeth that receives messages from God is so radical a departure from what really could happen that reality testing is seriously hampered. Such a thought is "crazy." To insist that you are the reincarnation of Alexander the Great shows a different kind of impairment in reality testing; in this case, grandiosity has gone overboard: this is a "megalomanic" distortion.

If the abnormality in reality testing is primarily in one's *thinking*, the condition will usually be called schizophrenia. If the abnormality affects predominantly *mood*, the condition will be called either mania (the mood is too elevated) or depression (the mood is unrealistically low). These distinctions are not always so clear-cut in real life: intermediate conditions may exist (thought and mood may both be affected). Some less common variants also exist. We have noted earlier that both schizophrenia and mania are associated with a heightened tendency to violence. The shock value of the violence may epitomize our notion of evil. This will be particularly true of schizophrenia, where one's judgment—and the violent crime that judgment may give rise to—may be so incomprehensible or bizarre, so unlike anything we have ever heard of before, that *crazy* or *evil* are the first words that come to mind.

One example concerns a woman who took a knife and eviscerated her mother through the genitals—in order to release the "good mother" who lay swallowed up and buried, like Jonah inside the whale—from the "Devil," which in her mind was the mother's visible body. The woman had never committed an act of violence, nor any other crime, before, so the abnormality lay primarily in the "thinking" part of the brain, corresponding for didactic purposes to the orbitofrontal cortex in our model (though what we mean by *thought* is not confined exclusively to this one area).

There are other, less common conditions, each reminiscent of schizophrenia, where *judgment* is radically impaired. Each may lead, on the rare occasion, to a similar kind of violence that smacks of the bizarre or the uncanny. One such condition is called *delusional disorder*, where the distortion in one's sense of reality, though profound, is confined to a comparatively small area of one's total thought. Not only that, but the peculiarity of thought is so cleverly constructed, so "reasonable" sounding—usually involving nefarious plots that *might just possibly* be true—that other people who hear the person's delusional tale may themselves be persuaded, or may be willing, temporarily at least, to give him the benefit of the doubt. Here is an example:

I once had occasion to interview a woman who was serving a long sentence for killing the man in whose house she lived as a lodger. A highly intelligent and deeply knowledgeable woman, conversant over a wide range of historical and other subjects, she had nevertheless developed (after the birth of her last child) the unshakable conviction that her landlord was secretly plotting to kill her by dropping poison pellets in her breakfast tea. Imagining herself locked in this kill-or-be-killed drama, she shot him to death one morning in the kitchen they shared, then proudly summoned the local police. To her astonishment, rather than celebrating with her this victory over so cunning an adversary, they promptly arrested her for murder. Though grossly delusional about the supposed machinations of the landlord (and certain co-conspirators hidden away in other parts of the country), she was sent to prison, rather than to a forensic hospital. She became the victim, ironically, of her own lucidity and normality on every other topic of conversation. It would have been most instructive to study the patterns of the woman's brain responses during a functional magnetic resonance imaging [fMRI] examination to see which areas of the brain "lit up" when the direction of questioning were shifted from, say, the dynasties of ancient Egypt (which she could discuss with professorial authority) to the execution-style murder of her landlord. Unfortunately, the budgetary constraints of the prison, as the warden informed me, left no surplus for scientific inquiry of that sort, however informative it may have proven.

Asperger's Syndrome

A milder condition within the spectrum of autistic disorders, Asperger's Syndrome is characterized by poor empathy, overly formal speech, and an all-absorbing preoccupation with just one area of interest. The condition is rare (perhaps 1 out of 5,000 children; boys are 3 or 4 times more likely to have the condition than girls); the language and communicational impairments are not as severe as in autism. Asperger's and autism have a strong genetic component, though there is no known gene or group of genes common to all cases. These conditions used to be grouped with schizophrenia because they involved aberrations of thinking rather than of mood, but they appear to be a separate group.[32]

There does not seem to be one distinct region of the brain where an abnormality could account for all the features of Asperger's, though some recent research suggests that a brain region called the *insula* may play an important role.[33] The insula, located in the internal area of the temporal lobe, serves a number of functions having to do with speech and also with the recognition of emotions in other people. The amygdala also plays a part, along with the insula, in this capacity for empathy. The cell architecture of the insula consists in part of the so-called *mirror* cells, which under normal circumstances allow us to imitate the gestures and expressions of others as soon as we see them. Some persons with autistic disorders show a lack of mirror-neuron activity. The problem may not be as simple as this: others have shown that some Asperger patients do not have an across-the-board empathy defect; rather, they have trouble recognizing emotions in other people that correspond to emotions they don't properly recognize in themselves.[34]

Autistic persons are rarely violent, but in the exceptional case where they commit a violent crime, the outburst will likely be a final act by someone who has been unable to sense what others feel, unable to relate to them in any meaningful way, let alone to form an intimate friendship with anyone. That was certainly the case with the mass murderer on the Virginia Tech campus in 2007.

Seung-Hui Cho had come to the United States from Korea with his family when he was eight. He was already considered "autistic" at that age; he was shy, nearly mute, never initiating a conversation. When he did speak, his speech patterns were strange, which led to his classmates making fun of him, the more so as he refused to participate in ordinary school routines. By the time he was in college, he had become a scowling, disgruntled loner who wrote "plays" of macabre and twisted violence, so disturbing as to frighten his teachers and make his fellow students wonder whether he would become the next "school shooter."[35] His behavior in class was bizarre and menacing: he took photos, unbidden, of girls, stalked several girls, and made harassing phone calls. Growing progressively more paranoid, he accused the other students of "debauchery," called them "deceitful charlatans."[36] His inability to fit in with others led to envy and hatred that grew to such proportions that on April 16, 2007, after writing a note saying that "you made me do this," he shot to death thirty-one students, a teacher, and finally himself.

The sense of evil in the Cho case stemmed of course from the snuffing out of the lives of the thirty-one students in the prime of life, along with one of their teachers (who had tried to save some of them). We can envision a pathway that led up to the massacre:

> Genetic impairment of empathy → Inability to fit in socially → Envy and hatred → Heightened drive for revenge → Impaired judgment about right and wrong (anterior cingulate) → Insufficient orbitofrontal inhibition → Implementation of murderous revenge fantasy acted out.

Perhaps there had also been a cultural element interwoven with these other adverse factors: had he remained in his native country, he might not have stood out as much as he did in the new environment. Some students picked on Cho, for example, because of his odd behavior, taunting him (and not even getting the country correct) with "Go back to China!" His age—twenty-three at the time of the murders—was just at the transition point between adolescence and adulthood. Neurophysiologically, the neurons in the frontal lobes, which are not fully coated with myelin until about that age or a little later, may have been a factor as well. As a result, the ability to inhibit destructive drives may not as yet have reached its optimal strength. This kind of neural immaturity was probably a factor in the spree murders of nineteen-year-old Charles Starkweather (mentioned in chapter 5).

Induced Mental Illness

There are several conditions where the tendency to violence has been sparked by factors that are not related to risk genes for schizophrenia, manic-depressive psychosis, delusional disorder, or autistic-spectrum disorders. Either that, or some genetic disadvantage related to one of those conditions is present, but to only a mild degree. The main cause stems from some other source. When obvious psychosis is present (with delusions, hallucinations, bizarre speech, and the like), we can call such conditions "induced mental illness." Here I am using the word *induced* to mean brought about primarily by causative factors other than the genetic ones directly related to schizophrenia, delusional disorder, manic-depression, or autism. Drug abuse, brain tumors, and serious head injury are examples of conditions that can induce a mental illness. Many practitioners in the mental health field will extend this admittedly vague term—*mental illness*—to cover certain other conditions that are quite serious (especially as to the risk of violence) but not so disruptive of one's grip on reality as to resemble a full-fledged psychosis. Let us focus here on some of the more prominent examples of this more broadly defined "induced mental illness."

Fetal Alcohol Syndrome

Mothers who abuse alcohol heavily during the early stages of pregnancy may give birth to babies with fetal alcohol syndrome (FAS), though some infants will show less serious signs of damage called fetal alcohol effects (FAE). In the full-blown syndrome, however, a baby may show characteristic facial features: small eye openings, a thin upper lip, and a smoothing of the fold from nose to mouth. But there may also be damage to neurons and brain structures, which may result in eventual memory impairment, attention deficit, impulsive behavior, inadequate cause-and-effect reasoning, delinquent behavior, and inappropriate sexual activity by the teenage years, heightened aggressiveness, and a tendency to drug and alcohol addiction, criminality, and violence. FAS is one of the most common causes of mental retardation.[37] The idea of a *multifactorial cause* is particularly apt in cases of fetal alcohol syndromes: the alcoholic mother may have also passed to her infant risk genes for familial alcoholism. Or the mother may have mated with a man who also abused alcohol or drugs. The mother is more likely than average to be "wild," promiscuous, inattentive to her child, and less competent in her ability to be a mother. As far as the risk for FAS or FAE is concerned, a child born into these circumstances has more than the one strike against him. The following case touches on many of these points.

Richard Clark was born in 1968 out of wedlock to Kathleen Feller, a severe alcoholic. Richard had FAE syndrome. Family life was chaotic.

Kathleen later had three quick marriages, before marrying for the fourth time to Bob Smith—an extremely abusive man who used to humiliate Richard by making him do such things as eat a cigar. Richard often stayed home from school so as not to show the scars from the beatings his stepfather gave him. When Richard was fourteen, his mother died while driving drunk. Dropping out of school at that time, he began robbing people and burglarizing homes. At twenty he tried to abduct and rape a girl of four but was intercepted by the mother. By then he was abusing alcohol, marijuana, LSD, cocaine, and methamphetamine—supporting his habits by theft. At twenty-seven he abducted a seven-year-old girl, the daughter of a drinking buddy, raped her and stabbed her to death and then dumped her body in some bushes where it was not discovered for a week. Because the murder occurred in the context of another felony (rape), and because he had stuffed a sock in the girl's mouth, his case was one of aggravated homicide, carrying the possibility of the death penalty (which is what the jury recommended). On the Gradations of Evil scale, Richard would be placed in Category 18, since some torture was involved, for a crime that was primarily sexual. Clark was considered a psychopath at trial, but whether he was a "born" or a "secondary" psychopath (because of his extraordinarily traumatic childhood) is impossible to disentangle.

Drug Abuse

All of the common so-called recreational drugs are capable of causing at least a temporary psychosis. In certain vulnerable persons, chronic abuse of these drugs can induce a lasting mental illness whose characteristics, depending on the drug, may resemble schizophrenia or mania. With the exception of alcohol, all these drugs are illegal. The most important ones for our purposes are marijuana, cocaine, amphetamine compounds (such as methamphetamine), phencyclidine (angel dust or PCP), and lysergic acid diethylamide (LSD). The latter belongs to a group of drugs called hallucinogens because of their ability to provoke hallucinations. Mushrooms of the *psilocybin* family also have this effect, by means of their metabolism in the body to the hallucinogenic compound *psilocin*. The other drugs, besides alcohol, can, in sufficient amounts, produce such reactions as well.

As we saw with the Richard Clark case, alcohol, the most readily available of these drugs, can create a vicious circle: the alcoholic mother possibly passed risk genes for alcoholism to her son and certainly exposed him to the (pathological) use of it. Then as he entered his adolescent years, he, too, became alcoholic—and prone to the same loss of inhibitions and self-control that are a regular part of the picture in chronic alcohol abuse. Alcohol's mechanism of action is to suppress the brain's serotonin activity, which ordinarily exerts inhibitory effects. Metaphorically, alcohol takes one's foot off the brake pedal, facilitating behaviors that one might otherwise have kept in check. Chronic abuse of alcohol can also lead to lasting damage of the higher cortical centers, leaving the brain even less able to weigh and measure the possible consequences of an intended action. In susceptible persons, alcohol may induce aggressive, including violent and murderous, behavior, via strong depletion of the brain's serotonin levels.[38]

Among the 145 serial killers in my study, alcohol abuse was a factor in 61 (42 percent), often serving to remove the last vestiges of self-restraint. This allowed them to do their bloody work without pangs of conscience. Here we can think of the alcohol as functioning as a kind of internal Lady Macbeth, goading her weak-willed husband to go ahead and murder Duncan. Macbeth, still worried about the consequences, asks, "If we should fail?" to which his wife responds: "We fail? But screw your courage to the sticking place, and we'll not fail."[39] Before her words loosened his inhibitions, Macbeth reminded himself that his murderous plan could backfire and destroy him: "We still have judgment here, that we but teach bloody instructions, which being taught, return to plague th'inventor."[40]

As for the illicit drugs, *cocaine* and *methamphetamine* have the effect of "hijacking the brain's reward centers, including a midbrain structure . . . the nucleus accumbens."[41] The end result is that the drug trumps other sources of pleasure (sex, food), such that the drug becomes the person's only source of pleasure. Thus rewired, the person may be willing to do literally *anything* to recapture that intense pleasurable, orgasm-like experience. Under the influence of these drugs, a normally law-abiding person may commit murders—including murders that rise in the public's conscience to the level of evil. Persons who are already psychopathic and chronically disposed to break the law may be driven to serial murder. An example of a previously law-abiding person is Martha Ann Johnson.

Thrice married by age twenty-two, all her marriages were marked by violent quarrels. Her childhood had been marked by beatings, neglect, and poverty. While still in her teens, Martha had a daughter by the first husband; a son by the second; and a son and daughter by the third. The first two children she killed in the hope of bringing Earl Bowen, her third husband, back home after he had left—as though he would feel sorry for her over her "loss" (she staged the murders to appear as sudden infant death [SIDS] cases).[42] Martha was sentenced to death in Georgia in 1990, though she was still in prison when I interviewed her in 2007. She had been abusing methamphetamine all during the years of her tumultuous marriages. On the Gradations scale, her acts place her in Category 5: *traumatized, desperate persons without marked psychopathic features*.

Jeremy Jones is an example of an already psychopathic person whose propensity to violence was aggravated by methamphetamine. A delinquent of the "childhood-persistent" type, he was at high risk for future poor adult adjustment.[43] Conduct disorder was apparent by age eight. As an adolescent he had assaulted a boy—and then the boy's mother when she came to her son's defense. At eighteen he killed the bride of a neighbor and erstwhile friend. Charged with rape at twenty-one and again at twenty-two, he was by then heavily addicted to methamphetamine. Unfortunately—because of poor communication between police in different locales—he was only put on probation for these crimes, making it easier for him to flee to another state and assume an alias. His use of crystal meth spiked both the noradrenaline and dopamine systems in his brain, rendering him hypersexual as well as increasingly violent. A psychopath of the charmer/con man type, he always had girlfriends who swore by him, even while he was committing one rape-murder after another, often burning down the homes of his victims so as to eliminate evidence. Utterly without remorse and contemptuous of the law or of ordinary human feelings, he boasted he could talk the panties off a nun, and that one day he would be free again (from the death row in Alabama where he now sits) to write a book and "laugh my ass off."[44] A serial killer in Category 18 on the Gradation scale, he is known to have raped and killed eight women but is suspected of having killed a dozen or more besides. He killed a married couple in Oklahoma and then murdered their sixteen-year-old daughter and her friend as well, throwing their bodies down a mine shaft. He later confessed to this, but for which they would never have been found.

The recreational drug phencyclidine (angel dust or PCP) was developed originally as an anesthetic of the ketamine family of anesthetics but was discontinued for medical purposes because of its potentially dangerous side effects. Phencyclidine has direct effects on dopamine D2 and serotonin 5HT2 receptors in the brain and is capable of producing symptoms suggestive of schizophrenia: hallucinations, loss of ego boundaries—and in some people—outbursts of rage and violence.[45] A common method of using the drug is to spray it on leafy material like marijuana or oregano leaves and then smoke it.

Sometimes the PCP is mixed with cocaine, resulting in a substance known on the street as "tragic magic." Tragic magic was the mixture smoked by the man mentioned in the introduction—the man who had killed one man and blinded another. The marijuana joint, laced with PCP/cocaine, had induced a state of rage and persecutory hallucinations that had precipitated the attack. It would be only fair to state that in his childhood he had been choked to unconsciousness and then sodomized by his father, and repeatedly whipped with an electrical cord by his mother for minor disobedience. This left him with a residue of vengeful feelings for the abuse he had suffered. The drug abuse with marijuana, PCP, and cocaine in his early twenties may have sufficed to provoke the violence unleashed in the murder and attempted murder. Whether he was additionally vulnerable because of adverse genetic peculiarities (to be discussed below) we do not know; the appropriate tests had not been developed at the time and are not commercially available even today. As a psychopathic man with poorly controlled rage and poor social skills, he belongs in Category 13 on the Gradations scale.

In the same way that schizophrenia, mania, and the other hereditary psychoses can occasionally spur outbreaks of violence, illicit drugs whose effects mimic these conditions can do the same in persons who have no prior history of violence or even of antisocial (or psychopathic) personality. That they may have been primed to violence by violence done to them earlier is another matter. This seems to have been the case with a man admitted to a forensic hospital after killing his mother. The mother had been diagnosed as a schizophrenic, though with what accuracy is not known. She had been alternatingly abusive and neglectful toward her son. In his twenties he began to use LSD with some regularity, which caused him to hallucinate both sounds and colors. During one of his visits with his mother, she became verbally abusive with greater than usual intensity. Still in his LSD-induced mental haze, he picked up a scissors and stabbed his mother to death, then eviscerated her—removing her heart and liver, parts of which he ate. His T-shirt soaked with blood, he then wandered in the street, where he was soon apprehended by the police, found to be "crazy," and remanded to the forensic hospital. Once the LSD was mostly cleared from his brain (a lengthy process, in the case of LSD), his behavior and personality returned to acceptable, nearly normal, levels. A gifted artist, he spent most of his days drawing and painting. He had no record of other violent acts. Eventually he was allowed to go to an ordinary psychiatric hospital, from which he was released back into the community a few years later. When I traced him, fifteen years after the murder, an art gallery was staging a one-man show of his artwork. The former patient was living a peaceful life, supporting himself through his art. The man had been psychotic because of the drugs, but was not psychopathic. He belongs in Category 6 or 8 on the Gradations scale.

Unlike alcohol, which contributes to violence largely through disinhibition (interfering with the brain's "top-down" ability to suppress violent behavior),[46] or cocaine and methamphetamine that intensify the ("bottom-up") drive toward violent "solutions," the effects of marijuana are less clear-cut and usually not so strong as promoters of violence. Some have suggested that marijuana may even reduce violence[47] or else that persons in a state of low-dose marijuana are more violence-prone than those in a higher-dose state.[48] But this is not true in a general way. The man mentioned in chapter 2, for example, who bludgeoned his mother to death, had abused marijuana extremely heavily every day for months on end—to the point where he developed a paranoid (persecutory type) psychosis that lasted long after he was hospitalized and no longer had access to the drug.

In my experience at a forensic hospital it was common to see men (and a few women) who had begun heavy marijuana use around age twelve or thirteen, sometimes as the only drug of abuse, more often admixed with alcohol or cocaine. They then went on to develop a psychosis mimicking schizophrenia. This was true of many of the patients who were remanded to a hospital because of murder (more often of a family member or sexual partner than of a stranger). Since these patients behave in ways very similar to the genuine "hereditary" schizophrenics, there is good reason to suspect that the drug has, over time, actually altered the genome, creating brain changes that are permanent—*as though they came about via inheritance*. Such changes are called *epigenetic*, and concern chemical "switches" that can turn certain genes on or off, thereby altering their expression. Environment, as we are now learning, can affect genes, as well as the other way around (though environmentally induced changes are not inherited). Genes and environment are a two-way street. Chronic cocaine use, for example, can cause more branching of the dendrite nerve endings in the nucleus accumbens, creating stronger connections to other neurons and, in this way, heightening the impact of subsequently used cocaine on the brain's reward system.[49]

In all these varieties of drug abuse, one has to take into consideration the brain's general state of maturity. Adolescent brains, less well myelinated in the frontal lobes than they will be a few years hence, are more vulnerable. This leaves adolescents (and young adults) more prone to violence than they might be later on—witness the fact that crimes of violence peak between the ages of eighteen and thirty.[50] In more than half of violent crimes (irrespective of the age of the attacker) alcohol has been a factor.[51] Examples are innumerable, but here is just one: In the summer of 1993, five high school dropouts in Houston, Texas, all age seventeen or eighteen and all with many prior arrests for violence (including assaults against teachers, for which they were expelled) formed a loose gang. One evening, after they had been drinking beer all day long, they first got into fistfights with each other by way of proving who was "macho" enough to belong to the group. They turned their attention a little later to two young girls walking home through the park where the boys were. All five boys raped, tortured, and stomped to death the two girls. All were quickly captured and ultimately given the death penalty. Alcohol was the catalyst to the crime (the only one in Texas history where five men were given the death penalty for the same crime), obviously not the sole cause. Some of the teenagers had been seriously neglected by their mothers, one—who had abused alcohol since he was five—had a father who was in prison for murder, three had murdered a man before they joined in the rape-murders of the girls, all had come from chaotically disorganized families. Most had conduct disorders present from an early age. All had committed previous violent crimes when under the influence of alcohol.[52] The torture of the girls was prolonged; the sexual attack preceded their being stomped to death. On the Gradations scale, the appropriate category is 22.

Brain Injury Related to Violence

Injury to the brain can come about in many ways. One common way is blunt trauma that, besides causing unconsciousness right after the blow, damages specific areas of the brain. Depending on which areas of the brain are involved, the effects on personality and behavior may be negligible or at least nondangerous. Or the damage may have profound effects on personality and behavior: there may be weakening of self-control and loss of inhibition. Brain tumors affecting certain areas may have similar effects. In addition, fetal distress at the time of birth may result from birth complications that interfere with proper oxygenation; the inadequate oxygenation, in turn, can damage key areas of the brain involved in behavior. These complications can occur toward the end of pregnancy or shortly after birth, and for this reason are often called *perinatal*, meaning "around the time of birth." The results can span the whole spectrum of possibilities, from docility to irritability to violence.

An important clue about such changes in behavior after brain injury came in the wake of a most unusual incident. A twenty-five-year-old Vermont construction foreman, Phineas Gage, was using a tamping iron to pack explosives into a rock. He inadvertently triggered an explosion that sent the iron bar, more than a yard long, through his left cheek and head. Unconscious only for a few minutes, Gage miraculously survived. But he underwent a profound change of personality. Having been a shrewd, energetic, industrious, and trustworthy worker before the accident, he was then described by the doctor who followed his case in these terms: "fitful, irreverent, indulging at times in the grossest profanity . . . impatient of restraint or advice when it conflicts with his desires . . . capricious and vacillating."[53] Gage also became alcoholic and grandiose.

Gage died some twelve years later, having taken on many traits of the psychopath—as a result of his brain injury. His skull has been preserved and studied extensively by Drs. Antonio and Hannah Damasio. They demonstrated that, besides his having been blinded in the left eye, Gage experienced selective damage to the prefrontal cortex on both sides.[54]

Recently, Gage's skull has been examined by other observers who concluded that the damage was limited to the left prefrontal cortex.[55] Specifically, it was the ventromedial prefrontal cortex region that was damaged in Gage; we now understand that this region plays an important role in normal decision making. Gage's inability, after the accident, to plan meaningfully for the future and to obey the social rules he adhered to when he was brought up, were the consequences of the bar passing through his brain in that area. Why, we may ask, did Gage not go on to become a violent criminal? Perhaps the answer to this question may be resolved by looking back to his childhood, which seems to have been fairly normal and nontraumatic.[56]

This scenario contrasts with that of the Texas Tower mass murderer, Charles Whitman (chapter 5), who at autopsy was found to have a tumor that impinged on the amygdala—irritation of which may lead to aggressive behavior.[57] But in his formative years, Whitman had been the object of punitive physical abuse by his father.[58] In Whitman's case the combination of the early environmental trauma coupled with the brain damage affecting the amygdala may have unleashed in him an explosion of murderous rage. As for the detonator to this rage, Whitman had experienced a number of recent stresses just before that fatal August day in 1966: strains at work and at school, and the impending divorce of his parents.

Given the "right" amount of damage to the brain, especially in the top-down areas (such as the ventromedial prefrontal cortex) that ordinarily put the brakes on socially inappropriate behavior, violence can be the outcome, even in the absence of known environmental traumas. This is a topic where research and forensic experience often pass each other by, because fMRI data before death and autopsy findings afterwards are seldom available in the cases of greatest interest to us. We wish we knew such details in the "Mr. Goodbar Murder" in 1973 about which a movie was made. Joe "Willie" Simpson, twenty-four at the time, sustained a brain injury and had become unconsciousness during a car accident when he was thirteen. He had been raised in a working-class family in Peoria, Illinois, by parents who, as far as we know, were not abusive. After the accident, Simpson underwent a drastic change in personality. He began to have headaches and nightmares. He ran away from home, became a thief and a vagrant; he conned people and lived a parasitic life as a male prostitute kept by a wealthy gay lover. Willie also had sex with women—

including a girl of sixteen he married (and then abandoned), by whom he had a child. Simpson could swing quickly between being sociable and charming—and explosively angry. He abused alcohol, LSD, and marijuana. Alcohol was in his system the night of New Year's Eve 1973 when he met a teacher, Kathy Cleary, in a bar in New York City. She invited him back to her apartment. He tried to have sex but was unable; he became enraged, strangled her to death, and had sex with the corpse. Once in prison for the murder, he hanged himself.[59] So we don't really know which parts of his brain were affected by the car accident; we can only make shrewd guesses based on what we know from cases where pertinent examinations had been carried out. Perhaps, judging from his impulsive lifestyle after the accident, the bottom-up drive centers, including the amygdala, had been damaged, though the blunt force of a car plowing into one most likely caused more widespread damage to the decision-making centers as well.

In a similar fashion, we don't know precisely which brain regions were damaged in Richard Starrett (chapter 7) after his episodes of head injury and unconsciousness, though we do know that he became hypersexual and preoccupied with pornography in his early teens, following the injuries. Whether these were signs of damage to the lateral prefrontal cortex (that may be associated with such symptoms) is unclear; Starrett has not to my knowledge been studied with MRI during his years in prison.

Hormones

On average, men are more apt to be aggressive than women, and tend to be less empathic than women. From the perspective of evolution, there are solid reasons for this. Men behave in ways similar to male lions (another social animal group), where the males guard the perimeter from would-be invading male lions who might be eager to take over the pride. Leaving his urine scent on trees and other objects in the pride's perimeter, the male lion signals that all within is his turf. Intruders trespass at their own peril.[60] Pissing contests of this sort are part of the repertoire of males in our species also—carried out sometimes just as crudely, though more often on a more symbolic level. Businessmen are fond of saying that their new product or new CEO is going to "kill the competition," by which is meant not murder (not usually, anyway) but rather an eagerness to prevail in the struggle for supremacy and for all the perquisites that go with beating the competition. Since ancestral times, before and after humans left the African savannahs fifty thousand years ago to try their luck in other parts of the world, men have guarded the perimeter of a social group. The women gathered in an inner circle, taking care of the children and preparing the food that their men, with any luck, dragged back from beyond the outer circle. Our tools, language, and dress have changed considerably since then; our brains have not.

Since testosterone in the fetus with the XY chromosome plays a crucial role in making that baby a boy, and in shaping his brain along lines associated with maleness, there has been a tendency to assume that males with higher testosterone plasma levels will be more aggressive than those with more modest levels. Taking this a step further, we often assume that murderers, who are far more likely to be men than women—by a factor of about 9 to 1[61]—would have particularly "off the chart" levels of male hormone. For a time it seemed as if violent criminals did tend to have higher testosterone levels,[62] but subsequent studies did not bear out such a neat relationship.

Because circulating testosterone levels increase in boys in lockstep with their advance into puberty—a period when antisocial behaviors increase markedly, as well—it seemed worthwhile to look at the hormone picture in boys between the ages of nine and fifteen. The expected increase in testosterone during those years turned out to have more to do with nonphysical aggression and social dominance (in the high-testosterone adolescents), and did not seem to relate to aggression.[63] Under certain circumstances there did seem to be a connection between high testosterone and aggression—but this occurred when, simultaneously, the brain serotonin level was low.[64] Severe aggression was related to the low serotonin level, not the high testosterone.

There are genes in the body cells that allow male hormone to become attached at the appropriate site: "androgen receptor" genes. Now that the human genome has been worked out in extensive detail, variations in the structure of different genes have been discovered. Some variations have fewer components (making for shorter alleles that one inherits from each parent); other variations have longer components. A person can inherit a "long" variant (i.e., allele) from both parents (creating an L-L, or long-long situation), or one long and one short (L-s), or a short allele from both (s-s). In a recent study in India, it turns out that rapists who went on to murder their victims were much more likely to have the s-s (double short) alleles for a particular sequence on the androgen-receptor gene, when compared with the men who only raped or the men who only murdered.[65]

Testosterone makes for maleness (women have levels of the hormone too, but it is much lower than in men). The bottom line in this discussion of the male hormone and violence is this: there is no clear-cut evidence that having *higher levels* of testosterone makes certain men extremely violent, though having higher levels may make certain men *socially dominant*—like the alpha males that become leaders in various groups (not just of men but of mammals in general). So the lopsidedness in male versus female aggression (including the extreme examples we associate with "evil") stems from the way male brains are configured from the earliest months in the womb.

As compared with the female brain, the male brain is—on average—readier for aggression (whether defensive or predatory) but less capable, oftentimes, in the matter of empathy. Now take this generally more aggression-prone, generally less-empathic postpubertal male and *add on* some of the factors we have been discussing here: maternal neglect, parental brutality, less favorable gene components for some of the neurotransmitters, alcohol and substance abuse, hereditary predisposition to antisocial or psychopathic personality (of which, more below) or mental illness. Given some or all of those add-ons, you may indeed end up with a killer of uncommon cruelty, prone to commit the acts we call evil. And this type of killer is more likely—7 or 10 times more likely—to be a male. But in men of this sort, we are talking about *predatory* aggression (the kind more associated with violent crime and, at the outer edges, "evil"), not the *social* (and ordinarily nonviolent) aggression associated with being dominant.[66] To become a *predatory* aggressor, the usual formula is maleness coupled with *other factors*—such as genetic risk for psychopathy and being brutalized in a violent household. Psychopathy carries us into the next topic: personality. But before we discuss personality, there is one more note about being male and violent: the matter of the XYY chromosome pattern.

It used to be thought that men who were born with the abnormal chromosome pattern XYY—that is, with an extra male (Y) chromosome—were particularly prone to violence. The condition is rare (perhaps one man in a thousand in the general population), so that even if the relationship were true, XYY couldn't be responsible for much of the violence we see in everyday life. Later, the notion that XYY men were likely to become violent criminals was seriously questioned.[67] A few XYY men were found in prisons, but for some time there were no large-scale surveys of how many XYY men were living peacefully in the community. Recently, a group of forensic psychiatrists in Germany looked at the chromosome pattern in a group of 13 men (out of a total of 166) arrested for sexual sadistic homicide. Three of the men were XYY (1.8 percent of the 166), which was higher than the percent found among men in general prison populations: about 0.8 percent, and much higher than for men in general.[68] So perhaps XYY does count for something in the arena of violent crime after all— but if so, these men are museum pieces. XYY has little explanatory value for violent crime, let alone for the phenomenon we call evil.

Personality

Thus far we have been looking at factors—mental illness, chronic drug abuse, head injury, and the like—that affect personality in ways that heighten the risk for criminal behavior. In extreme cases, the effects may be so great as to make aggressive impulses ungovernable. Or, empathy and compassion may be so seriously impaired that crimes that horrify us (and reach the level of "evil") lose all their shock value for the perpetrator. But in some persons who commit evil acts, these factors are either absent or of only minor proportions. Personality all by itself, with no "help" from mental illness or head injury, can account for the tendency to commit crimes of exceeding violence.

In general, personality is an amalgam of many different forces, some within us, some from our interaction with the environment. A useful equation in thinking about personality is that which we *inherit* accounts for about half of our personality; *environment* makes up the other half—especially the much larger portion of our personal lives that we do *not* share with our parents and siblings (as when brothers and sisters are in different grades in school, have different friends and different interests, etc.). In dealing with violent crime and evil, self-centeredness—narcissism—is common to almost all persons of either sex who commit serious crimes, the point being that they care only about themselves and care little or not at all about their victims. Because personality is the outgrowth of all the brain's intricate machinery operating at once, and is shaped by our ever-expanding bank of memories about all the experiences of our lives, it cannot be localized conveniently to this or that segment of the brain. The more normal and socially integrated the personality, the harder it becomes to "explain" the personality by pointing to certain areas of the brain, not even the bottom-up and top-down regions we looked at earlier. But in *abnormal* personalities, including those we confront again and again in criminal work and in reflections on evil, the search for underlying peculiarities of the brain often proves rewarding. Before we examine these peculiarities in detail, a word of caution.

The focus of this book is on evil in peacetime. In times of war and group conflict it is by no means "necessary" that the combatants exhibit abnormalities of personality. Some do, of course, and so do many of their leaders (Hitler, Stalin, Mao, Saddam Hussein, Slobodan Milošević, to pick just a few in recent history). Below the category of the leaders in war or group conflict is the group composed of gang members, mafiosi, drug runners, professional kidnappers, terrorists, and the like, for whom violence is a key ingredient in their everyday business. Many such men (and we are usually dealing with men here) are antisocial but not psychopathic. Some show the features of what Otto Kernberg has called "malignant narcissism."[69] In this personality we see "antisocial behavior, ego-syntonic sadism, and a paranoid orientation," yet with the capacity for loyalty to the group and for concern for other people. Here is an example where malignant narcissism, evil, and "business as usual" come together: Kidnapping is all too common in countries where poverty is rife. In Mexico, Maria Elena Morera, a dentist, recently spearheaded a large group of protesters demonstrating against the rash of kidnappings in her country. She had been touched by the crime personally. Her businessman husband had been abducted in 2001 and held for ransom by kidnappers, who, to speed up their extortion, severed a finger each week and sent each one to her house. Four weeks (and four fingers) later, the police were finally able to free her husband. One of the assailants was a medical doctor who had done the amputations.[70]

Some of the Common Disorders

Among the people we have encountered up to this point, almost all could be said to have a personality disorder of some sort, but in many instances the disorder was one *not* usually associated with violent crime, much less evil. The outburst of violence was usually a once-in-a-lifetime episode, not preceded (nor followed) by other such outbursts. John List (chapter 4) was obsessive-compulsive, for example; Nancy Kissel (introduction) was narcissistic; Robert Rowe (chapter 2) was depressive; Susan Wright (chapter 2) was histrionic; Gang Lu (chapter 2) was paranoid; Richard Minns (chapter 4) was hypomanic and narcissistic. Susan Smith, who pushed her car into a lake in South Carolina—causing her two sons in the backseat to drown so that she might be free (unencumbered by children) to marry the boss's son—had the features of borderline, narcissistic, and histrionic personalities all at once.[71] Contemporary neuroscience has not probed these disorders very extensively, partly because the brain-imaging techniques now available would probably not show much abnormality, and partly because the crimes connected with these personality types are *usually* not so extravagant and repugnant—not as evil, if you will, as to generate special interest in brain-research professionals.

Personality Disorders with a Connection to Violence and Crime

Three personality disorders have a close relationship to crime, particularly to violent crime. The evil actions described throughout this book are often the by-products of these disorders, whether singly or in combination. The three disorders are antisocial, psychopathic, and sadistic. A fourth—schizoid—deserves consideration as well because schizoid personality is seen in about half of the men committing serial sexual homicide. In the general population, schizoid personality is present only in about 1 percent. Among serial killers the situation is a little more complex: some of the men show autistic-spectrum disorders, including Asperger's, which resemble schizoid personality because of such qualities as aloofness and inability to form close relationships with other people.

If we set apart what we regard as evil from what we do not, the trait that really makes the difference is empathy. Here I am using the word *empathy* in the way it is often used both in everyday speech and in the language of psychiatry. Two different ideas are often merged as if they are synonymous. Strictly speaking, empathy refers to the ability to read correctly the emotions another person is experiencing, as telegraphed to us by the person's facial expression and gestures.[72] For this capacity, the mirror cells in the insula play a prominent role.

The other idea concerns *compassion*, which relates to the ability most people have: to feel distress at the distress or suffering of another person, and to feel moved to do something to alleviate that person's suffering. This particularly human sentiment probably requires an adequate capacity for empathy—as an initial step. Compassion is akin to sympathy, one of the four sentiments that are ingredients of the moral sense of which James Wilson speaks so eloquently in his book *The Moral Sense*,[73] the other three being fairness, self-control, and duty.

We see the division between these ordinarily coexisting concepts of empathy and compassion in the *psychopath*. Many psychopaths are rather good at reading people's expressions accurately, but they lack compassion. This *empathy sans compassion* allows them to take advantage of the tearful child who has gotten separated from his mother, the fragile-looking woman in the bar, and so on. Many autistic/Asperger persons and certain persons with schizoid personality (whose main trait is aloofness) lack both empathy and compassion. These handicaps make it difficult to form intimate relationships with other people, particularly with potential sexual partners. As a result, they live as loners or misfits. Half the men committing serial sexual homicide show this extreme inability to get emotionally close to anyone. Examples are numerous. One of the most moving accounts of a schizoid serial killer lacking the merest trace of compassion is that of Edwin Snelgrove Jr. M. William Phelps uses the word *evil* on many occasions in his book *I'll Be Watching You*[74]—one of the best of its genre—in describing the cruelty of Snelgrove, who, although raised in a unremarkable home alongside a normal brother and sister, experienced sexual arousal at the fantasy of murdering women since well before his adolescence.

In essence, the closer you are to having zero empathy and (especially) zero compassion, the easier it is to carve up a person as though you were whittling wood. We saw this with David Parker Ray and his Toy Box; John Ray Weber mutilating his sister-in-law while she was still alive; and Theresa Knorr torturing her daughters. I have occasionally encountered people who, while not devoid of compassion, exhibit this quality in an extremely constricted sphere of interpersonal contact. David Parker Ray, for example, was assisted in his torture of the women immobilized in his Toy Box by his much younger girlfriend, Cindy Hendy. In my blood-chilling interview with Hendy, she referred to their victims (all of whom were female), in her utterly expressionless manner, as "packages"—that is, as objects to be whipped, tortured, mutilated, and then tossed aside as packages (as one tosses out the garbage after a meal). When I asked her how she was able, as a woman herself, to treat victims of her own sex with such indifference and contempt—as not even human, she reiterated: they were just packages. But she was eager to be released from prison one day so she could be reunited with her daughters and grandchildren.

It is the actions of killers such as these to which we are least hesitant in applying the term *evil*. In the last few years, neuroscience has had a great deal to tell us about what is missing or malfunctioning in the brains of antisocial persons, especially those with the added characteristics that qualify them as psychopaths. If we wanted to narrow our focus to single out the personality configuration that is connected with particular closeness to our concept of evil, it would be at the place where psychopathy, sadistic personality, and schizoid/autistic-spectrum disorders all come together. We can show this as a map, as in figure 9.1, where psychopathy itself is seen as a "special case" of antisocial personality, since only perhaps a fourth of antisocial persons are also psychopaths. A few psychopaths manage to walk, without falling, the fence between breaking the law and not breaking the law—so a small part of the circle for psychopathy lies outside the large circle for antisocial personality. The same applies for sadistic personality: there are some cruel and demeaning parents, spouses, and bosses who are sadistic but who are not necessarily antisocial or psychopathic.

Turning our attention now to antisocial personality, and especially to that "inner circle" where psychopathy, sadism, and schizoid/autistic-spectrum disorders overlap, we can peer into this extreme, and sometimes evil, psyche—through the lens of neuroscience.

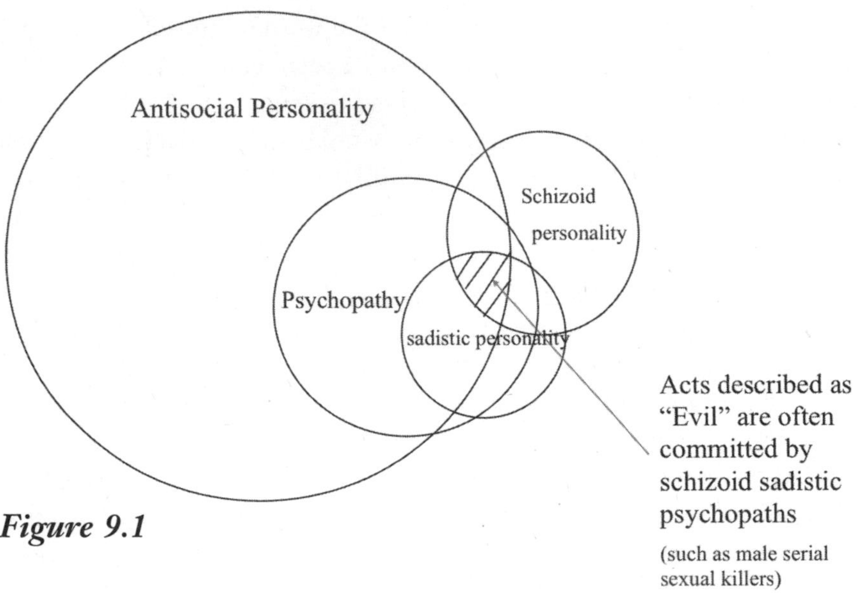

Figure 9.1

CONTEMPORARY RESEARCH

Adrian Raine and his colleagues have published a number of important papers over the past fifteen years touching on antisocial and psychopathic personalities and on criminality. In one such study they looked at the rates of adult violence in men who fell into one of three categories: one group had only obstetrical risk factors (pregnancy and birth complications); another group had grown up amid poverty risk factors. A third "biosocial" group had experienced early neuromotor deficits and unstable family environments. It was this last group that showed the greatest tendency to adult violence; the biosocial group accounted for 70 percent of all the crimes committed in the entire sample of almost four hundred men.[75]

Raine turned his attention to murderers of two different types: the predatory versus the "affective." This is akin to the distinction made in this book between those who kill methodically and with malice aforethought, and those who kill on impulse during some emotional crisis. As Raine and his team suspected, the affective (more impulsive) killers showed lower prefrontal functioning and heightened subcortical function. This suggested that in these men their drives were stronger and their "brakes"—their ability to monitor and inhibit violent ambitions—were weaker. The predatory killers had prefrontal function that was nearer to normal, though their "drive strength" was abnormally high, as in the impulsive killers. The predators, in other words, were more able to plot and scheme successfully, lowering their risk of doing something rash and getting caught.[76]

In a later study, Raine used magnetic resonance imaging to measure the white and gray matter in the prefrontal cortex in antisocial men and in several control groups. The antisocial men showed a substantial (11 percent) reduction in prefrontal gray matter. This deficit—the first evidence found for structural changes in the brain of antisocial men—helped to explain the low arousal (and tendency to boredom, the need for novelty and thrill seeking) in these men, along with their inadequate response to fear, their lack of conscience, and their poor decision-making skills. These features are characteristic of antisocial men; even more so, of psychopathic men.[77] Actually, the low arousal as a risk factor for antisocial behavior had been known for a long time. It is associated with low resting heart rate—the most reliable biological indicator of antisocial behavior in children and adolescents. This is presumably an inherited tendency, and when present it nudges the person in the direction of sensation seeking and risk taking—by way of spicing up a life that would otherwise be boring and flat.[78]

Taking the neuroscience approach a step forward is the recent work on the way children react to pictures that show people in a state of fear. Certain children show very little reaction to emotional stimuli and don't show remorse for doing bad or hurtful things. These "callous-unemotional" children seem in many instances to be the psychopaths of the future. When they are shown the fearsome pictures during an fMRI exam, it turns out that their amygdala response is notably reduced when compared with the responses of normal children or even children with just attention-deficit disorder (some children have both callousness and attention-deficit, and they do show the lowered amygdala response).[79]

Under ordinary circumstances, the amygdala communicates reward-expectance to the ventromedial prefrontal cortex: a bottom-up region "talking" with a top-down center that must decide whether the impulse to action is a good idea or a bad idea; whether the intended action is moral or immoral.[80] This connection is operating only weakly in the callous-unemotional children (and the same remains true in adult psychopaths). In a related study, children with psychopathic traits showed abnormal responses in the ventromedial prefrontal cortex—this seemed unique to them, since the abnormality was not found in healthy or even in attention-deficit children.[81]

We already know that *callousness* (which we can understand as the "negative" of which *compassion* is the positive) and *lack of remorse* are the hallmarks of the psychopath. It is likely that these children have strong inherited tendencies in this direction.[82] This does not condemn them to become violent criminals, but they are more likely than ordinary children to end up in trouble with the law for offenses that may include violence and even sadism. We know also that there is a stronger *genetic* influence operating in children who show early-onset delinquency in contrast to late-onset delinquency;[83] the same is true for aggressive versus nonaggressive children.[84] Yet, as Anderson underlines, the best antidote for a surplus of genetic predisposition to aggression is being raised in a stable, nurturing home.[85] We have of course no way of reducing the aggression, let alone the extremes of aggression that may get labeled as evil, by magically inserting children at risk into these optimal homes. In very rare circumstances, we may encounter a child with such genetic disadvantage, perhaps aggravated by perinatal complications, that his aggression cannot be curbed even by the most tender and devoted parents.

Bad Seed?

In chapter 8 we asked, were any of the persons mentioned examples of Bad Seed? This is the same as asking, Were any of them raised in families and in circumstances so free of abuse, neglect, negativity, head injury, hostile cultures, and so on, that we would have to ascribe their evil actions to *heredity alone*. We would even have to exclude cases where the mother abused alcohol, cocaine, or other such drugs during pregnancy, or where there was fetal distress, birth complications, and other unfortunate events that could adversely affect the developing brain. When I read Deborah Spungen's book *And I Don't Want to Live This Life* about her daughter Nancy (Nancy was the American girlfriend of the Sex Pistols'

Sid Vicious and was found stabbed to death at the Chelsea Hotel), I thought Nancy might be an example of Bad Seed. She turned out to be an uncontrollable, unsoothable, angry, violent child who was raised by warmly devoted, affluent, totally nonabusive parents. But Nancy was born a "blue baby," that is, she suffered from cyanosis due to the umbilical cord having been wrapped around her neck, plus she was born jaundiced from blood-group incompatibility.[86] This was the source of the brain damage (perhaps in both the bottom-up and top-down structures) that made her the "wicked" child she became (despite her genius-level IQ). This was not Bad Seed. I think cases of Bad Seed are rare. But consider the following case. It comes close.

The story is about a boy of twelve whom I shall call Edward. He was the only child of his mother's first brief marriage to a man who abused alcohol, and who even gave some alcohol to Edward when the boy was only two. Because her husband was at times menacing, at times physically abusive to her, Edward's mother left him to marry another man in what has so far been a stable and harmonious relationship. The couple now has a daughter of eight. The mother learned in the meantime that her first husband was an ex-con before she met him, though she does not know what he was incarcerated for. Because of his violent streak, she is still afraid he might come by one day and harm her or their son, though he has made no contact with her since she left him and moved to a different state. I was able to discover through Internet prison searches that her ex-husband had been imprisoned once again, this time for murder, and was serving a life sentence. His own father was also in prison for a violent crime. I thought she would be reassured to hear that she would never be in harm's way because of her ex. But her real fear came from Edward's behavior. He has all the traits of the callous-unemotional children of the research studies mentioned above. Edward talks continuously of hurting and killing people, which he finds highly amusing. He already shows the triad we referred to earlier, seen in a number of serial killers and other sexual criminals: he has tortured and killed cats and dogs, he still wets the bed, and he sets fires all over the house, which his mother has tried to deal with by putting extinguishers in every room. He has stolen large sums from other children at school and talks often of "revenge," though against what or whom is never clear. His parents find him manipulative, deceitful, and increasingly withdrawn and aloof. On several occasions he tried to strangle his sister. Edward knows nothing about his biological father but gives every sign of developing along very similar lines to those of him. There has been no abuse or neglect by his mother and stepfather; his intelligence is in the "brilliant" range.

At twelve Edward has not even reached puberty, let alone adulthood. Yet he has all the characteristics, in a less fully developed form, of a *sadistic psychopath* and, because he is so aloof and socially withdrawn, one with *schizoid features*. His personality, in other words, already places him at the epicenter of risk for becoming a violent criminal of the sadistic type. It is too early to tell whether his fantasies will take on sadistic sexual overtones. In the typical picture of an adolescent who commits sexual murders we see a boy who is "asocial, lacking in empathy, withdrawn to the point of isolation, and preoccupied with fantasies with sadistic sexual imagery."[87] Granted that Edward was exposed to some negative influences (his father letting him drink alcohol, perhaps beating him at times) before his mother remarried, those incidents from his first two years cannot account, as far as I can tell, for the frightening picture he now presents. Even if he does not represent a "pure" example of Bad Seed, this is as close as we are likely to encounter: a person whose predisposition to sadism, violence, and (if he continues along the same lines in the future) the actions we call evil—originated almost entirely from hereditary influences.

Bad Seed is of course a dreadful phrase, used in the popular language to condemn rather than to understand certain unfortunate, though dangerous, children. The phrase also tends to blind us to the realization that there are *other* children who survive prolonged parental torture, yet they emerge as healthy, integrated adults, highly valued for the benefits they bring society because of what we might metaphorically call *Good Seed*. Because of a lucky draw from the genetic lottery, these people remain resilient, invulnerable to the bad effects of abysmal parents, and are able, one feels like saying *miraculously*, to transcend the horrors of their early years. We don't get to hear so much about them. Virtue is not as fascinating as Evil.

There is a particularly heartwarming example of a "Good Seed" in the true story of Dave Pelzer.[88] A retired US Air Force crew member, Mr. Pelzer now lives with his wife and son in California, writing and lecturing about child abuse (including what he himself had endured) and what can be done about it. He had survived about ten years of torture—

beatings, starvations, burnings, stabbings, humiliations—from his sadistic alcoholic mother, while his passive father looked on and did nothing. Some kindly, understanding teachers finally caught on to what was happening (since as a schoolboy he was too afraid to talk to anyone), called Child Protective Services, and rescued him from his mother. If Mr. Pelzer did not have those special protective genes (about which we as yet know very little), he could easily have turned out to be a confirmed criminal. And people would have said: "Ah well, with a mother like that, small wonder . . ."

Some Hints about Protective Genes

We already know from research in the last few years that some children with attention deficit/hyperactivity (ADD/H) are prone to either property crimes or violence and often end up in trouble with the law. Other ADD/H children settle down eventually and never get in trouble. ADD/H runs in families presumably from genetic influences in most cases.[89] One factor that makes a difference: the ADD/H children who also had *conduct disorder* (unruliness, wildness, aggressive behavior) were the ones likely to end up in trouble. The ADD/H children who did not have conduct disorder had no higher rates of criminal behavior, when examined years later, than did ordinary children.[90] Since the tendency to childhood conduct disorder is itself often related to genetic influences, this suggests that the "combined" (ADD/H with conduct disorder) group of children (most of whom will be boys) will be especially at risk for criminal behavior as they enter their adult years. Did the boys who stayed out of trouble have some hitherto unsuspected "good" genes, or did they come from homes where there was no abuse? Or both? These questions have inspired research into a newly developing area concerning the *interaction* of genes and the environment. The old (simplistic and misleading) *Nature or Nurture* controversy is, finally, being replaced by the study of *Nature and Nurture*.

Avshalom Caspi and his wife, Terrie Moffitt, are at the forefront of research on gene-environment interaction as it relates to violence. In one of their approaches, they studied the gene for the monoamine oxidase-A enzyme (MAOA) whose task it is to metabolize (in this case, to inactivate) the neurotransmitters norepinephrine, serotonin, and dopamine. These neurotransmitters help convey nerve impulses from one neuron to another as the first impulse is conveyed to the thin barrier—the synaptic cleft—separating the first from the second neuron. In certain key pathways in the brain, the neurotransmitters may build up in the synaptic cleft to too high a level, leading to overexcitation of the next neuron—unless MAOA is doing its job efficiently, keeping the neurotransmitter level "just right." Plate 19 in the insert represents this process pictorially.

Deficient MAOA activity may predispose to hyperreactivity to threats of various kinds.[91] When MAOA levels were measured in a large group of boys and girls, some had high MAOA activity; others, low levels. The genes in question were found to have differences in their chemical composition, some persons inheriting a version of the gene that led to high activity; others, inheriting the less-favorable version, showed low MAOA activity. What is important for our purposes is their observation that boys who had been *maltreated* during their early years AND who had *low MAOA enzyme activity* (making them less able to inactivate excessive amounts of neurotransmitter in pathways related to impulse strength) were more likely to develop conduct disorder. Here, in other words, is a genetic link to the understanding of childhood conduct disorder. As these children were followed into adult life, the low-MAOA males were much more likely than their high-MAOA counterparts to be convicted of a violent crime. The children with high MAOA activity tended not to develop conduct disorder (not to get arrested for violence later on) *even if they had been maltreated*. Only one child in eight had the combination *maltreatment + low MAOA*, but those children were responsible for almost half the violent convictions.

Figure 9.2 shows in graphic form the relationship between the inherited MAOA pattern and childhood maltreatment. Because the neurotransmitters (such as serotonin[92] and dopamine) that MAOA acts on are involved especially in the bottom-up brain centers, we might expect that the ill effects of low activity would be linked with high drive or impulse strength, including (as in maltreated persons) the impulse to violent behaviors. In keeping with this idea, others have shown that persons who inherited a "small" allele from both parents for the serotonin-transporter gene have an overactive amygdala response to stress.[93] The job of the transporter is to carry serotonin that had been released into the synaptic cleft back into the first neuron where it originated. Inadequate function of the transporter would be another way of the transmitter piling up where it shouldn't, leading to overactivity and overfiring in the circuitry.

We don't know whether Dave Pelzer was blessed with inheriting the gene for high MAOA or whether there were other inherited protective factors that helped him survive the protracted torture at the hands of his mother. The fruits of contemporary research are seldom available to the people we read about in the crime literature. We have to hope that in the coming years tests of the sort Caspi and his colleagues are working on can be given to ever-larger numbers of young people, so that we may be able to spot "high-risk" children when there is still greater opportunity to help them cope more adaptively with the violent impulses they struggle with. Even so, there will probably be a residue of young persons (again, mostly boys) of the "life-course persistent" antisocial type, who, though they make up only 5 percent of the population, commit 50 to 70 percent of the crimes.[94] The problem, even with early detection, will be especially severe with the callous-unemotional youngsters: those with

The Association between Childhood Maltreatment and Subsequent Antisocial Behavior, in Relation to MAOA Activity
(adapted from Caspi et al: Science 297: 851-854, 2002)

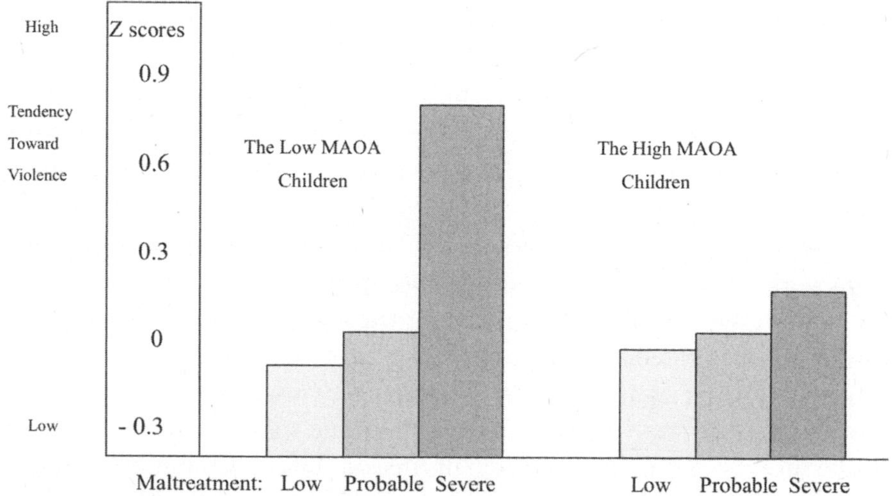

Figure 9.2

the strong genetic underpinning, low heart-rate and skin conductance, and so on—on whom parental punishment or admonition has little effect. Though such children cannot be punished into behaving better, it is becoming clearer now that some of them can improve socially with consistent and patient teaching.[95] Many of these children, in other words, respond favorably to parents who sit down and talk with them, calmly and without rancor, about the benefits of socially acceptable behaviors and the disadvantages of offensive behaviors. A young person with psychopathic tendencies who can be trained to do the right thing because it's to his advantage—even if he never *feels* it in his heart of hearts to do the right thing—may over time develop habits that incline him *away* from actions that are morally wrong and violent.

If you have read this far, you may be asking, where does neuroscience fit into the picture? It is a long and tortuous road from enzymes to evil. None of the unfavorable genes, frontal lobe abnormalities, limbic system irregularities, neurotransmitter peculiarities, and the like mark out a clear and predictable path toward evil actions. Instead of neat and unmistakable causes, we must settle for factors, such as the ones we have been looking at, that heighten the risk for someone to commit the kinds of acts—in peacetime—that so offend the "collective conscience" that we label them as evil. We have concentrated in this chapter on sadistic psychopaths since they have the "chemistry" and the personality that make them the most numerous occupants of the lowest circle—where evil is clearly present—of whatever Inferno that we might, in emulation of Dante, wish to create.

But some of the occupants of that circle are young runaways, lost souls with no moral center (but with no prior history of violence either, let alone of sadism), who find meaning through their worship of a truly evil leader. Easily led, they, too, enter this dark realm. How else to understand the former San Francisco go-go dancer Susan Atkins? Herself the mother of a one-year-old son, Atkins, under the spell of Charles Manson, broke into the home of the pregnant Sharon Tate, stabbing her to death while making sure the last words Sharon ever heard were: "Look, bitch, I don't care about you. . . . You're going to die, and I don't feel anything about it."[96] The sadism inherent in a young mother cruelly murdering a pregnant woman is baffling. Envy—the most corrosive of the Deadly Sins—was probably there, just as it was when Mark David Chapman shot John Lennon to death. But envy is common. Murders like the ones committed by Atkins and Chapman are rare. There must be other ingredients. For similar reasons, I find the *sadism* component of the sadistic psychopath harder to explain than the *psychopathy*—to which neuroscience has now turned so much attention. As I was finishing this chapter, however, I stumbled upon a book written by a psychologist who has studied sadism for a long time and who has some answers I find more convincing than most explanations I've come across thus far. "Stumbled" is the right word, because my discovery of her work was pure serendipity.

SOME HINTS ABOUT SADISM AND THE CORE OF EVIL

One of my colleagues at the forensic hospital was packing up his books, on his way to a much-deserved job promotion. On top of one of the boxes was Dr. Anna Salter's *Predators*.[97] It could just as easily have been at the bottom of the box, where I would never have noticed it. As I flipped through it, I found I could hardly put it down—it is that well written. But at the same time, it is hard to read, because the stories of the sadistic men and women she has encountered are extremely disturbing, in the same way I found David Parker Ray's taped monologue to his torture victims unbearable to read. A few days later I spoke with Dr. Salter by phone, and she graciously granted me permission to quote one of her examples here. I chose the same story I fixed on as I browsed through her book that has haunted my colleague, Vincent Spizzo, who has not been able to get it out of his mind since he read it five years ago. The story is that of a man who repeatedly suffocated his nine-year-old stepson, which I repeat here with some abbreviations.[98] The man made these revelations voluntarily.

> After about two years of molesting my son . . . I got my hands on some "bondage discipline" pornography with children involved. Some of . . . the pictures that I had seen showed total submission. Forcing the chil-

> dren to do what I wanted. And I eventually started using some of this bondage discipline with my own son, and it had escalated to the point where I was putting a large Zip-loc bag over his head and taping it around his neck . . . and raping and molesting him . . . to the point where he would turn blue, pass out. . . . I was extremely aroused by inflicting pain. And when I see him pass out and change colors, that was very arousing and heightening to me, and I would rip the bag off his head and then I'd jump on his chest and masturbate in his face and make him suck my penis. . . . While he was coughing and choking I would rape him in the mouth. I used this same sadistic style of the plastic bag and the tape two or three times a week, and it went on for I'd say a little over a year.

This man acknowledged to Dr. Salter that he knew he was going to continue this way, to victimize people "until someone killed me or I got locked up." He spoke of himself as "evil . . . I believed myself evil. Possessed by a demon . . . anything to justify my actions."[99] In the strange candor of this man, he went a step further than Tommy Lynn Sells (chapter 7)—who spoke openly of the "adrenaline rush" he felt when slitting the throats of young women. This man identified himself the way the public would—as "evil."[100]

Dr. Salter went on to say that she has noticed how many sadists talk about the "high" they experience when committing a sadistic act—likening it to the high of cocaine or a similar drug. Cocaine, as we learn from neuroscience, creates an impregnable blockade, preventing dopamine in the synaptic cleft from being taken up again by the first nerve in the pleasure pathway—thus magnifying the pleasure sensation. There are some sadistic persons who, having been victimized cruelly as children, later on take pleasure in victimizing others. This might underlie a psychoanalytic explanation for someone turning sadistic. But as Dr. Salter states, many confirmed sadists have no such history.[101] They may instead be the low-arousal, low-heart-rate, easily bored psychopaths who crave a "high" to make them feel alive and powerful. It helps, of course, to lack compassion and remorse and to be utterly callous—but this answers to the psychopathy part of the equation.

Some people, as we know, find the high in cocaine or meth and stop right there. For others, sex, food, or gambling fit the bill. And for some, this sought-after rush comes only from killing and from experiencing the godlike power that murder confers. This is not a new phenomenon. Reading Salter's comment about the sadist's high put me in mind of a French aristocrat who lived during the time of (who else?) the Marquis de Sade. Of Count Charolais it was said: "His heart was cruel and his actions were bloody. . . . Drunk more often than not, he killed peasants for sheer sport the way other men went hunting, and fired at workmen repairing roofs near his castle. . . . He once begged Louis XV's forgiveness for such murders. The monarch replied, 'The pardon you seek is granted . . . but I shall be even more pleased to pardon the man who kills you.'"[102]

In my review of serial sexual homicide, where the term *evil* is applied almost universally, I found only three men (Ian Brady, Leonard Lake, and David Parker Ray) who recorded the agony of their victims. But Dr. Salter has found that almost half of the sadistic men she has studied made "trophies" of this kind.[103] As we know, evil can be the final common path of myriad sources, some that we are now beginning to understand, others that remain mysterious. We have seen selfish, narcissistic wife killers, the mentally ill, the morbidly jealous, the cold psychopathic predators—schizoid ones as solitary as the leopard, gregarious ones who tell their wives they'll be late for dinner (as they go off in search of "prey"), some with obvious neurological and neurochemical abnormalities we are just beginning to understand, others as outwardly "normal" as the next-door neighbor (like Dave Pelzer's mother to most everyone else except Dave), some who shift gears into evil only after priming themselves with alcohol or drugs, others who need no such stimulation. When I think of the multiple routes to evil, I think of the dozen or so railroads, arranged like the spokes of a wheel, centered at Auschwitz-Birkenau that carried their victims from the four corners of Europe to the death camps. Think of evil as the common meeting ground where all the different pathways we have been looking at converge. Their common element is the horror that certain acts elicit in us, that provoke in us the emotion we identify as evil . . . and that make us utter the word: *evil.*

FINAL THOUGHTS

> We studied our serial killers, nonces and murderers in the same way we did our scientists, intellectuals and artists, looking for answers to the mystery of our nature.
>
> —Irvine Welsh, *Crime*[1]

In this book the spotlight has been on evil in peacetime: extreme violent actions, that is, committed by people who for the most part are outside the ordinary run of mankind. As we have seen, some are people ordinary in appearance and conduct before they explode into violence. They shock us not just by their actions but by the sheer unexpectedness of their actions. We tend to regard those whose violence moves or revolts us as *evil*—as "monsters." An acquaintance of mine from Sydney, Australia, for example, learned that her seemingly nice neighbor was a serial killer. With others who encounter violent persons, the shock doesn't come until a violent act has been performed because they already seemed quite different from ordinary folk—either because of mental illness, peculiarity of personality, or chronic antisocial behavior.

The situation in times of group conflict, especially in wartime, is different. To be sure, many of the leaders in such times, especially the aggressors, partake of this "otherness"—being awash in violence—to the point of becoming monsters. We must not forget the butchery carried out, or inspired, by Dr. Mengele at Auschwitz, Dr. Zawahiri from the caves of Afghanistan, or the recently captured Serbian doctor, Radovan Karadžic—a psychiatrist, no less. Yet much of the actual damage (or even carnage) is inflicted by ordinary people who become swept up in the tide of battle, their minds replaced temporarily, as it were, by the mind of the leader. The behavior of the soldiers or of other participants is uncharacteristic of their usual selves. Still, many of those "ordinary" soldiers who commit atrocities are *not all that* ordinary: they may have been the ones who beat their wives, were harsh or cruel with their children in such a way that they found war a welcome opportunity to give vent to sadistic tendencies that were kept somewhat under wraps in civilian life. These were not *good* men, that is; they were ordinary only in the sense that as civilians they had led unremarkable lives that garnered little attention. It is not likely that neuroimaging studies would reveal much brain abnormality in such men.

This crucial difference has been highlighted in a recent work by Croatian writer Slavenka Drakulic in her book *They Would Never Hurt a Fly*. One of her more interesting comments is, "War turns ordinary men into monsters."[2] She contends that in times of war and group conflict, men (and even some women) are transformed into moral zombies, capable of committing the most appalling atrocities upon the enemy—civilians included—only to revert, once the cease-fire has sounded, to their previous lives as grocery clerks, taxi drivers, farmhands, teachers, and, yes, doctors. But again, although they may revert to being *ordinary* people, they may not be *good* people.

As with *evil*, the word *monster* is one we reserve for behavior that is so unlike *our* behavior as to create a comfortable distance between our self-image and our perception of those freakish aberrations of nature, those monstrosities (as we prefer to regard them), who actually *are* inclined to behave like, well, evil monsters. The cartoonist Walt Kelly put it all very simply when Pogo, the main character of the titular comic strip—who happens to be an opossum—says, in a moment of reflection, "We have met the enemy—and he is us."

Since most of us go from cradle to grave without ever participating in evil acts, it is tempting to think—flattering to think—that many of us are truly inoculated against evil, as though there were some invisible divide separating the majority of us from those "others"—the monsters. Certainly it helps to come from a good family, surrounded by a supportive and accepting community, and to be blessed with the good fortune not to have inherited risk genes (either for mental illness or abnormal personality), nor to have suffered birth complications or sustained a serious head injury.

But put yourself in the place of twenty-four-year-old Dražen Erdomovic, a half-Serb, half-Croat soldier transported in mid-July with his unit in 1995 to Srebrenica, not knowing what his mission was. His commander, Brano Gojkovic, soon made his mission clear: he was to join with his mates in shooting to death some twelve hundred Muslim civilians, men and boys, who had been bused there for the purpose. As Drakulic tells the story, Dražen had no taste for this sort of thing. When he expressed his disinclination to take part in the massacre, his mates mocked him. He was after all only a half-Serb in their eyes: not someone they could readily trust. His commander then told him: "If you don't want to do it, walk over there and stand with the prisoners so we can shoot you too. Give me your machine gun."[3] Now Dražen is given the choice between a good and an evil. He could stand on moral high ground—and die. Or he could kill some innocent men and boys—and live, perhaps to tell the world of the still greater evil into which he was forced by his commander, who obeyed an even worse commander, General Mladic, who gleefully carried out the orders of Dr. Karadžic, who—ignoring the Hippocratic Oath ("First, do no harm")—happily obeyed the genocidal edict of President Slobodan Milošević. Dražen chose life—for himself, which meant the deaths of the sixty people he spent a quarter-hour shooting. He did tell the story, and because his story was believable, his sentence at court was reduced from ten years to five. Was it better that Dražen live to let the world know what happened on that killing field? Or would it have been better if he (and all the men compelled to take part in the massacre) died, leaving the truly evil and guilty commanders and generals and presidents to live out their lives unsuspected and unpunished? Because Dražen had a conscience, he lives on as a spiritually broken man. And Mladic and Karadžic live on, too—contented and unrepentant. In the young soldier's place, what would I have done? What would you have done? I ask this only as a rhetorical question. If we are honest, we cannot say what we would have done.

The banality of evil, of which Hannah Arendt spoke, was the banality of Adolf Eichmann, the oil company agent; of Josef Mengele, the doctor; of Joachim Ribbentrop, the champagne salesman; of Martin Bormann, the estate agent; of Hans Frank, the attorney; of Reinhard Heydrich, the violinist and navy officer. None of these men were mentally ill; none had suffered a head injury or any illness affecting the brain. Most of these men had what Dr. Kernberg has called malignant narcissism—they were egocentric, ambitious, ruthless, yet capable of loyalty to their group or within the confines of family. Several had been raised in virulently anti-Semitic families (Heydrich, Alfred Rosenberg) and were uncommonly arrogant. Of Ribbentrop it was said that he was disliked by everyone except his wife and Hitler; even Hitler found him tiresome. Only two of the top Nazis denounced Hitler during the 1945–1946 Nuremberg trials: the Hitler Youth leader Baldur von Schirach, and the architect Albert Speer. All these men had come under the sway of Hitler, but for which they would not have set in motion the Holocaust; all would have died in the same obscurity in which they had been born. Hitler was the catalyst that activated the potential for evil in these men. And I suspect all these men would have shown little or no abnormality if tested with MRI.

Hans Frank, who went on to become governor general of occupied Poland, was one of the war criminals hanged at the Nuremberg trials. His son Niklas was seven at that time and had been raised amid luxury in the castle his father had taken over. His mother used to take him in the chauffeured limousine to go into town and buy mink coats for a few złotys from Jewish women who were about to go, unknowingly, to their deaths at Auschwitz. Despite such beginnings, Niklas developed a strong moral center—how this happened is a mystery—and later wrote a book condemning his father, regretting that he was not privileged to witness his father's hanging.[4]

Niklas was almost alone among the children of the Nazi higher-ups to condemn, rather than excuse, their fathers.[5] Some twenty years ago I wrote him a letter, asking if he had any clue what helped him gain high moral ground in the face of the evils that both parents represented and that surrounded him on all sides. He responded, expressing how he felt red with both shame and joy at receiving my letter. He had no answer for how he retained moral integrity while growing up in that home. But he did comment how it was clear from his own text the danger we all are in, adding, "Who knows whether, if I had been born in my father's time, I wouldn't have ended up like my father?"[6] In his efforts to come to grips with the ordinariness of many who commit atrocities in wartime, Niklas Frank pondered the question in this way: "There are two people inside each German. One of them is well-behaved, hardworking, a solid citizen. That is the official version of the respectable German. But beneath it, behind it, as if made up of negative ions, there are the authentic Germans, a people of murderers."[7] Here he was too harsh in condemning his countrymen as a whole—especially those born after the war. But his remark does underline as if with yellow highlighter how vulnerable we are as human beings to shift in wartime from the honorable to the despicable; how easy is the transition in such times from a life of innocence to a life of evil.

What I am saying here does not lessen the responsibility of those who, in wartime, make the descent from the ordinary into the evil of atrocity, who selectively switch off their compassion—that essential ingredient of goodness—and end up blind to the humanity of the noncombatants, even of the children of the enemy. This means that Lieutenant William Calley of Vietnam's My Lai massacre was responsible;[8] Khalid Sheikh Mohammed, who confessed to beheading the *Wall Street Journal* bureau chief Daniel Pearl, was responsible; the American soldiers who tortured Iraqi prisoners at Abu Ghraib were responsible; the Russian guards who brutalized Ivan Denisovich in the gulag (the prisoner immortalized by Aleksandr Solzhenitsyn) were responsible; and so on in an endless list. All of these men started out as ordinary men. Ordinary men, carrying out the orders of their fanatical or sadistic leaders, or, in the case of the highly educated Khalid Sheikh Mohammed, radicalized by experiences in times of group conflict.

Ordinary men, briefly put, can turn into monsters in time of war or group conflict, committing acts that horrify and disgust—acts we label "evil." And then they can turn back again into ordinary men. Once the leader has dehumanized the enemy, the value system the followers may have brought to the conflict originally is scrapped and supplanted by the leader's value system. And that system is quite simple: the enemy is the enemy; the enemy is not really human. Uniformed troops, guerillas, combatants, civilians, men of fighting age, women and children . . . all are fair game. Thus the three thousand civilians killed on 9/11 were not "really" civilians; they were "soldiers" in the front lines of the Great Satan's infidel capitalist army. The North Vietnamese at My Lai were women who might be hiding bombs, children who might one day grow into enemy soldiers. Best not to take chances.

Apart from a declared war, there are innumerable instances of civil strife and politically inspired terrorism where we witness the transition: *ordinary man–torturer–ordinary man once again*. The Brazilian police during the military regime of 1964–1985 had been carefully instructed in torture and murder by way of suppressing those considered "subversives" in that era. Beggars were taken off the streets and tortured—for practice—the torturers having been carefully mentored by a US police officer.[9] The policemen involved showed "no evidence of premorbid personalities that would have predisposed them to such careers"; those with cruel tendencies were actually steered away from that work by the authorities.[10] This, from a chapter in *Violence Workers* entitled "Ordinary Men Doing Evil Deeds."

The behavior of the common soldiers in the Franco-Algerian war of 1954–1962 went along similar lines. The tortures taking place on both sides led French journalist Jacques Servan-Schreiber to write: "There is no one who is naturally evil. . . . There are situations which inflame the beast in man. . . . You have seen in Algeria how easily men can become the helpless playthings of the set-up into which they are thrown."[11] Servan-Schreiber is, I believe, *nearly* correct: the "naturally evil" are rare; they are the psychopathic men (and the still rarer women) who, in peacetime and without maltreatment or provocation, kill and torture for sport. Usually they occupy Category 22 of my Gradations of Evil scale, though the majority of them have been so brutalized in their younger years that it would be improper to call them "naturally evil."

In an earlier chapter we saw how uncommon it was to encounter a murderer whose acts could be attributed to Bad Seed alone. There is of course an intermediate group: persons who have spent all their adult lives (and much of their adolescent lives) doing one violent or socially repugnant act after another. These are the persons who seem "perpetually" evil. Some have endured neglect or humiliation in their early years (Charles Sobhraj, who killed a string of tourists in Southeast Asia; the Angel of Death nurse Jane Toppan; San Francisco's "Zodiac Killer" Arthur Allen; Florida serial killer Daniel Conahan; Francisco Montes, the Spanish man who sneaked into youth hostels in a dozen countries, raping and killing young women). Others came from apparently good homes (such as Vancouver's serial killer, Clifford Olson).

About certain others, we know little concerning their early years: Franklin Delano Floyd, who kidnapped a girl, kept her for many years as his "daughter" and then killed her when she tried to leave him and marry; Josef Fritzl, the Austrian man who imprisoned his daughter in the bunker under his house and had seven children by her. Then there is

Paul Schaefer, whose life was depicted under the arresting title "The World's Most Evil Man."[12] That is a gross exaggeration, though there is ample evidence to place Schaefer as *one among the most evil men*. A man of twenty-four at the end of World War II, he became a charismatic cult leader and moved with his flock from Germany to Chile. He created a compound, *Colonia Dignidad*, cut off from the rest of the country and ruled his subjects with absolute control—engaging in the sexual molestation of boys, forced labor, weapons trafficking, kidnapping, torture, and murder. A large but unknown number of murder victims lay buried in the hinterlands near Santiago. Through intimidation of his followers, the news of the unspeakable practices going on at the *Colonia* were so slow to reach the outside world that Schaefer was not arrested until 2006—when he was eighty-five. Given a twenty-year sentence, he will die in prison, but his crimes are no worse than those of David Parker Ray or Leonard Lake, described in an earlier chapter. There is no "most evil man"—though there are many serious contenders.

As for the men who have *fomented* the wars or the political conflicts, and in whose names atrocities were committed, their abnormalities were confined to the subtle area of *personality*. Sensitivity about short stature (Joseph Stalin) or physical abnormality (Joseph Goebbels, with his deformed leg from childhood osteomyelitis) affected some of these men.[13] Mental illness and brain injury were not a part of the picture; instead was a picture composed in varying fractions of grandiosity, hatred, sadism, vengefulness, bigotry, and a lust for power. Also, we should not overlook the *quest for fame*, as we see in many of today's terrorists who, nonentities at the outset, purchase fame through martyrdom, knowing that leading a blameless life earns no notoriety—but slaughtering a few innocents makes headlines.[14]

—~—

Evil in peacetime is quite another matter. In the absence of prior attack by an enemy bent on one's degradation and destruction, evil acts emerge neither from the aggressors nor from extremes of retaliation by the victims.[15] As outlined in the chapters of this book, evil in peacetime sometimes has its origins in aberrations of personality alone, but the more usual background picture is an amalgam of abnormal personality and other factors relating to mental illness or brain disorders. An extremely harsh early environment is commonplace (parental brutality, disparagement, or neglect), especially in the ranks of men committing serial sexual homicide. This was true of many of the *leaders* in wartime but is not a regular feature of those whom they inspire to carry out the atrocities against the enemy. Once the enemy has been demonized and dehumanized, the all-too-ordinary men committing these acts seldom regard them as atrocities.[16]

Evil in peacetime lends itself to neuroscientific study: the men involved in evil acts in peacetime are seldom the "ordinary" men of wartime soldiery.[17] As noted earlier, however, many of those "ordinary" soldiers committing these atrocities are *not all that* ordinary. Probably a good many were wife beaters, cruel and perhaps even sadistic to their children, men who found satisfaction in wartime situations where they could, now free of all restraint, unleash their sadistic desires.

But when we examine the persons who are responsible for the evil acts done in *peacetime*, we are usually looking at persons who have something decidedly the matter with them. Especially among those in whom mental illness, birth complications, and brain damage are *not* part of the picture, there will often be a "residue" of psychopathy. And as we have seen, psychopaths will often have abnormalities in certain key brain areas: the top-down areas mentioned in chapter 9, the paralimbic region that Dr. Kiehl is currently studying with fMRI.[18] Dr. Kiehl is optimistic that psychopathy will one day yield to treatment (including medications). I do not share his optimism. Even though brain abnormalities have been detected in some psychopaths via MRI, psychopathy as an aberration of personality is in *all* of the brain. Whether the condition arose on a genetic basis or on the basis of brutalization or extreme neglect (especially maternal neglect), the predatory nature of the psychopath and his deeply entrenched inability to care about the suffering of his victims will persist. And if the psychopath becomes a serial rapist like Fred Coe or James Bergstrom, or a serial killer like Ted Bundy or David Parker Ray, the idea of pardon and release for such dangerous men is completely out of the question.

Equally beyond the range of treatment and rehabilitation are the psychopaths who ruin the lives of others through a lifelong pattern of fraud, imposture, deceit, and theft but who either stop short of murder, or whose attempts to murder are thwarted at the last minute. Because murderous assault and actual murder are more likely to trigger the response of "evil," the imposter whose victims survive doesn't often make the headlines. Shock and horror stay confined to a narrower circle. This is evil too—but of a quieter kind. In her book *A Dance with the Devil*, Barbara Bentley gives a moving account of her marriage to a man, John Perry, who led her to believe he was an admiral in the navy and was the son of the famous Admiral Perry. He told her that he had won, among his many other medals, the Congressional Medal of Honor for his courageous exploits. A charming and clever parasite, he nearly bankrupted her with his extravagance, stealing her credit cards and charging huge sums, promising her that still huger sums were owed him and were about to come in any day, along with a substantial inheritance. Little by little she discovered he had spent three years in federal prison for impersonating an air force officer, that he actually *was* the son of Admiral Perry but had won no medals, and had used half a dozen aliases (one of the telltale signs of the psychopath). Nor was he was the heir to any fortune. As she began to learn the truth, he tried on several occasions, fortunately without success, to kill her. Barbara had to move mountains to win a favorable divorce (she actually got a law passed in California to protect victims such as herself). John was given five years in prison for attempted murder but was released after twenty-two months. He then continued as the same John Perry, this time tricking a wealthy widow into supporting him. As she began to realize he was defrauding her, he used the same ploy to win sympathy as he had with Barbara: faking a heart attack by taking a cocktail of pills. This time the cocktail killed him—a con artist and a killer manqué to the last of his sixty-seven years.[19]

Sexual crimes, particularly those involving children, readily trigger in us the "evil" response. Their perpetrators *usually* come from seriously troubled families, show multiple paraphilias, prime themselves with alcohol or drugs just before the crimes, and may be mentally ill besides. Yet even among them, there are a few who come from unremarkable, or even excellent, families: Dennis Rader and Richard Starrett are two examples.[20] Crimes of impulse, including those we regard as evil, often stem from problems in the brain's bottom-up areas. Drives go unchecked by the braking system. Murders committed by adolescents often have this characteristic, including the occasional "thrill-kill" by boys from respectable families. This seemed to be the case with the famous "Crime of the Century" by Richard Loeb and Nathan Leopold, eighteen and nineteen when they conspired to murder fourteen-year-old Bobby Franks.[21]

What is most important to remember, when considering the origins of violent criminal actions, is that the sociological explanations favored by many—that crime is an outgrowth of poverty and bad environment—is simplistic and misleading.[22] Some persons, consistently brutalized by parents in their formative years, do pass into the stage of *virulency*, described by Lonnie Athens (chapter 8 of Richard Rhodes's biography *Why They Kill*). But inherited factors may have paved the way for the ensuing brutality to have its devastating effects. Dr. Athens's own life gives the lie to his one-sided theory. He himself had been brutalized by his father in ways that would be sickening to describe here.[23] Yet he did not go on to become a violent (let alone virulent or evil) criminal. How can this be? The safest assumption is that Dr. Athens was dealt some genetic high cards that allowed him to endure his father's tortures without succumbing to a life of vengeance and criminality, becoming instead an eminent sociologist with some special insights into the lives of violent felons.

A similar case of "good seed" concerns Sanford Clark, the half-brother of Gordon Northcott. When Sanford was thirteen, he was taken by his much older brother (whom he was raised by their mother to believe was his uncle) to a California chicken ranch. There he was raped and beaten regularly by Gordon and forced at gunpoint to participate in the rape-murders of twenty Mexican boys. It was Sanford's job to flay the victims, crush their skulls, and dispose of their remains. After two years of this enslavement, he was able to escape and give evidence against Northcott, who was hanged two years later in 1930. After overcoming immense psychological traumas, Sanford was able to make a good recovery. He married and adopted two boys, afraid lest the taint of the family pass to any children he might have of his own (there were other violent and abusive relatives besides his half-brother). As with Lonnie Athens, Sanford Clark was able to lead an exemplary life—for reasons as mysterious as why Athens's father and Clark's brother were so consistently evil.[24]

We will find the fewest abnormalities in those who, driven by jealousy, murder a lover or spouse. This was the case with Clara Harris and Jean Harris, whom I have placed in Category 2 of the scale, where murder is a once-in-a-lifetime occurrence in an otherwise fairly well-integrated person. So far, we are speaking of the *external* aspects of evil: actions whose description, when we hear of them, make us wince in horror and disgust.

Equally important is the most significant *internal* aspect of evil: lack of *compassion*. Some professionals prefer the term *empathy*, but as I explained earlier, *compassion* is the more accurate word—and it is the word Drakulic emphasizes in her book. The evil acts of peacetime are only occasionally accompanied by a total and across-the-board lack of this vital human sentiment. In my experience the most striking example is that of the cannibal-killer, David Paul Brown/Bar Jonah. Going back to the time when he, while still himself a child, tried to kill another child, there is no evidence he felt compassion for anyone. This "liberated" him to perform the most unspeakable acts with utter nonchalance. Just as there are gradations of evil, there are gradations of compassion.

Of the persons sketched in this book, some had little compassion in general; others showed a kind of "splitting" in this regard: they had no compassion for their targeted victims, yet they retained a measure of compassion toward certain family members and friends. Serial killer Gary Ridgway, for example, felt close to his third wife (during that marriage, the frequency of his murders declined considerably), yet when interviewed by the authorities after his capture, he spoke of the women he killed as "garbage."

Sometimes an evil act arises unexpectedly in a person who is deficient though not devoid of compassion when subjected to an unanticipated stress relating to someone viewed as "them" but not "us." A common example is that of the parent who is kind to his own children but cruel to an adopted or foster child. Getrude Baniszewski is a case in point. A divorced and impoverished woman of thirty-seven in Indianapolis with seven children of her own, Gertrude took in other children as boarders to supplement her meager income.[25] Embittered, punitive, and mentally unstable, Gertrude was quick to use the switch with her own children, but her punishments fell short of "evil." When she agreed in the summer of 1965 to take care of a fifteen-year-old girl, Sylvia, and her younger sister while their parents were away, Gertrude's punitiveness suddenly rose to evil proportions. In a crime that was considered the most horrifying in Indiana's history at that time, she, along with her children and some of their friends, embarked on a campaign to torture. Sylvia—a virginal girl whose "offense" was to be prettier than Gertrude's eldest (and already pregnant) daughter Paula—was beaten, burned, scalded, booted in the groin, forced to eat and drink waste matter, and then branded with a hot needle that etched into her abdomen the words "I am a prostitute and proud of it." She was then tied to a bed in the basement and starved to death. At trial the prosecuting attorney, alluding to the branding of the victim, asked his counterpart on the defense side, "Where is the compassion, Mr. Nedeff?"[26] As with all those committing evil acts in peacetime, there was no Commander Gojkovic holding a gun to Gertrude's head. Her actions came from within. Gertrude died at age sixty-two still experiencing no remorse for the torture of Sylvia.

Cindy Hendy, the female accomplice of serial killer David Parker Ray, showed a similar compartmentalization of compassion. She referred to the women she lured to the Toy Box to be tortured by Ray and herself as "packages." A kind of "them"—as distinct from "us"—to be used and then thrown away.

No one held a gun to Hendy's head either, when she joined Ray in his systematic torture of his victims. In other killer teams—Fred and Rose West, Ian Brady and Myra Hindley, Gerald and Charlene Gallego, Doug Clark and Carol Bundy, Paul Bernardo and his wife, Karla Homolka—the women were not forced. Theirs was a volunteer army. Many had been incest victims, accustomed to control by an amoral "father figure." Their attitudes hugged the extremes: intense loyalty to, and vengeful feelings toward, the men on whom they depended. They were easily led into taking part in the evil actions of their lovers or husbands. Not all were strangers to compassion, but somehow after they had been sufficiently mesmerized by their men, their compassion went offline, sometimes for good. Myra Hindley had been a kindly, albeit very dependent woman before she met Ian Brady. Once under his influence, she did not demur when he recorded the screams of the children he strangled in front of her. She died years later in prison without a particle of remorse for what she and Ian had done.

Throughout the book I have placed particular emphasis on actions.

Horrifying actions elicit the reaction "evil"—it is the first word that comes to our minds when we learn of these acts of violence or extreme degradation. Yet as I hope to have shown, the persons behind these actions are not all the same. We can think of a kind of spectrum at one end of which are persons so devoid of human sentiments and so driven to commit evil acts repeatedly that we speak of both the *person* and his *actions* as evil. At this end of the spectrum, any idea of redemption is unthinkable, treatment ineffective, and release from incarceration a terrible mistake. Most of the persons who share these qualities are psychopaths; a few suffer from extreme forms of psychosis that do not respond to treatments currently available (or, if they were to be released, could not be trusted to continue taking their medications). At the opposite end of the spectrum, we confront persons for whom redemption, treatment, and eventual release back into the community are all feasible. Here are some examples, beginning with the unredeemable and progressing to those capable of rehabilitation:

- Lacking in human qualities, without compassion, not approachable in conversation, contemptuous of others, mendacious: David Paul Brown/Nathaniel Bar-Jonah; serial rapist, James Bergstrom; serial killers Jeremy Jones and Richard Ramirez
- Extreme egocentricity, though capable of being superficially friendly and affable but showing no remorse, incapable of redemption or release: Ian Brady, Arthur Shawcross, David Parker Ray
- Approachable, some capacity for relationships with a few people, remorse is meager and not altogether genuine; some honesty, though with a tendency to minimize or distort when recounting past crimes; still beyond redemption and release: Tommy Lynn Sells
- A capacity for remorse, candor, and self-reflection is present, as well as a limited capacity to care about others and to sustain friendships; release not appropriate: Dennis Nilsen
- Remorse and compassion along with improved self-control are present to such a degree that eventual redemption, rehabilitation, and release are possible (though many years may be required for the latter). The persons who share these qualities are usually antisocial—some with a few psychopathic traits—but are not full-blown psychopaths: Archie McCafferty

- The aforementioned positive qualities are all present; the act that inspired the reaction "evil" occurred just once and during a time of overwhelming stress. Redemption is assured, and eventual release is quite justified. Solid moral values are present, as well as a good capacity for close friendships and intimate attachments: Billy Wayne Sinclair, Clara Harris, Jean Harris

I hope these examples will illustrate the difference between evil in peacetime and evil in time of war and group conflict. In the latter is the element of subjectivity (with each side convinced that evil lay on their opponent's side). Also, the atrocities that inspire revulsion, that trigger the response of "evil," are most often committed by persons compelled by evil leaders: persons whose lives before and afterward were inconspicuous (though not necessarily innocuous). These are the soldiers and lower-ranking administrators of Hannah Arendt's *banality of evil*; the people who, as Slavenka Drakulic wryly put it, "would never hurt a fly."[27] The people behind the evil acts of peacetime often shock us all the more, *because they were acting quite on their own*. That is, they were not swept up in mob psychology, not caught like Dražen Erdomovic in a kill-or-be-killed situation; they were not like certain narcissistic leaders who, suddenly finding themselves at the top, become unshackled from moral constraints. In addition, there is little or no subjectivity at issue. The only person who would argue against the murder of a child as being evil is another child murderer. I am not being melodramatic here: Joseph Edward Duncan III, who began raping (and later murdering) boys when he was twelve,[28] after raping a boy at knifepoint when he was seventeen, spent the next fourteen years in prison. Highly intelligent (he later obtained a Phi Beta Kappa key from college), he authored a blog on the Internet, declaring: "[M]y reaction is to strike out toward the perceived source of my misery, society. My intent is to harm society as much as I can. . . . As an adult all I knew was the oppression of incarceration. All those years I dreamed of getting out . . . and getting even."[29] In his blog, Duncan advocated for release of sex offenders and for abolition of sex-offender registries, as well as recording many of his violent sexual fantasies.[30]

The other main ingredients of evil—that the act be shocking and that the perpetrator be lacking in compassion—are routinely present in both wartime and peacetime. But even here there is a difference. We grow up knowing the depths to which humanity can sink in wartime. The morning newspaper and the evening news teach us this. To most of us, these events seem far away. Our shock doubles, however, when a serial killer is our next-door neighbor (Gary Ridgway in Seattle), our church deacon (Dennis Rader in Kansas City), or our alderman (John Gacy in Chicago). I can personally attest to this doubling of shock: serial rapist and killer John Royster committed one of his near-murders in Central Park, across the street from where I live.[31]

EVIL IN PEACETIME: WHAT CAN BE DONE?

A great many of the vicious acts we witness in peacetime, the ones we register as "evil," are committed by men (and a few women) who have the characteristics of the psychopath. Some are born that way, as we have noted, others are transformed into psychopaths through environmental adversity. Rob a child of warm maternal nurturance and you rob the child of his humanity—usually. Compassion may fail to develop. Hatred toward the more fortunate majority may easily develop, along with the desire for revenge. But protective genes may prevent a bad outcome even in a brutalized child. There is little to be done, however, with the "born" psychopath—with persons, that is, whose inherited predisposition to psychopathy overrides even the most compassionate nurturing, as appears to have been the case with Gerald Stano and his adoptive parents. Such persons behave as though wired to break the law, no matter what the law is. A psychopath interviewed by Dr. Stanton Samenow told him, "If they made rape legal, I'd have to do something else."[32]

Many socially valuable strengths come naturally, that is, with little explicit instruction. Most young girls don't need to be taught to be maternal: they come by it naturally (helped by the affection and competence of their own mothers). Teaching "maternal adequacy" in our high schools would not likely accomplish much. But we could teach something about the disastrous effects of parental cruelty. We might even be able to get across the idea that corporal punishment meted out to the rebellious, let alone callous-unemotional child (who will usually be a boy), will be more likely to make him into the next Gary Gilmore than into a law-abiding citizen, respectful of the feelings of others.

Every generation will have a small but irreducible percentage of paranoid schizophrenic and other psychotic persons, a few of whom will commit—often at the urging of "command-hallucinations"—crimes of spectacular awfulness. Such was the case with David Tarloff, murderer of Dr. Faughey (mentioned in chapter 2, note 12), or with William Bruce, who killed his mother with a hatchet.[33] Both were paranoid schizophrenic men, released by an overworked and inattentive hospital staff in the first case, and by overzealous "patient advocates" in the second. Patient advocates (who are not trained psychiatrists) sometimes take patient rights to such an extreme as to interfere with a delusional patient taking appropriate medication or preventing hospital staff from communicating with family members—all to the detriment of patient care and to the increase in risk of violence to others. These tragedies could be minimized through better attention to the matter of dangerousness. Mentally ill persons who are chronically dangerous (as suggested by their past history) may need institutional care for prolonged periods. Not all can be trusted to comply with taking prescribed medications once they are released from a hospital. Patient rights need to be respected, yet the rights of the community must also be respected. There will always be some guesswork in the estimation of dangerousness, though the work of Dr. Hare and his colleagues, Dr. Monahan and his group, Dr. Hodgins, Drs. Caspi and Moffitt, and others has made our estimates more accurate than ever before. We can strike a more proper balance between the competing rights of the mentally ill and the community, in such a way as to reduce the violence to which certain patients might otherwise be prone.

The violent crimes committed by certain psychotic persons are often so bizarre as to elicit the label of evil even more readily than some of the (far more common) violent crimes committed by psychopaths—especially serial killers and wife murderers who take great pains to evade detection. Tossing your father's head out the window to make sure it does not get "reattached" and result in still more cruel behavior from your father is quite crazy. The public's first reaction is completely understandable. It is when closer acquaintance with the offender's illness becomes possible, after psychiatric examination, that the public becomes aware that the *act* was evil, but the *offender*—though perhaps still dangerous—was not so evil. The psychotic killer, for example, is often driven by fear and is not rational. To that extent he is less "evil" than is the rational and calculating psychopath who harms others not out of fear but out of self-aggrandizement or the quest for thrills.

An even greater problem than the premature or ill-advised release of certain mentally ill patients is the premature release of certain offenders in our prisons. Prisoners greatly outnumber the mentally ill. In my records of serial killers, fully a fourth have been, through carelessness or improper evaluation, released into the community after having been incarcerated for rape or murder or both. In rare instances (as in the case of David Paul Brown/Nathaniel Bar-Jonah), pressure was brought from the outside despite the grave warnings issued by the hospital or prison staff. Premature release of a serial killer often results in the subsequent murder of a dozen, or even many dozens of victims. Since the mentally ill seldom murder in such numbers, the consequences of releasing a psychopath who has committed a rape-murder are much more serious. Let us focus on seven of the more well-known serial killers for the moment, following their premature or otherwise unwarranted release from prison for serious violent sexual crimes: William Bonin, Ted Bundy, Gary Heidnick, Ed Kemper, Clifford Olson, Derrick Todd Lee, and Jack Unterweger. All went on to rape and murder at least an additional 107 victims.

One of the most egregious examples of the unwarranted release of a prisoner is that of serial killer Arthur Shawcross.[34] Described as "diabolical" and "evil" by his schoolmates, Shawcross came from a working-class family in Watertown, New York. Humiliated and physically abused by his mother, he also suffered at least six serious head injuries with prolonged unconsciousness during his early years. A moody, friendless outcast in school, he was kept back three grades, dropping out when he was seventeen. He showed the "triad" of prolonged bed-wetting, fire setting, and animal torture—setting dogs and cats on fire, tying up cats and hurling them into the river, and pounding squirrels and chipmunks flat. At twenty-two, he went to Vietnam, where he boasted of fantastical exploits ("beheading mama-sans and nailing their heads to trees, as a warning to the Vietcong"), when in fact he never saw combat. Back in the United States, he raped and killed a boy and a girl back in his hometown and was given a lengthy sentence at Greenhaven prison. Inexperienced social workers and staff considered him "no longer dangerous," and after serving twelve years he was given an undeserved release by the governor of New York in 1984. A few years later, prostitutes in Rochester, New

York, began disappearing—at least eleven that we know of. All were the victims of Arthur Shawcross, who, until his death in 2008, had been serving a life sentence (with no possibility of parole) at a different facility. Psychiatrists during his earlier incarcerations had assessed him (accurately) as a schizoid psychopath; their warnings about his dangerousness went unheeded. Shawcross was the embodiment of just about every risk factor mentioned in this book. A neuroscientist's nightmare, he was genetically disadvantaged, of below-average intelligence, brutalized, hypersexual, rageful, brain damaged, violent, and psychopathic—with all the callousness, grandiosity, deviousness, and lack of compassion that go to make up that personality configuration.

The two rape-murders when he was twenty-seven should have been enough to ensure a life in prison. Because sexual crimes tend to be repeated, men committing rape, especially if followed by murder, require much stricter treatment by the courts than was given to Shawcross or the dozens of other serial killers who, having been given a "second chance," used it to add to their list of victims.

A still more shocking example concerns serial killer Joseph Duncan, mentioned above. After a long series of rapes and murders of young boys, he was released as a "sex offender" (rather than as a "sex predator") thanks to a lax prison system. Reoffending shortly afterward (sexually groping a six-year-old boy), he manipulated a friend into putting up bail money—and then skipped bail. A month later, Duncan kidnapped a boy and a girl, after killing their mother, brother, and the mother's fiancé. Taking them from Idaho to Montana, he raped and tortured them for two months, making a video of the torture, and finally killing the nine-year-old boy. The sister managed to escape further abuse when Duncan was apprehended with her while in a convenience store. Convicting Duncan in 2008 in Idaho, the jury recommended the death penalty. Because the public's reaction to the torture and murder of children is stronger than its reaction to the murder of prostitutes, Duncan's case embodies evil to an even greater extent than does Shawcross's. Most have forgotten that Shawcross got his start by killing two children. In the words of the grandmother of the last boy Duncan tortured and killed, "I see nothing but an evil, empty, cold-hearted shell."[35] Both Shawcross and Duncan meet criteria for Category 22 on my scale; unlike Shawcross, Duncan came from a good home, was not abused, was very bright, and did not show the triad—though he did wet the bed until age thirteen. The factors behind his psychopathy seem attributable more to nature than to nurture. But it was the inappropriate release from prison that allowed both these sex offenders to continue their violent careers—their violence actually escalated in the postrelease years.

Mass murder is a different matter. Those responsible for mass murder, such as the men discussed in chapter 5—though typically paranoid, disagreeable men like Thomas Hamilton, Seung-Hui Cho, and George Hennard—usually explode into violence without much warning. Since mass murder is all but impossible without guns, better gun control might reduce this form of evil. In the United States, with two guns for every three people, it is quixotic even to think of such a solution, though we might at least aim toward making AK-47s and other repeat weapons less available. They are not instruments for hunting, after all; they are meant for killing people. A shocking case came to light recently: Quentin Patrick, an ex-convict in South Carolina somehow mistook for a robber a twelve-year-old boy who was trick-or-treating on Halloween night and rang his doorbell. Patrick, who, as an ex-convict shouldn't have had a gun in the first place, shot thirty rounds into the boy with his AK-47, killing him instantly.[36]

In chapter 9 there were illustrations of how alcohol and drugs like cocaine and methamphetamine can paralyze the "braking system" in persons contemplating acts of violence. It is an exercise in futility to aim at the eradication of the coca crop in Bolivia or the poppy crop in Afghanistan. "Meth" is home-grown in clandestine labs all around the United States. Cocaine and methamphetamine are, in effect, double evils, since they often ruin the lives of those addicted to them (leading them to turn to prostitution, robbery, and worse to maintain their habit), as well as the lives of those who are killed by the addicts during a violent crime. We would also have to include the lives lost to serial killers who prime themselves with such drugs before committing their murders. As a species, we evolved with brain wiring that makes us fear snakes, scorpions, spiders, and crocodiles. We cannot wait for evolution to solve the much more dangerous gun and drug problems. This becomes a task for the educational system. Since parents cannot always be relied on to instill the proper fear of these potential instruments of death and destruction, the schools should play a larger role in making children aware of the dangers.

We do try to "hardwire" moral values (the Golden Rule) and survival values (cross the street on the green light) into young children. It would be good if we could add avoidance of drugs to the list of survival values.

People summoned to jury duty are routinely taught how our Anglo-American justice system evolved from one of trial by fire or of draconian sentences for even minor offenses to a much fairer system based on the supposition of innocence until proven guilty. Sentencing was assigned in accordance with the seriousness of the offense; when an offender's time was served, his debt to society was paid. Our system offers justice to many but has proven at times inadequate when faced with certain repeat offenders, especially those with psychopathic personalities. Many such offenders know how to earn "time off for good behavior," and then resume their violent careers immediately upon release. Clifford Olson, currently residing in Vancouver's Supermax prison for the serial murder of eleven children, was asked by a journalist what he would do if he were ever released. Olson replied, "I'd take up where I left off," adding, when asked if he felt remorse toward the families, "If I gave a shit about the parents, I wouldn't have killed the kids."[37]

The Canadian system is such that eligibility for parole is considered every two years even in a case like Olson's; a life sentence tends to mean only twenty-five years; a murderer can apply for early release after fifteen years.[38] Olson's is not a debt that can ever be repaid, no matter the time he serves: he has put society on notice that he remains as dangerous as the day he was first incarcerated. This, and cases like this, argue for a justice system that is flexible enough to pay greater attention to the likelihood of continued dangerousness than to statutes stemming from earlier times, when some of the crimes most closely associated with the concept of evil (like serial sexual homicide) were scarcely known or rarely encountered.

The Olson case and those like it point the way to something we actually have in our power to do: reduce the amount of evil in society. If we accept that evil equates with criminal acts that shock and horrify us—the central thesis in this book—then evil will always be with us. We cannot change heredity. We cannot eliminate head injury, mental illness, and drug abuse. But if we hone our skills in spotting dangerousness, and make sure that those whom we deem most dangerous remain separated from society either permanently or for very long periods, then the most dangerous offenders, once apprehended, will be less free to repeat their crimes. This is especially so with violent psychopathic offenders, in whom the likelihood of rehabilitation and redemption is vanishingly small. Olson, for example, before he embarked at age forty on his career of serial sexual homicide of some eleven children, had been jailed and released and jailed and released several *dozens* of times for assault, animal torture, armed robbery, and the like. There was a lot of handwriting on the wall. The courts could have intervened and seen to it that his career—and the careers of many like him—were thwarted at the earliest stage.

Getting to know certain violent criminals through personal interviews and as their lives unfold over time can teach us another important—and more hopeful—point. Some persons regarded as evil early in their criminal careers do turn out to be capable of redemption as they mature over the years. We saw this in the example of Archie McCafferty (chapter 5). Despite the tumultuousness of his earlier years, he emerged as a man capable of compassion and a measure of remorse; his personality was clearly antisocial at first but lacked the psychopathic traits of utter callousness, conning, and the other extreme narcissistic traits. Early appearances to the contrary, he turned out to be salvageable. An even more compelling example is that of Billy Wayne Sinclair, mentioned in chapter 1.[39] Sinclair committed a murder during an armed robbery but proved himself in prison to be a man of strong moral values. He was the "whistle-blower" who exposed the corruption of the parole system in his prison. As I learned from him, the relatives of the victim will never forgive him. Though their sentiments are understandable, their hardheartedness is, I believe, misplaced: Billy Wayne Sinclair, now in his sixties, is clearly a redeemed man, an upright citizen, and a credit to the community.

Arthur Shawcross, who should never have been released, was—and went on to kill a dozen more people; Billy Sinclair, who should have been released after a reduced sentence, nearly died in the electric chair and was fated to die of old age in prison, until, nearing sixty, he finally was released. The system is not perfect. We need to pay more attention to the subtleties of personality, becoming more restrictive with the psychopathic killers and more liberal with the nonpsychopathic prisoners who begin to show genuine signs of remorse, reform, and redemption.

Redemption is not a possibility for all. Redemption is akin in the spiritual sense to what salvageability is in the realm of treatment. Essential ingredients would be remorse, a capacity for guilt, and some ability to make the transition from contempt to compassion for the kinds of persons one formerly singled out to victimize. Those who have made a career out of systematic torture—Theresa Knorr, David Parker Ray, David Paul Brown, Robert Berdella,[40] Mike DeBardeleben, Belgium's pedophile torturer Marc Dutroux, Spain's Francisco Montes—lacked those ingredients. Some (Brown, Berdella, Montes) had never established a friendship, let alone an intimate relationship, with anyone their whole life. All were at the far end of the scale (22) and were beyond redemption. Some had their humanity knocked out of them by extreme parental cruelty (Berdella, DeBardeleben); we can at least sympathize with the dehumanizing forces to which they were exposed in their earliest days. Others had decent parents and arrived at their inhumanity via less obvious routes.

But even among the torturers are some in whom we can spot islands of humanity, qualities that allow us to sympathize; they behaved monstrously at times, but, in line with Slavenka Drakulic's understanding, they were not simply "monsters." Ian Brady, mentioned briefly in chapter 1, is a case in point. For years, this man, who recorded the screams of the children he strangled in the English moor country, was my exemplar of the worst human being ever—in peacetime, that is. This was until I learned of the considerably worse tortures to which Leonard Lake and David Parker Ray subjected their victims. But Brady, one of the most intelligent and literate of the serial killers, wrote me a letter not long ago, now that he has spent some forty years in prison, in which he reminisced about the gourmet restaurants and delicatessens he enjoyed during his visits to the United States (before the murders). Brady has refused to eat these past few years and is kept alive by force-feeding through a stomach tube. He asked me for a map of the places he had visited in the United States, adding wistfully that, as he has no present nor future any longer, he has only the past. Prevented these past two-thirds of his seventy years from committing more of the vicious acts of the first third, these islands of humanity have become a bit more visible in this otherwise intensely narcissistic man. These islands are visible, if we peer long enough and hard enough, in a fair number of the men and women whose acts in peacetime reached the level of evil. More often this will be the case with those in the lower categories of the scale; occasionally, even with a serial killer who was not given to torture. This was something I learned only when I began to make personal acquaintance with a fair number of these otherwise "monstrous" killers. Getting to know murderers committing evil acts allows for distinctions one cannot draw from books alone. Actually this thought condensed in my mind only recently. The idea came in the form of a dream I had on August 17, 2008:

> I'm home with another man: an elderly, rather diminutive man dressed in a pajama-like outfit. We are trying to get the old man to talk about his past. He seemed to be on a pass from prison where he had been interred because he had been a serial killer. The man is very reticent to talk about his childhood, though he mentions that he was raised by his mother, since his father had absconded from the family. I go to the dining room at one point. The old man follows and gets into conversation with my wife, who, quite unafraid, chats with him in her usual amiable way. I feel nervous, wondering, what if he reverts to his old ways, what with all the knives in the dining room drawers? But he remains harmless, and moments later answers his cell phone—and begins crying. He mutters something in Russian. I ask him, in Russian, "Shto sluchcelos?"—What happened? He indicates that some woman he had been fond of had just rejected him. I feel sorry for him.

Shortly before the dream, I had been reading a letter that a former serial killer, Dennis Nilsen (mentioned in chapter 7), had sent me from the prison where he has been for the past twenty-five years. He closed his letter with a poem he had written that touched on his lifelong and intense loneliness. Nilsen had been raised mainly by his mother and her father, whose death was the traumatic event of Nilsen's early years. Here is a portion of his poem:

> Here I sit—long and long
> Quite alone—on the beach
> Besides the whispering sea
> Listening, waiting, hoping
> Tear-flecked patches on the sand
> As the tide gives up her dead.

. . . . .

As the sea gives up her life,
We creatures on the sand—
You—me
Always and always
Waiting for the man.[41]

His letter put me in mind of what my mentor in forensic psychiatry, Dr. Charles Smith, once said about evil: there are no evil people, only evil acts. I believe what he meant was that there are no people who shock us with their acts of violence and harm throughout the whole of their lives. He is largely right, but not entirely right. Many of the serial killers and other murderers I came to know around the country had been languishing in prison for a very long time. Capture having abbreviated their careers in evil, their human feelings had been able, in several of them, to rise to the surface. These were mostly the men and women who had led "double lives." They had friends, lovers, mates, but they sneaked off at odd hours to commit atrocious acts. This was true of Dennis Nilsen, Ian Brady, Dennis Rader, Tommy Lynn Sells, Sante Kimes, and Gary Ridgway. But then there were those—the exceptions that proved Dr. Smith's rule—who had no remorse, no redeeming features, no possibility of cure, persons in whom the propensity for evil was pervasive and without end. Here I think of David Paul Brown/Nathaniel Bar-Jonah, Ed Sexton, Dale Pierre, Phil Skipper, Charles Manson, Mike DeBardeleben, and Angels of Death such as Dr. Harold Shipman and Dr. Michael Swango.

Before that dream, I had also been reading the case histories of adolescent sex murderers in Niels Habermann's book *Jugendliche Sexualmörder* (Juvenile Sexual Murder). Most of these young men had committed their first rape-murder after having been rejected by a girl. Some were psychopaths and went on to become serial killers. Others, antisocial (but not psychopathic) while young, spent time in prison, were released, and did not reoffend. I had also seen a patient earlier that day who complained that, as far as she was concerned, most people weren't really "human." To her way of thinking, they were just animals. She asked if I didn't agree with her, especially since I worked with prisoners and forensic patients. I tried to make her understand that even those whose actions descended to evil were every bit as human as the rest of us. Or, as Nietzsche would have added, "Human, all too human." In his famous essay *Thus Spake Zarathustra*, Nietzsche created a powerful image relating to our task as human beings.[42] We pass through the years of our lives like a tightrope walker perched precariously on his rope. "Man," as he put it, "is a rope stretched between animal and the superior man; the rope lies over the abyss." We can fall back to the animal level—or we can strive toward the goal of self-transcendence and moral superiority. I am a little uncomfortable with the "animal" image. It is only we humans, not our animal cousins, who are capable of evil, though people (referring to some evil act) are accustomed to say, "He behaved like an animal." Perhaps a more up-to-date analogy might be: *We are a rope stretched between Bundy and the Buddha*. And the abyss is the descent to the evil of Ted Bundy and his like, where all regard for the welfare of one's fellow man evaporates, leaving one capable of immeasurable cruelty and harm. Harm that shocks us. Evil.

AFTERWORD

by Dr. Otto F. Kernberg

The present volume, I believe, is destined to become a classic in psychiatry and a landmark in our understanding of severe antisocial behavior and criminality. The early understanding of the psychopathic personality provided by Hervey Cleckley in his 1941 book *The Mask of Sanity* has evolved, in Michael Stone's book, to a comprehensive, updated, detailed, sophisticated analysis of what is implied in our intuitive concept of Evil. Dr. Stone provides instruments with which to differentiate evil actions from evil purpose, and a conceptual etiological frame that incorporates genetic and constitutional as well as environmental influences, personality structure, and psychiatric pathology. Stone defines, in the process, a broad spectrum of threatening, violent, and criminal behavior, pinpointing its severity and mapping out potentially preventive and prognostic features.

The nature of evil emerges as the shocking expression of primitive aggression, destructive behavior toward others that, in its violence, evinces a widely excessive quality, a radical callousness, and a lack of compassion that seem to defy the basic nature of humanity. Stone proposes a twenty-two-point scale that provides a fine differentiation of severity of antisocial behavior, with prognostic implications built into it. His proposed classification corresponds largely with the present DSM-IV system of the American Psychiatric Association, applying the concept of antisocial personality, in a broad sense, to refer to persons with chronic aggressive and/or exploitive behavior toward others. Within that broad spectrum this diagnostic scale further refines our understanding of the most dangerous and malignant group, the psychopathic personality, characterized by a total incapacity for compassion, combined with total lack of concern for others and self.

Because the entire spectrum of patients with severe antisocial behavior usually present an underlying narcissistic personality structure, I have preferred to classify this field into the narcissistic personality with antisocial behavior, the syndrome of malignant narcissism (referred to by Stone as occupying the intermediate zone of severity of his classification system), and the antisocial personality proper, using the latter term in a restrictive way that corresponds to the psychopath in Michael Stone's classification. He convincingly points to the fact that patients with schizoid and sadistic personality features also may enter the most severe group of psychopathy, and we do agree that the large majority of psychopaths present strongly predominant narcissistic features.

The great importance of Michael Stone's contribution resides not only in the detailed description of antisocial behavior along its entire spectrum but in the careful attention and updated review of the contribution to severe psychopathology of genetic factors, severely traumatic childhood experiences, and the social environment. He points to the mutual influences of genetic and environmental features that culminate in a personality structure that lacks a capacity for concern for self and others, for guilt feelings and remorse, and, in the worst cases, presents a fused experience of violence and lust as a fundamental pleasurable excitement in making others suffer.

Stone raises important questions regarding our present management of these cases in terms of a protection of both the civil rights of patients and those of the community. Patients with severely antisocial behavior who enter psychiatric inpatient services often prevent the hospital from obtaining crucial information about them from external sources. Confidentiality laws interfere with the possibility of gathering such information in order to arrive at an accurate diagnosis and an optimal treatment of that particular case. The need for protective, possibly lifelong custody for the most dangerous cases of those patients who enter the forensic system is hampered by the absence of the principle of "indeterminate sentencing," which would allow the legal system to individualize imprisonment and custodial treatment in terms of a realistic assessment of the dangerousness of patients along the dimensions specified by Stone. There are a few cases where psychiatric treatment, long-term psychotherapeutic engagement, and social rehabilitation may be effective, but in the immense majority of psychopathic criminals the possibility for successful treatment approaches zero. As Stone rightly observed, although we do not have absolute prognostic certainty at this time, we do have sufficient knowledge to decide what the optimal protective treatment should be once all the facts can be gathered and analyzed over a period of time.

Evil exists; it presents itself in the form of psychopathy, of blind violence geared to destroy without reason, often accompanied by an orgy of pleasure. But it also exists, as Stone points out, in the context of socially sanctioned mass murder and genocide, which, in turn, we have begun to understand in terms of the regressive nature of certain group processes, a psychological development in groups for which a potential exists in every individual. There are extreme social circumstances in which ordinary citizens, or rather, those with significant personality disorders that ordinarily would not show antisocial behavior, do become violent and destructive, evincing a total loss of compassion for an entire social group or oppressed minority. Here again, we have to differentiate social, political, and historical features from personality predispositions, and come to terms with the fact that our present-day understanding may exceed by far our capacity to influence those phenomena.

The core enigma of the psychopath, as Stone underlined, relates to the striking incapacity of compassionate reaction, of emotional empathy, and of concern for self and others. Neurobiological studies have pointed to certain cortical-limbic structures of the brain, particularly the complex relation between prefrontal and preorbital cortex, the anterior cingulum and the insula, with deeper layers of brain structures, particularly the amygdala and nucleus accumbens. While our knowledge of neurobiological systems and their specific functions is rapidly progressing, these structures and their functions may be indirectly related to complex behavioral, intrapsychic symbolic structures, with all of them implicated in influencing the capacity for empathy and for the internalization of moral values. As Stone points out, we have to advance simultaneously in research on the pathology of psychic structures embedded in the personality, and research on the personality determinants embedded in neurobiological structures.

This book is indispensable reading for all concerned citizens and all mental health professionals, particularly, of course, all those who deal with personality disorders at the boundary with forensic psychiatry. By the same token, it is hoped that all those in the legal system who deal with the social and legal problems involved in the management of antisocial behavior and criminality will find clear, updated information about an area that, unfortunately, still shows much discrepancy between our evolving level of new knowledge, on the one hand, and the practicality of dealing with the criminally ill, on the other.

ACKNOWLEDGMENTS

Major thanks, more than I can easily express, go to Linda Regan, executive editor at Prometheus Books, whose wisdom and guidance have been invaluable not only in matters of style but more importantly in matters of content. The subject of evil is problematical and sensitive, arousing strong emotions and inviting acrimonious disagreements. Some question whether a psychiatrist should broach the subject at all. Linda helped me avoid Scylla and Charybdis, keeping me in clear waters. Gratitude, also not easily expressed or measured, goes to Ben Carey of the *New York Times*, who featured my work on evil in a *Science Times* article he wrote in February of 2005. His article gave me a presence in this field that granted me access to journalists and to professionals in mental health and law enforcement around the world. Within a few months after the article was published, I was invited to serve as the host of a television program dedicated to educating the public about the often neglected "why" question of evil: What are the forces that prompt persons—civilians in peacetime—to commit the kinds of acts we label as evil? Through the program I had the opportunity to interview some of these men and women. Through these personal contacts it became more clear to me what were the ingredients that underlay the possibility of redemption and what were the ingredients that militated against it.

Even before Ben's article appeared, I had received encouragement to pursue this topic from leaders on psychopathy research: Dr. Robert Hare in Vancouver, and Dr. David Cooke in Glasgow. More recently I shared views and learned a great deal from some of the major writers on violence: Dr. Debra Niehoff and Dr. Katherine Ramsland. A number of prominent writers of true-crime biography gave me information about some of the high-profile murderers about whose crimes, designated evil by the public, I had only scanty knowledge of before. Among these writers: Carol Rothgeb-Stokes, Peter Davidson, Kieran Crowley, and Diane Fanning.

Thanks go to Mary O'Toole of the FBI, who invited me to participate in the First International Congress on Serial Killers, held in San Antonio in 2005. There I became reacquainted with Roy Hazelwood of the FBI, who taught me the fine points about sexual sadism—a topic that overlaps closely with the public's understanding of evil. There are a number of forensic specialists—Dr. Paul Fauteck, Dr. John Hume, and Dr. Norbert Nedopil—to whom I am indebted for more accurate biographical data about some of the persons mentioned in the book.

I owe great thanks to Dr. Charles Smith, former clinical director of the Mid-Hudson Forensic Psychiatric Hospital and my mentor in forensic psychiatry. It was through my work in forensics over the past twenty years that I developed a scale—the Gradations of Evil—by which I have attempted to place evil acts according to the degree of suffering of the victims and to the degree of horror evoked in the public.

As human beings, we are a members of a social species whose survival is threatened now and again by the forces of nature but to a much greater extent through the actions of other human beings. As a result, we have developed a rich vocabulary to depict the subtleties of badness. Our vocabulary for goodness is much skimpier. We do not distinguish between a dozen gradations of honesty, sweetness, amiability, since these qualities merely enhance rather than threaten our survival. But for someone immersing himself in the subject of evil, it is comforting to be surrounded by goodness as a counterbalance to the horror stories I confront daily. It is comforting to be reminded—daily—that there is much more goodness than evil in the world, even though evil is more apt to garner the headlines.

And it is here that my boundless love and gratitude go to my wife, Beth, who—were there a comparable Gradations of Goodness scale—would occupy a spot at its farthest end reserved for the very best of the Good. Beth's virtues are not confined to the spiritual; she read the manuscript as it evolved, made corrections, suggested changes in tone—all that were in line with Linda's recommendations and that contributed to a better manuscript. Better. Not perfect. The imperfections are mine.

NOTES

INTRODUCTION

1. Galatians 2:19–21.

2. As in Sura 10:27—"As for those who have earned evil, the punishment of an evil is the like of it . . ."

3. Mani was a third-century CE Persian religious preacher who emphasized two separate powers of Good and Evil. Derived from his name and influence was the heresy in the Christian world of "Manichaeism." St. Augustine had briefly been Manichaean before converting to Christianity.

4. Zoroaster, a Persian prophet of perhaps the seventh century BCE believed in a God of Good and Light (Ahura Mazda) and a God of Evil and Darkness (Ahriman).

5. Cf. *The Teachings of Buddha: Bukkyoh Dendoh Kyohkai* (Tokyo: Kosaido Printing Company, 1966).

6. Susan Neiman, *Evil in Modern Thought* (London: Transaction Publishers, 2002).

7. Ibid., pp. 8–9.

8. Andrew Delbanco, *The Death of Satan: How Americans Have Lost the Sense of Evil* (New York: Farrar, Straus & Giroux, 1995), p. 10.

9. Sura 4:79.

10. Brian Masters, *Killing for Company: The Case of Dennis Nilsen* (New York: Stein & Day, 1985).

11. Ibid., p. 19.

12. This is because there are no "evil genes." As we shall see in chapter 9, there are certain genetic factors that predispose to poor impulse control, low empathy, and certain other negative personality factors. But none of these are powerful in and of themselves to condemn one to behave in ways we consider evil. These factors heighten the risk that the person may later on behave in such ways, but they are not *determinative*.

13. Masters, *Killing for Company*, p. 187.

14. Lengthy biographies of mental patients begin to appear in the late eighteenth/early nineteenth century, such as Christian Spiess's *Biographien*

der Wahnsinnigen (Leipzig, 1796), or in K. W. Ideler, *Biographien der Geisteskranken* (Berlin: Schroeder, 1841).

15. Leviticus 19:15.

16. Ezekiel 7:3.

17. Matthew 7:1.

18. Matthew 7:3.

19. Ludwig Wittgenstein, *Philosophical Investigations*, trans. G. E. M. Anscombe (Upper Saddle River, NJ: Prentice Hall, 1999 [1953]).

20. Deuteronomy 22:25–30.

21. Elaine Pagels, *Adam, Eve, and the Serpent* (New York: Knopf, 1989).

22. Leviticus 18:21.

23. Many examples are recorded in George Ryley Scott's *History of Torture* (London: Bracken Books, 1940). Examples are the burning of the Albigensians in Provence in the thirteenth century and of the Jewish converts to Christianity during the Spanish Inquisition in the sixteenth century. In 1545 Calvin ordered twenty-three people burned at the stake for supposed witchcraft. To cite all such examples would require a separate book of considerable length.

24. This was the fear that inspired the witch trials in Salem and in other Massachusetts towns in 1692 during the judgeship of Cotton Mather. Cf. Cotton Mather, *Discourse on the Wonders of the Invisible World* (Roxbury, MA: WE Woodward, repr., 1866).

25. Neuroscientist Jean-Pierre Changeux supports this view, as he made clear in his discussion with philosopher Paul Ricoeur in Changeux, *What Makes Us Think: A Neuroscientist and a Philosopher Argue about Ethics, Human Nature, and the Brain* (Princeton, NJ: Princeton University Press, 2000), p. 284.

26. This topic is addressed in detail in the chapter 9.

27. Many of these we now call "psychopaths." I will have more to say about these in the next chapter.

28. Related words in German are *über* ("over," "atop"—as in "übermensch") and *übel* ("bad," "wicked").

29. *Insane* is no longer a medical term; it is a legal term meaning that the person in question, because of mental derangement, did not know the nature of his acts, not that these acts were wrong.

30. By no means are all mentally ill persons, even those with a poor hold on reality, "insane." Very few are, actually. For even when seriously mentally ill persons commit horrendous crimes, they usually know that what they have done was considered wrong by the community at large. Such persons are often viewed in the courts as being responsible, of course, yet with a lesser degree of responsibility, and are often sent to a secure forensic hospital rather than to a conventional prison.

31. Stephanie Stanley, *An Invisible Man* (New York: Berkley Books, 2006), p. 343.

32. Ron Franscell, *The Rape and Murder of Innocence in a Small Town* (Far Hill, NJ: New Horizon Press, 2007). Attorney Gary Spence made the comment about evil (on the back cover of Franscell's book), alluding to the author's experience as a child growing up in Wyoming who had heard about the murders and then wrote about them.

33. Chuck Hustmyre, *An Act of Kindness* (New York: Berkley Books, 2007), p. 223.

34. Joe McGinnis, *Never Enough* (New York: Simon & Schuster, 2007), p. 336.

35. Tina Dirmann, *Vanished at Sea* (New York: St. Martin's Paperbacks, 2008), p. 171.

36. David Reichert, *Chasing the Devil: My Twenty-Year Quest to Capture the Green River Killer* (Boston: Little, Brown and Company, 2004), p. 304.

37. Carlton Smith, *The BTK Murders* (New York: St. Martin's Paperbacks, 2006), p. 335.

38. Tom Henderson, *Darker than the Night* (New York: St. Martin's Paperbacks, 2006), p. 353. In a similar vein, Detective Morgan, commenting on Ann Brier Miller, who murdered her husband with arsenic, seemingly just to be "free," said, "There are certain kinds of criminals motivated by something that no ordinary person can truly understand—*evil.*" Cited in Amanda Lamb, *Deadly Dose* (New York: Berkley Books, 2008), p. 210.

CHAPTER ONE. EVIL IN PEACETIME

1. Julia Fox, *Jane Boleyn—The True Story of the Infamous Lady Rochford* (New York: Ballantine Books, 2007).

2. Ibid., p. 265.

3. Niccolò Machiavelli, *The Prince* (first published in 1513).

4. The full story is told in Emlyn Williams's biography *Beyond Belief: A Chronicle of Murder and Its Detection* (New York: Random House, 1968). Ian Brady gave still further details in a book he wrote himself—about a subject he knows best: serial killing. *The Gates of Janus* (Los Angeles: Feral House, 2001).

5. Not so rare a phenomenon, as it turns out. Dr. Salter's data suggest that about 45 percent of such men make recordings of these acts. Anna C. Salter, *Predators* (New York: Basic Books, 2003), p. 114. She cites J. L. Warren, "The Sexually Sadistic Serial Killer," *Journal of Forensic Sciences* 6 (1996): 970–74.

6. Alan Prendergast, *The Poison Tree* (New York: G. P. Putnam, 1986). Cf. *Seattle Times*, October 18, 1985.

7. Exodus 21:15.

8. Leviticus 20:9.

9. Malice aforethought is an aspect of *mens rea* ("guilty mind"), which must accompany an act of murder if an act resulting in death is to be regarded as murder in common law. Cf. Glanville Williams, *Textbook of Criminal Law*, 2nd ed. (London: Stevens & Sons, 1983).

10. The mechanism of overcoming humiliation by what the killer considers a "righteous slaughter" is brilliantly told by sociologist Jack Katz in *Seductions of Crime: A Chilling Exploration of the Criminal Mind—from Juvenile Delinquency to Cold-Blooded Murder* (New York: Basic Books), 1988.

11. Jean Harris, *Stranger in Two Worlds* (New York: Zebra Press, 1986). In this autobiography, Harris tells of discovering the panties of another woman, Lynn Tryforos, in a drawer in Tarnower's house, next to where Harris's clothes were kept.

12. C. P. Anderson, *The Serpent's Tooth* (New York: Harper & Row, 1987).

13. Stephen G. Michaud and Hugh Aynesworth, *The Only Living Witness* (New York: Simon & Schuster, 1983). There is some evidence that toward the end of his chain of murders, Bundy bit part of the breast off one of his victims. This would suggest that he began to escalate toward more pain-inducing, torturous acts before he was finally captured.

14. I expand on this point in chapter 9.

15. Vincent Bugliosi, *Helter Skelter: The True Story of the Manson Murders* (New York: W. W. Norton, 1994 [1974]).

16. Schizophrenia is currently defined in a narrower way—as a severe mental illness characterized by a marked *disorder of thought*, disorganized speech, delusions (often of a persecutory type) and hallucinations, and flattening of emotional expression.

17. It is better known in the United States by the name *Thorazine*.

18. The first such medication was lithium, developed by Cade in Australia and used in Europe in the 1950s before it was made available in the United States in the 1960s through the pioneering work of Dr. Ronald Fieve and Dr. Lothar Kalinowsky.

19. Developed in the mid-1970s, magnetic resonance imaging (MRI) is a technique used by radiologists to visualize bodily structures, in a way that yields greater clarity and definition than conventional X-rays. MRI is particularly useful in visualizing soft tissues, including brain tissues, whose detailed structures are often "opaque" to ordinary X-ray methods. The patient is placed within a powerful magnetic field capable of aligning the hydrogen atoms in the water of the body (water making up 70 percent of the body's volume). The

hydrogen atoms produce a rotating magnetic field that the MRI scanner can detect, resulting in an image of the body areas under examination, which can then be reconstructed. Cf. Mark Brown and Richard Semelka, *MRI: Basic Principles and Applications* (New York: John Wiley & Sons, 1999). The basic principle was discovered in 1946, but the use of MRI for imaging was pioneered by Paul Lauterbur (1929–2007) in 1973. He was awarded the Nobel Prize in 2003. Cf. Nancy Andreasen, MD, *Brain Imaging: Applications in Psychiatry* (Washington, DC: American Psychiatric Press, 1989).

20. V. L. Quinsey et al., *Violent Offenders: Appraising and Managing Risk* (Washington, DC: American Psychological Association Press, 1998).

21. http://www.trutv.com/library/crime/criminal_mind/sexual_assault/nathaniel_bar_jonah/13.html.

22. Though raised in a Protestant family, he claimed he wanted to take a Jewish name so as to have the experience of knowing what it was like to be the "object of prejudice." He made this change while incarcerated for sexual offenses in Massachusetts. When I interviewed him years later, he denied that story and said he did made the change because he liked the Jewish faith. It is common for "career" criminals to take on aliases by way of eluding justice and distancing themselves from their true and original persona.

23. Peter Davidson, *Death by Cannibal* (New York: Berkley Books, 2006).

24. It is important to note that Lundgren was a charismatic con man who was given to outrageous boasts of this sort, by which he managed to mesmerize and dupe his followers. He was not a psychotic person with delusions of grandeur; that is to say, he knew that he was not God or a prophet, but he chose for his own nefarious purposes to speak of himself in that fashion in order to produce the effect he wanted—to enslave and make puppets out of his followers, who would do his bidding, no matter what. By way of comparison, Hitler's mesmerizing abilities were far greater than those of Charles Manson, whose powers were far greater than those of Lundgren.

25. The entire story is told in the chilling biography by Cynthia Statler-Sassé and Peggy Widder, *The Kirtland Massacre: The True and Terrible Story of the Mormon Cult Murders* (New York: Donald I. Fine, 1991).

26. The situation with Lundgren and Luff is analogous in certain ways to that of Saddam Hussein and his closest followers, to whom he gave pistols and commanded that they shoot a number of their colleagues whom Saddam considered untrustworthy "conspirators." And shoot them they did—lest they be killed themselves by Saddam's guards. But the greater evil lay with Saddam, who sadistically trapped his followers into becoming murderers themselves, so they could no longer claim innocence. Cf. Con Coughlin, *Saddam: King of Terror* (New York: HarperCollins, 2002).

27. Billy Wayne Sinclair and Jodie Sinclair, *A Life in the Balance: The Billy Wayne Sinclair Story, A Journey from Murder to Redemption inside America's Worst Prison System* (New York: Arcade Publishing, 2000).

28. The original play was produced in 1938. William Drummond's novel was published in 1966. Drummond, *Gaslight* (New York: Paperback Library, 1966).

29. This was the meaning of the term *psychopathie*, used by the famous German psychiatrist Emil Kraepelin in his 1915 textbook *Psychiatrie*, 8th ed., 4 vols. (Leipzig: J. A. Barth).

30. The more specific definition derives from the monograph by American psychiatrist Hervey Cleckley. Cleckley, *The Mask of Sanity* (St. Louis: C. V. Mosby, 1941).

31. Robert D. Hare, *Psychopathy Checklist-Revised* (Toronto: Multi-Health Systems, 1991); T. J. Harpur, A. R. Hakstian, and R. D. Hare, "Factor Structure of the *Psychopathy Checklist*," *Journal of Consulting and Clinical Psychology* 56 (1988): 741–47.

32. The twenty items of the Hare Checklist are divided into *two main factors*. One concerns personality traits and emotional qualities. The qualities of both factors are found on page 117.

33. Michaud and Aynesworth, *Only Living Witness*.

34. Francine du Plessix Gray, *At Home with the Marquis de Sade* (New York: Penguin Books, 1998).

35. Jack Altman and Marvin Ziporyn, *Born to Raise Hell: The Untold Story of Richard Speck* (New York: Grove Press, 1967).

36. Michael H. Stone, *Abnormalities of Personality: Within and Beyond the Realm of Treatment* (New York: W. W. Norton, 1993).

37. Dante Alighieri, *The Divine Comedy of Dante Alighieri: Vol. One: Inferno*, ed. and trans. Robert M. Durling (New York: Oxford University Press, 1996).

38. Proverbs 6:16–19.

39. Some have considered Pride to be the worst, theologically, although from the standpoint of contemporary psychiatry, Envy often proves to be the most intractable.

40. Dante adhered to the orthodox Christian view of his era, one tenet of which was that beatitude was achieved via a "free gift of God predicated on faith in Christ" (cf. *Inferno*, Canto IV, p. 80, Durling's note to lines 34–42). As beatitude was not available to those who were born before Christ or who were not baptized, even if they lived some of their adult life during the early years of Christ's life (as was the case with Virgil), their souls remained in this First Circle as pagans. Some (like Virgil), albeit sinless, could not be considered "saved."

41. A simonist was someone who acted like Simon Magus, who offered money to the apostle Peter for the power of laying on of hands (Acts 8:9–24). As

Durling mentions, this man gave his name to the sin of *simony*: the selling of indulgences, by which priests in exchange for money gave various sacramental benefits (*Inferno*, Canto XIX, line 1).

42. Georges Bataille, *Dark Stars: The Satanic Rites of Gilles de Rais* (London: Creation Books, 2004).

43. Valentine Penrose, *The Bloody Countess: The Crimes of Erzsébet Báthory* (London: Creations Books, 1996).

44. See note 41 above.

45. *Inferno*, Canto XXXII, line 65.

46. Durling's notes to the *Inferno*, p. 510.

CHAPTER TWO. CRIMES OF IMPULSE: MURDERS OF JEALOUSY AND RAGE

1. Cf. Grover Goodwin, ed., *Criminal Psychology & Forensic Technology* (Boca Raton, FL: CRC Press, 2000).

2. Arthur P. Will, *A Treatise on the Law of Circumstantial Evidence* (Philadelphia: T. & J. W. Johnson & Company, 1896).

3. As in the life of the prizefighter Jake LaMotta, whose persecution of his innocent wife was depicted in the film *Raging Bull*, which accurately portrays a man in the grips of delusional jealousy.

4. Mass murder, according to criteria adopted by the FBI, is described as a number of murders (four or more) occurring during the same incident, with no distinctive time period between the murders, and occurring usually in the same location. An example is the 1984 mass murder at the San Ysidro McDonald's restaurant in San Diego, California, in which James Huberty shot twenty-one people to death within a very brief period. Cf. *Serial Murder: Multi-Disciplinary Perspectives for Investigators* (US Department of Justice, Federal Bureau of Investigation, Behavioral Analysis Unit, 2008), p. 11.

5. Cf. J. Reid Meloy, *Violent Attachments*, chap. 3 (Northvale, NJ: J. Aronson Press, 1992). Dr. F. Wertham first used the term in 1937, mentioning the stages a person in this crisis state goes through: first, a shattering experience, then the victim blames another person or situation. Carrying out a violent act seems like the "only solution." The violent act is committed, and the victim now feels relief of the original tension and a return to a state of apparent normalcy.

6. Cf. Jack Katz, *Seductions of Crime: A Chilling Exploration of the Criminal Mind—from Juvenile Delinquency to Cold-Blooded Murder* (New York: Basic Books, 1988).

7. Life as it may have been in the African savannah from which we all came is beautifully depicted in Nicholas Wade, *Before the Dawn: Recovering the Lost History of Our Ancestors* (New York: Penguin Books, 2006).

8. Cf. Baron Patrick Balfour Kinross, *The Ottoman Centuries* (New York: William Morrow), p. 146.

9. The nature and neurochemistry of love, including intense passion, is described in Helen Fisher, *Why We Love* (New York: Henry Holt/Owl Books, 2004).

10. Though some have cited William James or Ogden Nash as the author of the poem.

11. Chip Walter, *Thumbs, Toes, and Tears, and Other Traits that Make Us Human* (New York: Walker and Company, 2006), p. 40.

12. Exodus 20:7.

13. Matthew 6:13.

14. John Glatt, *Blind Passion. A True Story of Seduction, Obsession, and Murder: An American Beauty Falls for a Dashing Greek Sailor—with Deadly Consequences* (New York: St. Martin's Press, 2000).

15. Clifford Linedecker, *Driven to Kill* (Boca Raton, FL: America Media, 2003).

16. Lisa Pulitzer, *Fatal Romance* (New York: St. Martin's Press, 2001).

17. John Glatt, *Never Leave Me* (New York: St. Martin's Press, 2006).

18. Lisa Pulitzer, *A Woman Scorned* (New York: St. Martin's Press, 1999).

19. Emily Brontë, *Wuthering Heights* (New York: Barnes & Noble Classics Series, 2005 [1847]).

20. It was the presence of hallucinations that marked Rowe's depression as psychotic.

21. Julie Salamon, *Facing the Wind* (New York: Random House, 2001).

22. Eric Francis, *A Wife's Revenge* (New York: St. Martin's Press, 2005).

23. Jim Fischer, *Crimson Stain* (New York: Berkley Books, 2000).

24. Carlton Smith, *Bitter Medicine* (New York: St. Martin's Press, 2000).

25. Edwin Chen, *Deadly Scholarship* (New York: Birch Lane Press, 1995).

26. This stems from the 1843 McNaghten test in England, created after Daniel McNaghten, who, while targeting Prime Minister Robert Peel, killed his secretary, Edward Drummond, by mistake. McNaghten was declared not responsible because of his insanity; i.e., he had been laboring under such defect of reason as not to know the nature of his act nor that it was wrong.

27. According to US government statistics. Cf. http://www.ojp.usdoj.gov/bjs/.

28. Cf. http://www.psychlaws.org/BriefingPapers/BP11.htm.

29. Cf. http://news.bbc.co.uk/1/hi/health/24884/stm.

30. According to Sheilagh Hodgins, ed., *Mental Disorder & Crime* (London: Sage Publications, 1993). Also, John Monahan and Henry Steadman, eds., *Violence and Mental Disorders* (Chicago: University of Chicago Press, 1994).

31. The complexities of the issue are well discussed in Vernon Quinsey, Grant Harris, Marnie Rice, and Catherine Cormier, *Violent Offenders* (Washington, DC: American Psychological Association Press, 1998).

32. Cf. http://www.psychlaws.org/PressRoom/presskits/Kendra%27sLawPressKit/kendraslaw.htm.

33. Cf. http://www.omh.state.ny.us/omhweb/Kendra_web/Khome.htm. In New York State, for example, the court mandates assisted outpatient treatment for certain patients with mental illness who, in the court's opinion, would be unlikely to survive safely in the community without such supervision. Each patient is assigned a care-coordinator who monitors the patient's compliance with the prescribed treatment (including medications), with the understanding that lack of compliance would result in notification to the authorities, who might then take whatever steps were necessary to remedy the situation so as to safeguard both the patient and (in the case of potentially violent patients) the community.

34. Cited in http://blogs.kansascity.com/crime_scene/2007/03/15/index.html.

35. *New York Post*, April 20, 1989. This man had been living in Ms. Berle's apartment without paying rent. When she began to insist that he contribute to her expenses, he became angry and argumentative. This was the context in which he then killed her.

36. http://freedomeden.blogspot.com/2008/01/lam-luong.html.

37. Suzy Spencer, *Breaking Point* (New York: St. Martin's Press, 2002).

38. *New York Times*, September 8, 2001.

39. Peter Davidson, *Death by Cannibal* (New York: Berkley Books, 2006).

40. Such as the Association of Threat Assessment Professionals, founded in 1992 by the Los Angeles Police Department.

41. Cf. Hodgins, *Mental Disorder & Crime*; Quinsey et al., *Violent Offenders*. Also, John Monahan et al., *Rethinking Risk Assessment* (New York: Oxford University Press, 2001); and John Monahan et al., "Classification of Violent Risk (COVR)," *Psychiatric Services* 56 (2005): 810–15.

42. *New York Times*, February 20, 2008.

43. http://www.washingtonpost.com/wp-dyn/content/article/2006/09/04/AR2006090400430.html.

CHAPTER THREE. OTHER CRIMES OF IMPULSE: EMPHASIS ON ANTISOCIAL PERSONS

1. The case of Dr. Bruce Rowan from the previous chapter had the element of attempted cover-up (via a staged "car accident"), but in personality he was not antisocial and, although seriously depressed, was not grossly psychotic. The persons highlighted in this chapter tended to have more antisocial traits; some were more obviously mentally ill.

2. Soo Hyun Rhee and Irwin D. Waldman, "Behavior-Genetics of Criminality and Aggression," in *The Cambridge Handbook of Violent Behavior and Aggression*, ed. Daniel J. Flannery, Alexander T. Vazsonyi, and Irwin D. Waldman (New York: Cambridge University Press, 2007), pp. 77–90.

3. http://lifestyle.aol.co.uk/go-green/home-arson-linked-to-radical/article 20080304012.

4. Melissa Weininger, "The Trials of Lorena Bobbitt: A Study in Media Backlash." http://www.digitas.harvard.edu/~perspy/old/issues/2000/retro/lorena_bobbitt.html.

5. Bryce Marshall and Paul Williams, *Zero at the Bone* (New York: Simon & Schuster, 1991).

6. Roger Wilkes, *Blood Relations* (New York: Penguin Books, 1994).

7. *New York Post*, March 24, 1989.

8. Emmanuel Carrère, *The Adversary* (New York: Henry Holt, 2000).

9. *New York City Daily News*, November 7, 2006.

10. As in the case of Beatles star John Lennon, murdered by Mark David Chapman, December 8, 1980.

11. E.g., Colin Thatcher of Canada, former Saskatchewan premier, who shot his wife to death in 1983.

12. *New York Times*, July 6, 1999.

13. Cf. *Newsweek*, May 3, 1999.

14. http://www.albionmonitor.com/9907a/wcotc.html.

15. These cases involve psychopaths and are discussed further in chapter 6.

16. http://www.detnews.com/205/metro/0509/25DO1-326371.html.

17. *New York Observer*, January 28, 1991.

18. The technical term for throwing someone out a window. Historians will recall the famous defenestration in Prague in 1618 at the onset of the Thirty Years' War, when Protestant assemblymen threw two Catholic imperial governors out the window, in reaction to what the Protestants considered a violation of their rights.

19. http://www.nytimes.com/2007/03/11/magazine/11Neurolaw.t.html.

20. As Flynn relates in his book *Relentless Pursuit* (New York: Berkley Books, 2008).

21. The grotesqueness of Harrell's act—evisceration of his victims—would seem to place him at the extreme end of the Gradations scale. But torture and sexual crimes were not part of the picture, so he would be placed in category 16: multiple vicious acts.

22. Martin Daly and Margo Wilson, *Homicide* (New York: Aldine de Gruyter, 1988), p. 83. These authors estimate the risk may be greater by a factor of a hundred.

23. Judith A. Rudnai, *The Social Life of the Lion* (Wallingford, PA: Washington Square East Publishers, 1973).

24. The parent lion may then recognize these cubs as his own, by means of histocompatibility genes common to parent and offspring. Cf. R. Gadagkar, "Kin Recognition in Social Insects and Other Animals," *Proceedings of the Indian Academy of Sciences (Animal Sciences)* 94 (1985): 587–621.

25. Daly and Wilson, *Homicide*, pp. 87–89.

26. Ibid., pp. 107–10.

27. http://www.Psyih.com/2007/12/03/Kimberly-dawn-trenor-and-royce-zeigler.

28. The original is even harsher: "He that spareth the rod, hateth his son." Proverbs 13:14.

29. http://www.wkyc.com/news/news_article.aspx?storyid=78719.

30. Because the actions of this couple involved torture, although without the sexual element, the appropriate level on the Gradations scale is 18: torture-murder, though the torture element is not prolonged.

31. *Texas Prosecutor* 35 (July/August 2005): 1, 11–15.

32. *New York Post*, June 15, 2006.

33. *New York Daily News*, June 15, 2006.

34. *New York Post*, March 25 and 27, 1990.

35. Cf. Mark Gado, essay on Julio Gonzalez, Crime Library/Time Warner, 2007, http://www.trutv.com/library/crime/notorious_murders/mass/happyland/trial_7.html.

36. *New York Times*, December 4, 1998.

37. Jason Wright, Associated Press, December 7, 1998.

38. Dr. Katherine Ramsland, "About Evil," Crime Library, http://www.trutv.com/library/crime/index.html.

39. Blaise Pascal, *Pensées*, no. 894, 1670.

40. Cited at http://michellemalkin.com/2007/12/12/whitewashing-the-murder-of-aqsa-parvez/. Also, Ellen Harris, *Guarding the Secrets* (New York: Scribners, 1995), pp. 228–29.

41. http://riverfronttimes.com/2006/06/05/news/still-lips-still-whisper.

42. http://michellemalkin.com/2007/12/12/whitewashing-the-murder-of-aqsa-parvez/, based on *New York Times* article, October 28, 1991; also Harris, *Guarding the Secrets*, p. 149.

43. Erica Lynn Smith, "Zein Isa—Honor Killings and a Family Affair: The Murder of Tina Isa," http://www.bellaonline.com/articles/art47666.asp.

44. Zein Isa's place in the Gradations scale is problematical: he subjected his daughter to torture and terror, though without sexual violation. His act is closest to those of Category 18.

45. http://www.foxnews.com/story/0,2933,141121,00.html.

46. Because so little is known about Gale, it is not possible to situate him accurately on the Gradations scale. Perhaps Category 6 would be appropriate (impetuous, hot-headed murderer, without marked psychopathic features); if he showed strong psychopathic features, a level higher on the scale would be more appropriate.

47. "Erfurt, 26 April," *Der Stern*, April 30, 2000, p. 20: "*auffällig unauffällig*."

48. A full classification is provided in a book by Paul Mullen, Michele Pathe, and Rosemary Purcell, *Stalkers and Their Victims* (London: Cambridge University Press, 2000). Another excellent source is Reid Meloy, *Violent Attachments* (Northvale, NJ: J. Aronson Press, 1992. The relentless pursuit of a psychiatrist by a psychotic patient she had seen just once is described by Doreen Orion in *I Knew You Really Loved Me* (New York: Dell Publishers, 1997).

49. Wilt Browning, *Deadly Goals* (New York: St. Martin's Press, 1996).

50. What is meant here by *obsessive love* is what Meloy speaks of under the heading of *borderline erotomania* (*Violent Attachments*, p. 26). The original term *erotomania* referred to a delusional (psychotic) disorder where a person imagined that someone, usually of a higher social class, was secretly in love with that person. There is no real relationship between the two persons. In *borderline erotomania*, there *has* been a real relationship, but the object of the person's love is not as much in love with the erotomanic person, as the latter is with the love-object. That is: A loves B considerably more than B loves A—in this asymmetric and not-fully-requited love. I prefer the phrase *obsessive love* in this context. Persons showing this obsessional preoccupation with the love object are, of course, prone to feelings of overwhelming abandonment should the loved one break off the relationship. Intense jealousy is aroused also and may lead to violence, including murder.

51. D. T. Hughes, *Lullaby and Goodnight—The Blood-chilling Story of a Woman Who Wanted a Baby Badly Enough to Murder for One* (New York: Pocket Books, 1992).

52. Jacqui Goddard, "Mother Admits Killing Stranger to Steal Unborn Baby," http://www.rense.com/general60/unbon.htm.

53. M. William Phelps, *Sleep in Heavenly Peace* (New York: Pinnacle Books, 2006).

54. A race involving two cars coming fast toward each other on the median strip of a road, with the "loser" being the driver who is first to swerve to avoid being killed. That person is called, derogatorily, the "chicken."

55. http://pysih.com/2007/11/14/alexander-james-letkemann-and-jean-pierre-orlewicz/.

56. http://www.truecrimeweblog.com/2007/11/greater-evil-thrill-kill-in -michigan.html.

57. As described by the research group D. Lyman et al., "Longitudinal Evidence that Psychopathy Scores in Early Adolescence Predict Adult Psychopathy," *Journal of Abnormal Psychology* 116 (2007): 155–65.

CHAPTER FOUR. MURDER ON PURPOSE: THE PSYCHOPATHIC SCHEMERS

1. Donald Black, *Bad Boys, Bad Men* (New York: Oxford University Press, 1999).

2. Robert D. Hare, *Without Conscience—The Disturbing World of the Psychopaths Among Us* (New York: Pocket Books, 1993).

3. Robert I. Simon, *Bad Men Do What Good Men Dream* (Washington, DC: American Psychiatric Press, 1996).

4. Suzanne Finstad, *Sleeping with the Devil* (New York: William Morrow, 1991).

5. http://www.press-enterprise.com/newsarchive/2000/07/18/963897968.html.

6. http://www.spring.net/yapp-bin/public/read/tv/69.

7. Finstad, *Sleeping with the Devil*, p. 187.

8. Ibid., p. 207.

9. Ibid., p. 151.

10. Ibid., p. 135.

11. Ibid., p. 175.

12. J. R. Séguin, P. Sylvers, and S. O. Lillienfeld: "The Neuropsychology of Violence," in *The Cambridge Handbook of Violence and Aggression*, ed. D. J. Flannery, A. T. Vazsonyi, and I. D. Waldman (New York: Cambridge University Press, 2007), pp. 187–214.

13. Cf. A. R. Damasio, "A Neural Base for Sociopathy," *Archives of General Psychiatry* 57 (2000): 128–29.

14. Steven Levy, *The Unicorn's Secret* (New York: Prentice Hall, 1988).

15. Ibid., p. 280.

16. Ibid.

17. Ibid., p. 282.

18. *Times Herald Record*, October 18, 2002.

19. http://www.trutv.com/library/crime/notorious_murders/famous/einhorn/index_1.html.

20. Joseph Sharkey, *Death Sentence: The Inside Story of John List* (New York: Signet Books, 1990).

21. http://en.wikipedia.org/wiki/John_List.

22. http://www.trutv.com/library/crime/notorious_murders/family/list/8.html.

23. Kay Halverson, "The List Murders Stun Westfield in 1971," *Westfield Leader and Times*, February 17, 2001.

24. Ed Friedlander, http://www.pathguy.com/lbdsm.htm.

25. At a local production in Anaheim, California. John Glatt, *Deadly American Beauty* (New York: St. Martin's Press, 2004), p. 14.

26. The origin of the saying is George Herbert's 1651 *Jacula Prudentum* (Things Thrown to the Wise): "For want of a nail, the shoe is lost, for want of a shoe, the horse is lost, for want of a horse, the rider is lost." This was cited later by Benjamin Franklin, commenting on how small troubles can breed great mischief.

27. Glatt, *Deadly American Beauty*.

28. Seamus McGraw, "The Rose Petal Murder," http://www.trutv.com/library/ crime/notorious_murders/family/kristen_rossum/2.html.

29. As in the case of Martha Ann Johnson in Georgia, who killed her four children, http://www.crimezzz.net/serialkillers/J/JOHNSON_martha_ann.php.

30. T. E. Moffitt and A. Caspi, "Childhood Predictors Differentiate Life-Course Persistent and Adolescence-Limited Pathways among Males and Females," *Development and Psychopathology* 13 (2001): 355–75.

31. Carlton Smith, *Love, Daddy* (New York: St. Martin's Press, 2003), p. 56.

32. http://www.cbsnews.com/stories/2005/05/31/48hours/main698725_page2.shtml.

33. Smith, *Love, Daddy*.

34. Category 13 (inadequate, rageful psychopaths) is not covered in this chapter. An example is that of Richard Speck, discussed in an earlier chapter.

35. Leona Helmsley had earned public opprobrium for her comment that "taxes are for the little people."

36. Robert Scott, *Kill or Be Killed* (New York: Pinnacle Books, 2004).

37. Ibid., p. 95.

38. Ibid., p. 76.

39. Ibid., p. 135.

40. http://www.redding.com/news/2007/oct/21/murder-tale-to-air-on-tv/.

41. Adrian Havill: *The Mother, the Son, and the Socialite* (New York: St. Martin's Press, 1999).

42. Adrian Havill, http://www.trutv.com/library/crime/notorious_murders/women/kimes/1.html.

43. http://www.ojp.usdoj.gov/bjs/pub/pdf/spousmur.pdf.

44. Steven Long, *Every Woman's Nightmare* (New York: St. Martin's Press, 2006). The man Long was writing about was Mark Hacking.

45. R. Robin McDonald, *Secrets Never Lie* (New York: Avon Books, 1998). The husband of this story was attorney Fred Tokars, who hired a hit man to kill his wife.

46. http://www.physicsforum.com/archives/index.php/t-174914.html.

47. Clifford Linedecker: *The Murder of Laci Peterson* (America Media Inc., 2003).

CHAPTER FIVE. SPREE AND MASS MURDER: EVIL BY THE NUMBERS

1. For example, Clyde Barrow and Bonnie Parker were a team of outlaws who robbed stores and gas stations in the South during the Depression era between 1932 and 1934. Bonnie never shot anyone; Clyde killed approximately ten people in that time span, until they were gunned down by the police in Louisiana in May of 1934.

2. Incorrectly referred to as "mass" rather than as "spree" by author William Allen in his *Starkweather: The Story of a Mass Murderer* (Boston: Houghton Mifflin, 1976).

3. The figure "four" is used by the FBI in Robert J. Morton, ed., *Serial Murder—Multi-Disciplinary Perspectives for Investigators*, US Department of Justice, Federal Bureau of Investigation, National Center for the Analysis of Violent Crime/Critical Incident Response Group (June 2008): 11. The number is arbitrary. Some law authorities use the figure "three or more," but one must take into consideration that there are many instances of attempted mass murder in which an assailant shoots or stabs three or four or a dozen people in one incident, killing no one, or killing one or two, with the rest surviving. The intention in such cases is obviously mass murder; one may choose (as I have done here) to call these examples *mass murder manqué*.

4. Mark Fiore, *Daily Pennsylvanian*, 1996, http://media.www.dailypennsylvanian.com/media/storage/paper882/news/1996/09/30/Resources/Gun-Violence.Strikes.Campuses.Across.U.s-2175918.shtml.

5. Mikaela Sitford, *Addicted to Murder* (London: Virgin Publications, 2000).

6. Paul B. Kidd, *Never to Be Released: Australia's Most Vicious Murderers* (Sydney, Australia: Pan Macmillan, 1993).

7. Ibid., p. 57.

8. James Gleick, *Chaos: Making a New Science* (New York: Penguin Books, 1987).

9. Michael H. Stone, *Personality Disorders—Treatable and Untreatable* (Washington, DC: American Psychiatric Press, 2006).

10. Lindsey Marie Welch, "Charles Manson," http://ygraine.membrane.com/enterhtuml/live/Dark/Charles_Manson.html.

11. Ibid., p. 2.

12. Vincent Bugliosi, *Helter Skelter: The True Story of the Manson Murders*, afterword (New York: W. W. Norton, 1974), pp. 640–41.

13. Cf. Grant Duwe, "A Circle of Distortion—The Social Construction of Mass Murder in the United States," *Western Criminology* 6 (2005): 59–78.

14. Ibid., p. 75, note 14.

15. Shelly Leachman, http://truthasaur.com/local/secretcity48.html.

16. Duwe, "A Circle of Distortion," p. 75.

17. Ibid., p. 59.

18. Truman Capote, *In Cold Blood* (New York: American Library, 1965).

19. Duwe, "A Circle of Distortion," p. 72.

20. Brian Lane and Wilfred Gregg, *An Encyclopedia of Mass Murder* (London: Penguin Group, 1997).

21. James Fox and Jack Levin, *The Will to Kill* (Boston: Pearson Education, 2006), p. 167.

22. The percentages cited here reflect my analysis of 150 mass murderers from the last thirty years.

23. Fox and Levin, *Will to Kill*, p. 166.

24. Sanmarco killed six, as did P. J. Ford; Phan Thi Ai set fire to a house and killed five; Sue Eubanks killed four of her children (properly speaking, she committed infanticide); Jill Robbins shot one person to death at the University of Pennsylvania campus: this was mass murder manqué (she wounded some others), as was the case of Laurie Dann.

25. Joel Kaplan, George Papajohn, and Eric Zorn, *Murder of Innocence: The Tragic Life and Final Rampage of Laurie Dann* (New York: Warner Books, 1990).

26. The pun on Dann/Danai (an ancient name for the Greeks) didn't occur to me till later.

27. Demeter, "Thomas Hamilton and the Dunblane Massacre," http://www.everything2.com/index.pl?node_id=1011701.

28. Ibid.

29. Cf. Robert Merton, "Social Structure and Anomie," *American Social Review* 5 (October 1938). Merton characterized the intention behind certain dramatic crimes: to relieve the intolerable "anomie," or sense of being incapable of fulfilling one's goals.

30. http://www.huffingtonpost.com/jonathan-fast/steve-kazmierczak-the-sec_b_87031.html.

31. Yahoo! News, June 8, 2008.

32. AOL News, December 5, 2007.

33. http://massmurder.zyns.com/george_hennard_01.html.

34. http://www.users.on.net/~bundy23/wwom/hennard.htm.

35. *New York Times*, October 18, 1991.

36. Gary Kinder, *Victim—The Other Side of Murder* (New York: Atlantic Monthly Press, 1999 [1982]).

37. Jack Katz, *The Seductions of Crime* (New York: Basic Books, 1988), p. 282. Ordinarily *primordial* means "present from the very beginning, at the very origin of." I am not sure in what sense Katz was using the word here: perhaps to signify "quintessential" or "evil at its very roots," as though it is the example of evil by which all others are measured—a Platonic ideal of evil. Katz is probably reacting to the fact that it would not be easy to find an example of cruel and sadistic behavior in the crime literature that would match that of Pierre.

38. http://www.fbi.gov/libref/historic/famcases/graham/graham.htm.

39. http://www.trutv.com/library/crime/notorious_murders/mass/jack_graham/12.html.

CHAPTER SIX. THE PSYCHOPATH HARD AT WORK

1. We know that Gilles de Rais, the lieutenant of Jeanne D'Arc in the mid-fifteenth century, besides being the richest man in France, was also a confirmed and murderous homosexual pedophile, raping and killing hundreds of boys whom he brought to his castle—until he was finally hanged and burnt in 1440: George Bataille, *The Trial of Gilles de Rais* (Los Angeles: Amok Books, 1990). But this was a century and a half after Dante. The Countess Erzsébet Báthory, whose sexual sadism was practiced on young girls, was a figure of the late sixteenth century. Regarding whether there were examples of such serial sexual killers from Dante's time or before, information is sparse or lacking. The Roman emperor Caligula is known to have indulged in sadistic sexual practices, many with lethal consequences for the victims (who could be of either sex): George Ryley Scorr,

A History of Torture (London: Bracken Books, 1940), p. 142. What few examples of serial sexual killers we know of from the distant past belong to the nobility (however ignobly they behaved). We do not know of examples from men in the ordinary walks of life.

2. Elizabeth Daly et al., "Timeline on Kristin Gilbert," http://maamodt.asp.radford.edu/Psyc%20405/serial%20killers/Gilbert,%20Kristen%20-%202005.pdf.

3. William Phelps, *Perfect Poison* (New York: Pinnacle Books, 2003).

4. James Stewart, *Blind Eye* (New York: Simon & Schuster, 1999).

5. http://www.cbsnews.com/stories/2000/09/21/national/main235425.shtml.

6. It is not clear whether Swango was aware of Hitler's hatred of his violent and physically abusive father, though it is of interest that for both men, hatred of the father served as fuel to energize their murderous proclivities. Hitler, of course, was eventually able to murder on a scale incomparably greater than that of Swango. This is part of the reason I have purposely restricted the discussion of evil here to persons committing certain acts in peacetime. Hitler, Mao, Stalin, Saddam Hussein, Pol Pot, Ceauşescu, and the like belong to a different realm: evil in wartime—a vital topic that demands a separate book.

7. Kelly Moore and Dan Reed, *Deadly Medicine* (New York: St. Martin's Press, 1988).

8. M. H. Stone, M. Krischer, and M. Steinmeyer, "Infanticide in Forensic Mothers: An Evolutionary Perspective," *Journal of Practical Psychiatry* 11 (2005): 35–45.

9. Irene Pence, *No, Daddy, Don't: A Father's Murderous Revenge* (New York: Pinnacle Books, 2003).

10. http://www.csmonitor.com/2002/1018/p03s01-usju.html.

11. State of Illinois Review Board, October 2002 session, People's Response by Linda Woloshin and Catherine Sanders.

12. State of Illinois Review Board, October 2002 session, p. 25. Dr. Paul Karsten Fauteck granted permission for me to cite his observations.

13. Written after World War II by Ryonosuke Akutagawa and later made into a movie by Akira Kurosawa.

14. An apt phrase coined by Dr. Leonard Shengold, *Soul Murder: The Effects of Childhood Abuse and Deprivation* (New York: Fawcett Columbine, 1989).

15. State of Illinois Review Board, October 2002 session, p. 32.

16. Effectively, Duvalier's Gestapo.

17. Alan Hall and Michael Leidig, *The Natascha Kampusch Story: The Girl in the Cellar* (London: Hodden & Stoughton, 2006).

18. *New York Times*, January 18, 1993.

19. Mike Echols, *I Know My First Name Is Steven* (New York: Pinnacle Books, 1999).

20. http://en.wikipedia.org/wiki/Kenneth_Parnell.

21. *New Haven Register*, August 11, 1991, p. 1.

22. Gene Miller, with Barbara Jane Mackle, *Eighty-Three Hours Till Dawn: The Terrifying Chronicle of a Kidnapping* (New York: Doubleday, 1871), pp. 323, 387.

23. http://en.wikipedia.org/wiki/Kenneth_Parnell.

24. Barry Bortnick, *Polly Klaas: The Murder of America's Child* (New York: Pinnacle Books, 1995).

25. http://en.wikipedia.org/wiki/Richard_Allen_Davis, p.1.

26. Jack Olsen, *Son: A Psychopath and His Victims* (New York: Dell, 1983), p. 31.

27. Ibid., p. 39.

28. Ibid., p. 44.

29. Ibid., p. 464.

30. *Diagnostic and Statistical Manual of Psychiatric Disorders, edition III-R* (Washington, DC: American Psychiatric Press, 1987).

31. For an account of the Chambers case, see Bryna Taubman, *The Preppy Murder Case* (New York: St. Martin's Press, 1988).

32. Dina Temple-Raston, *Death in Texas: A Story of Race, Murder, and a Small Town's Struggle for Redemption* (New York: Henry Holt, 2002).

33. Faulkner Fox, "Justice in Jasper," http://www.salon.com/news/1999/02/cov_26news.html.

34. Chuck Hustmyre, *An Act of Kindness* (New York: Berkley Books, 2007).

35. http://www.trutv.com/library/crime/notorious_murders/classics/genore_guillory/6.html.

36. Ibid.

37. Cynthia Stalter-Sassé and Peggy Murphy, *The Kirtland Massacre* (New York: Donald I. Fine, Inc., 1991), p. 98.

38. Colin Wilson, *Rogue Messiahs: Tales of Self-Proclaimed Saviors* (Charlottesville, VA: Hampton Roads Publishing, 2000).

39. Stalter-Sassé and Murphy, *Kirtland Massacre*, p. 143.

40. I acknowledge some subjectivity here. I have shared this story with many people, including forensic specialists, psychoanalysts, and those in the general public. Opinion is divided as to which of the two fates were the worse: that Lundgren's wife died from a gunshot to the head, or that she suffer the memory all her remaining days of the horror and degradation she suffered from her husband's action. The pain from a slap or blow lasts but so long; the painful memory Lundgren forced her to acquire that day would live with her forever—like a "hot coal" in her brain. Admittedly, people differ as to their resilience. The most resilient could probably, after a long time, overcome the ill effects of such an experience;

the less resilient might be psychologically crushed for many years. Bear in mind that what Alice was made to experience was done to her by her own husband. In the aftermath of the Holocaust, many survivors—who suffered equal or even worse degradations and pains—knew that their camp guards were not family members; they were the enemy, whose sickening and depraved acts were perpetrated by the Other. And to that extent, the evil acts were easier to "discount" psychologically (as being no reflection on anything "wrong" with the victim). It is easier for the victim of torture to retain moral high ground when the torturer is from an alien force; not so easy when the torturer is one's spouse; perhaps most difficult of all, when one is young and the torturer is one's own father or mother. Subsequent chapters provide examples of the latter situation.

41. Stalter-Sassé and Murphy, *Kirtland Massacre*, p. 197.

42. Ibid., p. 288.

43. Arthur Herzog, *The Woodchipper Murder* (New York: Henry Holt, 1989).

44. Wensley Clarkson, *Deadly Seduction* (New York: St. Martin's Press, 1996).

45. M. William Phelps, *Sleep in Heavenly Peace: The Worst Crime a Mother Can Commit* (New York: Kensington Books, 2006).

46. David Krajicek, Crime Library, http://www.trutv.com/library/crime/notorious_murders/classics/ken_mcelroy/.

47. Harry MacLean, *In Broad Daylight: A Murder in Skidmore, Missouri* (New York: Harper and Row, 1988).

CHAPTER SEVEN. SERIAL KILLERS AND TORTURERS

1. This point was made at the 1st International Symposium on Serial Killing in San Antonio, Texas, July 2005. Public welfare must sometimes be put ahead of scientific rigor, hence the suppression of the news until the third similar murder took place.

2. As told by M. Cox, *The Confessions of Henry Lee Lucas* (New York: Pocket/Star Books, 1991).

3. Chemical name: phencyclidine.

4. K. Englade, *Cellar of Horrors* (New York: St. Martin's Press, 1988).

5. The triad was described by Hellman and Blackman in "Enuresis, Fire-Setting, and Cruelty to Animals. A Triad Predictive of Adult Crime," *American Journal of Psychiatry* 122 (1966): 1431–35.

6. L. D. Klausner, *Son of Sam* (New York: McGraw Hill, 1981).

7. The research in this area is well summarized by S.-H. Rhee and I. D.

Waldman, "Behavior-Genetics of Criminality and Aggression," in *The Cambridge Handbook of Violent Behavior & Aggression*, ed. D. J. Flannery, A. T. Vazsonyi, and I. D. Waldman (New York: Cambridge University Press, 2007), p. 86.

8. Philip Carlo, *The Night Stalker: The Life and Crimes of Richard Ramirez* (New York: Kensington Books, 1996).

9. The magisterial study of Murray A. Straus and Richard J. Gelles demonstrated the inverse relationship between socioeconomic status and the risk for physical violence (which was much less common among the well-to-do than in the disadvantaged). Straus and Gelles, *Physical Violence in American Families: Risk Factors and Adaptations to Violence in 8,145 Families* (London: Transaction Publishers, 1992).

10. I am indebted for this schema to Dr. Debra Niehoff and her excellent book on the roots of violence: *The Biology of Violence* (New York: Free Press, 1998).

11. Further details can be found in Ray Biondi and Walt Hecox, *The Dracula Killer: The True Story of the California Vampire Killer* (New York: Pocket Books, 1992). The infamous Jack the Ripper of London's Whitechapel District in the fall of 1888 killed, mutilated, and eviscerated five prostitutes, without having sex with any. In that way, he is similar to Chase: a serial killer with sex on his mind (in the Ripper's case, targeting prostitutes) but without raping his victims before or after death.

12. Flora Rheta Schreiber, *The Shoemaker: The Anatomy of a Psychotic* (New York: Signet Books, 1984). Dr. Katherine Ramsland in her account (found online at http://www.trutv.com/library/crime) adopts a more measured view, suggesting that "whether he was actually a serial killer or even psychotic is anyone's guess. Kallinger may have been a psychopath who liked to confuse and manipulate people."

13. Carlo, *The Night Stalker*.

14. http://en.wikipedia.org/wiki/Richard_Ramirez.

15. The full biography is by Paula Doneman, *Things a Killer Would Know* (Crows Nest, Australia: Allen & Unwin, 2006). Albert DeSalvo, the Boston Strangler, was another example of hypersexuality: he insisted on sex with his wife five times a day, which pushed her well beyond her comfort level. When she began to decline his favors, he embarked on a career of rape-murders of some eleven women in the Boston area (cf. G. Frank, *The Boston Strangler* (New York: New American Library, 1966).

16. This combination, with the preference for anal sex, is quite common in men with sexual sadism—as noted by Roy Hazelwood of the FBI and true-crime writer Stephen Michaud in their collaboration *Dark Dreams: Sexual Violence, Homicide, and the Criminal Mind* (New York: St. Martin's Press, 2001).

17. Scott Burnside and Alan Cairns, *Deadly Innocence* (New York: Time Warner Books, 1995). In this biography, the authors sketch a typical sequence of actions by sexual sadists: (1) spot a passive, naive, vulnerable woman, (2) charm her with attention and gifts, (3) persuade her to indulge in sexual acts beyond her previous experience—such as bondage, fellatio, anal sex, (4) isolate her from her friends and family so that she is totally dependent upon the man, and (5) make the woman into the object of the man's physical and psychological punishment. Bernardo's power over his wife, Karla, was such that he even got her to videotape him raping her younger sister—as a kind of "wedding gift" (Peter Vronsky, *Female Serial Killers* [New York: Berkley Books, 2007]).

18. The full story is told in Sondra London, *Killer Fiction* (Venice, CA: Feral House, 1997). The author had befriended Schaefer, who allowed her to collaborate with him on his short stories of sadistic murder.

19. As described in Dr. Katherine Ramsland's detailed account, "Dennis Nilsen," http://www.trutv.com/library/crime/serial_killers/predators/nilsen/stranger_1.html.

20. Ibid. Even Nilsen's seeming conflation of life and death as two not-so-separate states is not so much a sign of mental illness as carryover of his experience as a child at the time of his grandfather's death—which his mother explained as his "just having gone asleep," cf. Anna Gekoski, *Murder by Numbers* (London: André Deutsch, 1998), p. 187. Gekoski mentions Nilsen's lack of animosity as another manifestation of his "killing for company" (as emphasized in Brian Masters, *Killing for Company: The Case of Dennis Nilsen* (New York: Stein & Day, 1985), rather than for revenge or hatred. But murder is murder, and the judge who presided at the trial informed the jury that "a mind can be evil without being abnormal" (cited by Ramsland, "Dennis Nilsen")—which was the judge's way of dealing with the confusing testimony of psychiatrists on either side of the case.

21. Cf. Margaret Cheney, *Why? The Serial Killer in America: Stunning Revelations from the Mind of Serial Killer Edmund Kemper III and the Violent Society that Produces So Many* (Saratoga, CA: R-E Publications, 1992).

22. http://en.wikipedia.org/wiki/Ed_Kemper.

23. Cheney, *Why? The Serial Killer in America*.

24. According to *DSM-III-Revised* (1987), criteria for Sadistic Personality, where four or more of the eight descriptors are needed to make the diagnosis. Some persons had only three traits and were considered "subclinical" cases but were not entered into the percentages quoted here as being "sadistic."

25. Robert I. Simon, *Bad Men Do What Good Men Dream: A Forensic Psychiatrist Illuminates the Darker Side of Human Behavior* (Washington, DC: American Psychiatric Press, 1996).

26. Quoted in John Glatt, *Cries in the Desert: The Shocking True Story of a Sadistic Torturer* (New York: St. Martin's Paperbacks, 2002), p. 9.

27. As related by his fiancée-accomplice and almost-fifth wife, Cindy Hendy. Ibid., p. 12.

28. Glatt, *Cries in the Desert*; records from the investigation in New Mexico following the arrests of Ray and Hendy, 1999.

29. Glatt, *Cries in the Desert*, p. 159.

30. Ibid., p. 173.

31. From the transcription by Carol Crosley for the New Mexico state police, submitted June 3, 1999.

32. Attachment number 14 in the New Mexico state police dossier.

33. Berdella's biography is told in Tom Jackman and Troy Cole, *Rites of Burial* (New York: Pinnacle Books, 1992). The saga of Leonard Lake and his accomplice Charles Chitat Ng is recounted in Don Lasseter, *Die for Me* (New York: Pinnacle Books, 2000). Dennis Rader's story is told in Robert Beattie, *Nightmare in Wichita: The Hunt for the BTK Strangler* (New York: New American Library, 2005).

34. Others have made a similar point. Hazelwood and Michaud, *Dark Dreams*, pp. 9–14.

35. A full biography is Stephen Michaud, *Lethal Shadows: The Chilling True-Crime Story of a Sadistic Sex Slayer* (New York: Onyx, 1994).

36. http://www.psychiatryonline.com/content.aspx?aID=33062.

37. Dr. Katherine Ramsland, "Mike DeBardeleben: Serial Sexual Sadist," http://www.crimelibrary.com/serial_killers/predators/debardeleben/evil_3.html.

38. Marked rebelliousness in boys is often associated with "childhood-persistent" antisocial personality, low heart rate, need for novelty and thrill seeking, and a disobedience that does *not* respond to punishment. As Sheilagh Hodgins, professor of psychology at the Maudsley in London has shown, parents will often unwisely heighten their punishments in a vain attempt to make such sons obey—which only increases their rebelliousness in what ends up a (literally) vicious circle.

39. Ramsland, "Mike DeBardeleben: Serial Sexual Sadist," http://www.trutv.com/library/crime/serial_killers/predators/debardeleben/index_1.html.

40. Stephen Michaud, http://www.crimelibrary.com/serial_killers/predators/debardeleben/evil_5html.

41. Roy Hazelwood, http://www.crimelibrary.com/serial_killers/predators/debardeleben/evil_4html.

42. The full comment can be found in Hazelwood and Michaud, *Dark Dreams*, p. 88.

43. The point about the damaging effects of father absence and its connec-

tion with antisocial behaviors and "secondary psychopathy" in adolescence is well made in David Lykken, *The Antisocial Personalities* (Hillsdale, NJ: Lawrence Erlbaum Associates, 1995) pp. 197–212.

44. In Harry Harlow's famous experiments in the 1960s with rhesus monkeys, those reared with a "mother" made of cloth fared better than those reared with a monkey-shaped doll made of wire. The latter grew up severely handicapped in relating to other monkeys and in being able to perform sexually. Cf. Harry F. Harlow, "Development of Affection in Primates," in *Roots of Behavior*, edited by Eugene Bliss (New York: Harper, 1962), pp. 157–66.

45. Don Lasseter, *Die for Me* (New York: Pinnacle Books, 2000).

46. http://www.indopedia.org/Leonard_Lake.html.

47. Lasseter, *Die for Me*, p. 123.

48. Ibid., p. 217.

49. R. Biondi and W. Hecox, *All His Father's Sins* (Rocklin, CA: Prima Press, 1987).

50. Cf. Ann Rule, *Lust Killer* (New York: New American Library, 1983).

51. http://www.trutv.com/library/crime/serial_killers/predators/jerry_brudos/7.html.

52. When I had occasion to interview some men on death row in Florida, all of whom denied the murders of which they were convicted, the supervisor told me, "We have 348 men here—and they all say they're innocent. One of them probably is—but we don't know which one."

53. One of the full-length biographies of Sells is by Diane Fanning, *Through the Window* (New York: St. Martin's Paperbacks, 2003). Another, which is partly autobiographical, is by a woman who befriended Sells and writes under the name Tori Rivers. Rivers, *Twelve Jurors, One Judge, and a Half-Ass Chance* (St. Clair, MO: Riverbend Press, 2007).

54. http://www.geocities.com/verbal_plainfield/q-z/sells.html.

55. I believe that much of what falls under the heading of "homophobia" derives from the fear and hatred that heterosexual young men experience if forced into homosexual encounters (usually by stronger heterosexual men). I think this is a more powerful source of homophobia, since being "buggered" is a humiliating experience that can actually happen in a boy's life. The Judeo-Christian injunction against homosexuality and masturbation has more to do, I believe, with the great need for procreation if a small tribe is to survive (a point made by religious scholar Elaine Pagels); hence acts that steer away from procreation become forbidden. But that is a very abstract concern nowadays, compared with the fear a young man might experience at being overpowered and humiliated through forced sodomy.

56. http://www.amfor.net/killers/.

57. To get a better picture of what such a figure means, imagine a sample of a million boys, in which 50 turn out to become serial killers. Suppose also that 12,000 of the million boys had a father with a criminal record and the other 988,000 did not. Next, suppose that 3,000 of those 12,000 boys with a criminal father had been adopted (25 percent). In the larger group of 988,000 there were 17,000 adoptees. Out of the whole million, there were 50 who grew up to be serial killers. They were distributed as follows: of the 3,000 adoptees whose fathers had a criminal record there were six serial killers, and there were 32 in the 9,000 raised by their birth parents (where the father was a criminal). In the large group, suppose 2 of the 17,000 adoptees became serial killers, and 10 more among the 971,000 who had been raised by their birth parents. The numbers of serial killers is very tiny: 50 out of a million, but 8 of them had been adoptees—that is, *16 percent of the serial killers had been adopted.* But altogether there were 20,000 adoptees out of that million (2 percent) and only 8 became serial killers. So the risk of an adopted boy becoming a serial killer is 4 in 10,000. The risk of a nonadopted boy is 4.3 in 100,000. This means that the risk is very small in either group but measurably greater in the adoptees when compared with the nonadoptees. This is why it is worth looking into the adoption issue more closely.

58. Maria Eftimiades, *Garden of Graves: The Shocking Story of Long Island's Serial Killer, Joel Rifkin* (New York: St. Martin's Press, 1993).

59. John Gilmore, *Cold-Blooded: The Saga of Charles Schmid—the Notorious Pied Piper of Tucson* (Portland, OR: Feral House, 1996).

60. Cf. Anna Flowers, *Blind Fury* (New York: Windsor/Pinnacle Books, 1993); http://en.wikipedia.org/wiki/Gerald_Stano.

61. The story is told by David Lohr on the Crime Library Web site in the chapter called *Reckoning*, http://www.trutv.com/library/crime/criminal_mind/sexual_assault/thomas_soria/17.html.

62. Jared Diamond, "Vengeance Is Ours," *New Yorker*, April 21, 2008, pp. 74–87.

63. M. Cox, *The Confessions of Henry Lee Lucas* (New York: Pocket/Star Books, 1991).

64. Steven Naifeh and Gregory White Smith, *A Stranger in the Family: A True Story of Murder, Madness, and Unconditional Love* (New York: Dutton, 1995).

65. Carlton Smith, *The BTK Murders* (New York: St. Martin's Paperbacks, 2006).

66. Cf. Gail S. Anderson, *Biological Influences on Criminal Behavior* (New York: Simon Fraser University Publications, 2007), pp. 53–73. The author in her lucid presentation distinguishes between the inheritance of complex personality traits and the inheritance of simpler traits like eye and hair color, which depend on just a small number of genes and are less modifiable later on by environmental influences.

67. One can get a sense of Rader's dry, matter-of-fact recounting of the murders when speaking in court to the judge, by accessing http://www.ksn.com/news/local/3835926.html.

68. Smith, *The BTK Murders*.

69. In my experience, serial killers were at least four times as likely to have killed or tortured a cat than were the men who killed their wives.

70. Curiously, the triad was not noted in any of the fifteen homosexual serial killers I have studied—none of whom had set fires and only four of whom had tortured animals. The whole triad, and the combination of fire setting and animal torture, was noted only in the men who went on to kill women.

71. David Reichert, *Chasing the Devil: My Twenty-Year Quest to Capture the Green River Killer* (Boston: Little, Brown and Company, 2004).

72. http://www.kingcountyjournal.com/sited/story/html/148496.

73. I had occasion to see the tapes at the International Congress on Serial Killing, held in San Antonio in 2005 under the auspices of the FBI.

74. We saw this with Archie McCafferty and George Hennard, in chapter 5.

75. This point is convincingly argued by psychoanalytic experts in the field of sexuality Richard Friedman and Jennifer Downey in their article "Sexual Differentiation of Behavior," *Journal of the American Psychoanalytic Association* (to be published).

76. Original title: *Fegefeuer, oder die Reise ins Zuchthaus*. The story of his life is well told in John Leake, *Entering Hades: The Double Life of a Serial Killer* (New York: Sarah Crichton Books/Farrar Straus & Giroux, 2007).

77. http://en.wikipedia.org/wiki/Jack_Unterweger.

78. http://members.tripod.com/Fighting9th/History5.htm.

79. Recounted by Bruce Jackson, http://buffaloreport.com/020301abbott.html.

CHAPTER EIGHT. THE FAMILY AT ITS WORST

1. Kate Summerscale, *The Suspicions of Mr. Wicher: A Shocking Murder and the Undoing of a Great Victorian Detective* (New York: Walker & Co., 2008), p. 37.

2. Ibid.

3. Ibid., p. 75.

4. Wilkie Collins's famous novel *The Moonstone* (1868) owed a debt to the Road Hill House case.

5. A half-hour's drive to the east of Hitler's birthplace in Linz, one cannot help noticing. Linz was also home to another former mechanic with a talent for "disappearing" people: Adolf Eichmann.

6. http://in.ibtimes.com/articles/20080430/austria-incest-scandal-fritzl -father-daughter-cellar.

7. *New York Times*, May 9, 2008.

8. *New York Post*, May 3, 2008, p. 14.

9. *The Republic*, Book VII, the section sometimes called the Allegory of the Cave.

10. K. Englade, *Cellar of Horrors* (New York: St. Martin's Press, 1988).

11. Sacha Batthyany, "Das Böse ist unter uns" (Evil is underneath us), N22 Online, http://www.nzz.ch/nachrichten/international/das_boese_ist_unter_uns _1.725225.html.

12. Cf. D. J. Cooke and C. Michi, "Psychopathy across Cultures: North America and Scotland Compared," *Journal of Abnormal Psychology* 108 (1): 58–68. D. J. Cooke, A. E. Forth, and R. D. Hare, eds., *Psychopathy: Theory, Research & Implications for Society* (Dordrecht, The Netherlands: Kluwer, 1998), pp. 13–45. Cooke cites Cleckley's famous book on the psychopath, where the author mentions that "like the poor, psychopaths have always been with us" (p. 13).

13. The case of Latasha Pulliam and her boyfriend.

14. Wensley Clarkson, *Whatever Mother Says: A True Story of a Mother, Madness, and Murder* (New York: St. Martin's Press, 1995).

15. http://www.crimelibrary.com/notorious_murders/family%E2%80%99 theresa_cross/2html.

16. Ibid.

17. Ibid.

18. The mothers were Deanna Laney and Dena Schlosser. Their story is told by Jane Velez-Mitchell in *Secrets Can Be Murder* (New York: Simon & Schuster/Touchstone Books, 2007), pp. 41ff.

19. http://aolsvc.news.aol.com/news/article.adp?id=20050428232099003.

20. Charles Carillo, *New York Post*, June 23, 1990.

21. Ibid.

22. http://www.nydailynews.com/archives/news/1996/05/17/1996-05-17 _facing_father_from_hell__bur.html.

23. Ibid.

24. Lowell Cauffiel, *House of Secrets* (New York: Kensington, 1997).

25. Cf. Martin Daly and Margo Wilson, *Homicide* (New York: Aldine DeGruyter, 1988), pp. 83ff.

26. Carol Rothgeb, *No One Can Hurt Him Anymore* (New York: Pinnacle Books, 2005). Ilene Logan is not her real name but one used by the author to safeguard her identity

27. By Andrew's father. Ibid., p. 27.

28. http://goliath.ecnext.com/coms2/gi_0199-4414492/Prosecutor-writes -about-an-unforgettable.html.

29. Rothgeb, *No One Can Hurt Him Anymore*, p. 249.

30. Ibid., p. 299.

31. According to German psychiatrist Dr. Thomas Bronisch, the suicide rate among Holocaust victims was actually lower than average, after the war, compared with the rates in the general populations of the countries they had come from.

32. Any parents. I am not fond of the clinical word *caretakers*, so I am including under the label "parents": natural parents, stepparents, adoptive parents, foster parents, mother's boyfriends, etc.

33. Lonnie H. Athens, *The Creation of Dangerous Violent Criminals* (Urbana and Chicago: University of Illinois Press), 1992.

34. Gitta Sereny, *Cries Unheard: Why Children Kill* (New York: Henry Holt & Co., 1998).

35. Beth Kephart, "The Bad Seed," http://dir.salon.com/story/mwt/feature/1999/04/14/child_killers/index2.html.

36. Ibid.

37. Sereny, *Cries Unheard.*

38. http://en.wikipedia.org/wiki/Mary_Bell.

39. Beth Kephart makes this point in her essay.

40. To make it less abstract, Theresa Knorr once shot her daughter, Suesan, in the shoulder and then (being a nurse) extracted the bullet, patched up the wound, with no one the wiser. Had the bullet struck an artery, Suesan would have died then and there; her mother's crime would have been that much more depraved.

41. *New York Times*, http://www.nytimes.com/2008/03/18/nyregion/18cnd-nixzmary.html?_r=1.

42. http://kalimao.blogspot.com/2008/02/children-parental-abuse_11.html.

43. http://newsday.com/news/local/crime/ny-mynixz0202,0,5361314.story.

44. http://aolsvc,news.aol.com/news/article.adp?id=20050220141509990002.

45. http://exchristian.net/2/2005/09/detective-speaks-out-on-dollar.php.

46. http://nobloodforhubris.blogspot.com/2006/08/in-nightmares-begin-responsibilities.html.

47. http://aolsvc.news.

48. http://cnn.usnews.

49. http://nobloodforhubris.blogspot.com/2006/08/in-nightmares-begin-responsibilities.html. The power of religion cannot be underestimated in the area of Tennessee from which the Dollars hailed. Of interest: the famous Scopes

Trial of 1925 took place in Dayton, Tennessee, on the other side of Knoxville from the Dollars' former academy.

50. http://mydatanet.com/story/64536317.html.

51. http://exchristian.net/2/2005/09/detective-speaks-out-on-dollar.php.

52. http://news.bbc.co.uk/2/hi/uk_news/england/bradford/7203382.stm.

53. Ibid.

54. Dante Alighieri, *Inferno*, Canto XXXII 65–66. Sassol was a member of the Florentine family of Toschi. He murdered his cousin for the sake of an inheritance, which then fell to Sassol when the uncle died shortly thereafter. As Durling mentions in his 1996 translation for Oxford University Press, Sassol was punished by being rolled through the city in a barrel full of nails and then beheaded (p. 510).

55. Rachel Pergament, http://www.trutv.com/library/crime/notorious_murders/famous/menendez/murders_2.html.

56. Ibid., p. 9.

57. The defense attorney persuaded some of the jury that José had "sexually molested" the boys, hence their rage and thirst for retribution. This was farfetched, especially in light of the fact that José had many mistresses; sodomizing his sons was not on his mental map at all, ever.

58. Harold Schechter, *Fatal: The Poisonous Life of a Female Serial Killer* (London: Pocket/Star Books, 2003), p. 60.

59. Emily Allen, Alana Averill, and Emmeline Cook, "Jolly Jane," http://maamodt.asp.radford.edu/Psyc%20405/serial%20killers/Toppan,%20Jane%20-%202005.pdf.

60. Schechter, *Fatal*, p. 201.

61. Ibid., p. 305.

62. Ibid., p. xii.

63. Martin Gilman Wolcott, *The Evil 100* (New York: Kensington Publishers, 2003), p. 156. Since Wolcott conflates political killers with persons operating only in private life, his schema is not at all relevant to this book and is quite arbitrary. Jane is noteworthy because of the sheer number of victims, plus the unusual attribute of being "turned on" sexually by close contact with her dying victims—most of whose deaths were relatively painless (the arsenic cases aside). She does not compare in the malignancy of, or in the excruciating suffering caused by, the likes of David Parker Ray, Leonard Lake, Theresa Knorr, Herman Mudgett, John Weber, and many another "peacetime" sadistic killer reviewed here.

64. The novel was by William March; the play, by Maxwell Anderson, http://www.en.wikipedia.org/wiki/Jane_Toppan.

65. Publilius Syrus, writer of Latin maxims, 1st century BCE.

66. http://www.fenlandcitzen.co.uk/latest-east-anglia-news.

67. Roger Wilkes, *Blood Relations: Jeremy Bamber and the White House Farm Murders* (London: Pocket/Star Books, 1994).

68. Ibid., p. 440.

69. Ibid., p. 42.

70. For example: http://www.dailymail.co.uk/femail/article-455875/Is-Bambis-killer-innocent.html.

71. Some mothers who are truly overwhelmed with the prospect of losing their children or of being unable to care for them do commit murder-suicide. A few such mothers survive their own suicide attempt, are usually considered mentally ill, and are sent to a forensic hospital. Those mothers who kill their children for "wicked" reasons—like getting back at a husband who has left them—are the ones seen as "evil" by the public. An example: Dr. Debora Green (Ann Rule, *Bitter Harvest* [New York: Simon Schuster, 1997]), who burned down her house with her three children in it, two of whom died.

72. Bonnie Remsberg, *Mom, Dad, Mike and Pattie: The True Story of the Columbo Murders* (New York: Bantam Books, 1992).

73. Ibid., p. 340.

74. Ibid., p. 315.

75. Ibid., p. 127.

76. This special "chemistry" of obsessive love when thwarted is thoroughly discussed in Helen Fischer, *Why We Love: The Nature and Chemistry of Romantic Love* (New York: Henry Holt/Owl Books, 2004). Relevant points about her research will be mentioned in the following chapter.

77. Oliver Wendell Holmes Jr. (1841–1935): famous American jurist and Supreme Court justice.

78. http://www.ccadp.org/jimmyrayslaughter.htm. Slaughter was executed on March 15, 2005. The full story of his psychopathy and his crimes is told in Bill Cox, *Over the Edge* (New York: Pinnacle Books, 1997). The father of Melody Wuertz said at Slaughter's trial: "He's not a man. He's an evil and he must be destroyed. What this man has dumped into our lives is nothing short of a toxic bomb of evil," http://www.clarkprosecutor.org/html/death/US/slaughter955.htm.

79. Kieran Crowley, *Almost Paradise* (New York: St. Martin's Press, 2005).

80. *Obscene* is an apt word in this context. The origin of the word is obscure. The large Latin dictionary by Lewis and Short suggests the roots are *ob* plus *caenum*, the latter word conveying the meanings of "filth" or "loathsomeness." My Latin professor at university used to say the derivation was related to the Greek, meaning "tent," or "stage" (from which we get our word *scene*), the idea being that, as Aristotle advised, certain actions during a theatrical play were too horrifying or indecent to portray *on* the stage and therefore could only be hinted

at *off stage*; i.e., *ob* plus *scaenum*. Because the actions of John Ray Weber were to a great extent obscene (by whichever root meaning), they are properly alluded to only indirectly—off stage, as it were, not literally.

81. Lynard Barnes, in his 1995 review of Ray Garton's *In a Dark Place* (New York: Dell Publishing, 1992).

82. Peter Davidson, *Death by Cannibal* (New York: Berkley Books, 2006), p. 84.

83. As the philosopher Wittgenstein said, in a very different context, "Whereof we cannot speak we must be silent."

84. Barnes, review of Garton, *In a Dark Place*.

85. Cf. Hazelwood and Michaud, *Dark Dreams*. The authors point out that the longer the time the sadist fantasizes about the acts he wants to commit, the more specific the victim's characteristics will be (as to age, size, etc.), p. 36. As to the components of a ritualistic sadist like Weber, there are certain subtypes one encounters. Weber fits into the "paraphilic" sexual sadist category, practicing bondage, sexual sadism (with sexual excitement during killing), and cannibalism, p. 43.

86. Steven Daniels, coordinator of Annual Homicide Conference, personal communication.

87. Submitted by Wayne Wirsing for the Price County district attorney, as part of the case of *Wisconsin v. John R. Weber*.

88. Barnes, review of Garton, *In a Dark Place*.

CHAPTER NINE. SCIENCE LOOKS AT EVIL

1. Non-shared environment related to the fact that even siblings led largely separate lives, were in different classes at school, had different friends and different skills and interests, etc. "Shared" environment (the whole family sitting down to the same dinner table, taking a vacation together) accounts for barely 3 percent of the difference in our personalities.

2. Example: ex-con Jess Dotson killed his brother in an argument—plus five other family members. *New York Times*, March 9, 2008.

3. An exception might be in places like Brazil, where kidnap for modest sums of ransom money is something of a cottage industry. I once treated a Brazilian patient whose wife was kidnapped for about three days. This was fairly traumatic for him, since he had no idea when she would be released. The wife was rather calm throughout the ordeal, knowing that the kidnappers were not asking for much money and that her father was wealthy and easily able to afford the extortion.

4. Lee Butcher, *To Love, Honor, and Kill* (New York: Pinnacle Books, 2008).

5. Joseph Starkey, *Deadly Greed* (New York: Prentiss Hall, 1991).

6. Such as the man in chapter 1, who beheaded his father and threw the head out the window, for fear it might get reattached. Another example would be that of China Arnold, a mentally unstable woman in Dayton, Ohio, who in 2005 killed her baby daughter by burning her in a microwave because she was worried that her boyfriend would leave her if he found out the baby wasn't his. The reaction of the community ("evil—pure evil") may well have been more intense than in cases of infanticide where the child suffered no mutilation or disfigurement.

7. Such as Coy Wesbrook in Texas, who was invited for a supposed reconciliation with his estranged wife, only to discover that she was having sex with two men at once when he entered her apartment. Two other people were there also, both of them mocking Mr. Wesbrook. He went to his car, got his rifle, and shot all five to death. Had he caught his wife in flagrante delicto with just one lover and shot either the wife or the lover, a Texas jury would have been lenient (if they convicted him at all). But with five bodies, they could not in good conscience look the other way.

8. Example: a Jewish Vietnam vet was unable to afford the fee for Yom Kippur services at his temple. In a vengeful rage, he drew a swastika on the temple door. His arrest was attended with a lot of publicity.

9. As we saw with Sharon Tate in the Manson case.

10. As in the assassinations of John and Robert Kennedy and of Martin Luther King Jr.

11. In previous chapters we mentioned Richard Jahnke Jr., who shot his father to death but had been abused severely (as was his sister) by the father; also Mary Bell, whose mother had tried numerous times to kill her daughter, and who at age eleven killed two boys. The true victim in either case was the child.

12. As in the murder of psychologist Kathryn Faughey by the paranoid schizophrenic David Tarloff. *New York Times*, Feb. 13, 2008. Or the murder of the judge in an Atlanta courtroom by prisoner Brian Nichols in March 2005. Another example concerns the murder of Tennessee pastor Matthew Winkler by his wife, Maryann, as described in Ann Rule, *Smoke, Mirrors, and Murder* (New York: Pocket Books, 2008), pp. 386–484.

13. Ken McElroy, mentioned in chapter 6, is an example.

14. Among the numerous examples: the murder of Matthew Shepard in Wyoming by Russell Henderson and Aaron McKinney, who tied Shepard to a wire fence after stabbing and burning him.

15. As in the intentional bombing of the Bamiyan Buddhas in Afghanistan by the Taliban in 2001, or the mallet attack on Michelangelo's Pietà by the para-

noid Australian geologist Laszlo Toth in 1972. Toth was later declared "insane" and deported back to Australia.

16. Norman Mailer, *The Executioner's Song* (Boston: Little, Brown, 1979).

17. F. L. Coolidge, L. L. Thede, and K. L. Jang, "Heritability of Personality Disorders in Childhood," *Journal of Personality Disorders* 15 (2001): 33–40. If a twin has conduct disorder, for example, his co-twin is about twice as likely to have conduct disorder also if the twins are "single-egg" (monozygotic), as compared with dizygotic. Twins from two different eggs are no more alike than two siblings born at different times.

The close relationship between childhood conduct disorder and (adult) antisocial personality disorder (or at the extreme, psychopathy) can be glimpsed by noticing the similarity of behaviors: children (boys, usually) with conduct disorder are prone, for example, to lying, stealing, assaultiveness ("bullying"), cruelty to animals, arson, property destruction (such as vandalism), and aggression that may reach the level of severe violence.

18. Mikal Gilmore, *Shot in the Heart* (New York: Viking Press, 1994).

19. This was the view expressed by Nobel Prize–winning neuroscientist Gerald Edelman in Gerald Edelman and Giulio Tononi, *A Universe of Consciousness* (New York: Basic Books, 2000), p. 38; also in Gerald Edelman, *Bright Air, Brilliant Fire: On the Matter of Mind*, chap. 3 (New York: Basic Books, 1992).

20. A useful summary of her work can be found in "The Neural Basis of Addiction: A Pathology of Motivation and Choice," *American Journal of Psychiatry* 162 (August 2005): 1403–12.

21. Hippocampal damage and its attendant memory impairment is one of the key abnormalities in Alzheimer's disease.

22. Joseph LeDoux, article on the amygdala in *Scholarpedia* 3, no. 4: 2698.

23. http://en.wikipedia.org/wiki/Nucleus_accumbens.

24. *American Journal of Psychiatry* 157 (January 2000): 3.

25. A. Bechara et al., "Insensivity to Future Consequences Following Damage to the Human Prefrontal Cortex," *Cognition* 50 (1994): 7–15.

26. http://en.wikipedia.org/wiki/Orbitofrontal_cortex.

27. Lecture at the New York State Psychiatric Institute, 2007.

28. Lee Butcher, *To Love, Honor and Kill* (New York: Kensington Publishers, 2008).

29. Examples would be Tommy Lynn Sells, Leonard Lake, and David Parker Ray—serial killers sketched in chapter 7.

30. Émile Durkheim, "Forms of Social Solidarity," in *Selected Writings*, trans. Anthony Giddens, 29th printing (London: Cambridge University Press, 2007), p. 124.

31. Larry J. Siever, "Neurobiology of Aggression and Violence," *American Journal of Psychiatry* 165 (April 2008): 429–42.

32. http://www.ninds.nih.gov/disorders/asperger/detail_asperger.htm. Others have also pointed to the tendency of clinicians not familiar with Asperger's to misdiagnose persons with this syndrome as "schizophrenic": B. G. Haskins and J. A. Silva, "Asperger's Disorder and Behavior: Forensic-Psychiatric Considerations," *Journal of the American Academy of Psychiatry and the Law* 34 (2006): 374–84. About one such patient in five was preoccupied with violent themes (p. 377).

33. V. S. Ramachandran and L. M. Oberman, "Broken Mirrors," *Scientific American*, November 2006, pp. 63–69.

34. Tania Singer of the University of Zurich, Switzerland, cited in http://www.sciencenews.org/view/generic/id/31400/title/Asperger%E2%80%99s_syndrome.

35. http://news.yahoo.com/s/ap/20070418/ap_on_re_us/virginia_tech_shooting.

36. http://en.wikipedia.org/wiki/Cho_Seung-Hui.

37. www.freelibrary.com/Fetal+Alcohol+Syndrome+National+Workshop+2002-a0112129793.

38. A. Badawy, "Alcohol and Violence, and the Possible Role of Serotonin," *Criminal Behavior and Mental Health* 13 (2006): 31–44.

39. William Shakespeare, *Macbeth*, act 1, scene 7, ll. 59–61.

40. Ibid., ll. 8–10.

41. Edmund S. Higgins, "The New Genetics of Mental Illness," *Scientific American Mind*, June/July 2008, pp. 41–47.

42. http://www.francesfarmersrevenge.com/stuff/serialkillers/marthajohnson.htm. She is considered a serial killer of the nonsexual type, because the four murders took place over a five-year span between 1977 and 1982.

43. Terrie E. Moffitt, "A Review of Research on the Taxonomy of Life-Course Persistent versus Adolescent-Limited Antisocial Behavior," in *The Cambridge Handbook of Violent Behavior and Aggression*, ed. D. J. Flannery, A. T. Vazsonyi, and I. D. Waldman (New York: Cambridge University Press, 2007), pp. 49–74.

44. Sheila Johnson, *Blood Lust* (New York: Pinnacle Books, 2007).

45. S. Kapur and P. Seeman, "NMDA Receptor Antagonists Ketamine and PCP Have Direct Effects on the Dopamine D2 and Serotonin 5HT2 Receptors. Implications for Models of Schizophrenia," *Molecular Psychiatry* 7 (2002): 833–44. Also, M. A. Fauman and B. J. Fauman, "Violence Associated with Phencyclidine Abuse," *American Journal of Psychiatry* 136 (1979): 1584–86.

46. J. M. Kretschmar and D. J. Flannery, "Substance Use and Violent Behavior," in *The Cambridge Handbook of Violent Behavior and Aggression*, ed. Flannery, Vazsonyi, and Waldman, pp. 647–63.

47. A. J. Reiss and J. A. Roth, "Alcohol, Other Psychoactive Drugs, and Violence," in *Understanding & Preventing Violence*, vol. 3, Social Influences (Washington, DC: National Academy Press), pp. 182–220.

48. R. Myerscough and S. Taylor, "The Effects of Marijuana on Human Physical Aggression," *Journal of Personality and Social Psychology* 49 (1985): 1541–46.

49. Higgins, "The New Genetics of Mental Illness," p. 46.

50. In any case marijuana had been implicated in a 40 percent increase in the development of mental illness by adolescents who use it; the incidence of suicidal thoughts also is greater among adolescent marijuana smokers. These effects can in certain young persons contribute further to criminal (including violent) behavior. Cf. Jennifer Kerr, "Teen Pot Use Can Lead to Dependency and Mental Illness," http://news.yahoo.com/s/ap/20080509/ap_on_he_me/teens_drugs. The persistent effects of marijuana and other drug use in adolescence has also been highlighted by Brenda Patoine in "Teen Brain's Ability to Learn Can Have a Flip Side," *BrainWork/Neuroscience News*, November/December 2007, pp. 1–2.

51. D. Murdoch, R. O. Pihl, and D. Ross, "Alcohol and Crimes of Violence," *International Journal of the Addictions* 25: 1065–81.

52. Corey Mitchell, *Pure Murder: A Deserted City Park, A Vicious Killing Frenzy* (New York: Pinnacle Books, 2008).

53. From the observations of Dr. John Harlow, http://en.wikipedia.org/wiki/Phineas_Gage.

54. Antonio Damasio, *Descartes' Error: Emotion, Reason, and the Human Brain* (New York: Grosset/Putnam, 1994), p. 33.

55. P. Ratiu and I.-F. Talos, "The Tale of Phineas Gage, Digitally Remastered," *New England Journal of Medicine* 351 (December 2004): e21.

56. A "stable family home is a protective factor against crime"—as emphasized by Gail S. Anderson in *Biological Influences on Criminal Behavior* (New York: Simon Fraser University Publications, 2007), p. 112.

57. Joanna Schaffhausen, "The Biological Basis of Aggression," http://www.brainconnection.com/topics/?main=fa/aggression2.

58. G. Lavergne, *A Sniper in the Tower: The Charles Whitman Murders* (Denton, TX: University of North Texas Press), 1997.

59. L. Fosburgh, *Closing Time: The True Story of the Goodbar Murder* (New York: Dell Books, 1975).

60. Though when an intruding male lion does succeed, he behaves according to the script for new male lions, as mentioned in chapter 3.

61. Debra Niehoff, *The Biology of Violence* (New York: Free Press, 1998), p. 153.

62. Ibid., p. 155.

63. R. Rowe et al., "Testosterone, Antisocial Behavior, and Social Dominance in Boys: Pubertal Development and Biosocial Interaction," *Biological Psychiatry* 55 (2004): 546–52. A similar finding was made earlier by B. Schaal and colleagues in Montréal: "Male Testosterone Linked to High School Dominance but Low Physical Aggression in Early Adolescence," *Journal of the American Academy of Child & Adolescent Psychiatry* 35 (1996): 1322–30.

64. J. D. Higley et al., "Cerebrospinal Testosterone and 5-HIAA (Serotonin) Correlate with Different Types of Aggressive Behaviors," *Biological Psychiatry* 40 (1996): 1067–82.

65. S. Rajender et al., "Reduced CAG Repeats Length in Androgen Receptor Gene Is Associated with Violent Criminal Behavior," *International Journal for Legal Medicine* (March 2008).

66. Schaffhausen, "The Biological Basis of Aggression." She discusses predatory aggression (seen also in animals who stalk and kill other species), defensive aggression (as when a person or animal is "cornered"), and social aggression (associated with testosterone and the quest for social dominance).

67. Paul Aitken, "XYY—One Chromosome Too Many," http://www.alt-penis.com/penis_news/xyy.shtml.

68. P. Briken et al., "XYY Chromosome Abnormality in Sexual Homicide Perpetrators," *American Journal of Medical Genetics* (January 2, 2006). It should be noted that XYY is not even a heritable condition. It results from a random mutation when the sex cells (sperm and egg), each with twenty-three chromosomes, line up to reconstitute the full forty-six-chromosome cells of our species. One sperm cell in this rare mutation ends up with two "Y's" instead of just one; the fertilized egg becomes XYY. Cf. Anderson, *Biological Influences on Criminal Behavior*, p. 82.

69. Otto Kernberg, *Aggression in Personality Disorders and Perversions* (New Haven, CT: Yale University Press, 1992), p. 77.

70. "Global," *Time*, June 16, 2008, p. 10. Another example is the documentary by Ernestina Sodi Miranda, who had been kidnapped—and later freed—in Mexico in 2002: *Líbranos del Mal (Deliver Us from Evil)* (Mexico City: Aguilar, 2006).

71. Maria Eftimiades, *Sins of the Mother* (New York: St. Martin's Paperbacks, 1995).

72. A powerful study of empathy in this sense has been conducted by Professor Simon Baron-Cohen of Cambridge University in *The Essential Difference: Male and Female Brains and the Truth about Autism* (New York: Basic Books, 2004), pp. 187–99.

73. James Q. Wilson, *The Moral Sense* (New York: Free Press, 1993), pp. 29–54.

74. M. William Phelps, *I'll Be Watching You* (New York: Pinnacle Books, 2008). He refers to Snelgrove as the "embodiment of pure evil" (p. 9).

75. A. Raine et al., "High Rates of Violence, Crime, Academic Problems and Behavioral Problems in Males with Both Early Neuromotor Deficits and Unstable Family Environments," *Archives of General Psychiatry* 53 (1996): 544–49.

76. A. Raine et al., "Reduced Prefrontal and Increased Subcortical Brain Functioning Assessed Using Positron Emission Tomography in Predatory and Affective Murderers," *Behavioral Science and the Law* 16 (1998): 319–22. In a related study, psychopathic criminals showed overactivity in the fronto-temporal cortex for processing affective stimuli: Kent Kiehl, A. M. Smith et al., "Limbic Abnormalities in Affective Processing by Criminal Psychopaths as Revealed by Functional Magnetic Resonance Imaging," *Biological Psychiatry* 50 (2001): 677–84.

77. A. Raine et al., "Reduced Prefrontal Gray Matter Volume and Reduced Autonomic Activity in Antisocial Personality Disorder," *Archives of General Psychiatry* 57 (2000): 119–27.

78. A. Raine and P. H. Venables, "Tonic Heart Rate Level, Social Class, and Antisocial Behavior," *Biological Psychiatry* 18 (1984): 123–32.

79. A. Marsh et al., "Reduced Amygdala Response to Fearful Expressions in Children and Adolescents with Callous-Unemotional Traits and Disruptive Behavior Disorders," *American Journal of Psychiatry* 165 (2008): 712–20.

80. J. Moll et al., "Morals and the Human Brain: A Working Model," *Neuroreport* 14 (2003): 299–305.

81. E. C. Finger et al., "Abnormal Ventromedial Prefrontal Cortex Function in Children with Psychopathic Traits during Reversal Learning," *Archives of General Psychiatry* 65 (2008): 586–94.

82. H. Larsson, E. Viding, and R. Plomin, "Callous-Unemotional Traits and Antisocial Behavior: Genetic, Environmental and Early Parenting Characteristics," *Criminal Justice and Behavior* 35 (2008): 197–211.

83. J. Taylor, W. G. Iacono, and M. McGue, "Evidence for a Genetic Etiology of Early-Onset Delinquency," *Journal of Abnormal Psychology* 109 (2000): 634–43. Also, L. Arsenault et al., "Strong Genetic Effects on Cross-Situational Behavior among 5-Year-Old Children According to Mothers, Teachers, Examiner-Observers, and Self-Reports," *Journal of Child Psychology and Psychiatry* 44 (2004): 832–48.

84. T. C. Eley, P. Lichtenstein, and J. Stevenson, "Sex Differences in the Etiology of Aggressive and Nonaggressive Antisocial Behavior: Results from Two Twin Studies," *Child Development* 70 (1999): 155–68.

85. Anderson, *Biological Influences on Criminal Behavior*, p. 112.

86. Deborah Spungen, *And I Don't Want to Live This Life* (New York: Ballantine Books, 1983).

87. Niels Habermann, *Jugendliche Sexualmörder (Juvenile Sexual Murder)* (Lengerich, Germany: Pabst Science Publishers, 2008).

88. David J. Pelzer, *A Child Called "It": An Abused Child's Journey from Victim to Victor* (Deerfield Beach, FL: Health Communications, 1995).

89. S. K. Loo et al., "Genome Wide Scan of Reading Ability in Affected Sibling Pairs with Attention-Deficit/Hyperactivity Disorder," *Molecular Psychology* 9 (2004): 485–93.

90. Finger et al., "Abnormal Ventromedial Prefrontal Cortex Function," p. 593.

91. A. Caspi et al., "Role of Genotype in the Cycle of Violence in Maltreated Children," *Science* 297 (2002): 851–54.

92. C. M. Filley et al., "Toward an Understanding of Violence: Neurobehavioral Aspects of Unwarranted Physical Aggression," *Neuropsychiatry, Neuropsychology and Behavioral Neurology* 14 (2001): 1–14; also R. Cadoret, L. D. Levé, and E. Devor, "Genetics of Aggressive and Violent Behavior," *Psychiatric Clinics of North America* 20 (1997): 301–22.

93. A. R. Hariri et al., "A Susceptibility Gene for Affective Disorders and the Response of the Human Amygdala," *Archives of General Psychiatry* 62 (2005): 146–52.

94. Sheila Hodgins, lecture at the Jephcott Forensic Symposium, Royal Society of Medicine, London, UK, April 22, 2008.

95. Ibid.

96. Vincent Bugliosi, *Helter Skelter* (New York: W. W. Norton, 1974/1994), p. 125.

97. Anna C. Salter, *Predators: Pedophiles, Rapists, & Other Sex Offenders* (New York: Basic Books, 2003).

98. The full story is found on pages 98–99 in ibid.

99. Ibid., p. 100.

100. This man, who would be at Category 22 on the Gradations scale, represents a particularly heinous form of evil because his victim was his own son. If a stranger had abducted and violated the boy in a similar fashion—provided the boy's parents were warm and loving—the boy's capacity to trust others would not be as shattered as it would be knowing that he was violated by his own father, who was supposed to be his guardian and protector.

101. Examples are the serial killers Edwin Snelgrove Jr., mentioned above, and Dennis Rader (known in the press as BTK—for bind-torture-kill). Both these men came from normal homes and became sexually aroused from sadistic fantasies when still quite young. Dennis Rader was able to lead a "split" life, marrying and raising a family, while also leading a secret "double-life" as a sadistic killer. Edwin Snelgrove was a loner, unable to relate intimately with women—whom he grew to hate, as though it were their fault that he couldn't form close attachments to them.

102. Francine du Plessix Gray, *At Home with the Marquis de Sade: A Life* (New York: Penguin Books, 1998), p. 30. Aristocrats could not be executed in those royal times; this was the same reason why the Countess Báthory was simply immured in her castle, when arrested, rather than being executed.

103. Salter, *Predators*, p. 114.

FINAL THOUGHTS

1. Irvine Welsh, *Crime* (London: Jonathan Cape, 2008), p. 255. "Nonce" is Scottish slang for "pedophile."

2. Slavenka Drakulic, *They Would Never Hurt a Fly* (New York: Penguin Books, 2005), p. 189.

3. Drakulic, *They Would Never Hurt a Fly*, p. 111. The very same story about Erdomovic is also mentioned in a book by German social psychologist Harald Welzer, who discusses how ordinary men can end up committing mass murder: *Täter—Wie aus ganz normalen Menschen Massenmörder werden* (Perpetrators—How quite normal men become mass murderers) (Frankfurt am Main: Fischer Verlag, 2008), pp. 242–45.

4. Niklas Frank, *Der Vater: Eine Abrechnung* (Munich: Bertelsmann, 1987). Later translated as *In the Shadow of the Reich* (New York: Alfred Knopf, 1991).

5. One of Eichmann's sons condemned his father's actions but did not write a book about him, http://www.jewishf.com/content/2-0-/module/display/story_id/20954/edition_id/431/format/html/displaystory.html.

6. My translation from his 1992 letter.

7. Frank, *Der Vater*, p. 350.

8. Lieutenant Calley's character structure left something to be desired even before he went to Vietnam. Outwardly, however, he certainly seemed like an "ordinary man." Not surprisingly, when he was brought to trial for the massacre, he showed his moral meagerness when he said in his defense, "What the hell else is war than killing people?" This was cited in Welzer, *Täter*, p. 245.

9. The officer was one Daniel Mitrone. Martha Huggins, Mika Haritos-Fatouras, and Philip G. Zimbardo, *Violence Workers* (Berkeley: University of California Press, 2002), p. 239.

10. Huggins, Haritas-Fatouras, and Zimbardo, *Violence Workers*, p. 240.

11. Cited by Rita Maran, *Torture: The Role of Ideology in the French-Algerian War* (New York: Praeger, 1989), p. 83.

12. Bruce Falconer, "The World's Most Evil Man," *American Scholar* 77 (2008): 33–53.

13. Niels Habermann in his book on adolescent sexual murder (*Jugendliche Sexualmörder* [Berlin: Pabst Science Publishers, 2008]) drew attention to how a third of the nineteen adolescent murderers he studied had deformities of one sort or another that contributed to their poor self-image and shyness, and played a role in their eventual crimes.

14. One of the rare forms of evil in peacetime partakes of this dynamic: consider Hinckley's attempt on the life of President Reagan, or David Mark Chapman's murder of John Lennon. A brilliant comment on this kind of anomie-driven evil was made by Martin Amis in his piece "Terrorism's New Structure," *Wall Street Journal*, August 16, 2008, pp. W–1, 6.

15. Among myriad examples: Napoleon's troops committed atrocities against the Spanish when they invaded Spain (1807–1812); the Spanish citizenry retaliated by flaying alive or sawing in two some of the invading troops. David A. Bell, *The First Total War* (Boston: Houghton Mifflin, 2007), p. 290.

16. As Welzer (*Täter*, p. 263) points out, killing (whether of soldiers or civilians) in wartime is reduced to a job that unfortunately has to be done. Here he echoes Himmler's pep talk to the SS (cited in ibid., p. 23) in referring to the mass murder of the Jews as an unpleasant task that the Fatherland needs to perform for its salvation. In his address to SS leaders in 1943, Himmler waved aside any accusation of "anti-Semitism," speaking of the Jews as "lice"; their eradication simply a matter of cleanliness, or "delousing" (Katrin Himmler, *The Himmler Brothers* [New York: Macmillan, 2007], p. 231). Violence, in this perverse and topsy-turvy schema, is no longer something destructive but rather a "constructive" exercise in social hygienics.

17. I am using the word "men" here, for brevity's sake, to refer to both men and women. Men enormously outnumber women when we speak of evil, whether in peacetime or war. And as we have seen, serial sexual homicide and mass murder are anyway almost exclusively male phenomena.

18. John Seabrook, "Suffering Souls," *New Yorker*, November 10, 2008, pp. 64–73.

19. Barbara Bentley, *A Dance with the Devil: A True Story of Marriage to a Psychopath* (New York: Berkley Books, 2008), pp. 351–52.

20. Professor of English Harold Schechter insists that "there is no such thing as a serial killer who has come from a healthy, happy home. All of them are the products of distinctly dysfunctional backgrounds." *The Serial Killer Files* (New York: Ballantine Books, 2003), p. 256. Schechter is simply wrong. Examples of the contrary come not only from my own records and clinical experience, but also from the clinical observations of Niels Habermann (*Jugendliche Sexualmörder*). He gave vignettes of nineteen adolescent sexual murderers, including a few who became serial killers. Most did come from dysfunctional

homes, but several, such as his case of "Matthias," did not. These boys did tend to be schizoid loners from birth—meaning that they inherited risk genes for this personality type that interfered severely with their ability to connect with, and develop intimacy with, girls as they entered puberty. They came from good homes, as did US serial killer, adoptee Joel Rifkin, whose schizoid personality also stood in the way of his developing closeness with women.

21. Simon Baatz, *For the Thrill of It: Leopold, Loeb, and the Murder that Shocked Chicago* (New York: HarperCollins, 2008). Leopold, sensitive and sexually in the thrall of the more psychopathic Loeb, conspired to kill a boy just for the excitement of doing it. Loeb was killed in prison by another inmate. Leopold, remorseful, was freed after thirty-four years and then led a socially useful life.

22. This point is made convincingly by Dr. Stanton Samenow in *Inside the Criminal Mind* (New York: Times Books, 1984), pp. 175–90.

23. The details can be found in the biography of Athens by Richard Rhodes: *Why They Kill* (New York: Random House, 1999).

24. Anthony Flacco with Jerry Clark, *Slave in the Necropolis* (Martin Literary Management, 2008, preprint of book to be published, 2009), pp. 16–62.

25. John Dean, *House of Evil* (New York: St. Martin's Paperbacks, 2008).

26. Ibid., p. 218.

27. Her original title read "*Oni ne bi ni mrava zgazili*": They wouldn't step on an ant, but the idea is the same.

28. Gary King, *Stolen in the Night* (New York: St. Martin's Press, 2007). Also http://news.aol.com/article/confessed-child-killer-sentenced-to/141596?icid=100214839x1.

29. http://fifthnail.blogspot.com/.

30. http://en.allexperts.com/e/j/jo/joseph_e_duncan_iii.htm?zlr=4.

31. His story is recorded in the *New York Times*, June 14, 1996.

32. Samenow, *Inside the Criminal Mind*, p. 177.

33. The murder took place in 2006 in the state of Maine, after he was inappropriately released from a mental hospital at a time when he was harboring murderous thoughts about his mother. *Wall Street Journal*, August 16, 2008, pp. A–1, A–8; also http://www.nylj.com/nylawyer/probono/news/07/080307a.html.

34. Joel Norris, *Arthur Shawcross: The Genesee River Killer* (New York: Windsor Publications, 1992). Also, Jack Olsen, *Misbegotten Son* (New York: Dell/Island Books, 1993).

35. http://news.aol.com/article/confessed-child-killer-sentenced-to/145196 ?icid=100214839x1.

36. http://mediahangout.blogspot.com/2008/11/Quentin-patrick-halloween-arrest. html-220k.

37. http://www.allserialkillers.com/clifford_olson.htm, p. 6. Cf. also W. Leslie Holmes and Bruce Northrup, *Where Shadows Linger: The Untold Story of RCMP's Olson Murder Investigation* (Surrey, BC: Heritage House Publishing Company, 2000).

38. According to Section 745.6 of the Criminal Code, as mentioned by the stepfather of thirteen-year-old murder victim Colleen Daignault, who was raped, tortured, and killed by Olsen in 1981. The stepfather has urged the repeal of that statute. http://www.owl125.com/colleen.html.

39. Billy Wayne Sinclair and Jodie Sinclair, *A Life in the Balance: A Journey from Murder to Redemption Inside America's Worst Prison System* (New York: Arcade Publishing, 2000).

40. His story is told in Tom Jackman and Troy Cole, *Rites of Burial: The Shocking True Crime Account of Robert Berdella, the Butcher of Kansas City, Missouri* (New York: Windsor Publishing/Pinnacle Books, 1992).

41. Reprinted here with Dennis Nilsen's permission: his letter of July 31, 2008.

42. Friedrich Nietzsche, *Also Sprach Zarathustra*, ed. and trans. Stanley Appelbaum (Mineola, NY: Dover Press, 2004 [1883–85]), p. 10. The original reads "*Der Mensch ist ein Seil, geknüpft zwischen Tier und Übermensch—ein Seil über einem Abgrunde.*" *Übermensch* is often translated "overman" to avoid the word *superman*, which has overtones either of the comic-book character or the goose-stepping Nazis. Nietzsche did not have in mind brutish men like the Nazis; rather, an independent, morally superior, artistic man—*beyond* or *more than* the ordinary person. For easier comprehension, I prefer the phrase "superior man" here: one who would be at the farthest remove from the commission of *evil*, in the sense I have been using it in this book.

EPILOGUE

1. See chap. 2, p. 62.

2. "ISIS Burns 19 Yazidi Women to Death in Mosul for Rejecting Sex Slavery," Behind the News (blog), June 10, 2017, https://behindthenews israel.wordpress.com/2017/06/10/isis-burns-19-yazidi-women-to-death-in-mosul-for-rejecting-sex-slavery/.

3. *Wikipedia*, s.v. "Akihabara Massacre," last modified April 25, 2017, https://en.wikipedia.org/wiki/Akihabara_massacre.

4. BBC News, July 15, 2016; "What We Know about the Bastille Day Killings," *Wall Street Journal*, July 15, 2016.

5. *People v. James F. Cahill*, Court of Appeal Report, November 25, 2003, p. 3: "Pursuant to CPL 400.27, the court conducted the jury trial in two phases. In the first phase, the jury found the defendant guilty of both counts of first degree murder, first degree assault (based on the April 1998 beating) and related charges."

6. D. J. Krajicek, "Wife and Death: Doc Gives Murder and Adultery a Shot," *Daily News*, August 29, 2015.

7. Terrence McCoy, "With His Dying Words, Alexander Litvinenko Names Putin as His Killer," *Washington Post*, January 28, 2015.

8. Iris Chang, *The Rape of Nanking* (New York: Basic Books, 1997).

9. Ibid., p. 11 of the illustrations.

10. Shi Young and James Yin, *The Rape of Nanking: An Undeniable History in Photographs* (Chicago: Innovative Publishing Group, 1997).

11. Ibid., p. 56.

12. V. N. Dadrian, *The History of the Armenian Genocide* (Providence, RI: Berghahn Books, 1995); P. Balakian, *The Burning Tigris: The Armenian Genocide and America's Response* (New York: HarperCollins, 2003), B. N. Ketchian, *In the Shadow of the Fortress: Survivors' Memoirs; the Genocide Remembered*, no. 1 (Cambridge, MA: Zoryan Institute Survivors' Memoirs, 1988).

13. "Marriages and Divorces, 1900–2012," Infoplease, https://www.infoplease.com/us/marital-status/marriages-and-divorces-1900a2012.

14. Association of American Medical Colleges, "U.S. Medical School Applicants and Students: 1982–83 to 2011–12," 2012, https://www.aamc.org/download/153708/data/; Staff Care, "Women in Medicine: A Review of Changing Physician Demographics, Female Physicians by Specialty, State and Related Data" (white paper), 2015, https://www.staffcare.com/uploadedFiles/women-in-medicine-changing-physician-demographics-white-paper.pdf.

15. D. J. Besharov and A. West, "African American Marriage Patterns," Hoover Institution, 2001), p. 96, http://www.hoover.org/ sites/default/files/uploads/documents/0817998721_95.pdf.

16. G. D. Sandefur, Molly Martin, Jennifer Eggerling-Boeck, Susan E. Mannon, and Ann M. Meier, "An Overview of Racial and Ethnic Demographic Trends," chap. 3 in *America Becoming: Racial Trends and Their Consequences*, vol. 1 (Washington, DC: National Academies Press, 2001), available at https://www.nap.edu/read/9599/chapter/4.

17. C. Brandon, *Murder in the Adirondacks: An American Tragedy Revisited* (Utica, NY: North Country Books, 1986).

18. Betsy Kepes, "Infamous Murder Revisited," review of *Murder in the Adirondacks*, by Craig Brandon, Adirondack Explorer, March 2017, https://www.adirondackexplorer.org/book_reviews/murder-in-the-adirondacks.

19. *Murderpedia*, s.v. " Dr. Bennett Clarke Hyde," http://murderpedia.org/male.H/h/hyde-bennett.htm; Nadia Pflaum, "Dr. Bennett Clarke Hyde's Trial in the Swope Family Poisonings Provoked Media Frenzy," *Pitch*, March 23, 2010, http://www.pitch.com/news/article/20586923/dr-bennett-clark-hydes-trial-in-the-swope-family-poisonings-provoked-media-frenzy.

20. *New York Times*, February 11, 1910, p. 1a.

21. T. E. Gaddis, *Birdman of Alcatraz* (New York: Random House, 1955); "Robert 'the Birdman of Alcatraz' Stroud," Alcatraz History, http://www.alcatrazhistory.com/stroud.htm.

22. *Encyclopedia Britannica*, s.v. "Robert Stroud: American Criminal and Ornithologist," last updated March 31, 2017, https://www.britannica.com/biography/Robert-Stroud.

23. H. Schechter, *Deranged: The Shocking True Story of America's Most Fiendish Killer* (New York: Pocket Books, 1990), p. 85.

24. *Wikipedia*, s.v. "Albert Fish," last modified May 12, 2017, https://en.wikipedia.org/wiki/Albert_Fish.

25. Harold Schechter, *The True Story of America's Most Fiendish Killer* (New York: Pocket Books, 1990).

26. Leslie Margolin, *Murderess! The Chilling True Story of the Most Infamous Woman Ever Electrocuted* (New York: Pinnacle Books, 1999).

27. Troy Taylor, "The 'Dumb-Bell Murder,': The Crime of Ruth Snyder & Judd Gray," Dead Men Do Tell Tales, 2004, http://www.prairieghosts.com/ruth_judd.html; cf.: Margolin, Murderess.

28. Anthony Flacco, *The Road Out of Hell* (New York: Sterling Books, 2009).

29. Diane Wagner, *Corpus Delicti* (New York: St. Martin's Paperbacks, 1986).

30. William Allen, *The Story of a Mass Murderer* (Boston: Houghton Mifflin, 1976).

31. Ibid.

32. Robert Greenfield, *Timothy Leary: A Biography* (New York: Harcourt, 2006).

33. Ryan McMaken, "FBI: Us Homicide Rate at 51 Year Low," *Mises Wire* (blog), Mises Institute, June 15, 2016, https://mises.org/blog/fbi-us-homicide-rate-51-year-low.

34. Michael H. Stone, "Mass Murder, Mental Illness, and Men," *Violence & Gender* 2 (2015): 51–86.

35. Kate Zernicke, "Jury Finds Spying in Rutgers Dorm Was a Hate Crime," *New York Times*, March 16, 2012.

36. *Wikipedia*, s.v. "Suicide of Audrie Pott," last modified August 4, 2017,

https://en.wikipedia.org/wiki/Suicide_of_Audrie_Pott.

37. Michelle Dean: The Story of Amanda Todd. The New Yorker October 18, 2012.

38. CBC News, April 12, 2013: US Teen's death eerily similar to Rehtaeh Parso's story.

39. Sandra Constantine, "South Hadley, MA Superintendent Gus Sayer Says DA's Findings in Phoebe Prince Case Consistent with School's Investigation," *Republican* (Springfield, MA), March 31, 2010.

40. Mark Dunphy, "Phoebe Prince Death Inspires Anti-Bullying Bill in New York," *Clare Herald*, May 11, 2010.

41. Laura Crimaldi, "DA: School Knew of Brutal Bullying of Phoebe Prince," *Boston Herald*, March 29, 2010.

42. Waldon R. Porterfield, "Little Charlie Ross and the Crime That Shocked the Nation," *Milwaukee Journal*, October 2, 1974; Norman Zierold, *Little Charlie Ross* (Boston: Little, Brown, 1967). Shortly after the kidnaping, the boy's father, John E. Potter, wrote *The Father's Story of Charley Ross, the Kidnapped Child*, in 1876.

43. Rupert Cornwell, "The Lindbergh Mystery: Could America's Most Famous Crime Be Solved at Last?" *Independent*, October 19, 2012, http://www.independent.co.uk/news/world/americas/the-lindbergh-mystery-could-america-s-most-famous-crime-be-solved-at-last-8215537.html.

44. Tim O'Neil, "A Look Back: 1953 Bobby Greenlease Jr. Kidnapping Ended in the Missouri Gas Chamber," *St. Louis Post-Dispatch*, October 4, 2009; cf.: J. J. Maloney, "The Greenlease Kidnapping," Missouri Death Row, http://missourideathrow.com/doc history/the-greenlease-kidnapping.

45. Gene Miller, *83 Hours 'Til Dawn* (New York: Doubleday, 1971); cf.: *Wikipedia*, s.v. "Barbara Mackle Kidnapping," last modified February 1, 2017, https://en.wikipedia.org/wiki/Barbara_Mackle_kidnapping.

46. *Wikipedia*, s.v. "Kidnapping of Jaycee Dugard," last modified May 7, 2017, https://en.wikipedia.org/wiki/Kidnapping_of_Jaycee_Dugard.

47. Phil Garrido's father, personal communication with the author, 2009.

48. John Glatt, *The Lost Girls* (New York: St. Martin's Paperbacks, 2015); "Ariel Castro Kidnappings," *Wikipedia*, last modified May 14, 2017, https://en.wikipedia.org/wiki/Ariel_Castro_kidnappings.

49. Susan Claremont, "A Murder, Two Accused, But No Body," *Hamilton Spectator*, May 21, 2009.

50. Kristina Sauerwein, *Invisible Chains* (Guilford, CT: Lyons Press, 2008).

51. Associated Press, "Life in Prison for Kidnapper of Smart," *New York Times*, May 25, 2011; cf.: *Wikipedia*, s.v. "Elizabeth Smart Kidnapping," last modified May 6, 2017, https://en.wikipedia.org/wiki/Elizabeth_Smart

_kidnapping.

52. Shamita Das Dasgupta, "Acid Attacks," in *Encyclopedia of Interpersonal Violence*, vol. 1, 1st ed., ed. Claire M. Renzetti and Jeffery L. Edleson (Thousand Oaks, CA: SAGE Publications, 2008).

53. Beth Stebner, "Linda Pugach: Woman Blinded by Burton Pugach Dies Aged 75 in New York" (obit.), *Daily Mail* (London), January 24, 2013, http://www.dailymail.co.uk/news/article-2267638/Linda-Pugach.

54. Anne O'Neill, "Acid Death Case Goes to New Trial," *Los Angeles Times*, July 5, 1994.

55. Jill Young Miller, "The Cruelest Cut of All: Marla Hanson Carries a Visible Reminder of the Night Her Face Was Slashed. But She Says It Was What Came after the Attack That Left the Deepest Scars," *Sun Sentinel*, http://articles.sun.sentinel.com/1987-11-23/features/8702070506_1_invisible; cf.: Dean Balsamini, "Chelsea Slashing Is Chilling Reminder of 1986 Nightmare," *New York Post*, January 9, 2016.

56. Bill Mayer, "The Plain Dealer," Associated Press, February 11, 2009; Adam Sullivan, "Rodgers Sentenced for Lye Attack," WCAX.com, Local Vermont News, February 11, 2009.

57. Thomas Erdbrink, "Iranian Woman Blinded by Spurned Suitor Persuades Court to Punish Him Similarly," *Washington Post*, December 14, 2008.

58. Jeff Barker, "Judge Calls Sifrit 'Butcher,' Gives Him 38 Years in Prison," *Baltimore Sun*, July 8, 2003.

59. Doyle Murphy, "Texas Killer Convicted of Murder in Burning Death of 8-Year-Old Sex Abuse Victim," *New York Daily News*, February 9, 2015.

60. Madeline Baro Diaz, "Man Convicted of Killing 9-Year-Old Florida Girl," *Sun Sentinel*, March 8, 2007.

61. Christie Blatchford, "The Chilling Online Posts That Luka Magnotta Jurors Were Not Shown," *National Post* (Canada), December 15, 2014; cf.: Petti Fong, Andrew Chung, and Hilda Hoy, "Foot and Hand Sent to Vancouver Schools," *Toronto Star*, June 5, 2012; "Head Found in Montreal Park Belongs to Jun Lin," CBC News, July 4, 2012; "'Canadian Psycho' Murder Suspect Arrested in Berlin," RNW Media, June 5, 2012; Brian Daly, "Personality Disorder Best Explains Luka Magnotta: Crown Expert Magnotta Trial," *Toronto Sun*, February 9, 2015.

62. Cara Lee Carter, *Canadian Psycho: The True Story of Luka Magnotta*, Crimes Canada, vol. 5 (Canada: VP Publications, an imprint of RJ Parker Publishing, 2015).

63. Ibid., pp. 58, 100ff.

64. R. D. Hare, *The Hare Psychopathy Checklist-Revised* (Toronto: Multi-Health Systems, 1991).

65. Peter Davidson, "Albert Fentress: Middle School Madman," chap. 2 in *Death by Cannibal: Minds with an Appetite for Murder* (New York: Berkley Books, 2015).

66. Ibid.

67. Roy Hazelwood and Stephen Michaud, *Dark Dreams: Sexual Violence, Homicide, and the Criminal Mind* (New York: St. Martin's Press, 2001).

68. In their article on Asperger's disorder and criminal behavior, "Asperger's Disorder and Criminal Behavior: Forensic-Psychiatric Considerations," *Journal of the American Academy of Psychiatry and the Law* 34 (2006): 374–84, Barbara Haskins and J. A. Silva mention studies showing a modest increase in criminality among (male) Asperger patients—that does not justify the public's worry about violence in that population (despite the few dramatic cases in the recent press).

69. Stone, "Mass Murder." In my study of 302 mass murderers from the United States and other countries, Asperger's syndrome and other forms of autistic disorders were present only in four cases (1.5 percent), whereas other forms of psychosis were present in forty-two other persons (16.4 percent). Grant Duwe, in *Mass Murder in the United States* (London: McFarland, 2007), cites (pp. 139 ff) percentages from TV coverage (males account for 94 percent of mass murderers) and *New York Times* (95 percent male) and weekly news magazines (100 percent), so my 97 percent is a reasonable estimate.

70. Dinesh Ramde, "Wisconsin Temple Shooting: Oak Creek Incident Leaves at Least 7 Dead," *Huffington Post*, August 5, 2012; cf.: *Wikipedia*, s.v. "Wisconsin Sikh Temple Shooting," last modified May 12, 2017, https://en.wikipedia.org/wiki/Wisconsin_Sikh_temple_shooting.

71. "Male Headwear," Raqs, last updated April 22, 2015, http://www.raqs.co.nz/me/clothing_headwear_male.html.

72. Kristina Savali, "Adam Lanza's Possible Motive: Mother Cared More about Sandy Hook Students Than Him," NewsOne, 2013; cf.: Michael Daly, "We Already Know What Adam Lanza's Real Motive Was at Sandy Hook," *Daily Beast*, November 26, 2013; Alison Leigh Cowan, "Adam Lanza's Mental Problems 'Completely Untreated' before Newtown Shootings, Report Says," *New York Times*, November 21, 2014. For other background details, see "Adam Lanza: Murderer," Biography, last updated June 13, 2016, http://www.biography.com/people/adam-lanza-21068899.

73. T. Moran, "Inside Cho's Mind," ABC News, August 30, 2007.

74. Stone, "Mass Murder." In my survey of prominent mass murders from 1900 to 2016 in the United States and other countries, I noted that in the decades from 1900 to 1959, there were between five to seven such murders per decade; in the decade 1960–69, there were twelve. In the following decades, the

figures rose from twenty-two (1970s) to forty (1980s) to eighty-eight (1990s), and then tapered somewhat to sixty (2000s). But in the years 2010–2016, not even a complete decade, there were already fifty-nine. Semiautomatic pistols and rifles accounted for most of the mass murders.

75. John Cloud, "The Troubles Life of Jared Loughner," *Time*, January 15,2001, http://content.time.com/time/magazine/article/0,9171,2042358,00.html.

76. Georgina Lloyd, "Chapter 13: The Snuff Movie Murder," in *Murders Unspeakable* (1992; repr., London: Robert Hale, 2008), pp. 153–61.

77. Ibid., p. 161.

78. David A Gibb, *The Shocking Double Life of Canadian Air Force Colonel Russell Williams* (New York: Berkley Books, 2011); Timothy Appleby, *A New Kind of Monster: The Secret Life and Shocking True Crime Story of an Officer . . . and a Murderer* (New York: Broadway Books, 2011).

79. Dennis McDougal, *Angel of Darkness: The True Story of Randy Kraft and the Most Heinous Murder Spree of the Century* (New York: Warner Books, 1991).

80. *Murderpedia*, s.v. "Dr. Teet Härm," http://murderpedia.org/male.H/h/harm-teet.htm .

81. Nancy Dillon, "California Chef David Viens Who Ate His Wife's Boiled Corpse Sentenced to 15 Years to Life in Prison," *Daily News*, March 22, 2013, http://www.nydailynews.com/news/national/california-chef-15-years-life-killing-eating-wife-article-1.1296775.

82. Christine Pelisek, "David Viens Murder Trial: Chef Says He Slow-Cooked His Wife's Body," *Daily Beast*, September 20, 2012, http://www.thedailybeast.com/david-viens-murder-trial-chef-says-he-slow-cooked-his-wifes-body; James Nye, "Revealed: Wife Who Was Murdered and Cooked in a Pot by Her Chef Husband Had Been Saving Up Money as 'Escape Fund,'" *Daily Mail*, February 2, 2014, http://www.dailymail.co.uk/news/article-2550485/How-wife-trying-escape-marriage-weeks-killed-cooked-California-chef.html.

83. "Brazilian Goalkeeper Charged with Murdering Ex-Girlfriend," *Daily Telegraph* (London), July 30, 2010.

84. Jonathan Watch, "Outrage after Brazil Football Team Signs Goalkeeper Convicted of Killing Girlfriend," *Guardian*, March 13, 2017; Emily Shugerman, "Brazilian Goalkeeper Charged with Torture and Murder of Ex-Girlfriend—'Mistakes Happen. I'm Not a Bad Guy,'" *Independent*, March 21, 2017, http://www.independent.co.uk/news/world/americas/bruno-fernandes-de-souza-brazil-goalkeeper-torture-murder-ex-girlfriend-boa-esporte-mother-child-a7641836.html.

85. Kieran Crowley, *The Surgeon's Wife: A True Story of Obsession, Rage, and Murder* (New York: St. Martin's Paperbacks, 2001).

86. John Glatt, *To Have and to Kill: Nurse Melanie McGuire, an Illicit Affair, and the Gruesome Murder of Her Husband* (New York: St. Martin's Press, 2008).

87. Camille Kimball, *What She Always Wanted: A True Story of Marriage, Greed, and Murder* (New York: Berkley Books, 2010).

88. Cliff Linedecker, *The Murder of Laci Peterson* (Boca Raton, American Media, 2003).

89. Linda Rosencrance, *An Act of Murder* (New York: Pinnacle Books, 2006).

90. Christopher Lasch, *The Culture of Narcissism: American Life in an Age of Diminishing Expectations* (New York: W. W. Norton, 1977).

91. Jean Twenge and Keith Campbell, *The Narcissism Epidemic: Living in the Age of Entitlement* (New York: Atria Books, 2010).

92. Jean Twenge, *Generation Me: Why Today's Young Americans Are More Confident, Assertive, Entitled—and More Miserable Than Ever Before*, rev. and updated ed. (New York: Atria Books, 2014).

93. Justin Heckert, "A Positive Life: A Son Survived Being Injected with HIV by His Father," *Gentleman's Quarterly*, April 28, 2016, http://www.gq.com/story/son-survives-hiv-injected-by-father-brian-stewart.

94. Ian Lovett and Adam Nagourney, "Photos Led to Arrest in Abuse of Pupils," *New York Times*, January 31, 2012, http://www.nytimes.com/2012/02/01/education/former-teacher-61-arrested-in-california-on-abuse-charges.html.

95. Victoria Kim and Howard Blume, "L.A. Unified Alerted to Possible Sexual Misconduct by Berndt in 1983," *Los Angeles Times*, September 26, 2014.

96. Paul Thompson, "Father 'Decapitated and Dismembered Cerebral Palsy Son, 7, with a Meat Cleaver and Left His Head at Side of Road,'" August 16, 2011, *Daily Mail*, http://www.dailymail.co.uk/news/article-2026318/Jeremiah-Lee-Wright-decapitated-cerebral-palsy-son-Jori-Lirette-7-meat-cleaver.html; "Father 'Who Hacked His Disabled Son's Head Off and Left It by the Road for His Mom to See' Ruled Insane and Found NOT Guilty of Murder," *Daily Mail*, February 14, 2014, http://www.dailymail.co.uk/news/article-2559816/Father-hacked-disabled-sons-head-left-road-mom-ruled-insane-not-guilty-murder.html.

97. John E. Douglas, *Journey into Darkness* (New York: Pocket Books, 2010).

98. Michael Benson, *Murder in Connecticut: The Shocking Crime That Destroyed a Family and United a Community* (Guilford, CT: Lyons, 2008).

99. Shama Alexander, *Nutcracker: Money, Madness, and Murder; A Family Album* (New York: Dell Books, 1983).

100. Jonathan Coleman, *At Mother's Request: A True Story of Money, Murder, and Betrayal* (New York: Athenaeum, 1985).

101. Alexander, *Nutcracker*, pp. 326–27.

102. Ibid., p. 327.

103. Wesley Clarkson, *Whatever Mother Says* (New York: St. Martin's Paperbacks, 1995).

104. Keith Laidler, *Ranavalona: Female Caligula—the Mad Queen of Madagascar* (Chichester, West Sussex, England: John Wiley & Sons, 2005).

105. Leonard Shengold, *Soul Murder: The Effects of Childhood Abuse and Deprivation* (New Haven, CT: Yale University Press, 1989).

106. Cf. the Babylonian Talmud: Tractate Sanhedrin, folio 57a; three main crimes punishable by death are *Giluy Arayot*, *s'phikut haDam*, and *birkat haShem*—equating, respectively, with incest, murder ("spilling of blood"), and blasphemy.

107. Roger Scruton, *On Human Nature* (Princeton, NJ: Princeton University Press, 2017), p. 134.

108. Ibid., p. 135.

109. Ibid., p. 137.

110. Ibid.

111. Hazelwood and Michaud, *Dark Dreams*, p. 88.

112. *Wikipedia*, s.v. "Rape in English Law," last modified May 15, 2017, https://en.wikipedia.org/wiki/Rape_in_English_law.

113. Ecclesiastes 1:9.

114. See chap. 3, p. 111.

115. Thomas H. Cook, *Early Graves: The Shocking True Story of the Youngest Woman Sentenced to Death* (New York: Dutton, 1990).

116. Chris Berry-Dee, *Monster: My True Story* (London: John Blake, 2004).

117. "An Updated Definition of Rape," Department of Justice Archives, January 6, 2012, https://www.justice.gov/archives/opa/blog/updated-definition-rape.

118. David Lohr, "Amanda Johnson, Valerie Bartkey Allegedly Sexually Assaulted High School Student with Pliers," *Huffington Post*, February 2, 2012, http://www.huffingtonpost.com/2012/02/02/valerie-bartkey-amanda-johnson_n_1248510.html; Keith Edwards, "Woman Gets Probation in Bizarre Sexual Assault Case," WQOW, July 27, 2012, http://www.wqow.com/story/19132589/woman-gets-probation-in-bizarre-sexual-assault-case.

119. Brett Bodner, "Ohio Woman Charged with Raping, Robbing, Taxi Driver Who Was Held at Knifepoint by Accomplice," *Daily News*, April 10, 2017, http://www.nydailynews.com/news/crime/ohio-woman-charged-raping-robbing-taxi-driver-article-1.3039994.

120. Scruton, *On Human Nature*, p. 55.

121. À propos war, it is worth recalling that President Wilson spoke of the

events of 1914–1918 as a "war to end all wars." This was a tragic error rendered all the more fanciful for being uttered by a former professor of history. There hasn't been a year since (or before) 1918 during which the world has not witnessed a war.

122. It is noteworthy in this regard that the Golden Rule: "Do unto others as you would have them do unto you"—was a cornerstone of Jesus's teaching (Matthew 7:12). Akin to that was his message: "Love thy neighbor as thyself" (Matthew 19:19). The sentiment embodied in the Golden Rule was espoused also by Confucius several centuries earlier, and the message is also implicit in the Old Testament. Jesus spoke of the rule as summarizing what was already in the laws of Moses and in the teaching of the Old Testament prophets. We meet it again in the categorical imperative of Immanuel Kant in his 1785 *Groundwork of the Metaphysics of Morals*, where it stated that one should treat others as one wishes to be treated (or, in the negative: "Do not impose on others what you do not wish for yourself"). Even in wartime, one's actions can be proper and just, rather than evil—as noted in Lord Krishna's advice to the warrior Arjuna in the *Bhagavad Gita* (chap. 2, verse 45).

EPILOGUE

The framework for the *Anatomy of Evil* was a scale I had created called the "Gradations of Evil." Divided into twenty-two compartments, the scale began with Category 1—set aside for situations that were not evil at all. This represented acts of justified homicide or killing in self-defense, and established a dividing line between "evil" and "not evil." Category 2 was for crimes of passion, as when a spouse is caught in flagrante delicto with a stranger—and one or the other is killed by the discovering spouse. Because I defined evil the way the word is used in everyday language—namely, as an emotion-word we invoke when confronted with a crime that is startling and horrifying—even a crime of passion may evoke this response. Here is an example of a Category 2 crime: when Clara Harris drove to the hotel where her husband had been spending the night with his mistress—and then ran him over with her car as he left the hotel.[1] This was a "least evil" crime. At the far end of the scale, Category 22, I placed men (and the occasional woman) who subjected their victims to extreme torture or disfigurement before finally murdering them. Most of the persons occupying the latter categories—roughly from 10 through 22—showed strong psychopathic personality traits: they were for the most part callous, exploitative predators devoid of remorse for what they did to their victims. I also emphasized that the concept of evil is peculiar to the human species, given our big brains, and our awareness of death, we are able to kill others of our own species, with malice aforethought, and resulting from motives of Pride, Anger, Envy, Lust, or Greed—five of Saint Gregory's Seven Deadly Sins. (I can't get myself worked up much over Sloth and Gluttony.) We are very different from one of the other social species, namely, the lion. The mother lion chases after gazelles to put food on the table, so to say, for the family. The daddy lion establishes his "territory" and restricts his aggression to actions designed to ward off intruders that invade his turf. How different are these acts from our own?

But lions do not kill for sport or out of animosity or prejudice or hatred. Perhaps some of the higher apes—chimpanzees, for example—have a capacity for (human-like) trickery to gain advantage over rivals. Whether they know in some fashion that they will one day die—and that they can hasten the death of a rival—remains unclear.

What I did not emphasize in *The Anatomy of Evil* was the historical—or, in contemporary times, the chronological—aspects of evil. I also restricted my examples (with a few exceptions) to evil in peacetime. Evil has always been with us, both among individuals in peacetime and among warring enemies and other manifestations of group conflict. And evil will always be with us. As regards war and group conflict, I am not referring to "fair fights" between opponents who kill one another in hopes of persevering, but who avoid committing atrocities—as in the 1415 battle between the English and the French at Agincourt. I am referring to the innumerable campaigns of genocide and torture committed by the likes of the Roman emperor Caligula; by Pope Innocent III in his crusade against the Albigensians in the early thirteenth century; and by Tomás de Torquemada and the Spanish Inquisition. Other examples include the 1572 St. Bartholomew's Day massacre of the Huguenots in Catholic France; the persecution of the Spaniards by Napoleon's troops in 1809; the 1915 Turkish genocide of the Armenians; the Nazi atrocities of the 1940s; and Pol Pot's genocide against his fellow Cambodians in the 1970s. And then there was Brazil's torture and persecution of suspected "leftists" in the 1970s, the tortures and genocidal acts against the Bosnians by the Serbs under Slobodan Milošević in the 1990s, and now the acts of the Islamic jihadists in our day (of which, more below). This list just scratches the surface. The full story of evil in wartime would require a second book—and a very thick one at that.

What has made our species special is, of course, our ingenuity. We learned to control fire, and—much later—to control ice. When the mother lion fells a gazelle or an antelope, she cannot cook it to make the meat more digestible; she cannot put the remains in the fridge for next Thursday. She and her family must have their dinner then and there. We are able to use fire for cooking, and for innumerable other good things—but also for evil. Examples of the latter are legion, but we can mention just a few: when in France King Philip IV was in debt, he called the Knights Templar "heretics" and took their money. He arrested their leader, Jacques de Molay, on Friday, October 13, 1307 (the true origin of our phobia about "Friday the 13th"), and had him burned at the stake five months later. A century later, the nineteen-year-old heroine Jeanne d'Arc, who led the French to victory over the English—was burned at the stake in 1431. In our time: the pogrom in 1941 when, during the Nazi regime, 340 Jews were locked in a barn in the Polish town of Jedwabne and burned to death; the immolation of the Czech people in the town of Lidice as punishment for their killing the Nazi SS general Reinhard Heydrich in 1942; and the crematoria of Auschwitz. In June 2016, another evil use of fire occurred, namely, the burning of nineteen Yazidi women who had been locked in iron cages in Mosul, Iraq, by their Islamic State (ISIS) captors.[2]

It is hard to think of any product of human ingenuity that cannot be used for evil purposes, as well as for good. We use fire for smelting ore to extract metal with which to make, among other things, knives—to cut our meat or to behead our opponents. We use rope to tie packages, or to hang our enemies. Trains, cars, and planes—they speed our travel but can be put to evil purposes as well. Trains took victims to concentration camps; cars are used to run people over (as when Tomohiro Katoh ran his car into a crowd, killing ten,[3] or when on Bastille Day in 2016 Tunisian jihadist Lahaouiej-Bouhlel drove his truck into a crowd of celebrants in the French city of Nice, killing eighty-nine people[4]); planes were used by the German Luftwaffe in April 1936 as they practiced the efficacy of bombs (for future use in their eventual Blitzkrieg in Europe) by obliterating the Basque town of Guernica—the atrocity later immortalized by Picasso in his masterpiece by the same name. We have created medicines through plant extracts and our own chemical genius that render surgery painless—using ether and cocaine and opiates. We have learned to kill rats and other pests with arsenic and cyanide and a host of other agents—all also poisons, used in innumerable murders. A particularly chilling example comes from my hometown of Syracuse, New York, in which James Cahill III, the feckless (and jobless) husband of Jill, struck her on the head with a baseball bat in the spring of 1998 during an argument prompted by her plan to divorce him and marry another man.[5] He intended to kill her, but she survived and was making a gradual recovery in a hospital. Several months later he sneaked into the hospital, dressed as a female janitor—wearing a wig, and carrying a mop—entered her room, and poisoned her to death with cyanide that he had obtained under false pretenses as though for use in a photo lab. Furthermore, several murders of spouses have been committed by doctors and other hospital personnel, using the curare-like agent succinylcholine, which is used in surgical procedures. The most notorious case occurred in 1965, when thirty-two-year-old Dr. Carl Coppolino murdered his wife, thirty-two-year-old Dr. Carmela Musetto, so he could be free to marry his lover.[6]

Another example of the evil aspect of something otherwise good concerns radioactivity. Now that we live in the atomic age, for example, much of our power is generated by nuclear fuels, which are good for mankind because they are more environment-friendly than burning coal. As always, there is an evil downside. In the early years of this century, for example, Alexander Litvinenko, a former officer in the Russian Federal Security Service and the KGB, had some unflattering things to say about how Vladimir Putin came to power. On the first of November 2006, as Litvinenko was lunching on sushi at a restaurant in London's Piccadilly Circus, another Russian agent poisoned him with polonium-210. Polonium-210 is a highly radioactive metal that does have some "good" properties (as a heat source for thermoelectric generators), but it also has a potentially evil property (as a poison with no possible antidote). Litvinenko died three weeks later.[7]

The preceding remarks will, I hope, convince the reader that events of the sort that elicit in us the reaction, "That is evil!" stretch back to antiquity and continue not only to the present day but also beyond, as an unwelcome but ineradicable element in the tangled skein of human interaction. À propos antiquity, I could have begun with persons or groups well before Emperor Caligula from scarcely two millennia ago. It's just that Caligula is one of the few evil men in antiquity about whose repugnant (and evil) acts of sadism we have ample written records. A confounding factor is the tendency for persons of the "older generation" to suppose that the younger generation is somehow less worthy and more apt to indulge in reprehensible actions. There is a long history here. The fourth-century ascetic preacher St. John Chrysostom (349–407), whose name means "golden-tongued," believed that the adolescent boys of his day, wearing their hair so long and living (as he saw it) frivolous lives, were of a generation worse than his own. Yet here we are, sixteen centuries later, still inventing wonderful, life-enhancing things, still—for the most part—leading commendable lives. In trying to assess whether or not life is getting worse, I recently prepared two PowerPoint presentations. One focused on "Evil in the Good Old Days"; the other I called "The New Evil." Both dealt with evil in peacetime, as it would have been absurd to dwell on evil during wartime. I can think of no century in human history as horrific and atrocity-ridden as the twentieth century. Besides the genocidal outbreaks alluded to above, there were the persecutions of the leftists in Argentina under Juan Perón; in Chile under Augusto Pinochet; and in Colombia during *La Violencia* in the 1950s. There was the massacre of Ibos in southern Nigeria in the 1960s and the genocidal mass killing of Tutsis by the Hutus in Rwanda in the 1990s. There was the starvation of the Ukrainians under Stalin (and, later, the Gulags in Siberia) and the massacres in China's "Great Leap Forward" under Mao Zedong in the late 1950s.

The human suffering, the dreadfulness of the atrocities, and in many instances, their pornographic quality of the sadism and torture make it impossible—unseemly, even—to assign gradations to the level of awfulness. But there is something special about the Japanese invasion of Nanking during the Sino-Japanese wars of 1937–1945—so thoroughly and disturbingly documented by Iris Chang in her 1997 book *The Rape of Nanking*.[8] Earlier I mentioned the good versus the evil use of metal knives. Shortly after the invasion of Nanking, in 1937, the Japanese soldiers instituted a beheading contest with swords. Which soldier could behead the most Chinese townspeople in a ten-minute period? The goal was to reach one hundred. The winner: a soldier named Mukai (106 victims), who bettered his rival, Noda (only 105).[9] Their accomplishments were cheered, alongside their photos, in the Japanese newspapers. As for the suffering and indignities of the thousands of women, young and old, who were raped and tortured by the Japanese soldiers, those who have the stamina to read Iris Chang's book can learn the details. Mercifully, Chang's book contains only a few photographs of the atrocities. Also published in 1997, the book by the same name, *The Rape of Nanking*, by Shi Young and James Yin contains much greater photographic documentation—but also a commentary on the "killing as entertainment" by the Japanese soldiers, with their *Bushido* mentality. As the authors put it: "One way in which the Japanese fascists overshadowed their German counterparts in massacre was the abnormal enjoyment they derived from the killing. . . . Many Japanese soldiers carried heads severed from refugee victims on the ends of their rifles and strolled down the streets, exhibiting their achievement with great joy."[10] Compounding the evil of Nanking is the refusal of the Japanese to acknowledge, let alone express remorse, for what happened there—with the exception of Emperor Hirohito's youngest brother, Prince Mikasa. In an interview with the newspaper Yomiuri Shimbun, the prince, an outspoken pacifist—who died in 2016 at age one hundred, gave details of the atrocities against the Chinese and openly condemned the actions of the Japanese soldiers. Copies of his statements were later quashed and destroyed by the military authorities—except for one copy discovered by a Kobe University professor.[11] The behavior of the Japanese stands in marked contrast to that of the Germans, who in the post-Nazi era have written a whole library of books offering full accounts of, and expressing deep regret for, what their countrymen did during the Holocaust. We still await expressions of acknowledgment and regret from the Turkish government for the genocide of Armenians, a third of whose population were killed by shootings, burnings, and death marches a hundred and two years ago (and thirty years before Hitler employed the same techniques).[12]

As terrible as the twentieth century was during times of war and group conflict, if we look at America in the era of the Armenian and Nazi genocides (1915–1945), the situation is much less grim. But in reviewing newspaper archives and other sources beginning in 1900, I sensed that I could discern a difference in the nature and varieties of evil acts—in peacetime, that is—within our country, even when our soldiers were engaged in foreign wars. There seemed to be a coarsening during the latter half of the century, especially after the mid-1960s. Certain evil acts occurred then that either were very rare or had no parallel in the earlier decades.

Societal changes are difficult to discern when they are just beginning to happen; often they are hard to spot even in retrospect. But a number of changes, especially regarding gender roles, took place in the United States after World War II that may have played a role. During the war, in the absence of men, many women had to work in jobs traditionally held by men (Rosie the Riveter comes to mind). Many of these women achieved a measure of financial independence as a result, and they were less at the mercy of husbands who were domineering or cruel. The divorce rate, which was at 0.7 per 1,000 people in 1900, rose gradually to 2.2 in 1960; then it increased rapidly to 3.5 in 1970 and to 5.2 in 1980. It has remained between 3.5 and 4 ever since.[13] In 1960, the oral contraceptive pill (often called just "the pill") became available, giving women still-greater freedom over their private and reproductive lives. Further rights to privacy came in 1973 with the landmark *Roe v. Wade* ruling by the Supreme Court, which granted women the right to a decision regarding abortion. These changes (divorce, birth control, and abortion) have sparked controversy in many quarters. The abortion-rights decision has been fought mostly on religious grounds. But underneath the rhetoric is a perhaps even deeper psychological issue. Men can no longer take comfort in the "Me Tarzan, You Jane" mentality that has been prominent ever since the dawn of our species; men, being physically stronger and charged up with testosterone-laced aggressiveness, have for millennia felt like the "boss." Even a working-class man was king in his own house. For example, in my medical-school class of 1954, there were seventy-nine men and four women; the latter were resented because they were, so it was said, taking a good job (being a doctor) away from four deserving men. Six decades later, the ratio is about even; perhaps the women outnumber the men a bit.[14] I have noted in other publications that the numbers of men committing serial sexual homicide (almost all of whom come from the working class) began to rise precipitously in the 1960s. Before that time, there were, since that type of evil began in the 1870s, only two or three cases per decade. I see this dramatic increase as a kind of male backlash against this new crop of "uppity" women who dare to take control over their own lives. I see this kind of male backlash even more commonly in the contemporary custody disputes, in which the divorcee fathers (especially rich fathers) often prevail over affectionate and deserving mothers of young children. The fathers, relying on trumped-up charges (such as "parental alienation") against their former wives, gain custody of the children, with whom they then spend little time—to the detriment of the children's psychological health. This is one form of the "New Evil" in my PowerPoint presentation. A related problem is the high divorce rate and the phenomenon, more prevalent since the 1960s, of women raising children alone, without fathers (or even without knowing the fathers)—which heightens the risk significantly for the sons to become wayward and to have criminal records by the time they enter their twenties.[15] Actually, until 1970, black men and women were only a little less likely to have been "ever married" than white men and women.[16] But since 1970 that changed drastically: white men and women were two to three times more likely to have been in the ever-married category. There are other factors as well that predispose people to crime, violence, and the acts that we call evil. But this is a good moment to compare evil in peacetime in the years before the 1960s—and evil as it manifests itself in the contemporary period.

EVIL IN THE "GOOD OLD DAYS"

Reviewing the crime records in our country starting in 1900 and working our way through to 1960, I found that there were some that carried the shock value worthy of the word *evil* as I have defined it here. But these cases were comparatively few and far between.

The earliest one in my collection is the murder of Grace Brown, a coworker in the skirt factory owned by the uncle of Chester Gillette, who took a job there when he dropped out of prep school.[17] A sexual relationship developed between Chester and Grace, and she became pregnant. In this pre-pill, pre-abortion, pre-any-alternative era of 1906, she naturally urged him to marry her. Chester was not so inclined. Instead, he invited her to a rowboat lunch in one of New York's Adirondack lakes. When they were far enough out in the lake, Chester struck her with a tennis racket and shoved her into the water to drown. He was arrested the next day, when her body was found. He was tried, convicted, and executed in the electric chair in 1908.[18] This became the basis for Theodore Dreiser's famous novel: *An American Tragedy*, published in 1925. Gillette would rate a Category 10 in my scale of evil: *killers of people "in the way" . . . egocentric, but not totally psychopathic*. A selfish man, that is, who lacked the courage and moral center to "man up" and do the right thing. But he was without the extravagant features of sadism and torture, where unequivocal evil resides.

A few years later, in 1910, Dr. Bennett Hyde was hoping for a life of luxury with his bride of the year before, Frances Swope—the niece of an elderly millionaire.[19] But her uncle had entrusted his estate to another man. This spurred Dr. Hyde to embark on a program of what I call "accelerated inheritance"—to which end he poisoned to death old Thomas Swope with pills. He also poisoned five other beneficiaries (one died) and the executor of the will—who also died. Arrested and tried (in three separate courts), Hyde was convicted at first but later cleared when the last jury did not consider Hyde's guilt as proven beyond doubt. He had used cyanide and arsenic to dispatch his victims, lying to the Court that he used the cyanide to remove silver nitrate stains from his fingers, or else to kill cockroaches in his office.[20] In personality, Hyde was quite a departure from his father, who was a Baptist preacher. The doctor would be placed in Category 14: *a ruthlessly self-centered psychopathic schemer*. He represents a variety of evil, surely, but not much out of the ordinary among those committing murder.

The notorious case of Robert Stroud stands in contrast to that of Dr. Hyde. Where Dr. Hyde's murders represented malice aforethought prompted by greed—a prototypical example of evil—Stroud's murders appear as reactions on the part of an impulsive man seeking revenge for what he saw as wrongdoings of others. Born in 1890, Stroud, when he was thirteen, ran away from his abusive father, working later as a pimp in an Alaska bar some five years later.[21] Stroud was sentenced to twelve years in prison, where he gained a reputation as an angry, confrontational inmate. In 1916 he killed a prison guard, a crime for which he was sentenced to hang—though later the sentence was revised to life imprisonment at Leavenworth in Kansas. It was there that he began to raise and treat injured sparrows, eventually publishing a book titled *Diseases of Canaries*—in 1933. When it was discovered that he had been making alcohol in his cell, he was transferred to Alcatraz in the San Francisco Bay, where he spent the remainder of his life.[22] Toward the end of his seventy-three years, and with his genius-level IQ of 134, Stroud had written a second book on the history of the penal system. He had become a modest man, no longer a danger to society, and an example of self-improvement and rehabilitation—thanks in no way to the penal system, but to the effects of aging. Though he was diagnosed repeatedly as a psychopath, I regard him as what is sometimes called a "secondary" psychopath, a person who suffered intense abuse in childhood, to the point of developing certain psychopathic-like traits, yet without the incapacity for remorse and empathy. Unlike the famous serial killer Ted Bundy (a true psychopath), Stroud (whom we know as the "Birdman of Alcatraz") would fit in my Category 8: *nonpsychopathic persons with smoldering rage, who kill when the rage is ignited.*

And then there was Albert Fish, a mentally ill (psychotic) man born in 1870 in Washington, DC, into a family of other mentally ill persons. From age five, he was raised in an orphanage where he was treated with great cruelty—which he experienced as sexually arousing. That became one of a whole menu of paraphilias he exhibited, that is, conditions in which sexual arousal depends on engaging in behaviors that are atypical and extreme. Being aroused by enforced suffering would be called masochism, but Fish also experienced arousal by inflicting pain (sadism), from ingesting urine and feces (urophilia and coprophlia), from sex with children (pedophilia), from eating human flesh (cannibalism), and from sending obscene letters to women (scatologia). He was bisexual, having married and fathered six children, yet engaging in sex with children (mostly boys) under age six; Fish was, however, devoted to his own children, and never beat or abused them.[23] He mutilated himself (injecting dozens of needles into his groin: "infibulation")—but also subjected others to torture (sadomasochism). Fish was subject to auditory hallucinations, imagining himself under the direct influence of St. John the Apostle or else imagining that God was commanding him to sexually mutilate children. In 1928, he lured an eight-year-old girl, Grace Budd, to an empty house in the suburbs around New York City. There, he stripped her naked, strangled her, and then cut her body into small pieces. He then sent her mother a letter (under an alias) telling her ". . . how sweet and tender her little ass was, roasted in the oven."[24] When finally captured and arrested, he spoke of having had two involuntary ejaculations while killing her (sexual sadism). Fish had earlier been a patient at Bellevue Psychiatric Hospital. But instead of keeping him permanently in that facility, he had been released—free to kill and cannibalize Grace and several other children. There was a trial, at the end of which the jury concluded that he was insane but should be executed anyway, given the gruesomeness and repugnance of his murders. He was executed in the electric chair in Sing Sing in 1936.[25] Nowadays a man like Fish would have been remanded for life to a forensic psychiatric hospital, since (a) he could never be restored to normalcy, and (b) the public would have every right to protest against the release of such a man. On my scale, he would be in Category 20: *Torture-murderers, with torture the primary motive, but in psychotic persons.* Unlike the preceding three cases, Fish was clearly an "exotic"—not at all an "ordinary" murderer of the sort the police encounter in their tours of duty.

In the same era as Fish, Ruth Brown Snyder, born in New York City in 1895, had become furious with her husband, Albert, for keeping a picture of his ten-years-deceased fiancée, Jessie Guishard, on the wall of their home, for also naming his boat after her, and for constantly extolling her virtues as "the finest woman I ever met."[26] Ruth began an affair with Henry Gray, in the meantime persuading her husband to take out a life-insurance policy. She then inserted via forgery a double-indemnity clause—were the death to occur by violence. Ruth and Henry embarked upon a plan to kill Albert. Like the proverbial cat with nine lives, Albert survived their first seven bungled attempts at murder. But on the eighth (March 20, 1927), the pair garroted him and stuffed chloroform-soaked rags on his nose, ultimately killing him. Ruth and Henry were apprehended the next day, and they tried to pretend that a burglar had killed Albert. The crime attracted a lot of attention. Among those attending the trial was the author Damon Runyon, who called it the "dumb-bell murder case" because it was indeed very stupidly carried out.[27] Both received the death penalty and were duly executed in the electric chair on the same day (Ruth first) a mere 298 days later—in Sing Sing, on January 12, 1928. To the astonishment of contemporary audiences, murder was murder and the death penalty was a death penalty in that era—even for so unexceptional a crime as the murder of a spouse for spite and greed. Nowadays the death penalty is more apt to be carried out, if at all, for crimes more spectacular and heinous than spousal murder in which no torture was involved. Ruth Snyder would be an example of Category 8 in my scale: *rage-ignited in nonpsychopathic persons, who kill when the rage is ignited.*

A much more exceptional crime for the mid-1920s was that committed by Gordon Northcott, who was born in Canada in 1906.[28] In 1924, Gordon moved with his parents to Los Angeles and then asked them to purchase a chicken farm in Wineville, not far from the Mexican border. He went to the Wineville farm with his thirteen-year-old cousin, Sanford Clark. Gordon was a gay man with marked sadistic tendencies;

he molested his cousin, and also made Sanford an accomplice in luring boys (often from Mexico) to the farm, where he would rent them to pedophiles. The rent-monies helped keep the farm going, unbeknownst to his parents until later, when he was arrested. Gordon would rape some of the young boys himself (perhaps as many as twenty), then kill them with an axe. He would then dissolve the bodies in lye and discard the remains in the desert, compelling his cousin to help. There may have been a genetic component to his psychopathology: Gordon's father died in an insane asylum; his uncle died in San Quentin after being convicted for murder; and even his mother, Sarah Louise Northcott, helped in burning the body parts of the murdered boys, in hopes of destroying evidence against her son. He was finally arrested in 1928, thanks in part to the testimony of his cousin, Sanford. Northcott's crimes—of serial sexual homicide (rather new for the time), sodomy, and torture sent him to the gallows; he was hanged in 1930. There was no hesitation in calling his crimes evil; the bad publicity surrounding the name of Wineville, where the "Chicken Coop Murders" occurred, led to the name of the town being changed to Loma Mira. Northcott's crimes are examples of Category 22: *psychopathic torture-murderers, with torture the primary motive.* Most persons in this category are male serial killers.

Whereas the Northcott crimes were motivated by Lust, the crime in the next example was prompted by another of the Seven Deadly Sins: Greed. Little is known about the early years of Leonard Ewing Scott (who was born in 1897, locale unknown).[29] As an adult, he acquired a reputation for preying on wealthy older women. When he was fifty-two, he married Evelyn Kiernan Lewis Pettit Mumper (née Throsby)—a twice divorced, twice widowed wealthy woman of sixty-three whom he had met at a society party in Mexico. Soon after the marriage, Scott took over control of Evelyn's finances, telling her broker that he, as a "skilled investor" could better handle her affairs. He also intimidated Evelyn physically, and he told her friends that she was a serious alcoholic and becoming quite ill—all of which was untrue. He made up more fanciful, and apocalyptic, stories about a possible atomic war—which he claimed "necessitated" converting her holdings into more liquid assets, ostensibly for her protection, but actually for his nefarious purposes. After five years of marriage, in May 1955, Evelyn disappeared. Scott told people she had either been hospitalized or else had run off. Evelyn's brother became suspicious and began an investigation. No body was ever found, though Evelyn's dentures were discovered among the ashes near the incinerator on their Los Angeles property. Scott was convicted—in a landmark case (murder convictions are difficult to obtain, absent a body)—and sentenced to life in prison. He was released in 1978 because of his age, and he died at the age of ninety-one in 1987. Scott would be in Category 14—though the level of evil was greater than that of Ruth Snyder: Scott was a psychopath motivated also by greed, prompted not by the "hot" emotion of rage but by the "cold" mind-set of malice aforethought.

Born to a poor Nebraskan family in 1938, the third of seven children, Charles Starkweather had been bullied at school because of his bowed legs and a speech impediment.[30] Though of average IQ, he was so nearsighted that he was barely able to read. He got into many fights at school and was deeply ashamed of his poverty. In his late teens, he got into a verbal battle with his father, which left him feeling humiliated. His personality gradually changed: at first he was described as "the kindest person you've ever seen . . . he'd do anything for you."[31] But eventually he became harsh and cruel. At age nineteen, he befriended a fourteen-year-old girl, Caril Fugate. His wish to marry her was quashed by her parents. At that point, the young couple embarked on a theft-and-murder spree, as they drove toward California. Both were fired by two hopes: to get away from their parents, and to end their poverty by commencing a life of (lucrative) crime. They committed a spree of eleven murders in rapid succession, the first being that of a gas-station attendant in Lincoln, Nebraska, in November 1957. They had robbed him of one hundred dollars. Charles then felt transcended, as though he were able to live outside the law and commit any crime without guilt or fear of repercussions. Two months later, he killed Caril's mother and stepfather. One of his next victims was a wealthy Nebraska businessman. The couple stole the man's expensive car, then abandoned it because it was so recognizable. Another stolen car got them as far as Wyoming—but when the car stalled, Charles got into a fight with a motorist who stopped to help him. A policeman came, and, after a gunfight, the young killers were arrested. Charles and Caril were tried in a Nebraska court where he received the death penalty, and Caril, because of her young age, was given a life sentence and later paroled. Starkweather was executed in the electric chair at age twenty-one in June 1959, seven months after the trial. I had placed Starkweather in Category 15: *psychopathic cold-blooded spree or multiple murderers*. Had he lived in prison into his fifties or sixties, it is not clear whether Starkweather would still appear as a callous psychopath. The harsh circumstances of his early life may have nudged him into becoming a kind of "secondary" psychopath, still capable of changing into a more socially acceptable person once he grew past the impetuosity and impulsivity of adolescence.

Starkweather's execution in mid-1959 can serve as a dividing line between the preceding era and what I have designated as the "New Evil," commencing in or shortly after the 1960s. Besides the aftereffects of World War II—the emergence of women's rights, the surge in the divorce rate (and consequently a larger number of children no longer raised in two-parent families), the increase in murder rates also (more than doubling between 1960 and 1980), and the drop in the marriage rate—there were other factors that appear to have had an influence on evil in American culture. Some of these factors were dramatic, such as the Vietnam War and the demoralization that accompanied what the public saw largely as an embarrassingly wasteful and brutal expedition. Also, there was the surge in drug abuse; the "just alcohol" culture of the earlier era was replaced with the shift toward marijuana, cocaine, LSD, amphetamines, phencyclidine ("angel dust"), hallucinogens like psilocybin ("shrooms"), and a host of other substances created in the recent years. The drug epidemic was helped along by the misplaced enthusiasm of drug-promoting gurus like Timothy Leary (who in the early 1960s popularized the catchphrase *turn on*, *tune in*, *drop out*—with the "help" of LSD) and Richard Alpert (who reinvented himself as a "Hindu" guru, Ram Dass, meaning "God's Servant").[32] The spike in the murder rate in the 1980s was due in good measure to the crack-cocaine epidemic in that decade. The culture in America in the 1980s took a more narcissistic turn and became coarser—which has contributed, I believe, to an increase in the kinds of heartless and sadistic murders and other acts of hitherto rarely encountered selfishness (as in many of the current custody cases) that have occurred over the past half century. This has been happening even as the murder rate itself has begun to dip down from a height of 10.7 per 100,000 persons annually in 1980—to about half that in the recent years (i.e., since 2010).[33] The shockingly evil crimes of Northcott and Fish, which were once or twice a decade phenomena in the pre-1960 era, are now occurring several times a year. In particular, mass murders in the United States have risen exponentially since 1960—largely as a result of the greater availability of semiautomatic guns—from about 29 notable (i.e., making big headlines) mass murders between the start of the century and 1960 to 215 between 1960 and 2016.[34] In the examples that follow, I have grouped them within a few categories, focusing on some men and women the nature of whose evil acts was rarely encountered in the pre-1960 period. Many of these crimes beg for a new set of adjectives, beyond the usual—*gruesome*, *heinous*, *atrocious*—we resort to in speaking of evil acts. We feel as though we are in presence of the devil incarnate or a devouring beast. More appropriate words might be *diabolical*, *satanic*, *fiendish*, or else *savage* and *barbaric*.

THE "NEW EVIL"

Casualties of the Internet: The modern Internet had its origins in the early 1960s; its use became widespread in the late 1980s. Among its numerous good uses is that of being a readily accessible, worldwide encyclopedia. But, like all human inventions, there comes with it a potential for evil. Slanderous comments and embarrassing images can be posted and go "viral"—to the detriment of certain "target" individuals. This was the case with two students at Rutgers University in September 2010. Dharun Ravi made a secret closed-circuit TV film of his gay roommate, Tyler Clementi, kissing another man.[35] The film was put on the Internet and viewed by many. Three days later, Tyler committed suicide by jumping off of the George Washington Bridge. There was a trial, and Ravi faced only a modest fine and jail sentence for cyberbullying, but no additional charges for the resultant suicide. This was a new kind of crime, and the law is not yet able to deal with it adequately. There is a common principle in law, called "But . . . for"—which relates to proximate cause. In this case, *but for* the broadcast of the invasive film footage by which Ravi meant to cause his roommate extreme embarrassment, Clementi would not have committed suicide. Granted, not every gay man subjected to this form of public shaming would have taken his life. But Tyler Clementi did, so making and showing the film constituted proximate cause of his death—and equates, therefore, to murder. More problematical from a legal standpoint are the suicides of four adolescent girls between 2010 and 2013: Audrie Pott, Amanda Todd, Phoebe Prince, and Rehtaeh Parsons—all of whom had been the victims of bullying. In several instances, sexually explicit photos were distributed via the Internet. In the case of Audrie Pott, three boys, having raped her at a party, took photos and distributed them.[36] A then-unknown man blackmailed Amanda Todd into exposing her breasts via webcam.[37] Images of Rehtaeh Parsons, who was also raped, were released to the media.[38] Half a dozen classmates of Phoebe Prince put "unkind words" on Facebook.[39] All four of the girls committed suicide. In the latter case, envy seemed to be the force behind the bullying: Phoebe was unusually attractive (as were the other three girls); those who bullied her were quite plain. But because of the young age of the perpetrators who could be identified in these four cases (with the exception of Todd's bully), the judges at their trials did little more than sentence them to community service or probation.[40] In 2017, the man responsible for blackmailing Amanda Todd was identified (only the name "Aydin C." has been revealed). A Dutch court found him guilty of cyberbullying and sentenced him to eleven years in prison; he faces yet another trial in Canada for extortion and possession of child pornography. Suicide by public shaming is not "inevitable" the way murder by shooting or stabbing is, so lawmakers remain flummoxed regarding how best to deal with this variety of New Evil.[41]

Kidnapped for Sex: In times gone by, the usual motive for kidnapping was greed, which was to be satisfied by the paying of ransom money. The first American case to receive wide attention was that of the abduction in 1874 of four-year-old Charlie Ross in Philadelphia by two men who demanded a ransom of $20,000.[42] The kidnappers were killed, the ransom never paid, and the boy never found. More notorious was the kidnapping in 1932 of Charles Lindbergh's baby, Charles Lindbergh Jr., for which a $75,000 ransom was paid, though the child had been killed.[43] In Kansas City in September 1953, six-year-old Bobbi Greenlease was abducted by Austin Hall and his accomplice, Bonnie Hendy.[44] Hendy posed as Bobby's "aunt" so as to fool the nun at his school into releasing the boy, as if to visit his "suddenly hospitalized" mother. The father paid a $600,000 ransom, but the boy was killed; the kidnapping murderers were tried and executed eighty-two days later. In the post-1960 era, Gary Krist kidnapped Barbara Mackle, a twenty-year-old Emory University student, then buried her underground with air pipes and food; he offered to release her, pending the payment of a $500,000 ransom.[45] The sum was paid, and the young woman rescued. In less affluent countries, ransom money is still the main motive. The kidnappings in Juarez, Mexico, and other Central and South American countries come to mind. But, in America, sex has recently replaced money as motive. Among the most notorious of cases is Phil Garrido's kidnapping of eleven-year-old Jaycee Dugard in 1991.[46] He kept her as a sex slave in his backyard for eighteen years, siring two daughters by her, before she and the girls finally managed to escape in 2009. Phil had been a fairly normal boy until, at fourteen, he crashed his brother's motorcycle, suffered a head injury with frontal-lobe damage, and began to develop rape fantasies, along with abusing drugs heavily.[47] Ariel Castro, in contrast, was a psychopath (without head injury) who, starting in 2002, kidnapped three adolescent girls in Cleveland, Ohio.[48] He kept them imprisoned, and often chained, in his house for ten to twelve years (he had a child by one of them, Amanda Berry), until they managed to escape. Castro committed suicide in prison. In Canada, twenty-eight-year-old Michael Rafferty and his accomplice, Terri-Lynne McClintic, abducted eight-year-old Tori Stafford in 2009, as the girl was leaving school to go home.[49] After sexually assaulting the girl, Rafferty beat her to death with a claw hammer. Both he and McClintic were convicted and sentenced to life in prison. In 2002, thirty-seven-year-old Michael Devlin, a gay man who worked in a pizzeria in Kirkwood, Missouri, kidnapped an eleven-year-old boy, Shawn Hornbeck, as he was riding his bike to a friend's house.[50] He kept the boy sequestered as his sex slave for five years, until 2007—when Devlin was arrested four days after kidnapping yet another boy, William Ownby. He had also made pornographic films of one of the boys—for which he was sentenced to 170 years in prison, years that were added to the 1,850 years he was already sentenced to for the multiple other crimes against the two boys. Also in 2002, Brian Mitchell, a middle-aged man with religious delusions of being a "Davidic King" broke into the Salt Lake City home of the Smart family, and abducted at knifepoint fourteen-year-old Elizabeth Smart.[51] After installing her in his camp, he would pray aloud for her to have sex with him, as if to fulfill some divine obligation. Police rescued Elizabeth nine months later. Both Mitchell and his accomplice, Wanda Barzee, were later convicted. Mitchell received life in prison, while Barzee was given fifteen years. The cases cited here, and many similar ones (including several highly publicized ones in Europe) over the past thirty years constitute one of the most dreadful forms of the New Evil. It's a double evil, in a way, since not only do the kidnapped victims suffer, but their families suffer—torment, for months or for years, of not knowing whether their children are alive or dead.

Criminal Disfigurement: Intentional use of corrosive substances to disfigure someone is a crime with a long history. Acid attacks with sulfuric acid—an ingredient of vitriol (used to purify gold)—were know in sixteenth-century Europe. In some crimes of passion, fueled by jealousy and betrayal, a woman might toss the acid at the face of a female rival or a disloyal mate. Such women were called *vitrioleuses*; in the nineteenth century, Art Nouveau artists at times painted portraits of such women. But now, for the most part, it is persons in low- or middle-income countries who commit such crimes, especially India, Bangladesh, Jamaica, Pakistan, and Iran.[52] More often, it will be a man who disfigures a woman who has rejected him; lye may be used as often as acid. These are malicious crimes involving premeditation and prompted by vengeance, usually against some actual or perceived romantic rejection. They are now rare in affluent countries like the United States or Britain, where most cases known to me have occurred in the past half century. And since beauty is more prized in women than in men, this crime is now more apt to involve a jealous or rejected man seeking to exact vengeance by destroying a woman's beauty. At the dawn of the New Evil era, Burton Pugach, who was married at the time, fell in love with another woman, Linda Riss, then in her twenties.[53] Burton kept stalling in his promises to leave his wife and marry Linda. When she finally tried to leave him, he tossed lye in her face, saying: "If I can't have you, no one else will, and when I get finished with you, no one will want you!" Linda was left blinded in the 1959 crime. Pugach spent fourteen years in prison for the assault. But, as Ovid once wrote—*Amor omnia vincit*. "Love conquers all." When he was finally released, he and Linda actually married—and lived happily from that time forward, until her death at seventy-five in 2013.

In 1980 a lye assault went beyond disfigurement and blindness. Thirty-four-year-old Patricia Worrell, studying for a law degree in California, had been engaged to Richard Morton Gilman—a forty-seven-year-old law school graduate who had failed his bar exam.[54] She broke off the engagement, but when Gilman insisted that she return the engagement ring (it had been his grandmother's), she refused. They quarreled violently, and he then hired a "hit-man" to throw lye in her face. The assailant threw a whole quart of lye at her, some of which she inadvertently swallowed. The lye burned through her esophagus and then an artery; she died ten days later. Gilman, now in his late eighties, is serving a life-sentence in prison.

In 1986, a less dreadful fate awaited twenty-four-year-old Marla Hanson, a New York fashion model and aspiring actress.[55] After Marla rejected the advances of her landlord, twenty-eight-year-old Steven Roth, he contrived to have two men accost her, one of whom slashed her face with a knife. The three men each received a fifteen-year sentence. Marla, after extensive plastic surgery, went through a long period of depression but eventually made an excellent recovery. She is now married; the couple have a teenaged daughter, and Marla is a strong advocate of anti-stalking laws.

Much less fortunate was Carmen Tarleton, the estranged wife of Herbert Rodgers. In 2007, he broke into her Vermont house and doused her with lye, giving her chemical burns over 90 percent of her body; he also beat her with a baseball bat—all on the false assumption that she had been "cheating" on him.[56] Rodgers was sentenced to thirty years in prison, for what the police said was one of the most brutal cases they had ever seen. Advances in plastic surgery in the recent years have allowed Carmen a face transplant. Though this advancement has not restored her appearance to anything like it had been prior to the attack, it has considerably improved her life.

Another case of disfigurement via acid attack is the that of Ameneh Bahrami, an Iranian woman of thirty-four who had refused to marry a former university classmate, Majid Movahedi.[57] Movahedi dealt with his rejection by tossing acid at her face, causing horrific disfigurement and blindness. Islamic sharia law permitted her via the rule called qisās ("retaliation") to have his eyes blinded, too, and she initially pursued such recourse. She nevertheless pardoned him in 2011. The Iranian government has paid part of the $200,000 she has spent for plastic surgery to repair her injuries. All of these crimes of disfigurement—each committed with malice aforethought—while relatively new and not so common in the West, are relatively common and not so new in Islamic countries.

Sadistic Perversity: Certain crimes have occurred in the past half century in which elements of paraphilia and sadism are fused within an outer shell of narcissistic disregard for the feelings of others—in such a way as to strike us as repulsive almost beyond our imagination, and also as somehow "new" in the sense that we can scarcely find similar cases in the past. Again, I refer to crimes committed in peacetime. These crimes do not exceed the tortures sometimes inflicted on enemies and noncombatants in wartime, but they make us suspect that the perpetrators have relished creating their own private Nanking or Auschwitz.

Benjamin Sifrit, a former Navy SEAL, was a psychopathic thrill seeker, bigot, and extreme paraphilic sadist.[58] In 1998, when he was twenty, he married Erika Grace (also twenty). Erika had been an honors student and a basketball star at her college. But she too had psychopathic traits and was emotionally unstable and totally dependent on Ben. Earlier, Ben had been given a bad-conduct discharge from the Navy because of insubordination, wearing unauthorized insignia, and frequent absences. In 2002, he and Erika, both twenty-four, were now living in Ocean City, Maryland, where they met another couple—Josh Ford and Martha Crutchley—and invited them to their condo. The visitors were then held at gunpoint, ordered to strip naked, and then murdered. Both victims were decapitated. Then Ben proceeded to have sex with Martha's severed head—the details of which we have, fortunately, been spared. As for the male victim, Ben wanted Erika to cook Josh's leg so that he could eat it; it is unclear whether she did this. Ben and Erika did cocaine and ecstasy (methylenedioxymethamphetamine, or MDMA) daily, and Ben made Erika take photos of him holding the heads of the two victims. Arrested a week later, Ben was sentenced to thirty-eight years in prison. Erika was sentenced to life plus twenty-five years. The crime fits well into the notion of a New Evil: necrophilia with a decapitated head is a paraphilia never before encountered.

In 1998, in the tiny town of Splendora, Texas (population 1,615), near Houston, Donald Collins, who was thirteen at the time, raped an eight-year-old boy, Robbie Middleton. Then, two weeks later, Collins tied him to a tree and poured gasoline over him in an attempt to burn him to death and perhaps eradicate the nature of the crime.[59] Though Robbie was not expected to survive a total-body burn, he did, amidst unimaginable suffering—and innumerable operations and grafts. Despite his suffering, Robbie did not name his attacker. Thirteen years later, Robbie died of cancer related to the severely burned skin; but, with his last breaths, he finally named his attacker—whose identity had hitherto been undetected. Collins, now recognized as a psychopathic and sadistic homosexual pedophile, was sentenced to forty years in prison (his youth at the time capped the sentence at no more than that). Collins showed no emotion in court. The jury heard one man testify that Collins had once raped him; and a woman spoke of how Collins had stomped kittens to death. Even the pre-1960 crimes of Northcott and Fish do not rise to the level of cruelty of the Collins case.

Another uncommonly cruel rape/murder, this time by a heterosexual pedophile, was that committed by John Evander Couey in 2005.[60] At age forty-seven, Couey had twenty-four arrests (for burglary and indecent exposure) when he sneaked into the home of nine-year-old Jessica Lundford, kidnapped her, and then raped her in the evening and once again the next morning. Afterward, Couey placed her in a garbage bag and buried her alive in a shallow grave. Her body, discovered three weeks later, showed that Jessica tried to claw her way out of the bag but died of suffocation. With reference to Couey, there had been several miscarriages of justice in years before he attacked Jessica. When Couey was twenty, he molested a girl and was sentenced to ten years—but was paroled after only two. At thirty-three, he molested another girl and was again prematurely released because of the inappropriately lenient laws at the time. For Jessica's murder, he was given the death penalty, but he died of anal cancer in prison when he was fifty-one.

Born in Canada in 1982, Erik Kirk Newman changed his name to Luka Rocco Magnotta when he was twenty-four, though he used innumerable other aliases at other times, including on Facebook.[61] Bisexual, but more gay than straight, Newman once impersonated a woman while applying for a credit card—which he then used to purchase $10,000 worth of goods. He received a minimal sentence for theft in 2005 and was out again the next year, which is when he then became Luka Magnotta. He served as a male model and a homosexual prostitute, using his charm and buoyancy to attract a high-paying clientele. At one point, he placed a post on a white-supremacist website denouncing Chinese people. Among his many offenses—which drew the attention of animal-rights groups—was an online video of him killing kittens by stuffing them in plastic bags and then suffocating them by sucking the air out with a vacuum cleaner. The crime that drew international attention occurred in May 2012. In this case, Magnotta waylaid a Chinese engineering student, Lin Jun, whom he murdered. He also made and released online a video of the crime, which showed a naked Lin Jun tied to a bed and being repeatedly stabbed and dismembered—followed by acts of necrophilia. Magnotta cut off some portions of flesh, postmortem, and fed them to a dog; he is suspected of having indulged in cannibalism as well.[62] The truly bizarre part of the crime consisted, however, of Magnotta mailing Lin's hands and feet to half a dozen governmental sites, such as the headquarters of the Conservative Party of Canada. A month later, Lin Jun's head was discovered near a small lake in a Montreal park. His torso had been stuffed in a suitcase that was found by a janitor for a building in Montreal.

What establishes Magnotta as the Mount Everest of narcissism is the manner of his eventual capture less than two weeks after the murder. Once an international manhunt had begun, Magnotta had fled to Europe—first to Paris, then to Berlin. There, he was apprehended at an Internet café while reading the lurid news stories about his crime. At his trial back in Canada, there was an attempt by his defense attorneys to claim "diminished responsibility" on the grounds of "mental illness." He was once diagnosed as a "paranoid schizophrenic" in his adolescence, at a time when he was abusing illegal drugs, the effects of which could mimic that condition. During the trial, six psychiatrists rendered diagnoses: three for the prosecution side and three for the defense. Those for the prosecution called him "borderline with histrionic traits"; those for the defense called him "paranoid schizophrenic."[63] All six missed the obvious point that Magnotta is a psychopath—one whose score on the Hare Psychopathy Checklist–Revised measures 33 (a score of 30 out of a possible 40 is needed for the diagnosis), even with a "not applicable" on the 2-point item "revocation of conditional release" and a "0" on "many short-term marital relationships."[64] He was sentenced to life in prison, but with the possibility of parole after twenty-five years. That one could imagine Magnotta suitable for release at age forty-eight, as though no longer a threat to society, bespeaks a naiveté that needs, I believe, serious rethinking. His sheer savagery and contempt for ordinary social rules and behavior mark Magnotta as more than just an exemplar of the New

Evil. There was no one like him in the pre-1960 period. And there is something unique about his use of the Internet to commit terrible crimes (the torture of kittens and the video of dismembering his victim, released shortly after the murder) and to assist in his own arrest—by watching himself on . . . the Internet.

In August 1979, Albert Fentress, a teacher in upstate New York, lured an eighteen-year-old student, Paul Masters, onto his property.[65] He proceeded, at gunpoint, to bind the young man to posts in his basement, and then, during a torture session including verbal intimidation, he severed the young man's genitals with a razor. After cooking and eating the testicles, Fentress shot Masters to death, and then tried, unsuccessfully, to haul the body upstairs and into his car. Soon after, he was arrested and sent to a forensic hospital, on the grounds that to have committed such an act must signify a psychotic disorder. The idea that the condition underlying this act of cannibalism and murder was one of sexual sadism and pedophilia—rather than "schizophrenia"—was not understood at the time. In the years preceding the crime, Fentress, at an "after-school" club he ran, had molested several other boys—some of whom came forward twenty years later and testified to that effect at a trial concerning whether Fentress merited release from the hospital where he was still held. Release was denied. Ironically, what makes Albert Fentress's sexual sadism different from that of Albert Fish's similarly shocking crimes half a century earlier—is that Fish, though placed in prison, was truly psychotic and belonged more properly in a forensic hospital, whereas Fentress was never psychotic. Had this been appreciated at the time of his arrest, prison would have been the more appropriate setting. The Fentress case has been described accurately in Peter Davidson's 2006 book *Death by Cannibal*[66]; and sexual sadism—and its difference from psychosis—has been clearly delineated in the 2001 book *Dark Dreams* by the former head of the FBI's Behavioral Science Unit, Roy Hazelwood, and the true-crime author Stephen Michaud.[67]

Mass Murder: As mentioned above, what is "new" about mass murder beyond the 1960 dividing line is mainly its frequency—which has increased substantially and at a rate faster than the increase in the US population. There are proportionally more mass murders in the United States than there are in other countries. Easy access to guns—particularly to semiautomatic pistols and rifles—is a factor, considering that they are less readily obtainable in most other countries. Some have expressed concern about the mass murders committed in recent years by men with Asperger's syndrome, a form of autistic disorders.[68] These cases (e.g., the shootings by Seung-Hui Cho at Virginia Tech, by Adam Lanza in Newton, Connecticut, or by Elliot Rodger in San Barbara, California) have been very rare, but so dramatic as to create headlines that then distort the public's perception of the frequency and risk of such disorders.[69] Men account for about 97 percent of mass murders. Mental illness (in the sense of a psychosis) occurs in approximately a quarter of mass murderers. A more common background is that of a disgruntled worker or a jilted lover or spouse, either of whom then plans a do-or-die act of retribution. Some mass murderers have accompanying psychopathic traits; very few are "primary" psychopaths such as Jack Graham, described in chapter 5 of this book. About half of mass murderers either commit suicide or are killed in the act by the police (a circumstance sometimes referred to as "suicide by cop"). Many other instances of mass murder have been carried out by Islamic extremists, ever since Iran's Ayatollah Khomeini assumed control in 1979. But these acts are not really acts of evil in peacetime; they are acts of a guerilla warfare waged on a continuing basis over the past four decades. Here I offer a few examples of mass murder by men in everyday life, outside the arena of warfare.

Wade Michael Page was a man of forty when he barged into a Sikh temple in southeast Wisconsin in 2012 and shot to death six worshippers with his semiautomatic pistol. He then shot himself to death as the police closed in.[70] Twenty years earlier, Page had served in the US Army but was discharged because of misconduct (including being drunk and going AWOL). Page became a neo-Nazi brand of white supremacist and was involved in a neo-Nazi group in his area. An unreliable worker, he had recently been fired from his job, and he had also been jilted by his girlfriend (who was also a neo-Nazi). He had talked of an "impending racial holy war," but it is not clear why he targeted Sikhs. Was it because, although Caucasian, they are not quite "white"—or because he thought they were Muslims? In the days after 9/11, many Sikh taxi drivers in New York, for example, were attacked and beaten up because their turbans were thought to be Muslim headwear.[71] Most Americans are woefully ignorant about distinctions concerning Muslims (some of whom wear a skullcap/Taqiyah), Hindus, and Sikhs; it is not likely that Page was sophisticated in these matters. Why he targeted that peaceful group will remain a mystery.

In December 2012, the country was electrified by the actions of twenty-year-old Adam Lanza, who had invaded a school in Newton, Connecticut, with a cache of semiautomatic weapons, and killed twenty elementary-school children, six teachers, and then himself.[72] Later the police discovered that Adam had earlier that day shot his mother to death with six bullets from an AK-47 rifle—the "overkill" signifying that he was in a state of intense rage against her. Manifesting a severe form of Asperger's syndrome, he had always been incapable of conventional social interactions but had grown increasingly paranoid and delusional in the months leading up to the massacre. He was living with his divorced mother in a home where they communicated only via computer; he kept to his own room, where the windows had been blackened. His mother, Nancy Lanza, was herself a disturbed person—a doomsday prepper survivalist preoccupied with the need to maximize her ability to withstand apocalyptic destructive events. She had five semiautomatic rifles and was giving yet another to Adam as a Christmas present. In typical paranoid fashion, Adam blamed society for his misery. This was a more comforting illusion than to realize that he had been born with a serious brain disorder that does not allow one to understand others or to make satisfying emotional contact with them. The most likely reason for Adam's decompensation and the mass murder was barely mentioned in the press. After the massacre, an informant said that Nancy had gotten to the end of her tether—because of the increasing gravity of her son's condition—such that she was finally talking about having him institutionalized. She had apparently planned this, after years of avoiding any attempts at taking therapeutic steps that might have been of some benefit to her son. Adam would then be facing a decrease in human contact from one to zero—from alienation to complete isolation. This seems to have been the trigger.

The situation with Seung-Hui Cho, the twenty-three-year-old Korean immigrant who shot thirty-two people to death in 2007 on the Virginia Tech college campus where he was a student, was similar in many ways.[73] His relatives described him as extremely shy; he wouldn't say much or mix with other children. His family thought that he showed "selective mutism" or autism. While at college, his teachers noted that he had a mean streak; he would intimidate female students by taking pictures of their legs without their permission and by writing obscene and violent poetry. Toward the end of 2005, he was depressed and showed a flat affect—that is, a deadening of all emotional display—and was briefly hospitalized. By the time of the shooting, he had grown increasingly angry at the "rejection" he experienced from others. Like Lanza, he was unable to grasp that it was his repellent and strange behavior that led to their distancing themselves from him, and he came to feel, as did Lanza, that people were "against" him. Cho and Lanza, and, later, Elliot Rodger—the student who killed six other students in Santa Barbara in 2014—had the unfortunate effect of prejudicing the public against persons with Asperger's syndrome and other forms of autism. This, despite the fact that persons with either of these disorders are in general not prone to violence.

The prevalence of autism in the general population has increased in recent decades, partly because of an increased awareness of autism-related disorders and improved ability to diagnose them. The contribution of autism to the upsurge of mass murder since the 1960s is minimal, almost negligible—but the few such cases that have occurred have been dramatic. A more prominent social factor in provoking such killings is the greater risk of working-class men losing their jobs, and, given the high post-1960 divorce rate and generally greater instability of sex-partner relationships; the greater the number of men suddenly losing jobs, mates, and status, the greater the likelihood that these men will "even the score" via mass murder.[74] The substantial increase in post-1960 abuse of illicit drugs may also play a role, not in the murder rate in general (which has declined since 1980), but in the bizarre nature of some of the violent crimes. Jared Loughner, for example—who in 2011 at age twenty-two killed six people in Arizona during his attempt to kill Congresswoman Gabrielle ("Gabby") Giffords (whom he seriously wounded). He had begun to abuse psychotomimetic and hallucinogenic drugs (such as LSD and psilocybin, which induce a psychosis), since age fourteen.[75] This was after a girlfriend jilted him. He became paranoid and delusional, was expelled from school, and felt persecuted by the federal government—which precipitated his descent into violence. He was called "schizophrenic," but his condition was, if anything, a drug-induced psychosis that mimicked the authentic condition.

Sadistic Serial Sexual Homicide: Although the phrase *serial killer* most often refers to men committing serial sexual homicide, it also covers women who kill one infant after the other; hospital personnel (called "angels of death") who kill a series of patients with various drugs; and persons who kill others, one at a time, for nonsexual reasons. I have already covered several serial killers (of the male/sexual type) in the text of the present work, including such "iconic" ones as Ted Bundy, John Wayne Gacy, Leonard Lake, Dennis Rader, and David Parker Ray—all of whom committed their crimes during New Evil post-1960 years. About 90 percent of serial killers are psychopathic, which means that they inhabit the outermost edge of the narcissistic spectrum. In that sense, they may be said to be simply the most morbid representatives of what has been an increasingly narcissistic culture over the past half century. A few serial killers (and murderers of other sorts) have boasted of making videos of victims while they are dying. Actual "snuff films" are, fortunately, rare, and I know of none in the pre-1960 era. One serious claim came to light in Birmingham, England, in 1985, when Geoffrey Jones, a bachelor of forty-nine, lured a young woman to his home on the pretext of offering her a modeling job. As described in Georgina Lloyd's 1992 book, *Murders Unspeakable*,[76] once Jones had the young woman in his home, he told her he was making a film about hanging—to which end he persuaded her to place her head in a noose he had arranged for the purpose. He told her this, only once they were back at his home. As Jones delicately put it at his trial: "After all, no girl in her right mind would go to the house of a chap she didn't know from Adam and put her head in a noose." But hang her he did, and he filmed her death. Jones was a particularly warped individual: impotent with women, an admirer of Hitler and Nazi atrocities, and preoccupied with extreme perversions and with fantasies of hanging women. As for his narcissism and indifference to the suffering of others, he said when receiving a life sentence at this trial: "It's all been a bit of a giggle. But I knew that in the end I would have to pay a price for the good time."[77]

Another man who made snuff films was the Royal Canadian Air Force colonel Russell Williams—a serial killer manqué (his murders fell short of the four required by the FBI for that appellation) from Ontario.[78] As a pilot, he had an illustrious career and was privileged to fly Queen Elizabeth on her tours in Canada. But he also had a secret life as a transvestite. Married (without children) to an older woman, at forty Williams began to sneak into homes in Ontario and steal girls' panties and bras—storing huge numbers of them in boxes at home. He progressed to raping young women, and then, at age forty-four, he invaded the homes of two women whom he bound, raped repeatedly, and filmed with elaborate photographic equipment he set up. He dressed himself in their panties and bras during their torture; and then he killed them. Crossdressing of this sort does not generally start in a man's forties; presumably, he had been doing so, or thinking about doing so, since adolescence but was hitherto able to keep the paraphilia under wraps. Some transvestites appear to develop their paraphilia in response to a longing for a mother they lost when young or who was cold and unemotional; by dressing briefly in women's clothing, they "become" the mother they wished they had. Williams's mother was said to be of the cold and unemotional sort, but his brother, now a physician, has led a more normal life. When arrested and tried in court, Williams made a thorough confession, so there was no examination by psychiatrists for the prosecution or the defense. There is much we don't know about this man, apart from his transvestism, and the boundless narcissism that led him to his make his morbid snuff films for his "enjoyment."

Randy Kraft, a serial killer from California, was born in 1945 into a middle-class family of staunchly conservative political views.[79] He realized he was gay during adolescence, at a time when the subject was taboo and public animosity against homosexuality much stronger than it is today. He had his first liaisons with other men while in college, and once was arrested for propositioning an undercover policeman. Since he had no previous record, the charges were dropped. Kraft joined the Air Force after college but later was given a general discharge when he acknowledged his homosexuality. Between 1971 and 1983, Kraft murdered dozens of men—perhaps as many as sixty-seven. Many had been Marines. His victims ranged in age from thirteen to thirty-five. The sadistic manner in which he dispatched his victims was almost without parallel, exceeded perhaps only by what David Parker Ray had done to women. Kraft would use a cigarette lighter to burn some of the men about their genitals or face—or else their nipples; some were killed with blunt trauma to the head, while others suffered genital mutilation or castration—or dismemberment. He inserted foreign objects into the anus of some victims, but he would also insert glass tubes in the penile urethra and then stomp on then penis, shattering the glass and the surrounding tissues. The FBI suspected the killer was a highly organized man with superior intelligence (Kraft's IQ was superior: 129). Although he began killing in 1971, Kraft was not arrested and charged with the mutilations and murders until 1983. The trial was lengthy because of the large number of victims. He was finally convicted and given the death penalty in 1989, since which time he has remained in San Quentin Prison on "Death Row"—basically serving a life sentence without parole, since California no longer carries out the death penalty. One of the few men to survive an attack by Kraft has both spoken and written to me about the tortures he suffered decades ago. He has spent many of the intervening years recovering, in and out of hospitals, from the effects of the trauma. He and his wife have been planning to write a book about male-to-male victimization by rape.

Kraft, it occurs to me, as I wear my psychoanalytic hat, had likely become one of the self-hating homosexuals of his day—a man aggravated probably by the rage his father expressed when he learned of his son's predilection. It is as if Kraft spent the next thirty years torturing and killing gay men, by way of punishing himself by proxy for his "sin," and administering the death penalty his father might have fantasized about. Only, Kraft administered that penalty to other gay men, instead of to himself. This would be the same psychodynamic manifested in Albert Fentress. These men appear boundless in their narcissism and in their capacity for cruelty. But it is worth noting that the tortures by Albert Fish in the 1930s were carried out by a man who was legally insane. Kraft was—and is—a sane man.

Most of the persons whose crimes I have discussed in the preceding sections, whose crimes bespeak a cruelty and narcissism not often encountered until the past half century, came from the United States. A few others were Canadian, as with Colonel Williams and Luka Magnotta, or British, like Geoffrey Jones. But even in Scandinavia, where the murder rate is considerably lower than in the United States, there are a few examples. In Sweden, we have Dr. Teet Haerm (or Härm), a pathologist allegedly turned serial killer.[80] Born in 1953, Haerm allegedly raped and strangled some eight prostitutes in the mid-1980s. It is believed that he then did autopsies on his victims and cleverly covered up his crimes by reporting innocuous causes of death. Furthermore, the trial showed that he possibly also committed vampirism (drinking the blood of his victims) and cannibalism. Allegedly, he sawed off the head of one woman—

Catrine da Costa—in front of his own five-year-old daughter. At his 1988 trial, the jury rendered a guilty verdict; but, because some jurors gave interviews to the press before the final verdict came down, the judge overturned the conviction on that technicality. Haerm is now a free man. In the next section we turn our attention to some current and unusual crimes involving persons in intimate relationships.

The Murder of Lovers and Spouses: Spousal murder is not new. There are myriad examples before 1960. About 1900 years before 1960, for example, Emperor Nero killed his first wife, Octavia, and he is said to have also killed his second, Poppaea Sabina. In the sixteenth century, Henry VIII had his second wife, Anne Boleyn, killed on trumped-up charges of adultery (her real crime was that she failed to produce a son); he also had his fifth wife, Catherine Howard (at age seventeen), killed on pretty accurate charges of adultery. We reviewed some of the pre-1960 s murders of lovers and spouses here: Chester Gillette (his lover). Ruth Snyder (her husband), and Leonard Scott (his wife). These were efficient "no frills" murders aimed at freeing someone to be with another partner. Newspapers were in wide circulation all through the early 1900s, and archival material from the papers are now accessible on the Internet. Nonetheless, I have not found proportionally as many gruesome murders of lovers and spouses in the pre-1960 era as I have since then. I suspect the papers would not decline to print news of spousal murders of a sensational nature back then, though I can't be certain. It does appear, however, that in the past half century there has been an increase in murders of spouses and sexual partners that involve measures of torture, diabolic attempts to "disappear" the bodies, and other bizarre features never previously encountered. Here are some examples.

In 2009, David Viens, a forty-nine-year-old California chef, had been in a tempestuous relationship with his wife, Dawn.[81] He was angry about her alcohol problem and had accused her of taking money from their sandwich shop. Then Dawn, thirty-nine at the time, disappeared without a trace. It emerged eventually that David had killed her (we don't know by what method), then cooked the corpse slowly over a four-day period in a fifty-five gallon drum filled with water—and had eaten part of her body. He had hoped to make her disappear completely, and indeed her remains were never found. Viens may have escaped justice had not his daughter Jacqueline revealed to the police in August 2010 that her father had admitted to her that he had killed his wife.[82] The irony was not lost on the judge that here was a chef who had cooked and eaten part of his wife. David Viens was sentenced to fifteen years to life in prison.

The following year, twenty-five-year-old Bruno Fernandes, a prominent soccer goalie in Brazil had gotten his mistress, Eliza Samudio, pregnant.[83] He urged her to have an abortion, lest the situation become embarrassing to his wife, Dayna—but Eliza refused. A few days after she gave birth, Bruno strangled her, and then, with the help of friends and relatives (including his wife) he dismembered the body and fed the pieces to ten Rottweiler dogs to make the remains vanish. Later, Bruno's cousin had a pang of conscience and confessed, whereupon Bruno and Dayna were arrested. As an indication of his regret and remorse, Bruno is alleged to have said (while sitting in prison): "Now I won't be able to play in the 2014 World Cup!" Though sentenced originally to twenty-two years for the assault, torture, and murder of Eliza, he was released after only six and a half years, at which point he uttered another expression of "regret": "What happened, happened. I made a mistake. Mistakes happen in life. I'm not a bad guy."[84]

What distinguishes some of the spouse/lover murders in recent years from those of the pre-1960 era is the exotic and devilish means by which the murders were carried out. There have been several cases, for example, in which an intimate partner disposed of a no-longer-wanted partner by dismemberment, with the body parts then being dumped in the ocean, presumably never to be recovered, hence a "perfect crime." In one case, a surgeon named Dr. Robert Bierenbaum disposed of his wife in this way in 1983, when she planned to get a divorce.[85] Her body parts were never found; his subsequent arrest and conviction depended on strong circumstantial evidence. As a surgeon, he had the skills to carry out the dismemberment in a more anatomically "correct" way. Women, too, have been known in recent years to dispose of an unwanted husband by murder and dismemberment. Melanie McGuire, a nurse in a New Jersey fertility clinic, had fallen out of love with her husband, Bill McGuire, and had fallen in love with Dr. Brad Miller, one of the physicians at the clinic.[86] When Bill wanted to move to a different state, Melanie realized that this would put an end to her affair with Dr. Miller. So she bought a pistol, gave Bill a "mickey" of chloral hydrate and alcohol, which put him into a coma. She then shot him to death and cut him up with a power saw (a less refined method than that carried out by the surgeon). She placed the three large pieces in three suitcases, each also containing a five-pound weight, and tossed them into the Chesapeake Bay. Apparently she was not aware that it takes much more than a five-pound weight to keep such a parcel submerged (because of the post-mortem gases); she was eventually arrested when the suitcases surfaced and were found bobbing in the water.

The case of Marjorie Orbin is similar: A former Las Vegas showgirl sought to solidify her financial future by murdering her wealthy husband, Jay, and inheriting his fortune.[87] On his forty-fifth birthday in 2004, Marjorie shot him to death in their Phoenix, Arizona, home, and then dismembered his body with a jigsaw. She was arrested when, a month later, parts of his body were found in a plastic container at the edge of the city. Upon her conviction, Marjorie was given a life sentence.

The notorious case of Scott Peterson, who in 2002 killed his wife, Laci, who was eight months pregnant at the time, also involved dismemberment and disposal of body parts in the ocean.[88] The premeditation of her murder is chilling. Prior to killing her, Scott had lied to his wife, telling her he was in Paris at a work conference. She could hear the sounds of water during the phone conversation, so he told her that's because he was near the Seine. Really he was in the San Francisco Bay near their home, checking out the tides to determine where best to toss her body.

In another not so perfect "perfect crime," Kimberly Hricko, a surgical technician, had grown bored with her husband of nine years, Steve Hricko.[89] She had begun an affair with a US Marine named Brad Winkler. To bypass the nuisance of divorce, Kimberly tried to hire a hit man to kill her husband. She offered $50,000, but he declined. She had assumed she'd still have $350,000 left over from her husband's $400,000 life insurance policy. Forced now to take matters into her own hands, she planned a "romantic" Valentine's Day weekend at a hotel. While there, she poisoned him with the curare-like drug succinylcholine—which she had swiped from the hospital surgical cart. She then set fire to the hotel room with an accelerant, propping up the scene with a cigar and a bottle of liquor, as though Steve accidentally set the fire himself. Actually, Steve neither smoked nor drank. Furthermore, it was shown at autopsy that he had stopped breathing before the fire started (there was no soot in his trachea or bronchi, for example). Kimberly was arrested and sentenced to life plus thirty years. She has never confessed to the murder.

Granted that since 1960 some chemicals, biological agents, and weaponry have become available that were not accessible or even known earlier, the new discoveries and developments have at times been incorporated into previously unheard-of methods of violence and murder. But beyond these changes, American culture itself appears to have become more self-centered. Dozens of new books on narcissism have appeared in the last few years, adding to the sentiments—and warnings—expressed by Christopher Lasch in his 1979 book, *Culture of Narcissism*.[90] Among the newer books is Jean Twenge and Keith Campbell's *The Narcissism Epidemic*,[91] which addresses what they consider the "pernicious spread of narcissism in today's culture." Some of this may be a reaction to positive changes in our culture. For instance, in an earlier book by Twenge[92] she showed, via a graph, that since 1960 women's achievements in education have been such that currently more than half of college degrees in the United States are earned by women, and women earn almost half of law and medical degrees (as opposed to only 5 percent before 1960). As I mentioned in connection with the serial killer epidemic staring in the 1960s, these changes, which are favorable to women, may have provoked resentment and discontent in some males, especially less successful males. À propos the latter, I will close this section with a final example, that of Brian Stewart, a man who wanted his wife dead, but who attempted to kill his infant son when his wife sued for divorce.[93] In 1990, when she was pregnant with their son, Brian had once shoved his hand in her vagina, saying he would "ruin her for anyone else." Clearly, this was narcissism writ large; but worse was to come. After the boy was born, Stewart, who was working in a hospital as a phlebotomist, obtained a sample of HIV blood and injected it into his son, in an attempt to kill him with AIDS. Stewart was described as a diabolical character during his trial (for attempted murder) that took place later; his two ambitions were to hurt his ex-wife grievously and to eliminate the need for child-support payments, figuring the boy would be dead in five years. As with many narcissistic killers, Stewart assumed that no one was smart enough to convict him. He was wrong on both counts: the boy, now aged twenty, has survived and done well, thanks to antiretroviral drugs that are now much more effective than what was available when he was born. And

Stewart was convicted and sentenced to life in prison for what was one of the most sickening crimes before or after the 1960s. The Stewart story serves not only as a conclusion to this section but also as an introduction to the last section, on crimes showing remarkable contempt for the feelings of others.

Heartlessness: Many of the crime stories I have related in this epilogue concern persons, both before and after, but particularly after, the year 1960, the watershed year that I have used as my dividing line between Evil in the Good Old Days and the New Evil. But there are crimes that have taken place in recent years for which the details are breathtaking in their display of evil, leading sometimes to murder, yet at other times to a kind of psychological torture more dreadful than death—because the victim must go on living with the painful memories.

One of the nonfatal cases involved Mark Berndt, a sixty-one-year-old Los Angeles elementary school teacher with extreme sadistic paraphilias, who committed multiple lewd acts against his seven-to-ten-year-old pupils.[94] He would place large cockroaches on their faces, or he would hold his semen under the nose of a blindfolded young girl after binding her mouth with masking tape—and would then photograph her. Others, he fed cookies laced with his semen. When arrested, police found in his home, where he lived alone, hundreds of photographs of his pupils in the various situations he had put them in. He had molested at least twenty-three children. Berndt is now in prison, but, meanwhile, many of the children and their parents have had to receive counseling and support for the psychological damage he inflicted on them.[95]

In Thibodaux, Louisiana, thirty-year-old Jeremiah Wright was arrested in 2011 after he beheaded his seven-year-old son, Jori, with a meat cleaver, and then left the head in the driveway for his wife to find when she returned home.[96] Jori was born with cerebral palsy and was unable to talk or walk, and he needed feeding tubes. The night before the murder, Jeremiah and his wife had argued, and she had told him she was moving him out of the house. At trial, he was considered psychotic (or legally insane) and was remanded to a forensic psychiatric hospital. It is not clear whether he was truly psychotic, or was considered so (as was Fentress years earlier) because it was assumed that only a person who was "crazy" could commit such a revolting and heartless act. It is not easy to imagine the memories the wife must carry with her for the remainder of her days.

There is nothing new about rape. Going back three thousand years, the Bible, in Deuteronomy 22:25–29 declared what the punishments for raping a young woman should be: if she were already betrothed, "then the man who forces her and lies with her shall die," whereas if she were not betrothed, "he shall give to the young woman's father fifty shekels . . . and she shall become his wife, for he has humbled her." Considering the psychological (and, often, physical) traumas women who have been sexually violated in this way experience, the Bible was not far off in its view of rape (at least of a betrothed woman) as a capital crime, like murder. I think of the man I evaluated at a forensic hospital—who had eighty-four "priors" (incarcerations for either violent crimes or mental illness) and whose last offense was to have attempted the rape of a woman he encountered in an apartment elevator in Brooklyn. Unable to maintain an erection (as happens in about a third of rapists), he instead thrust a metal pipe in her vagina, causing serious lacerations and blood loss. How was that not a capital crime? He would not face execution, as Deuteronomy insisted, but I at least recommended that he never be released for so cruel and heartless a crime. That brings me to Sedley Alley, a thirty-year-old man who in 1985 accosted a nineteen-year-old Marine, Suzanne Collins, as she was about to graduate the next day from the aviation school.[97] As she was walking in the park the night before her graduation, she was bludgeoned in the head by Alley, who then thrust a thirty-one-inch-long, two-inch thick tree branch through her vagina—all the way to her lungs, killing her. He had also bitten her left breast. This was the most violent and degrading sexual assault on record, surpassing in heartlessness, in inhumanity . . . in evil—the worst of known sexual violations of women (in peacetime) recently, or in the pre-1960 era. Alley was given the death penalty. But his execution was delayed to the point that he spent more years (twenty-one) awaiting his June 2006 execution than the nineteen-year-old Suzanne had been alive.

Another crime that involved rape and murder, but which received much wider attention, took place in Cheshire, Connecticut, in July 2007. Steven Hayes (aged forty-four) and Josh Komisarjevsky (twenty-six), each with long criminal records, invaded the home of Dr. William Petit, after having already extorted money from his wife at a bank earlier in the day.[98] In the home, they proceeded to rape Mrs. Petit and her two daughters, and then kill them. The two men attempted to kill Dr. Petit, who somehow survived. They then set fire to the house, as if to destroy evidence of their crime, which is regarded as one of the most heinous in Connecticut history. One reason for the robbery/murder was to garner enough cash to maintain their cocaine and methamphetamine habits. The death penalty, though awarded, is not carried out in Connecticut, so their sentence is actually life in prison without parole. As one crime expert commented, you must never believe that you've seen the limits of man's inhumanity against man. This is akin to my comment that there is no bottom to human depravity—though the crimes of the past fifty years have made a furious effort to reach the bottom of this bottomless pit.

The last case in this section concerns a woman who committed what one can call murder without death—though she was also responsible for a "regular" murder. Born in 1938 in Salt Lake City to a Mormon father named Franklin Bradshaw and a Unitarian mother, Berenice née Jewett, Frances Bradshaw was their last (and unwanted) of their four children. Frances's father was a Scrooge-like workaholic who amassed what would today be a billion-dollar fortune in the auto-part and oil and gas business ($400 million, at the time of his death in 1978). The full story of the case has been set forth in two books, which combine to almost 1,100 pages; the first is by Shana Alexander[99]; the second, by Jonathan Coleman.[100] Frances, a prickly, narcissistic, tyrannical, and greedy woman with (what was eventually discovered to be) bipolar disorder, had two sons, Larry and Marc, both born at opposite ends of 1960 to her Italian husband. A psychiatrist opined that she had a "psychopathic personality which is probably by now too late to treat." The marriage did not last, and in 1969 she married a Dutch man and became Frances Schreuder (pronounced SHROY-der), by whom she had a daughter, Ariadne. Frances had moved to New York City, where she added to her scant allowance from her mother by urgent appeals for additional funds—and by forging checks and credit cards from the family. Her demands for extra money were partly to ensure that her children went to good private schools in the city, lest they end up in public schools with all the "niggers, Jews, and white trash."[101] She grossly favored Marc, her younger son, and often forbade Larry entrance to her apartment, which frequently meant that he had to sleep rough. She had amassed enough money through her manipulations that she could then indulge her fascination with ballet. To that end, in the mid-1970s, she gave Balanchine's New York City Ballet its largest donation—of $330,000—to help launch a new production. Despite her abrasive and garrulous personality, she was awarded a patronage in the company, even though the other patrons found her insufferable. As her fortieth birthday approached, she became obsessed with the worry that her father might cut her out of his will. To head such trouble off at the pass, she persuaded Marc, who had grown totally dependent on her, to go to Utah and kill her father. So in July 1978, when he was still only seventeen, he made the trip—armed with a .357 pistol he had acquired—and shot his grandfather with two bullets, killing him. He fled, in the meantime giving the gun to a family friend for safekeeping. It took three years for the police to amass enough evidence to arrest Frances and Marc as the responsible parties. Around the time of the murder, Frances had become hateful and rejecting toward her then five-year-old daughter. When the girl could not recall from her day at school what the definition of a sentence was, Frances flew into a rage, humiliating her daughter in a bone-chilling way—a confrontation which Marc happened to record secretly from an adjacent room. This is what Frances yelled at the girl—and which was later replayed at her trial:

> You'll never have friends! You'll never go to pretty parties with nice girls. . . . You're stupid, disobedient, a liar, and it's all your fault! . . . You decided to talk to those little Jew girls. . . . You won't have love from me! Or from Mr. Balanchyne's [*sic*] school or Brearly or Spence or any other nice school. You'll be sad the rest of your life. . . . I will make you *really* cry! I HATE you, stupid! I'll put you in a hospital for stupid children and you'll never get out. . . . You'll never see your mother again. . . . They have special hospitals for children who are disturbed and cuckoo. . . . They are not permitted to go out EVER. . . . Children like you don't go to a school with other children. . . . You have to go to a nigger school where there are only poor kids and little Jew kids. . . . You belong in a zoo with the animals and monkeys![102]

It was not this diatribe, of course, that sent Frances to prison, but rather the evidence against her about conspiracy to commit murder. I cite her words as an example of a mind inclined to evil. At the trial, Marc was sentenced to twelve years; Frances, to thirteen. After serving her sentence, she died in her house in New York City in 2004—remaining one of the most consistently cruel and sadistic women in the history books, along with Teresa Knorr[103] and Madagascar's Queen Ranavalona (who had people who opposed her tossed off high cliffs to their death).[104] Frances committed what Dr. Leonard Shengold has called "soul murder," which is also the title of his book on the effects of childhood abuse and deprivation.[105] Ariadne, who later changed her name, is thankfully still alive. Many another child subjected to a parental tongue as venomous as Frances Schreuder's would end up committing suicide. Perhaps there have been parents as wicked as Frances in the pre-1960 days. Probably so. But their tirades were not recorded, for want of easy access to the electronic devices we have now. But unlike Dharun Ravi, described above, who I believe did not want Tyler Clementi to commit suicide, Frances's tirade, because she did want the girl to die, was the product of malice aforethought, unfathomable heartlessness—or, to use a more apt phrase, sheer evil.

In the introduction to this book, I mentioned my reluctance to rely, for my definition of evil, upon the works of religious and philosophical texts. This was because of their inherent vagueness—speaking in generalities, for example, and seldom providing what we would consider "case histories." There were, for example, in ancient Jewish law three acts punishable by death: the spilling of blood (murder), uncovering the nakedness (of family members; viz., incest), and uttering the Lord's name.[106] These were among the most unconscionable of evils, but they do not coincide closely with how we use the word *evil* in everyday life. It was for this reason I suggested a definition of evil rooted more in contemporary usage both in speech and in writing. I defined evil as an emotional word—reserved for acts that are "breathtakingly horrible" (along with three other attributes cited in the introduction). Recently, however, I encountered a philosophical work whose author is more willing than most of his predecessors *to get down to cases*. I refer to the refreshingly au courant Roger Scruton. In his treatise, *On Human Nature*, Scruton uses evil not as an emotional word so much as an abstraction that distinguishes evil persons from those who are merely bad. Ordinary people, for example, will from time to time do bad things—but they are still part of the human community; they can still be reasoned with and improved.[107] Evil people, as Scruton explains, are "not like us, since they do not belong to the community even if residing within its territory. . . . Their faults are not of the normal remediable variety—they are visitors from a different sphere."[108] He goes on to say: "Even their charm (and evil people are often charming) is further proof of the Otherness . . . the negation of humanity"; he then adds that "evil people are not necessarily threats to your body—but are threats to your Self." We saw this with Frances Schreuder, who was a threat to her daughter's self (or soul, if you will), not to her body. Most of the persons described in the earlier portions of this epilogue—the various killers and torturers—were of course threats to the body. Scruton's description of the evil person accords well with the psychiatric concept of the psychopath—for whom "superficial charm and glibness of speech" are among the defining characteristics (as we saw with Ted Bundy, Ira Einhorn, and Larry Bittaker earlier in the text). Elsewhere, Scruton adds another, and defining, feature of evil—one that runs like a red thread through both his definition of evil and the descriptions in this book of (primarily) psychopathic persons given to committing evil acts. This red thread consists of the dehumanization of the victim. This was a prominent feature of Nazis and other perpetrators of genocide: the treating of the "others" as vermin, bacilli, lice—no longer human—and whose elimination was no longer "murder," any more than stepping on a bug in one's kitchen.[109] Scruton also makes it plain how rape may be understood as "an easy way to genetic investment on the part of the male [which] also involves triumph over the other's subjectivity—a delight in wresting sexual pleasure from an unwilling donor."[110] This dehumanization—here, of the rape victim—was mirrored also in the remarks about sadism expressed in the manifesto of serial killer Mike DeBardeleben, a man as articulate as he was vicious. As I cited earlier in this book, he wrote that sadism has as it central impulse "the complete mastery over another person," adding that "there is no greater power over another person than that of inflicting pain on her."[111] Note the "her." DeBardeleben was referring to rape as it is usually understood, as in English law[112]—where the offense of rape is created when person (A) "intentionally penetrates the vagina, anus, or mouth of another, non-consenting, person (B) with his penis." The rapist, as the definition indicates, is a male.

In the spirit of this epilogue, I found myself thinking about the famous words of the pseudonymous author of Ecclesiastes, Koheleth ("the preacher"): *ein kol hadash tahat ha-shemesh*—there is nothing new under the sun.[113] In keeping with my assertion that during the past half century we have witnessed some hitherto never (or almost never) encountered evil acts, Koheleth's statement may need some revision. I have found no descriptions of a woman who cut open a pregnant woman's belly in order to steal the fetus, prior to that of Darci Pierce in 1987.[114] And the women's liberation movement of the current period, besides enabling women in developed countries to become doctors and lawyers and judges and scientists and chairmen of large companies to a far greater extent than ever before, has also seen among its ranks a few women who have sought to emulate the worst—and evil—actions of their male counterparts. There are now a few female serial (nonsexual) killers, such as Judith Neelley[115] and Aileen Wuornos.[116] And there are now several examples of women committing rape, in such a way as to require a new and updated definition of the offense—such as might surprise even Koheleth: "The penetration no matter how slight, of the vagina, anus, or any body part or object, or any penetration by a sex organ of another person, without the consent of the victim; perpetrator and victim may be of any gender—and even if the victim was rendered incapacitated by drugs or alcohol."[117] Here are two examples: (1) Recently, in Wisconsin, two sisters forced a male high-school student to drink their urine and endure their twisting of his penis with pliers when he refused to have sex with them.[118] (2) In Ohio, twenty-five-year-old Brittany Carter, with the help of two accomplices, allegedly held up a taxi driver at knifepoint, and, as the man was held down, performed a sexual act on him.[119]

It is easy to understand why Scruton focused on rape as a crime to illustrate his point about dehumanization. Among the various parts of our bodies, we are heavily invested in our sexual parts—as defining who we are, our sense of self, our identity, our "I" (as Scruton speaks of it). Scruton is referring, from a philosophical understanding, to the certainty we develop about our being—each of us—a unique individual or, from a psychological frame of reference, a Self. As he explains, "I am this thing that you too observe and which can be understood in two ways—as an organism and as a person. In addressing me as 'you,' you address me as a person and are asking me to respond as an 'I.'"[120] Losing a toe or a finger or even an ear to some knife-wielding assailant would not damage our sense of identity so much as would the loss—or the violation—of a sexual part through rape. As most victims of rape survive the experience, they must continue on with painful memories, disillusionment about the benevolence of people—sometimes to the point of their lives, after the sexual assault, being permanently shattered. This is true at times also of victims of incest, which is another form of rape. It goes without saying that the greater the violence toward the victim and the greater the contempt for the victim's self-hood or "I" in those who survive, the greater will be the degree of evil in my gradations scale. In retrospect, my scale may be understood as oriented, in large part, toward the pain and suffering of the victims—and on the psychological reactions (the horror) of ourselves as observers. For Scruton the spotlight is on the dehumanizing aspects of evil. There are gradations also to this aspect of evil: the degree, that is, to which our uniqueness, our identity, our "I" is damaged or crushed by an evil act. I hope in a forthcoming work to expand on the broad concept of evil, joining the philosophical to the psychological counterparts. I would want to add a scale relevant to the evils inflicted by parties engaged in group conflict and war. Hints of such a scale are offered in this epilogue: the evils of Agincourt pale, for example, when compared to the evils of the genocidal acts of the past century. As a social species with a consciousness couched in language—a collection of "I's" inescapably dependent as we are upon the family and the community (that constitute the "we")—there will always be among us those who, in their struggle for survival, far exceed behaviors that are acceptable and transgress the boundary separating the acceptable from the evil. Evil will always be with us—both in times of peace, as highlighted in this book, and in times of war.[121] To our credit, a number of the great and wise among us—Moses, Buddha, Confucius, Jesus, the philosopher Kant—have each offered us a guideline for living in harmony with one another and for refraining from evil, that is, from actions that cause suffering and dehumanization of others.[122] They have given us, in effect, a prescription for a good life. A prescription. But not a cure.

INDEX